JORDAN
WALKS, TREKS, CAVES, CLIMBS AND CANYONS

About the Authors

Di Taylor and Tony Howard have been climbing and trekking in the mountains of North Africa and the Middle East for well over 40 years. In 1984 they were responsible for the discovery of Wadi Rum in south Jordan as a climbing and trekking venue, and have written the guidebooks to that area. Since then they have returned to Jordan every year, always managing to find time to explore other parts of the country between world-famous sites of antiquity such as Pella, Ajloun, Karak and Petra, and in Jordan's recently formed Nature Reserves, in particular in the mountains and canyons of Dana and Mujib and also their favourite desert area of Wadi Rum, which now has Protected Area status.

Photo: The authors with HM Queen Noor (right)

Cicerone guidebooks by the same authors
Treks and Climbs in Wadi Rum, Jordan
Walks in Palestine and The Nativity Trail

JORDAN
WALKS, TREKS, CAVES, CLIMBS AND CANYONS
IN
PELLA, AJLOUN, DEAD SEA HILLS, DANA, PETRA AND RUM

by

Di Taylor and Tony Howard

2 POLICE SQUARE, MILNTHORPE, CUMBRIA LA7 7PY
www.cicerone.co.uk

Second edition 2008
ISBN-13: 978-1-85284-520-9

© Di Taylor and Tony Howard 2008

First edition 1999
ISBN-10: 1-85284-278-4

A catalogue record for this book is available from the British Library.

Maps, photographs and rock art illustrations by the authors unless otherwise acknowledged.

Floral watercolours by Mary Hartley

Dedication
To the people of Wadi Rum and elsewhere in Jordan who, throughout out travels and explorations, have been the epitome of Arabic hospitality.

Have you gazed on naked grandeur where there's nothing else to gaze on,
Set pieces and drop-curtain scenes galore,
Big mountains heaved to heaven which the blinding sunsets blazon,
Black canyons where the rapids rip and roar?
Have you swept the visioned valley with the green stream streaking through it,
Searched the Vastness for a something you have lost?
Have you strung your soul to silence? Then for God's sake go and do it;
Hear the challenge, learn the lesson, pay the cost.

From *The Call of The Wild* by Robert Service

Advice to Readers
Readers are advised that while every effort is taken by the authors to ensure the accuracy of this guidebook, changes can occur which may affect the contents. It is advisable to check locally on transport, accommodation, shops, and so on, but even rights of way can be altered. The publisher would welcome notes of any such changes.
   Mountain walking can be a dangerous activity, carrying a risk of personal injury or death. It should be undertaken only by those with a full understanding of the risks and with the training and/or experience to evaluate them. Whilst every care and effort has been taken in the preparation of this book, the user should be aware that conditions can be highly variable and can change quickly, thus materially affecting the seriousness of a mountain walk.
   Therefore, except for any liability which cannot be excluded by law, neither Cicerone nor the authors accept liability for damage of any nature (including damage to property, personal injury or death) arising directly or indirectly from the information in this book.

Front cover: Descending the Canyon of Zerqa Ma'in to the Dead Sea (Route 31)
Back cover: The view from the north exit of the Canyon of Abu Khashaba, Wadi Rum (Route 136)
Back cover insert: The first view of the Treasury in Petra is unforgettable (Route 81)

CONTENTS

Foreword by HM Queen Noor al Hussein of Jordan 10
Preface to the second edition 11
Thanks to all concerned 12
Permissions 13

Introduction 15
History 15
The people and places that inspired the book 16

Environmental and Cultural Awareness 17
Culture clash 17
Who's who? 18
Cultural tips for travellers 19
The environment – a plea from the authors 19
Environmental tips for the traveller 22

The Royal Society for the Conservation of Nature 23
Visitor code 24
How to make a booking 24

Wildlife in Jordan 26
What sort of birds might you see? 26
What animals might you see? 26

The Lie of the Land 27
Geographic and historical boundaries 28
    North Jordan 28
    The Dead Sea Hills 28
    The Dana Area 28
    The Petra Area 31
    Wadi Rum and the Aqaba Mountains 31

On the Move 31
Going to Jordan 31
Getting in 31
Where to go 32
When to go 33
On the road 33
Accommodation 34

Other Things Worth Knowing 35
Holidays and holy days 35
Language and communication 35
Money matters 36
Food and drink 36
Water 37
Clothing and equipment 37
Mountain biking 38
Guides 38
Maps 39
Maps and topos in this guide 39
GPS 39

Be prepared! 39
In an emergency 40

Using this Guide. 41
Route descriptions. 42
Grading of walks and treks 42
Grading of canyons. 42
Caving in Jordan 44
Grading of caves 44
Rock climbing in Jordan 44
Grading of scrambles and rock climbs 44

North Jordan 47
The Jordan Valley Hills 49
    The Ajloun Area 50
    The RSCN Ajloun Woodland Reserve. 59
    The Yabis and Pella Area 62
    The Yarmuk Area 73
The North Eastern Desert 79
    RSCN Nature Reserves in the Northeast 79
    Around Azraq 82
The Capital Area 84
    RSCN Dibeen Forest Reserve 85
    The King Talal Dam Area 86
    Around Amman 88
    The Northern Dead Sea 90

The Dead Sea Hills 95
The Madaba Area 98
The RSCN Mujib Nature Reserve. 109
The Karak Area 129

The Dana Area 141
The Northern Dana Area 143
The RSCN Dana Nature Reserve 153
Shaubak Area 163

The Petra Area 175
Petra 179
    The Northern Approaches to Petra 192
    The Western Approaches to Petra 201
    Jebel Harun and the Southern Petra Area 206
Humeimah 227

Wadi Rum and the Aqaba Mountains 231
Wadi Rum. 235
    The People of Rum 237
    The Rum Protected Area. 242
    The Rest House Area 244
    Jebel Rum, 1754m 251
    Jebel um Ishrin, 1753m 263
    Eastern Rum. 269
    Burdah, Khazali and the South. 271
    North of Rum. 282
The Aqaba Mountains 283

Caving in Jordan 287

Climbing in Jordan 297
The Saqeb Area 301
The Ajloun Area 306
The Karak and Shaubak Areas 313
The Petra Area 315
The Wadi Rum Area 316
The Aqaba Mountains 317

Appendices
1 Guides and Adventure Tourism Operators in Jordan 318
2 Relevant Reading 320
3 Some Useful Arabic/English Words 322
4 Climber's Glossary 322
5 Index of Routes 323
6 Place-name Index 326
7 Index of Maps in the Guide 329
8 Animals and flowers of Jordan 330

Map key

═══	Roads
─ ─ ─	Tracks
··········	Walks, treks and canyons
⌒	Wadis
⌣	Contours
─·─·─	Borders
⬭	Lakes and seas
▬ (green)	RSCN Reserves
▬ (dotted)	Deserts
▬ (tan)	Rum mountains and canyons
○ (orange)	Towns and villages
■	Sites of antiquity
▲	Mountains
○	Caves
△	Campsites
●	Other relevant places
• (blue)	Springs
══▶ ? / ─ ─▶ ?	Destination not known

1. Areas covered in this guidebook

Areas and route locations (walks, treks and canyons)

	Routes
North Jordan	
1. Jordan Valley Hills	1–3
2. North Eastern Desert	14–17
3. The Capital Area	18–28
Dead Sea Hills	
4. Madaba Area	29–36
5. RSCN Mujib Reserve	37–51
6. Karak Area	52–60
Dana area	
7. Northern Dana Area	61–65
8. RSCN Dana Nature Reserve	66–72
9. Shaubak Area	73–80
Petra area	
10. Petra	81–103
11. Humeimah	104–118
Wadi Rum and the Aqaba Mountains	
12. Wadi Rum	119–142
13. Aqaba Mountains	143–144

FOREWORD
by HM Queen Noor of Jordan

Over the past 15 years I have watched with vicarious pleasure as Tony Howard and Diana Taylor have been trekking, climbing and leading safaris in the deserts of Wadi Rum. More recently they have spread their explorations to other areas of Jordan. They have taken others with them, but their love of the land and landscape is such that they wanted to share it with a much wider audience. The result is this book, the first to present to the world the walks and other adventures to be had in the little-known but infinitely varied scenery of our land. I am sure that connoisseurs of travel from all corners of the globe, as well as many Jordanians, will find this book fascinating. In these pages you will discover travels to suit every taste: gentle walks amongst ancient 'Roman' olive groves, and rambles over dales as green and beautiful as any in England, or down valleys that rival the Swiss Alps in their kaleidoscope of spring flowers. There are walks through canyons as impressive as the world-renowned Siq of Petra, but previously only known to the Bedouin people, or treks, camel and horse rides, even 4WD journeys along the ancient caravan routes used for bringing incense and spices from Arabia.

If you have the skills you can descend into the recently discovered cave of Zubia hidden in the oak forests of the north, or the dark chasm of the Mujib Siq in the mountains of Moab, abseiling through waterfalls to the Dead Sea 400m below sea level. In the south in Wadi Rum you can climb to the spectacular Rock Bridge of Burdah, brought to the world's attention by the authors after their Bedouin friends showed it to them back in 1984. You can even make the ascent of Jebel Rum following a route which is more than 2000 years old, or scramble to the summit of the highest mountain in Jordan, Jebel um Adaami, in a remote part of the desert near Saudi Arabia. And in the quiet and wild mountains, canyons and valleys around Petra the experienced trekker can discover true wilderness.

As Patron of the Royal Society for the Conservation of Nature, I am particularly pleased that the authors have included walks and treks in the beautiful Dana and Mujib and other Nature Reserves, helping to support these precious but little-known areas, while introducing them to the outside world. In Wadi Rum, too, their efforts have been directed towards benefiting the local people and encouraging them in their effort to protect the desert and mountain habitat for future generations. The thoughtful introductory notes on environmental and cultural awareness are especially relevant in these areas, but are useful throughout the country.

This book demonstrates that ours is a land well worth discovering, where you will find a wealth of natural beauty and warmth of welcome rare in this day and age. I am pleased to add my welcome to Jordan and to wish you a safe and pleasant journey as you explore our ancient trails and scenic wonders – even if you never leave the comfort of your armchair.

HM King Hussein with Queen Noor in Wadi Rum

PREFACE TO THE SECOND EDITION

Since this book was first written in 1999 Jordan has continued to play a major role in our lives; the hot sun, the welcoming people and the promise of new discoveries are always irresistible after a grey English winter.

Our annual (and sometimes biannual) visits have enabled us to add numerous GPS points to this second edition, which should be of benefit as maps are not publicly accessible. We have also explored and documented more unexpected wonders such as a walk in pine-forested hills above the Jordan Valley, a remote lava tube in the Eastern Desert, some surprising canyons above the Dead Sea, wild valleys around Dana and Petra and exciting scrambles on Bedouin hunting routes in Wadi Rum. The limestone cliffs near Ajloun Castle continue to reveal new climbs, now being developed as sport routes by our friend, French mountain guide Wilfried Colonna, who also provided information on other new cliffs near Karak and Dana.

We have added new maps and updated others to include recently constructed roads or forgotten tracks not marked on the maps provided for us by the Ministry of Tourism or HM Queen Noor. At the suggestion of Cicerone Press we have also added colour to the maps, hopefully making them easier to use. The updated Appendices include numerous new Jordanian adventure travel companies, many operated by our Bedouin friends in Petra and Rum – and who better than they to benefit by sharing their local knowledge with others. A comprehensive index has also been added.

Jordan itself is also changing. The Ajloun area is targeted for tourism development and there has already been massive urban development, in particular in Amman and Aqaba; despite the problems that beset the surrounding Middle East, Aqaba is now an international-class holiday resort attracting unprecedented numbers of visitors and with further plans for new man-made lagoons and resorts. Similarly Jordan's Royal Society for the Conservation of Nature has benefited greatly from adventure tourism, which was non-existent prior to the publication of our climbing and trekking books. Their new Reserves, Protected Areas and Eco-Lodges are described in this new edition, together with information on plans for more in the Petra Mountains and the Jordan Valley, bringing this book fully up to date.

Di Taylor and Tony Howard, 2008

The delightful walk to Pella through the shaded pine woods of Wadi Salih (Route 8)

THANKS TO ALL CONCERNED

Numerous friends have been involved in our explorations, enjoying the excitement and new discoveries and paying the sometimes inevitable price of being rained on, snowed on (yes, it can snow in Jordan), sunburnt, dehydrated or absolutely worn out at the end of some very long days. In particular we would like to thank Wilf Colonna, Bernard Domenech, Mick Shaw and Al Baker for the early years in Rum; Wilfried and Bernard also contributed considerably to the chapter on climbing in Jordan. We were also lucky to enjoy the company of Sami Sabat, Hanna Jahshan, Adam Messer, Paul and Mandy Taylor, Mike Searle, Brian Hodgkinson and Mark and Julie Khano of Arabian Escape on various trips throughout Jordan.

We give special thanks to the people of Rum, especially the late Sheikh Atieq and his sons Defallah, Eid, Mazied and Sabbah; also Hammad Hamdan and his sons, including in recent years Mohammad, now an aspirant mountain guide who, like his father and grandfather, Sheikh Hamdan, is a first-class climber. Sabbah Eid, his family and his brothers have also played a major role in our explorations. Atieq Auda, the youngest of the three Bedouin guides who came to England on the guide's training course in the mid-1990s has also been a good friend, as has his mentor on the mountains, Sheikh Kraim. Still in Rum we must thank Ali Hillawi and Atta who, for many years, were synonymous with the Rest House hospitality, and all the mothers, wives and sisters of our Bedouin friends for preparing the innumerable *mensefs*, the excellent Bedouin bread, and for making us part of the Rum family.

In the Petra area the late Mr Kamel Mehadine and Mr Suleiman Farajat of The Petra Authority provided helpful advice and entry permits, whilst Wendy at Petra Moon Travel, Ismael at La Bedouina Tours, Khalil of Petra Caravan Tours and Nyazi of Nyazi Tours went out of their way to be of assistance with information on southern Jordan. More recently Yousef Hasanat and Sufian Amarat of Jordan Beauty Tours have been of particular help, sponsoring our explorations between Dana and Petra, whilst Nawaf Awad al Fageir and Harun Daqlalah and family also provided friendly hospitality and advice. Further south in Aqaba, William Sawalha and Gill Balchin of the Alcazar Hotel have been good friends since our first visit in 1984, always providing warm hospitality and good company whenever we needed some relaxation.

Elsewhere, the Royal Society for the Conservation of Nature welcomed us into their Nature Reserves and provided knowledgable guides and much-appreciated hospitality. In particular we must thank Khaled Irani (now Minister of the Environment), Chris Johnson (now head of Wild Jordan), Yehya Khalid (the Acting Director) and the RSCN staff, as well as their staff at the Ajloun, Dibeen, Dana and Azraq Reserves. Information on the Azraq Lava Tube was provided by Jadd Younis and Samer Mouasher of Discovery, whilst Raouff Dabas – then of Friends of the Earth, Middle East (FOEME) – took us even further east, to Burqu and a nearby curiosity, the Begaaweyeh Tree. More recently Monqeth Meehear (also of FOEME) has helped with information, as has Adnan Budieri of Ecotech and Birdlife International who, like Khaled Irani, has been a long-time supporter of our work. The Terhaal team have also helped with up-to-date canyon information, and James Garrett provided details of new climbs around Rum and Petra, whilst Ruth Caswell of www.jordanjubilee.com saved the day when other sources of information failed.

For the success of our two visits to finalise the first edition in 1998 we are particularly grateful to our good friend Sami Sabat who not only provided his house for our base but also gave us additional backup transport whenever we needed it, making life so much easier, whilst his mother and brother made sure we were well looked after in his absence. Also in Amman, Rami Khouri (then of Al Kutba Publishers) gave his support when the project looked like faltering, as well as his encouragement and provision of archaeological information. Hanna Jahshan and Qusai Shaath (then of Cheval and Outdoors Unlimited) freely provided hospitality, whilst in recent years Brian and Andjelka Hodgkinson and Mark and Julie Khano made us welcome in their homes as well as providing transport. Anne Meauve and Mattar Auda of Teva Services also provided hospitality in both Amman and Rum, and Geraldine Chatelard shared her wealth of knowledge of Bedouin life and culture and kindly contributed the section on the Bedouin of Wadi Rum.

The Ministry of Tourism was of particular help in the 1980s when the late Mr Nasri Atalla supported not only our original explorations in Rum, but also those elsewhere in Jordan when he was Director of Tourism. More recently, the sponsorship of Jordan Tourism Development (SIYAHA) – helped by USAID – was also invaluable, Ramez Habash and Shukri Halaby providing support whenever it was needed.

Back home, Christine Evans helped with some French translations for the 1st edition as did Al and Kate Carne for the 2nd edition, whilst Mary Hartley of Sansome and Hall Architects, Milton Keynes, provided the floral artwork, which enhances the book, and helped with 1st edition typing. Meanwhile the late St John Armitage provided new and, as always, interesting historical information on our Bedouin friends in Wadi Rum as well as early climbing on Jebel Rum, whilst M .C. A. MacDonald provided fascinating translations of Thamudic inscriptions in Rum.

Even closer to home, Suzanne Troop and Dave Cummins of Bank Creative Consultancy gave us assistance when lost in the complexities of our computer, whilst Troll Climbing Equipment provided equipment and clothing for our early travels in the equally complex mountains and canyons of Jordan. For getting us there we are indebted to Royal Jordanian Airlines, and to Emma Bodossian at their London office for her always helpful, friendly and invaluable assistance.

Finally, we would like to thank Lt Colonel Omar Damra and the Royal Jordanian Air Force for the wonderful helicopter flight over the canyons of Moab near the Dead Sea, arranged with the help of HM Queen Noor of Jordan without whose support the first edition of this guidebook could not have been written. We are also deeply indebted to Her Majesty for kindly contributing the Foreword, and to Dana Toukan at the Office of HM Queen Noor for her constant help and reliable efficiency and for smoothing the way whenever the going became difficult; also Salameh Awamleh, our 'Palace Driver', who happily and willingly accompanied us to more places in Jordan than he ever knew existed – we hope he enjoyed it as much as we did!

To all the above and to everyone in Jordan we are indebted for 23 years of fascinating adventures in a beautiful country with wonderful people. We trust this book will be some small recompense.

Thanks – it's been great!
Di Taylor and Tony Howard, 2008

n.o.m.a.d.s

NEW OPPORTUNITIES FOR MOUNTAINEERING, ADVENTURE AND DESERT SPORTS
www.nomadstravel.co.uk

PERMISSIONS

We thank the following copyright holders for permission to quote from their books:

Al Kutba *The Antiquities of the Jordan Rift Valley* by R.G. Khouri
Alpine Club Library *Mountains in the Desert* by C. Longstaff
Fawzi Zayadine *The Journey of Sultan Baibars* by F. Zayadine
Harper Collins *Portrait of a Desert* by G. Mountfort
Iris Davies (née Service) *Call of the Wild* by R. Service
Methuen *In the Steps of the Master* by H. V. Morton
Seven Pillars of Wisdom Trust *Seven Pillars of Wisdom* by T. E. Lawrence

Many of the other quotations used in this book are now out of copyright, whilst other authors, publishers or copyright holders proved impossible to trace despite our very best efforts. We thank them here for their works, which inspired us to seek out little-known places.

Entering Numeira Siq (Route 57)

INTRODUCTION

The time has surely come when the world will 'discover' the real Jordan and the charm of its proud but hospitable people. When it does so it will find a country more rich in historical heritage than Egypt of the Pharaohs, with more archaeological treasures than Greece and a scenic magnificence rivalling the Grand Canyon and Yosemite.

Portrait of a Desert Guy Mountfort (1965)

Jordan is a land of unexpected beauty and vast variety. Discovering its savage river-filled canyons, awesome mountains and deserts, delightful flower-filled springtime meadows and pine-forested northern hills can be a life-changing experience. Add to this the remarkable hospitably of its people, particularly the Bedouin with their contagious good humour, and any visit to this remarkable Middle Eastern country is guaranteed to more than fulfil expectations. Welcome (*Ahlan wa sahlan*) to Jordan, its land and its people.

As its title implies this guidebook describes walks, treks, caves, climbs and canyons in Jordan, the majority of routes being half- to one-day walks or multi-day treks. There are also descriptions of over 30 canyons, all of which involve walking and scrambling in rivers, usually in inescapable surroundings subject to flash floods and sometimes requiring abseils. Very few caves are described since a limited number have so far been discovered, but Jordan's climbing potential outside Wadi Rum is revealed for the first time and five 'new' climbing areas are covered with pointers to others (climbing in Wadi Rum is described in our book *Treks and Climbs in Wadi Rum*, Cicerone, 4th edition 2007).

In total 150 routes are covered along the length of the country, mostly in the western hills above Jordan's extension of Africa's Rift Valley, the location of Jordan's border with Israel and the West Bank (Eastern Palestine); whilst in the southeast of Jordan along its border with Saudi Arabia 24 desert and mountain walks and scrambles in Wadi Rum are described.

There are routes to suit all abilities in all categories, though there are as yet no 'difficult' caves; nevertheless it should be remembered that all caves are hazardous and more may yet be discovered. Any route requiring special skills, equipment and/or a guide is identified as such in its introduction. Any reasonably fit person should be capable of doing the short walks, although a degree of route-finding ability is sometimes necessary due to the lack of available maps other than those in this book. It is difficult, however, to imagine any reader having problems following the most popular walk, the Petra Siq, and most will be happy on the easy to moderate grades in any category. Note that guides should always be considered if recommended.

Highlights include springtime excursions in the flower-carpeted 'alpine meadows' of the north; the spectacular Dead Sea canyons; the multi-day Dana–Petra treks; the superb walks and treks in and around the ancient city of Petra, one of the recently proclaimed 'New Seven Wonders of the World'; caving and climbing in Jordan's exotic limestone regions often reminiscent of the south of France; and for the full Bedouin experience a night in a real Bedouin camp in Wadi Rum combined with the ascent of a Bedouin hunting route, perhaps to the Rock Bridge, the summit of Jebel Rum or Jordan's highest mountain, Jebel um Adaami, with a Bedouin guide – finish it all off with a snorkelling or diving trip on the coral reefs of the Red Sea and what more could you want!

Prior to the first edition few of the routes had been documented yet – apart from the few climbs, caves and more serious canyons – this is largely a book of ancient trails, some originating as far back as Iron Age times or even before, as early man spread across the land making his home in sheltered valleys and constructing dolmens and forts to guard the heights.

History

Stone tools from the Palaeolithic era possibly dating back 250,000 years were left in Jordan by early man who wandered the hills and valleys hunting large game animals now only found in Africa. Settlements dating back 10,000 years have been excavated. The Edomites, Moabites,

JORDAN

Amorites and Ammonites settled these lands around 1200BC. Moses and the Israelites reputedly passed through the mountains and deserts of Jordan about this time, though expert opinion differs as to exactly when.

The Nabataeans ruled here from 500BC to AD100, controlling the trade routes and the transport of precious silks and spices from the Orient and distant Arabia Felix (Yemen). The ubiquitous Greeks and Romans left their imprint, as did the Byzantines and the soldiers of Islam, the forces of Saladin and the invading Crusaders. Hardly changed by time and the swirl of events, the wandering nomadic tribes of Bedouin settled or passed through on their migrations, in search of grazing and hunting. Their black tents still adorn the windswept plateaux, open deserts and hidden green valleys, moving with the seasons, although their numbers are falling and life is getting harder as the government endeavours to settle them.

Travellers like Sultan Baibars, el-Bakr, Burton, Burkhardt, Doughty, Musil and Lawrence have journeyed through the land, documenting their adventures. It has been fascinating to read these stories of discovery, and to follow in their footsteps and those of the shepherds who still wander Jordan's quiet hills and valleys. Hopefully you too will share in the delights of treading these routes, both ancient and modern.

The people and places that inspired the book

As well as the basic directions necessary to follow the routes each description is accompanied by information giving a taste of the history and extraordinary variety and beauty of the land they pass through, enhanced by quotations from the poetic and romantic writings of those earlier travellers in the nineteenth and early twentieth centuries. Their words inspired our explorations and took us to some quite unexpected places that most Jordanians didn't know existed.

Most people find something uniquely special about trekking in Jordan, identified in 1938 by Louis Golding in his book In the Steps of Moses the Conqueror: 'It is idle to compare phenomena like the Wadi Mojib and the Wadi Hasa and the Grand Canyon at Colorado in terms of figures and say this is the most impressive because it is the deepest and the broadest. Each is a unique experience, compounded out of its own elements of colour and proportion. There is, however, the element of the spiritual significance one rather than another may hold for the onlooker.'

Remarkably little has changed in the wilder parts of Jordan: the Bedouin are just as likely to appear from nowhere as they did 70 years ago when Louis Golding observed 'Every now and then the totally uninhabited landscape would yield up a sudden crop of Bedouin who would

The Bedouin trail from Rajif to Wadi Bahra (Route 113)

16

ENVIRONMENTAL AND CULTURAL AWARENESS

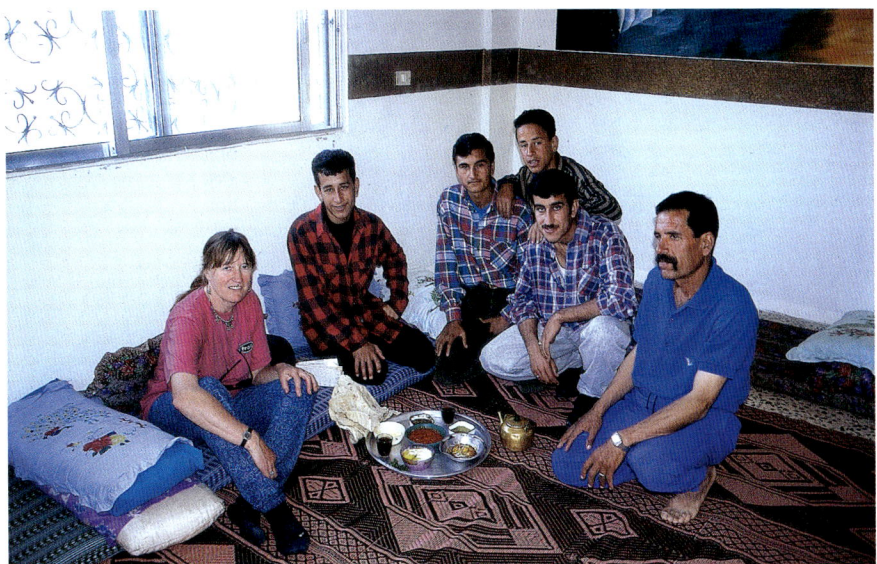

Jordanian hospitality to passing strangers, Kufr Abil, Jordan Valley Hills (Routes 2, 5)

hasten up to us to find out what we were all about.' The inhabitants of the deserts and mountain valleys are fortunately less warlike these days than they were at the turn of the century when tribal squabbles were still common and guns and daggers seemed *de rigueur*. Thompson, in *The Land and The Book* (1859), describes the Bedouin as 'land-pirates', though most considered them to be as hospitable as they are now. Charles Doughty's description, in his classic two-volume *Arabia Deserta*, of his arrival at an encampment in the late 1800s is typical and timeless: 'The sun was setting and the camels wandered in of themselves over the desert, the housewives at the tent milked the small cattle. By the ruins of a city of stone they received me, in the eternity of the poor nomad tents, with a kind hospitality.'

Of course the cities and villages of Jordan have grown in size; paths have sometimes become drivable tracks; tracks have become roads; roads have multiplied. The Desert Highway, only a rough road 20 years ago, is now a motorway and the Dead Sea Highway has appeared from nowhere since our first descent of the Mujib Gorge. Even so, 'off the beaten track' you will find not only a contrasting land of harsh yet sometimes surprisingly delicate beauty, but also a people who will welcome you with a warmth of custom that has its roots in the not-so-distant hard life of the desert, as Geraldine Chatelard describes in her chapter on the Bedouin of Wadi Rum.

Be as good to this land and its people as they will be to you and perhaps it is not too altruistic to hope that both you and they, and thereby the world, will be a little better for your journey.

ENVIRONMENTAL AND CULTURAL AWARENESS

Culture clash

A good holiday is one spent among people whose notions of time are vaguer than ours.

J. B. Priestley

The lack of awareness shown by many tourists concerning the impact of their actions on the cultures and environment of the places they visit is quite often astonishing: girls riding camels or sitting in Bedouin tents dressed in beachwear; picnic boxes and drink cans discarded from 4WD vehicles or left at campsites, toilet paper protruding from beneath stones, names carved on the rocks. The list is long and gives our hosts a very poor impression of our society.

One of the great joys of travel is meeting people from different countries – if we want to be accepted by them it is up to us to behave in a way that is acceptable to them. Make yourself aware of other people's customs and traditions, and act accordingly. Maintain the generally good reputation of trekkers and climbers.

Who's who?

The vast majority of Jordan's 6 million population is Sunni Muslim. According to the late King Hussein's website http://www.kinghussein.gov.jo/people1.html (from which some of this information was obtained) 'this includes many Circassians, a non-Arab Islamic people originally from the Caucasus region of western Asia who first arrived en masse in what is now Jordan in 1878, where they settled in Amman, Wadi Seer and Na'ur. Nowadays, Circassian populations can also be found in Jerash, Sweileh, Zarqa, Azraq and other parts of northern Jordan. Estimates of the Circassian population vary from 20,000 to 80,000. Today, Circassian Jordanians are a well-educated people who continue to play a role in Jordan's political, economic and social life, larger than their numbers would indicate.'

The Arab Christian minority, many of whom were Palestinian, is less than 3 percent of the total population, around 150,000 mostly living in Amman, Ajloun and Karak. There is also a small community of Druze living in Jordan, mainly near the Syrian border but also in Azraq, whist Amman is home to several thousand Armenians. The north Jordan Valley hosts a small community of Turkomans and Baha'is, who moved from Iran to Jordan to escape persecution in 1910.

According to IRIN News (UN Office for the Coordination of Humanitarian Affairs) Jordan hosts about 1.7 million Palestinian refugees from 1948, around 28 percent of Jordan's 6 million population. Many live in 10 impoverished camps around the country, relying on UN aid, which imposes a degree of segregation from the rest of the population. An additional 130,000 Palestinians (IRIN) who were forced to leave their homes during the 1967 Middle East war are more integrated into Jordanian society, as those from the West Bank had lived under Jordanian rule between 1950 and 1967, when Israel seized the land. Many now have Jordanian citizenship. Agence France-Presse has a higher estimate and comments that 'almost half the Jordanian population are of Palestinian origin'. There are also around 0.5 million Iraqi nationals who, like the last wave of Palestinians, tend to be well educated and mainly reside in the capital. Whilst some of the West Bank Palestinians are Christian, most of the Iraqis are Sunni Muslims from Baghdad and many plan to emigrate to a third country.

Although there are many Jordanians whose ancestors inhabited the land before the creation of Transjordan in 1921 and the establishment of the Hashemite Kingdom of Jordan in 1946, large numbers of the population are of ancient Arabian ancestry, which includes the Bedouin. Many (including the Royal family, direct descendents of the Prophet Mohammed) arrived from Saudi Arabia in the 19th century. According to the late

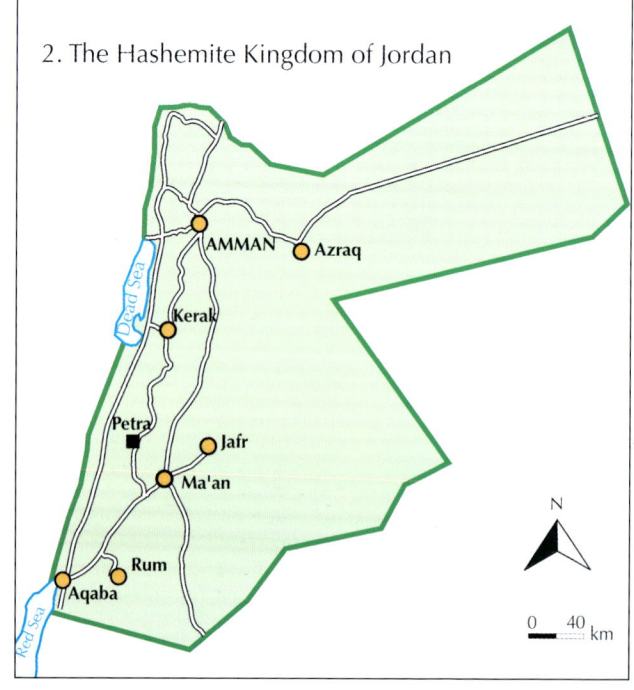

2. The Hashemite Kingdom of Jordan

ENVIRONMENTAL AND CULTURAL AWARENESS

King Hussein's website, 'The Bedouin are undoubtedly the best known of Jordan's population, their communities being marked by characteristic black goat-hair tents. Though often stereotyped as constantly wandering the desert in search of water and food for their flocks only a small portion of Bedouin can still be regarded as true nomads, while many have settled down to cultivate crops [or work with tourism as in Petra and Rum]. It can be said that many of the characteristics of the Jordanian and Arab society are found in their strongest form in Bedouin culture. For instance, Bedouins are most famous for their hospitality, and it is part of their creed – rooted in the harshness of desert life – that no traveller is turned away.'

This pervades the whole of Jordanian culture. The people are welcoming and liberal minded. All religions are respected; some women wear the veil, though the majority do not; indeed, Amman is like any other modern international city. Smaller towns and villages tend to be more conservative, but everywhere the people will respect you as you respect them and their customs.

Cultural tips for travellers

The following notes are a modified version of a checklist from the Ecological Centre, Leh, Ladakh, India, the original source being confirmed by Tourism Concern as 'A Third World Stopover – The Tourism Debate' by Ron O'Grady.

The environment – a plea from the authors

The true servants of the most gracious are those who tread gently on the earth.
The Qu'ran Sura 25, verse 63

The idea for this book germinated in 1984 when we were invited by Jordan's Ministry of Tourism to assess Wadi Rum in South Jordan for its rock-climbing and adventure-tourism potential. With the help of the local people who were still, at that time, predominantly semi-nomadic Bedouin, we quickly identified Rum's huge potential for climbing, trekking and camel safari. This led to the publication of *Treks and Climbs in Wadi Rum* in 1987, followed by *Walks and Scrambles in Wadi Rum* in 1993.

TRAVEL TIPS

- Travel in a spirit of humility and with a genuine desire to learn more about the people of your host country. Be sensitively aware of the feelings of other people thus preventing what might be offensive behaviour on your part. This applies very much to photography – do not take photographs of people without first asking for their permission.
- Instead of the Western practice of 'knowing all the answers', cultivate the habit of asking questions, listening, observing and learning, rather than merely hearing and seeing.
- Realise that often the people in the country you visit have time concepts and thought patterns different to your own. This does not make them inferior, only different.
- Instead of looking for that 'beach paradise', discover the enrichment of seeing a different way of life, through other eyes.
- Acquaint yourself with local customs. What is courteous in one country may be quite the reverse in another. People will be happy to help you.
- Remember that you are only one of thousands of tourists visiting this country and do not expect specific privileges.
- If you really want your experience to be a 'home away from home', it is foolish to waste money on travelling.
- When you are shopping remember that 'bargain' you obtained possibly because of the low wages paid to the maker or because the poorest merchant may sooner give up his profit than his dignity.
- Do not make promises to people in your host country such as sending photos when you get home unless you intend to carry them through.
- Spend time reflecting on your daily experience in an attempt to deepen your understanding. It has been said that 'what enriches you may rob and violate others'.
- Enjoy yourself, but remember that an extravagant display of wealth is insensitive to local people who may have to manage on much less money than you have. Nevertheless, respect and accept genuinely given hospitality – do not taint your hosts by offering money when none is required but discreetly establish first what is expected.

Whilst all this was going on we made further trips into Jordan's other mountain areas, finding a wild and beautiful country unspoiled by tourism. In 1985 we walked through Wadi Dana from what was then a ruined village with few inhabitants – it has since become one of Jordan's first Nature Reserves. Tremendous work has been done by Jordan's Royal Society for the Conservation of Nature (RSCN), not only to identify the indigenous flora and fauna, but also to ensure that the village was restored to its original state and the inhabitants helped by bringing into the area traditional work such as agriculture and crafts. It is one of Jordan's success stories. On that same trip we returned to Petra via Wadi Siyyagh, from the wilderness of Wadi Araba. This was another astonishing journey, discovering waterfalls, deep pools and palms where the maps showed only desert and rocky ravines.

Other exploratory trips in the following years were equally or even more astounding: the spectacular Siq of Tibn, the oasis of Sabra, the 'Grand Canyon' of Mujib, the hilltop ruins of Selah, the Cave of Zubia, the forests and 'alpine' meadows of Ajloun and Pella and numerous cliffs of limestone, granite, basalt, conglomerate and sandstone. The list goes on: all 'new', all exciting and beautiful, all different. Coupled with the treks and scrambles we were still discovering in Rum with the help of our Bedouin friends, such as that to Jebel Adaami, Jordan's highest mountain, we soon realised we had a unique collection of adventures which deserved publication.

The dilemma for guidebook writers is, however, a real one: do we say nothing and hope these places will stay 'undiscovered' and pristine, or do we tell all and risk the hidden jewels being destroyed so that others can share our discoveries and the local people can benefit from their visits?

Our experience in Rum has been salutary. In this day and age it is extremely rare that a truly 'new' area such as Rum once was is revealed in a guidebook. In the ensuing 20-plus years we have watched the changes that have taken place, partly as a result of our work. This has given us cause for considerable soul-searching: the bad news is that, despite our advice in the guidebook, places like the Rock Bridge and the summit of Jebel Rum have been vandalised by graffiti. Some of the ancient rock art has gone the same way. The tracks of 4WD vehicles now cover most of

Inside the maze of Rakabat Canyon (Routes 128, 129, 130)

ENVIRONMENTAL AND CULTURAL AWARENESS

The Monastery, Petra: the figure on the central finial gives the scale (Routes 83, 84)

the desert, destroying fragile ecosystems. Litter can be found at popular tourist sites. A few shiny rock climbers' safety bolts have appeared in unsightly places.

The good news is that the local people have benefited tremendously, although the direct benefits of their homeland being designated a Protected Area have yet to be proven. The damage to the rock art and desert has reached a point where others are becoming concerned and are supporting efforts to stop it. The destruction could be contained and the worst of the damage could be removed. Thousands of people have had wonderful, memorable experiences in the desert and mountains, and many have struck up lasting friendships with the Bedouin to the benefit of all.

We hope that the growth of visitors has been less destructive than it may otherwise have been had we not stressed the cultural and environmental considerations in our books. Even so, we are very concerned that the success of Jordan's tourism will mean that the local people are put under ever-increasing pressure by outside commercial interests who sometimes want their own slice of the pie at the expense of others. Wherever possible, please use local guides and amenities.

As far as environmental damage goes, we believe it has usually, if not always, come from the uncontrolled growth of mass tourism (from Jordanians themselves, as well as from abroad), rather than from the relatively small numbers of, hopefully, 'aware' trekkers and climbers. Tour guides, usually from outside the area and perhaps lacking in environmental awareness, are also responsible, as are sometimes the local people; the irreparable damage caused to Zubia Cave is a tragedy (see Caving in Jordan), as was the destruction of a World War 1 Turkish train out in the desert near Wadi Rum. Until a few years ago it was still standing on rusted tracks after being blown up by 'Lawrence of Arabia', a relic of history that should have been treasured but which was thoughtlessly cut up for scrap metal – what an attraction it would have been! Those involved in tourism in Jordan should take note before other precious resources are lost.

Nevertheless, none of us can be complacent; few of us are entirely blameless and we should be aware at all times that our actions will inevitably impact on the environment and cultures of the

21

places we pass through. It is up to us all to make our impact a positive one, and we hope that readers of this guide will act in a way that will be a credit to them.

You should find little or no litter on the trails in this book (if you do, please remove it), no new waymarks, no toilet paper, few signs of fire other than perhaps a few burnt sticks left by shepherds enjoying their regular cups of shai. The people you will meet will inevitably be welcoming and friendly. Please do everything you can to keep it this way. Jordan is a haven of peace. Have fun, take care and tread gently!

Environmental tips for the traveller

The world is green and beautiful and Allah has appointed you as his stewards over it. He sees how you acquit yourselves.

Sayings of the Prophet Mohammed

USEFUL HINTS

- Observe restrictions and access agreements negotiated by National Mountaineering Federations (or, in Jordan's case, Nature Reserves and other RSCN zones), and avoid any actions which might endanger access.
- Limit desertification – make no open fires and discourage others from doing so on your behalf.
- Remove litter, burn or bury paper and carry out all non-degradable litter. Keep campsites clean. Graffiti are permanent examples of environmental pollution.
- Keep local water clean and avoid using pollutants such as detergents in streams, wells or springs. If no toilet facilities are available make sure you are far away from water sources, and bury waste. Burn toilet paper or use water instead.
- Do not disturb nesting birds or other wildlife and respect sites of geological or other scientific interest. Plants should be left to flourish in their natural environment – do not take cuttings, seeds and roots. It is illegal in Nature Reserves and bad practice elsewhere.
- Do not disturb livestock or damage crops or vegetation.
- Avoid actions that cause unnecessary erosion (such as taking short cuts on footpaths).
- Wear lightweight boots or trainers and tread carefully, especially in descent. Do not leave unnecessary waymarks.
- Rock climbers should respect established mountain traditions in ethical matters such as the use of chalk, pitons or bolts, and so on. Avoid indiscriminate or excessive use of fixed equipment.
- Help your guides and porters to follow conservation measures.

The following guidelines have been compiled from information given in the International Union of Alpine Associations (UIAA) Mountain Code, the British Mountaineering Council's conservation booklet *Tread Lightly*, and the Himalayan Tourist Code published by Tourism Concern, sponsored by *The Independent* and Rough Guide publications. By following these simple rules (see box) you can help preserve the unique environment of the places you pass through.

For information on fighting exploitation in tourism contact:
Tourism Concern
Stapleton House
277–281 Holloway Road
London N7 8HN
Tel: +44 (0) 20 7133 3330
Fax: +44 (0) 20 7133 3331
E-mail: tourconcern@gn.apc.org
Website: www.tourismconcern.org.uk

For information on mountain tourism and the ethics and responsibilities of trekkers and climbers, contact your national mountaineering body, which (in the UK) is:
The British Mountaineering Council
177–179 Burton Road
Manchester M20 2BB
Tel: 0161 445 6111/0870 010 4878
Fax: 0161 445 4500
E-mail: office@thebmc.co.uk
Website: www.thebmc.co.uk

For information on environmental action in Jordan and the Middle East contact:
Friends of the Environment An independent non-profit-making NGO encouraging the younger generation to take an active part in conserving and improving their natural environment:

THE ROYAL SOCIETY FOR THE CONSERVATION OF NATURE

PO Box 1554
Amman 11118
Jordan
Tel: 00 9626 5514430
E-mail: foes@nets.com.jo
Website: www.cns.com.jo/org/foe/index.htm

EcoPeace A consortium of Egyptian, Israeli, Jordanian and Palestinian environmental NGOs working jointly to promote sustainable development in the Middle East region:
2 El Akhtal Street
East Jerusalem 97400
PO Box 55302
Israel
Tel: 00 9722 6260841/3
Fax: 00 9722 6260840
E-mail: ecopeace@Netvision.net.il

Friends of the Earth, Middle East (FOEME)
PO Box 840252
Amman 11181
Jordan
Tel: 00 9626 5866602/3
Fax: 00 9626 5866604
E-mail: info@foeme.org
Website: www.foeme.org

For archaeological information contact:
Friends of Archaeology
PO Box 2440
Amman 11181
Jordan
Tel/fax: 00 9626 696682
E-mail: foa@nets.com.jo
Website: www.foa.com.jo

For information on Jordan's Nature Reserves contact:
The Royal Society for the Conservation of Nature
PO Box 1215
Jubeiha-Abu-Nusseir Circle
Amman 11941
Jordan
E-mail: rscn@rscn.org.jo
Website: www.rscn.org.jo

THE ROYAL SOCIETY FOR THE CONSERVATION OF NATURE

The RSCN is a non-profit-making organisation, using the income it receives from visitors to directly support its conservation work. The following information was kindly supplied by them.

Jordan is blessed with a wide range of climates, resulting in an unusually large number of different habitats and great biological diversity for a country of its size, but many are extremely fragile and can be easily disrupted. There are substantial local climatic variations, largely due to the extensive differential in heights from the country's lowest point at the Dead Sea, 400m below sea level, to the high mountaintops at around 1800m. Other contributory factors include the different soil types (rich agricultural soil to desert sand) and the varying rainfall levels from a mean annual total of 50mm in the eastern badia to nearer 800mm in Ajloun. Runoff from the mountains is high, and much water soaks into the valley floors, which support a far denser vegetation than would be expected from the low rainfall figures. All these factors combine to create multiple wildlife habitats and a complex ecology, resulting in a wonderfully varied and beautiful country, with many different species of flora and fauna: an environment that needs to be carefully protected.

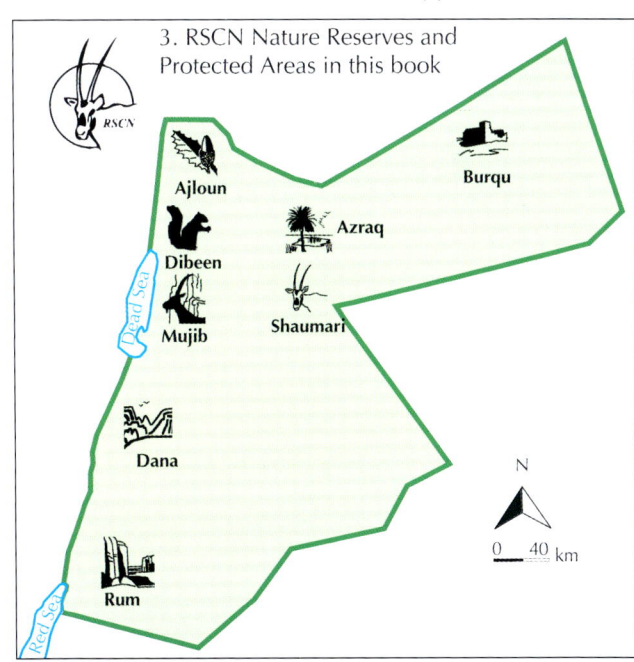

3. RSCN Nature Reserves and Protected Areas in this book

Founded in 1966, the RSCN has since set up a system of wildlife Reserves and Protected Areas as part of its environmental protection scheme. Its mission is to protect wildlife habitat in Jordan and to promote an understanding of the natural environment. It is currently involved in a six-year project in the Jordan Rift Valley where new Reserves are to be opened covering a total area of 570sq km in the Yarmuk River basin in the north of the Jordan Valley, Fifa in Ghor Safi by the Dead Sea, and Qatar and Jebel Mas'uda (south of Petra) in and above Wadi Araba. The JD13 million Rift Valley Project was launched in November 2007 to protect the various environments with their unique ecosystems and threatened species and to improve the living conditions of the area's inhabitants as well as to examine the impact of climate change on the country's ecosystems. By 2013 there will be 11 such 'sanctuaries'.

The Reserves offer visitors a chance to experience some of the country's most beautiful landscapes, including the spectacular sandstone cliffs and wild valleys of Dana, the flowing streams of Mujib, the woodlands of Dibeen and Ajloun, the desert grassland of Shaumari and the marshes of Azraq, with new Reserves proposed for Wadi Araba and the mountains south of Petra. The Protected Area of Wadi Rum has its own particular regulations. Whether you enjoy hiking, climbing, canyoning, birdwatching, archaeology or simply a quiet picnic, RSCN's Nature Reserves offer something for anyone who loves nature and wild places. They also have their own code of ethics (◄ see box).

CODE OF ETHICS

- **Beauty without crowds** In order to protect the environment within the Nature Reserves, the number of visitors allowed to enter each day is limited and cars are required to park outside, so you can experience the wonders of nature in peace and quiet.
- **A chance to learn about nature** RSCN offers trained guides who can accompany visitors and tell them about the wildlife, landscape and history of the area.
- **A chance to explore unspoiled landscapes** There are hiking trails in all the Reserves, enabling visitors to experience the beautiful places and special character of each one; some trails can be self guided, others need a tour guide.
- **A sense of adventure** For small groups seeking a challenge, adventure treks can be arranged in the more dramatic and remote wild places of Jordan.
- **Specialist tours** A number of these are being developed on topics such as birdwatching and botany to cater for those visitors seeking more in-depth knowledge. Adventure trekking is also being offered.
- **A way to support the conservation of wildlife** All the money visitors contribute through entrance fees, accommodation charges and buying crafts is used to further the work of RSCN and help protect the wildlife and wild places of Jordan.
- **A way to help local people** RSCN has a policy of employing local people where possible and to create opportunities for them to earn income from the Nature Reserves.

Visitor code

To ensure that the Reserves are protected for future generations, visitors are asked to respect all regulations, and particularly to:
- Obtain a valid permit before entering the Reserve.
- Leave vehicles in designated parking places.
- Protect all nature (don't hunt or collect flowers, rocks, fossils or archaeological artefacts).
- Camp only at official sites.
- Keep to permitted hiking trails and access routes.
- Enjoy the sounds of nature (don't use radios or musical instruments, or play noisy games).
- Leave nature's beauty for others to enjoy (don't damage trees or rocks).
- Refrain from making open fires (firewood collection damages trees and shrubs; many creatures make their home in dead wood).
- Keep the reserve clean (don't leave litter or pollute watercourses).
- Dress modestly and ask permission before taking photographs of local people.
- Respect local cultures and traditions and you will be rewarded with warmth and hospitality.
- All tour operators should ensure that potential visitors are made aware of these regulations.

How to make a booking

Advance booking is essential to stay, or trek, in a Reserve, and is best done by contacting the RSCN or their tourism organisation Wild Jordan

Camp in the Mujib Gorge at end of Day 1, before entering the Reserve (Routes 48, 49)

(see Appendix 1). Enquiries can be dealt with in person in downtown Amman at the new Wild Jordan Centre, which also has a café. It is located beyond the 1st Circle, down Rainbow Street past the British Council, then left at the Jordan River Designs shop (worth a visit), beyond which a small side street and steps lead down to the Centre.

The RSCN Headquarters is about 10km from the 3rd Circle in Amman to Jubeiha-Abu-Nusseir Circle. Turn right there, then right again a short distance up the road at the next circle, then right again. The RSCN building with its oryx head logo is on your left.

Note that (with rare exceptions, which are noted) an RSCN approved guide must accompany every tour in the Reserves. This, the limited visitor numbers and the need to book well in advance can hinder those experienced in trekking and canyoning, some of whom have been deterred by what they see as unnecessary restrictions; as a result the RSCN loses income and people miss some of Jordan's most beautiful places. Luckily there are no such Draconian rules in Wadi Rum where the Bedouin had already developed the concept of adventure tourism.

WILDLIFE IN JORDAN

Jordan sits at the junction of three continents – Europe, Africa and Asia – and birds from these regions are often seen in the same vicinity. The country has a remarkable variety of habitats from rugged mountains and evergreen woodland to scrubby steppe and hot desert. Each of these has its special complement of birds. Jordan's Great Rift Valley is a 'bottleneck' on the main route for birds migrating from Eastern Europe and Russia to Africa. At certain times of the year the skies over the Rift Valley are full of circling birds of prey.

Birdwatching tours in Jordan are organised by the Royal Society for the Conservation of Nature, the partner in Jordan of Birdlife International. By joining one of their Wild Jordan tours you are helping to finance the conservation of the country's finest nature areas (see Appendix 1).

What birds might you see?

The eastern part of the country consists mainly of desert habitats and contains the Azraq wetland. While the wetland holds aquatic species and is packed with migrants in spring, the surrounding area supports characteristic desert birds, such as the Temmiinck's horned lark, desert lark, hoopoe lark, desert wheatear and trumpeter finch. In winter cranes and imperial eagles roam across this area. While walking around the desert castles, thick-billed lark and red-rumped wheatear can be spotted.

In the west, the highlands contain typical Mediterranean habitats, usually surrounded by open steppe country. In the wooded areas (such as Ajloun, Rumeimin, Zubia, Dibeen, Salt and Dana) Palestine sunbird, Upcher's, Orphean and Sardinian warbler can be found, while the more open, steppe habitats typically hold spectacled warbler, long-billed pipit, black-eared wheatchat, shrike and linnet.

The Rift Valley margins on the western side of the highlands and the wadis cutting into and crossing the mountains – the crossroads of four bio-geographic zones (Mediterranean, Irano-Turanian, Sudanian and Sahara-Arabian) – often hold a wide range of birds. Wadi Shu'eib and Wadi Mujib contain perennial watercourses which are home to the beautiful Smyrna kingfisher, whilst the magnificent rocky gorges of Wadi Rum, Dana, Mujib and Petra are home to griffon vulture, Bonelli's eagle, Hume's tawny owl, blackstart, different wheatears, scrub warbler, Sinai rose finch, house bunting, Tristram's grackle and fan-tailed raven, to mention a few.

Last but not least, the Dead Sea area and Wadi Araba contain mainly Arabian and African species: sand partridge, bar-tailed dunn, hoopoe lark, little green bee-eater, blackstart and Arabian warbler.

What animals might you see?

The endangered ibex, once that most prized creature of the Bedouin hunter, is now being bred by the RSCN in their Mujib Reserve for reintroduction to the wild, but they can – if you're lucky – still be seen in the mountains of Rum and other high, remote places, despite illegal hunting. The beautiful and highly endangered oryx, together with the ostrich, are subjects of another RSCN breeding programme in the Shaumari Reserve and Wadi Rum, as is the goitered gazelle in the Ajloun Reserve. Elsewhere, fleet-footed gazelles, mongoose, porcupines, snakes, rare wolves and even rarer striped hyenas still lurk in shaded corners of the mountains, canyons and deserts.

The large, long-legged, fast-moving camel spider can empty a Bedouin tent in seconds! It is not harmful to humans but can anaesthetise a sleeping camel long enough to eat a hole in it. Scorpions can be found almost anywhere (beware of sitting on them; be careful when picking up sticks and stones; and, if you sleep out, check your shoes before putting them on). You are much less likely to see snakes – although horned and Palestinian vipers are not too uncommon – and according to the RSCN there are also Egyptian cobras, whilst we saw a large

Montpellier snake near the Yarmuk Gorge. Gerbils and lizards (including the blue Sinai lizard), as well as hedgehogs and rock hyrax, are fairly common; there are also chameleons, and wherever there is water there may be frogs and even freshwater shrimps and crabs, even in the most remote pools and streams no longer connected to the sea.

Wild boar roam by the Jordan River and in the forested hills of the north, and some have been reported near a spring north of Rum. The desert cat and fox (fennec) are extremely reclusive, as is the rabbit, though you may see the greyhound-like saluki, which is used by the Bedouin for hunting. (You may even come across a captive peregrine falcon being trained for hunting, for eventual sale to Saudi Arabia, although this is illegal). Finally, of course there are camels and finely bred, high-spirited Arabian horses, either of which you may be tempted to ride in Petra or Rum.

THE LIE OF THE LAND

Sometimes I have seen the desert referred to as a dead land without life, a barren waste or a landscape of the moon. Nothing could be further from the truth, for the desert is in reality indescribably beautiful with its pure air, its distant blue horizons and its rolling hills and valleys covered with shrubs. There is a magical fascination about the desert which fills one with a wild elation.
A Soldier with The Arabs Glubb Pasha (c1930)

Jordan is generally perceived as a 'desert country'. Don't be deceived! There are, of course, vast and generally arid deserts to the east and northeast, bordering Saudi Arabia, Iraq and Syria. Wadi Araba, which descends to both Aqaba and the Dead Sea, 400m below sea level, can be as hot and dry as almost anywhere on the planet, but elsewhere Jordan has different stories to tell: the desert of Rum in the southeast is a land of great isolated mountains, its steep-walled 'jebels' rising like battleships from coloured sands which are dotted with vegetation and, after the spring rains, carpeted with flowers.

The hills that form the east side of Jordan's extension of the Rift Valley run the full length of the country. Though increasingly arid to the south, above Araba, they and their upper plateaux are riven by beautiful gorges and canyons often concealing rivers. Oak forests, junipers and small green fields cultivated by

Ancient olive groves, Wadi Yabis

JORDAN

Bedouin or local farmers give an unexpected Mediterranean charm to these otherwise seemingly inhospitable wild hills.

At the northern end of the Dead Sea – and also below sea level – the continuation of the Rift, now the Jordan Valley, is lush and green year-round with crops of fruit and vegetables. The hills above are generally less rocky than their southern counterparts with thick forests and pinewoods sheltering rich carpets of springtime anemones and other flowers, which appear as winter's snow melts or the spring rains finish.

Amongst this vast varied landscape archaeological sites abound. Prehistoric man inhabited the Jordan Valley at Pella 250,000 years ago; 10,000-year-old settlements, dolmens, great tumuli or tells, castles, fortresses, abandoned villages, once-lost cities and Biblical sites exist throughout the country. Add to that the world-renowned Petra, the magnificent Islamic hilltop fortress at Ajloun, the great Roman city of Jerash, Herod's fortress at Mukawir, the Crusader castle of Karak, the tomb of Aaron, brother of Moses, on a hilltop high above Petra… the list is endless. The journeys in this book follow trails ancient and modern through this ever-changing landscape, often far from the nearest road. They are journeys of discovery both of nature's wonders – deserts, mountains, canyons, caves and hot springs – and of the history of man.

Trekking below the cliffs of Thôr Motlagh, Ajloun (Routes 1, 2 and Climbing in Jordan)

Geographical and historical boundaries

East of the River Jordan and its southern continuations, the Dead Sea and Wadi Araba, the mountains explored in this guidebook are divided by three steep gorges with perennial rivers. These districts correspond roughly with the Kingdoms of the Old Testament, and are described as follows:

North Jordan

This chapter is divided into the Jordan Valley Hills, the North Eastern Desert and the Capital Area. The former includes the modern district of Ajloun (the Biblical land of Gilead), which lies between the Yarmuk River marking Jordan's border with Syria, and Wadi Zerqa (the Jabbok of Biblical times). The area abounds with famous Greek and Roman ruins as well as castles from the Crusader period and Iron Age remains. The region between Zerqa and the north end of the Dead Sea including the capital, Amman, was originally the land of the Ammonites and is described as the Capital Area. The oases and castles in the North Eastern deserts are also covered, and the whole area is easily accessible from Amman. The Jordan Valley Hills have some excellent trekking as well as climbing and caving.

The Dead Sea Hills

The mountains above the Dead Sea (once the Old Testament land of Moab and consequently holding a considerable number of important sites from that period) are nowadays mostly part of the district of Karak and extend from the hills immediately north of the Mujib Gorge to Wadi al Hasa. Amman and Madaba are the bases for the region north of Mujib, otherwise the town of Karak with its magnificent Crusader castle is ideally located for trips in the south. The area is described in three sections: the Madaba Area, the RSCN Mujib Reserve and the Karak Area. All have superb canyon trips and some climbing possibilities.

The Dana Area

The District of Ma'an (the land of the Edomites and later the Nabataeans) stretches south from

THE LIE OF THE LAND

Entering the Upper
Hidan Gorge (Route 39)

On the Cave Trail near
Dana campsite (Route 69)

29

Exploring Petra's many tombs (Route 81)

View south from the Thamudic Route (Route 124)

Wadi al Hasa to the Gulf of Aqaba. The northern part of this area is the Northern Dana Area; moving south the RSCN Dana Reserve with its unique ecosystems and traditional village is passed, then the Shaubak Area beneath its eponymous castle, beyond which is Petra. There are first-rate treks in this area, some continuing all the way to Rum and Aqaba; some surprising canyons cut through the hills and climbing areas have been discovered recently.

The Petra Area
Petra itself needs no introduction, but in the surrounding Shara Mountains there is excellent trekking, not to mention the numerous Biblical, Nabataean, Roman and Crusader sites. All are accessible from Wadi Musa, the gateway to Petra. Southeast of Petra the great expanse of the Hisma extends to the border with Saudi Arabia, but other than treks and safaris through from Petra to Rum there is little here to interest the traveller.

Wadi Rum and the Aqaba Mountains
South of Petra the mountains and canyons continue all the way to Aqaba, bounded on their west by the barren Wadi Araba, which extends from the Dead Sea to the Red Sea. Bases for exploration of this area are Wadi Rum or Aqaba. Rum is now world-famous as a climbing area, including some magnificent ways to its summits following unique Bedouin hunting routes, 'amongst the world's best mountain adventures'. A selection of these mountain routes and desert treks are described along with other routes in the Aqaba Mountains.

ON THE MOVE

Going to Jordan
There are numerous travel guides available giving advice on international travel (see Appendix 2). British Airways now fly to Jordan from London Heathrow, whilst other airlines fly from Manchester to Jordan via major European cities. Costs are around £500 return, though better prices can be obtained by shopping around; try Turkish Airlines, for example. Royal Jordanian Airlines (Space One, 6th Floor, 1 Beadon Road, London W6 0EA tel: 0207 878 6333, fax: 0208 748 2426, website: www.rj.com) fly daily from London, Paris and many European cities to Amman, and on to Aqaba.

Voyages Jules Verne fly charters from London Gatwick to Aqaba in the spring and autumn, which may have seat-only options at around £300 return, e-mail: sales@vjv.co.uk

There are also inexpensive charter flights to Eilat in Israel, which is next to Aqaba. If you search around you will find other comparatively inexpensive fares to Jordan but financial savings have to be considered versus the inconvenience of, say, flying via Moscow, or having to take various taxi and bus rides from Eilat Airport (which is about 60km from Eilat), then having to pay an Israeli exit tax before entering Jordan and getting another taxi to Aqaba – and the same complicated journey on your way home.

Travel by the most convenient route and you can be in Jordan in six hours and on the hills the next day. Go a cheaper way and it may well take one or two days. Such is life!

For British travellers tourist information is available from the Jordan Tourism Board, 1st Floor, Kennedy House, 115 Hammersmith Road, London W14 0QH tel: 020 7371 6496, fax: 020 7603 2424, brochure line: 0870 777 3553, e-mail: info@jordantourismboard.co.uk, website: www.visitjordan.com/uk

At the time of writing costs for direct Royal Jordanian Airlines flights from New York to Amman are $900–1300 dependent on season, and around $1200–1700 from Montreal, Canada. European operators can be more expensive, and include a European stopover.

For climbing and trekking holidays in Wadi Rum from the UK, contact High Places, Globe Centre, Penistone Road, Sheffield S6 3AE, tel and fax: 0114 275 7500, website: www.highplaces.co.uk; or KE Adventures tel: 01768 773966, website: www.keadventure.com; or contact any of the Jordanian adventure travel companies in Appendix 1, or try Jordan's Ministry of Tourism, PO Box 224, Amman 11118, Jordan tel: 00 9626 4642311/4 fax: 00 9626 4648465, website: www.tourism.jo/inside/Main.asp

Getting in
European citizens can buy a month-long visa on arrival at the airport or other point of entry to Jordan for 10JD. Alternatively, British citizens can purchase one in advance from the Visa Department at the Jordanian Embassy, 6 Upper Phillimore Gardens, London W8 7HB (visa information tel: 0870 005 6952). For stays exceeding one month you will need a visa extension, which

JORDAN

can be obtained from the police station in most large towns, or from the offices of the Aqaba Authority (ASEZA) in Aqaba.

If entering from Israel be aware that an Israeli stamp or even a Jordanian or Egyptian entry stamp from an Israeli border crossing point precludes entry to countries such as Syria.

Where to go

As outlined above, this guidebook will introduce you to all of Jordan's mountains, although there are still gaps on the map when it comes to adventure tourism. We have, for example, been told of interesting walks between archaeological sites in the great basalt deserts of the northeast, and of others in the eastern deserts or in the mountains north of Aqaba that may be less harsh than they first appear. *Trekking & Canyoning in the Jordanian Dead Sea Rift* (see Appendix 2), published soon after the first edition of this book appeared, covers the canyons of the Rift Valley in great detail; if that is your specific interest that title supplements this book perfectly.

If you visit these areas and find anything new, exciting or interesting, please let us know. Alternatively, if you want to experience the many excellent trips that are already 'on the map' then look no further. If you find any errors in the descriptions please advise us about those too; remember, landslips and changes to canyons are not uncommon due to annual flash floods and, sadly, new roads can often replace old paths.

The routes are described from north to south. Generally those in the north are in a greener, kinder environment and demand the least experience. Most are in the vicinity of sites of antiquity and many can be reached from Amman, returning to the city in the evening.

Moving south there are still some short walks available, but the big canyons of the Dead Sea Hills in central Jordan are the pièce de résistance of this area – do not consider them unless you are an experienced walker and do not go alone; some may require the use of ropes. These canyons offer truly spectacular and often unexpected, even tropical, scenery and are truly rewarding for those seeking real adventures and who have the skills to extricate themselves if things go wrong: anything can happen, from broken ankles and snake or scorpion bites to flash floods and even encounters with hyenas.

In southern Jordan around Dana and Petra there are options for everyone with a range of short walks and multi-day treks starting from places such as the Dana campsite or the town of Wadi Musa outside Petra. Specialist adventure travel companies offer guided trips to some very remote areas, usually in the company of local Bedouin, and even treks on foot or by horse or camel from Petra to Rum. Whatever you are looking for – spectacular and beautiful scenery, wilderness adventure, wildlife or archaeology – you will find it here in abundance.

Last but by no means least is Wadi Rum, the land of Lawrence of Arabia, a mountain desert par excellence. Here you will find awe-inspiring treks and climbs, 4WD journeys and camel and horse safaris amongst unsurpassed

Bedouin children in Petra (Route 81)

landscapes. A group of two or more can walk and climb unguided if they have the necessary skills and equipment, though many prefer to hire local Bedouin guides for a real desert experience.

When to go

There was a time when travellers chose only to visit Jordan in autumn and spring. April is undoubtedly a favourite month: water is at its most plentiful and the land is green and carpeted with flowers in the northern pinewoods and, if you're really lucky, in the southern deserts too. Spring is definitely the best time to wander amongst the flower-filled northern meadows, forests and valleys, and to discover your own short walks in this generally gentle terrain. However, it may not be the time for trips into the great canyons such as Mujib and Hidan that are prone to flash floods from rain falling on near or distant hills up to late April (and in some years later). See the box below for weather records in Jordan.

Apart from avoiding the hotter summer months from June to August, travellers today seem to take to the trails throughout the year. Note that in the hills north of Amman there may well be snow in the winter months and there will inevitably be some rain almost anywhere in Jordan from early November through to the end of March or even late April, especially in the north. A few years ago it even snowed in Aqaba and there were winter floods of unprecedented proportions in Wadi Rum. In the winter of 2006–7 there were blizzards in the mountains of both Petra and Rum, trapping two climbers for two days just below the summit of Jebel Rum. Global warming has caused the weather to become less predictable.

Daylight hours in winter are short and it's not the best time to go (although some climbers and trekkers are not deterred). The best seasons are spring and autumn, late March through to the end of May, and late September to mid-November. If you are considering any canyon trips remember that people are killed by flash floods in these inescapable places. Go there when the weather is fine; late spring should be fine, the safest time of all being summer and early autumn when the water is low and before the onset of the winter rains. Due to climate change extra caution is required; two people were killed in Wadi Zerqa Ma'in by a flash flood in late April 2007, and four in a canyon in Israel in early May 2007. In mid-May that year there were floods in Jerusalem and violent electric storms over Amman followed by days of rain, all very unusual. The world is changing – take care!

On the road

From Amman airport there are currently regular JETT (Jordan Express Tourist Transport) bus services to Abdali bus station in Amman for 3JD leaving every hour from 6am to midnight, running less frequently through the night. (The airport bus may soon be changing its destination to Tabarbor, an out-of-town bus station, to allow for redevelopment of the Abdali area; if so, getting a taxi into town from the airport is probably your best bet as you would need one anyway to get there from the bus station.) The cost is around 20JD to Amman, or nearer 80JD to Wadi Rum or Aqaba.

Public transport is much cheaper in Jordan than in Europe, for example 6JD from Amman to Aqaba with Trust or JETT air-conditioned buses with hostesses (from 7th Circle and Abdali respectively). These services are fast, punctual and efficient, though it is usually necessary to book in advance; for reservations contact JETT on 00 9626 5664146, and Trust on 00 9626 5813427. The regular public bus services, on the other hand, do not require pre-booking and although there are usually plenty they tend to go when they're full, stop frequently and arrive at their destination after a sometimes rattling journey. However, they are very cheap and you may well meet lots of friendly Jordanians en route.

Service-taxis also ply regular bus routes on a similar basis. They are a bit more expensive but they'll get you there quickly – you may wish you'd gone by bus, depending on the driver!

WEATHER RECORDS

Place	Month	Average Temp (°C) Min	Max	Average rainfall (mm) Min	Max
Amman	Dec–Mar	4	16	30	75
Amman	Apr–Nov	9	32	0	5
Aqaba	Dec–Mar	5	33	2	5
Aqaba	Apr–Nov	11	43	0	2

Private taxis: you're in control, and if the driver goes too fast you can ask him to slow down; you can go when and where you want but, as always, it costs; establish the price first. Alternatively you can hire a car: prices start from 25JD per day. Fuel prices are lower than in Europe, but are expected to rise considerably in 2008. In January 2008 prices were: diesel 0.315JD per litre, petrol super 0.605JD per litre, petrol regular 0.43JD per litre, petrol unleaded 0.64JD per litre (see Money Matters below).

It's worth knowing the Arabic words for different types and grades of fuel: *benzin* (regular), *super* (high octane), *khali min rassas* or *khali*, (unleaded), *solar* or *diesel* (diesel). The costs of public transport and vehicle hire are well covered in general travel books to Jordan (see Appendix 2).

Accommodation

As with most things in life you get what you pay for: small hotels are available in most towns charging as little as 10–15JD a night for a double room, sometimes with en suite shower and toilet.

Bedouin camp, Wadi Rum

Generally speaking such rooms will be adequately clean (though not always). If you move up nearer the 20JD bracket you may even get breakfast. Beyond that the sky's the limit, and if you really want you can stay in one of the excellent RSCN Eco-Lodges or experience the luxury of Jordan's ultra-modern hotels. Contact details and prices for most will be found in travel guides such as the relevant Rough Guide or Lonely Planet guide, or via the Internet.

Places such as Wadi Rum and Dana have official campsites with prices ranging from 2JD a night at the Rum Rest House to 25JD B&B at Bedouin camps near Petra; all camps have showers and toilets. Out in the deserts and mountains you can camp or bivouac for free.

In Wadi Rum camping is possible almost anywhere. In the RSCN Nature Reserves camping is only permitted in RSCN tents on their campsites. In Petra camping (or sleeping in the 'caves') is not permitted in the old city or its immediate vicinity. However, in the outlying areas sleeping out seems to be allowed except on the top of Jebel Harun, which is a holy place.

In other parts of Jordan camping does not seem to be a problem although professional

OTHER THINGS WORTH KNOWING

travel companies need permits and it is probable that individual trekkers and campers would be moved if camped near roads and villages. The official position is unclear, but if you camp in remote places it is highly unlikely that you will have any problem with officialdom, whose main concern is for your safety in times of Middle East instability. Fortunately Jordan always seems to be a haven of peace.

OTHER THINGS WORTH KNOWING
Holidays and holy days
Ramadan commemorates the revelation of the Qu'ran to the Prophet Mohammed. Ramadan lasts for 28 days and follows the lunar calendar, moving back about 11 days each year. During this time nothing is allowed to pass the lips, including cigarettes, from dawn till dusk. During Ramadan it may not be quite so easy to get guides, or to shop, or carry out normal business as most Jordanians observe the fast.

Ramadan is followed by the holy day of Eid al-Fitr to celebrate the end of fasting. The next holy day is Eid al-Adha, which marks the time of the *haj*, or pilgrimage to Mecca, when many businesses may be closed for four days.

Dates move back about 11 days each year dependent upon the sighting of the moon from Mecca (see box below).

There are also traditional Christian holidays celebrated by the Christian community, as well as 1 May, Labour Day and 25 May, Independence Day. Otherwise Jordanians work a six-day week (though a five-day working week is currently being debated). At the time of writing the only day off is Friday when banks, offices and many shops are closed.

Language and communication
Jordanians speak Arabic, but English is the second language and many people speak it very well indeed. Most have sufficient English words to be able to offer advice and have a simple conversation. However, try to speak a few words of Arabic – it always helps even if it's only 'Hello' (*Marhaba*), 'How are you?' (*Kayf halak*) and 'Very well thanks' (*Quais el Hamdulillah*, or more easily *Quais*, or *Quaisa* if you're female). 'Thanks' (*Shokran*) is another useful and oft-needed word. Have a go – at the very worst you'll make someone smile! Most travel guides have a section with key words and phrases, or there are pocket guides to Arabic such as Berlitz or Penguin or the BBC language series supported by tapes (see also Appendix 3).

The daily English newspaper is the *Jordan Times*, and the leading European and American papers can be bought in Amman and Aqaba and at the international hotels. Radio Jordan (in English) with news, interviews, weather forecasts and a variety of music is broadcast on MW 855 KHz, FM 96.3–99 MHz, and MOOD FM on 92.00MHz plays almost continuous 'easy listening' popular music. Jordan TV also broadcasts several English and French programmes, whilst satellite TV with programmes such as CNN News can be seen at the larger hotels and in many houses (even in Wadi Rum, which not too long ago was a Bedouin encampment!).

There are Internet facilities and cafés in most towns including the popular Books@Cafe in Amman, which also has a book and music shop and reading room. Head down to the 1st Circle and continue along Rainbow Street, in old Amman, past the British Council. Continue past the sign for two craft centres – Jordan River Designs (and the turning for Wild Jordan) and the Bani Hamida House. Books@Cafe will be found a little further on, down the hill and along the last street to the right before the T-junction. The British Council, mentioned above halfway along Rainbow Street, also has computer facilities and a useful library of books on Jordan.

International phone calls can be made at a reasonable price from telecommunication offices in Amman and Aqaba and some of the other larger towns, as well as from hotels (where

ISLAMIC HOLIDAYS

Prophet's birthday	Ramadan begins	Eid al-Fitr (Ramadan ends)	Eid al-Adha (Festival of Sacrifices)
20 March 2008	2 September 2008	2 October 2008	9 December 2008
9 March 2009	22 August 2009	21 September 2009	28 November 2009
27 February 2010	11 August 2010	10 September 2010	17 November 2010
16 February 2011	31 July 2011	30 August 2011	6 November 2011

JORDAN

it will cost more). Mobile phones work almost everywhere in Jordan except in some of the more remote areas. SIM cards and top-up cards are available in every town at the numerous Fastlink and Mobilecom outlets, which were taken over by Zain and Orange respectively in autumn 2007. There are also prepaid cards such as Ma'ak cards which enable you to make calls from a land line in Jordan to a land line in UK and other EU countries for as little as 2JD per hour.

Money matters

In January 2008, 1JD was worth £0.71 sterling (£1 = 1.41JD); against the Euro, 1JD was 0.95E (1E =1.05JD) and against the US dollar, 1JD was US$1.41 ($1 = 0.71JD). The dinar is split into 1000 fils or 100 piastres; make sure you carry some small currency, including coins, everywhere outside major cities as change always seems to be in short supply. Credit cards are increasingly accepted, but still mostly confined to businesses dealing with tourists on a regular basis.

Money can be changed at Amman airport (near the visa office), and in all major cities at money exchange offices and most banks. Prices do vary a little and if you're changing a large amount it can be worthwhile to seek out the best deal.

Food and drink

The major towns generally offer a huge selection of both lightweight provisions (dehydrated food) and fresh food. In the bigger towns there are supermarkets and off licences selling alcoholic drinks. The smaller villages offer less choice but you can usually find bread, vegetables (usually, though not always, fresh), powdered milk (usually in very large cans), tinned fish and other foods, biscuits, tea, coffee, sugar and bottled water. Quite often you will find a small shop selling fresh eggs and chickens (killed for you on the spot). A vegetarian diet is the cheapest, and the best place to shop for fresh fruit and vegetables is always the local market.

The larger towns also have a good choice of restaurants and cafés of all standards serving international or local Arabic foods, with a range of prices to match. The more expensive are also likely to sell alcoholic drinks. Many of the smaller villages have at least one street café for locals and these are always friendly and inexpensive. Most of the best cafés and restaurants are mentioned in the travel guides (see Appendix 2).

In areas popular with tourists, such as Aqaba and Wadi Musa outside Petra, you will find numerous eating places and shops. In Wadi Rum there are a couple of 'Bedouin cafés' (not always open) as well as the restaurant and bar at the Rest House and at least three small grocery shops and a chicken shop. Other tourist sites such as Um Qais, Pella, Ajloun, Jerash, Karak and so on all have their own restaurants. Some are excellent, and most tend to be a bit pricey. Any street café popular with locals is likely to be good and cheap. Almost regardless of where you go, it should cost less to eat in Jordan than it does in Western Europe; and if you eat

The Waters of Tibn, another key to survival in these wild mountains (Routes 110, 111, 112)

OTHER THINGS WORTH KNOWING

in street cafés and buy local produce for your treks, it will cost you far less.

There is good drinkable water on tap in Wadi Rum, so there is no need to buy bottled water. The tap water throughout Jordan is usually drinkable but most people prefer to buy bottled spring water.

Remember that during Ramadan most food shops and cafés are closed during daylight hours, smoking is frowned upon and alcoholic drinks are banned except in some international restaurants.

Water

When walking in a hot climate it is vital to understand the need to keep up your fluid intake. Dehydration is the biggest threat to walkers and trekkers and a major cause of fatigue and loss of energy. Drinking plenty of water is the answer. It's dangerous to take salt tablets – sufficient salt is usually obtained via food. (Some of the very dilute rehydration drinks do contain salt – not to replace what has been lost in sweat, but to speed up the absorption of water through the gut and to maintain plasma volume and assist the drinking reflex.)

The official advice is to carry at least 2 litres of water per person for a 4hr walk and have regular drinks along the way, whilst keeping some in reserve for emergency. It's also important to drink water before setting out, rather than waiting until you are thirsty; your body doesn't recognise dehydration until it's too late. On a long day, the downside of carrying so much water is the fact that each litre weighs 1kg. If you risk less, top up whenever you can along the way – which is not often in Jordan – and drink well on your return. Problems arise if the journey takes longer than expected; your stamina and reserves will be severely put to the test, and dehydration can be a killer. Expect a lack of water en route, even if wells or springs are indicated in this book. If you are returning to a guaranteed water supply at night and drink well before starting you might just manage on 2 litres (or even 1 litre) for a full day, but it's a gamble! If you plan to camp away from water, the absolute minimum to take with you is 4–5 litres a day. If you hope to get water from wells carry 6–7m of cord, and a suitable container to which it can be fastened.

Clothing and equipment

Jordan can be cold at night, especially in the north or on the mountains (it may even snow in midwinter), so carry some warm and windproof clothes. Waterproofs can be useful in north Jordan in the winter, but otherwise are rarely necessary: it seldom rains for long periods, though the occasional storm can be very severe, bringing waterfalls down the mountains and flash floods through the canyons. If you get caught out in a storm, it can be exciting – shelter under a rock and keep out of the canyons and narrow gullies or *siqs*.

For most of the routes in the book (except in midwinter) lightweight clothing, with a fleece jacket, windproof top, sunglasses and sunhat will

Snow on the summit domes of Jebel Rum, winter 2006 (Routes 124, 125, 126).
Photo: Rob Durran

be adequate. Shorts and vests are fine on the mountains, weather permitting, though on a hot day you may suffer sunburn and will lose precious body moisture quickly (without noticing it), leading to speedy dehydration. Whatever you wear remember to dress with respect for local traditions if you want to be welcomed into Bedouin camps or the houses of local people; that means (particularly for women) no shorts, no bare midriff or shoulders. If you do dress like that, carry something lightweight so that you can cover up quickly when necessary.

Trainers or modern lightweight trekking boots are suitable; trekking sandals can be worn on easier walks but you could regret it if you disturb a scorpion or, worse still, a snake (there are plenty of snakes – mostly Palestinian vipers and the much more venomous horned viper – but we have never heard of anyone being bitten.) Additionally you will need a comfortable 40–50 litre rucksack, a lightweight sleeping bag and tent and the usual camping gear, including a Swiss knife or similar, a headtorch with spare batteries and a cooking stove (though it may be possible to cook on a small open fire when trekking). If sleeping in a Bedouin camp they will be happy to cook for you and provide blankets.

Wood is a scarce commodity and should be used sparingly if at all – and never in Nature Reserves. Whether or not you feel that using wood for fires is environmentally acceptable is another matter. When only a few people pass by, burning a little wood may not appear to be a problem; when the number of trekkers reaches the hundreds it becomes an environmental disaster. At the moment, in some places, a small fire for cooking, the ashes of which are covered afterwards, may be acceptable. If you disagree you'll need a multi-fuel stove or a Gaz stove. Either of these options means carrying extra weight. Cylinders can be bought in Amman supermarkets, in Wadi Musa and in Aqaba in the street below the vegetable market. The standard French blue cylinders cost around 3JD. There are also red cylinders that fit the stoves but these do not last as long.

Whilst it is possible to do all but the hardest routes in this book without any specialist equipment, ropes and climbing equipment, if required, can be provided by some of the more experienced Bedouin guides and specialist trekking companies. Make sure you always carry your own small first aid kit and water bottle. It's also worth having a compass, although good maps are difficult to obtain. The maps in this guidebook should be adequate for the routes described, although a local guide with knowledge of the area is always worth having and usually good company.

A few of the trips in this book are considerably more serious undertakings. If you're crossing Jebel Rum, descending the whole length of the Mujib Gorge, exploring a cave or climbing, you're going to need additional specialist kit. Any necessary extra equipment is mentioned in the route description – ignore this advice at your peril!

Mountain biking
Mountain biking is a fairly new sport in Jordan; it's only in the last few years that groups have started exploring the old hill trails by bike. Some of the routes described would be possible by mountain bike and some have already been used, including tracks from Dana to Petra, Wadi Rum and Aqaba. There are many more old tracks that could be followed – the best way would be to link up with a company that knows the terrain and can offer back-up services. Nyazi Tours, La Bedouina and Petra Moon (all in Wadi Musa) have worked with mountain bike groups, as have Bedouin Roads and Rum Guides (both in Wadi Rum) and Desert Guides (Aqaba and France). There are also two new companies in Amman: Arabian Escape (Cycling Jordan) and Terhaal (see Appendix 1).

Guides
Guides are recommended for many of the routes as the terrain is off-the-beaten track and can be quite complex; inexperienced parties could well have problems. Many visitors to Jordan are sufficiently experienced to do any of these routes without guides. Others come to Jordan with qualified climbing and trekking guides from Europe or elsewhere, and an increasing number of Jordanians now offer guiding services on many of the treks and easier scrambles. Some, usually Bedouin from Wadi Rum, also guide on rock climbs (see Appendix 1). In the RSCN Reserves approved guides are usually compulsory (unless noted otherwise). The downside of this is not just the cost, but the need to pre-book; as the number of visitors is limited this can be very frustrating for those who are experienced enough to trek unaccompanied.

If you are going on a scramble where a rope is recommended, for example Wadi Siyyagh in Petra or the harder scrambles in Wadi Rum, check that your guide has a rope and any other necessary equipment and knows how to use it.

OTHER THINGS WORTH KNOWING

Three Bedouin from Rum have been on training courses in the UK. Other Bedouin in Wadi Rum and Petra are also very good natural climbers and are rapidly acquiring the necessary guiding skills for mountain terrain. There are also several local people and travel companies elsewhere in Jordan who are approved as trek and safari guides, and others are training as canyon guides with the necessary rope skills (see Appendix 1).

Guiding fees – whether for safaris, treks or mountain climbs – can vary from 40JD to over 100JD per day depending on the size of the group, the difficulty of the route and whether vehicles, camels or horses are involved.

Maps

There is an English 1:50,000 map series to Jordan (code K737) dating from the 1960s and 1970s, and a new series in Arabic to the same scale. Both are almost impossible to obtain, but you can try contacting: The Royal Geographical Centre, PO Box 20214, 11118 Amman, Jordan tel: 009626 5345188, fax 009626 5347694, e-mail: rjgc@rjgc.gov.jo, website: www.rjgc.gov.jo. The relevant K737 series map numbers are given at the beginning of each section.

Geological maps at the same scale can be bought for 4JD from: The Natural Resources Authority, 8th Circle, PO Box 7, 11118 Amman, Jordan tel: 009626 5857612, fax: 009626 5811866, e-mail: marwanmd@nra.gov.jo, website: www.nra.gov.jo/side.htm

The Royal Geographical Centre also produces and sells tourism maps such as the 1:750,000 road map of Jordan, and an excellent 1:5,000 map of Petra (also available in Petra). Travel guides such as Lonely Planet and Rough Guide have road and town maps. Maps of this type can also be obtained from the Tourism Ministry, large hotels or bookshops. You could also contact specialist map suppliers in Europe or elsewhere.

There are sketch maps of Wadi Rum in *Treks and Climbs in Wadi Rum* (see Appendix 2) and also a larger scale map of Rum (1:38,500) obtainable in bookshops; unfortunately the area covered by the latter is inadequate for most purposes as it only details the central area of Rum. The 1:50,000 maps covering the whole Wadi Rum area are on display on the Rum Rest House wall.

There are also more technical ways of locating objectives, such as that used by Adam Messer who used radar elevation data from NASA's Shuttle Radar Topography Mission (SRTM) to find a meteor crater in the Eastern Desert (R17). Data can be downloaded from the US Geological Survey site. The SRTM maps are geo-referenced, so you can determine where a point of interest lies. In this instance, the maps indicated the alignment of the main Azraq–Ma'an highway, plus a lot of tracks in the desert enabling GPS co-ordinates to be fixed. Without the SRTM data, the crater could have been missed. Adam also pointed out quite rightly that the new Jordanian topo maps use an unusual grid reference system, so it's difficult to mesh these with satellite images. Knowing where to look he found the crater on the topo map, but otherwise it would have been obscure.

Maps and topos in this guide

The combination of route descriptions, maps and topos (topographical diagrams of mountain scrambles and climbs) should be adequate to find and follow the routes, though route-finding skills will be needed for the more complex treks and climbs due to the inevitably small scale of the maps and consequent limited information. In particular the 'contour' lines are not precise. The scale also is always approximate.

GPS

Since writing the 1st edition GPS has come into fairly common use. Wherever possible GPS waypoints have now been added to route descriptions using a Garmin eTrex with MGRS Position Format and WGS 84 Map Datum, giving the start and finish points and relevant points along the route. This correlates reasonably well with the old K737 map series. However, for users of this book (most of whom will not be able to obtain this or any other large-scale map) the Position Format has been converted to degrees, minutes and decimal minutes, whilst keeping the WGS 84 Map Datum. GPS altitude figures have also been given although there is a 50m margin of error, so if other information was available from maps that has been used instead. Not all routes have GPS points included, so if you manage to add some please let us know.

Be prepared!

Some of the walks described are easy low-level strolls (sometimes far below sea level) taking only a couple of hours. Others are more serious undertakings of two or three days or more, sometimes crossing complex terrain, perhaps with no reliable water sources and always with inadequate maps.

39

View south into the northern amphitheatre of Barrah Canyon (Route 131)

It may well be that you have no maps other than those in this book. On top of that there are often only vague shepherds' paths, or sometimes none at all. It's likely to be hot and, because of the water situation and the need to take camping gear and food, you may well be carrying around 15kg. If trekking between hoped-for water sources you could be in for a long day and must be prepared for the worst.

You also need to be self-sufficient as on some of the routes you may be far from any villages and the only people you meet are likely to be Bedouin shepherds. If you have an accident or get lost it will be up to you to get yourself out, bearing in mind that there is no official mountain rescue service in Jordan. What you carry will be a compromise between weight, comfort and safety. Your pack should always include a first aid kit and other items such as water purifiers (not essential, but worth having), sun creams, insect repellents and so on (see Clothing and Equipment above).

Be aware that as well as mosquitoes – which can be a nuisance – it is also possible (despite tents with mosquito nets) to be bitten by minute sandflies which may carry Leishmaniasis. The result is unsightly scabs that appear three or four months later and take another eight months or so to disappear, possibly leaving a small scar. To avoid sandflies it is always best to sleep away from water and vegetation. It is, apparently, also possible to get malaria – check with your local travel clinic – and insect repellent creams are a wise precaution if sleeping out near wadis and pools. Bilharzia may be present in some rivers, especially near and below agricultural areas, so leave footwear on when wading through. There are also snakes (including poisonous vipers and cobras), though they are seldom seen; scorpions are much more common, so take care when sleeping out or moving stones or wood for a campsite or other purpose.

No vaccinations are needed when visiting Jordan.

In an emergency

Despite the above note on rescue facilities the Royal Jordanian Air Force have carried out a number of helicopter rescues from the mountains of Wadi Rum and Petra. As mobile phones now work in most areas outside the more remote parts of Wadi Rum and the deeper mountain valleys and canyons leading down to the Rift Valley, it is now possible to phone directly for help in emergency. Don't abuse the system; it's best to be self-sufficient if at all possible.

If you need assistance in Petra go to the Visitor Centre near the Forum Hotel, or the Emergency Centre in Wadi Musa: Petra Visitor

USING THIS GUIDE

USEFUL TELEPHONE NUMBERS

- Police tel: 191/192
- First aid and ambulance tel: 193
- Public Security tel: 196, ext. 4561 (or '0') for tourism police
- Civil Defence Emergency tel: 199/4617101
- Emergency (mobile phones only) tel: 112

Centre tel: 03 215 6020, 8.30am–3pm; Petra Emergency Centre tel: 03 2156 299, 24hrs. The Wadi Rum Tourist Police office closes at 8pm. There is no 24hr emergency English-speaking phone number available. The only number for emergencies is: Rum Visitor Centre tel: 03 209 0620, daytime only.

They will pass any message on to the appropriate service, but your best bet may be to contact one of the Bedouin mountain guides mentioned in this book (see Appendix 1). Three of them – Sabbah Atieq, Sabbah Eid and Atieq Auda – have had some rescue training in the UK, though as yet there is little modern rescue equipment available to them. However, they and other Bedouin are ready to help and have done so whenever necessary in the past. Any climbers in the area should also be willing to join a rescue call-out. Insurance for helicopter rescue is advisable.

Outside Petra and Rum you will have to get to the nearest police post or place with a phone and ask for assistance. It may take time, though everyone will be as helpful as possible. There is a small hospital for Bedouin in the northeast corner of Rum village where you can get medical help in an emergency, and there are good hospitals in Aqaba and Amman as well as medical centres in most towns.

Other useful emergency numbers are shown in the box above.

Make sure you let someone know not only where you're going, but also when you expect to be back. Having made this commitment, don't go somewhere else and do check in on your return! **Remember – there are no specialist mountain, canyon and cave rescue teams in Jordan.**

USING THIS GUIDE

The walks, treks and canyons are described first, starting from Amman (where most visitors to Jordan will arrive), then proceeding north along the Jordan Valley Hills to the Yarmuk Gorge on the Syrian border, before heading east to the

Poiensiana tree on the shore of the Dead Sea at Ghor Mazra'a below Karak (Routes 55, 56)

routes in the North Eastern Desert and continuing clockwise back to the Capital Area. In the following chapters the routes to the south are covered: first the canyons of the Dead Sea Hills, then the superb trekking country of Dana and Petra and the magnificent desert mountains of Wadi Rum, concluding with the Aqaba Mountains and a dip in the Red Sea at Aqaba.

The caving and climbing sections follow, and in both the routes are also listed from north (mostly around Ajloun) to south.

Route descriptions

The introduction to each route description (apart from the climbs) commences with comments on special features, attractions and risks, followed by details of special equipment and/or skills needed and whether or not guides are advisable (or compulsory). Next is the grade of difficulty, followed by distance covered with altitude changes (not applicable to caves) and the time required to complete the route for an average party (two or three people at most on the harder canyons and rock scrambles with abseils). The approach is then described before giving details of the route followed by, if necessary, the return. GPS points are given wherever possible. In some instances grades, distances and times are not mentioned as the route may be a short walk or of indeterminate length or, in a few cases, may not yet have been done by us and there are insufficient details available.

The climbing descriptions follow the traditional format with a description of the cliff, its location and aspect (shade is usually important) and approach, then the route description with a note on climbing style (many were top-roped due to lack of protection). The French system of climbing grades is used, that being commonly understood worldwide (and definitely applicable to the limestone cliffs of the north).

The terms 'true left' and 'true right' apply when looking down a mountain, canyon, wadi, valley or cliff, whereas directions to go 'left' or 'right' apply to the direction of travel, whether in ascent or descent. Compass points are abbreviated to N, S, E, W for north, south and so on, whilst route numbers on the maps are prefixed by R.

Distances and heights are given in metric, as is altitude (abbreviated to alt.). These are quoted in kilometres (km) or metres (m), and are as accurate as possible given the difficulties of obtaining good (or any) maps to most parts of Jordan. Four-wheel drive is abbreviated to 4WD, and times in hours and minutes shown as hrs and mins.

The term 'exposed' indicates that the climbing or scrambling is above a steep drop, needing a head for heights, and use of a safety rope and associated equipment should be considered. The routes in this guidebook are predominantly those which we have travelled; a few are based on notes supplied by others and in this case the words 'Not checked by the authors' appear in the route introduction. Anyone doing any routes and having useful comments to offer, or anyone with details of new routes, should send their notes for inclusion in future editions of this guidebook to either Cicerone Press, 2 Police Square, Milnthorpe, Cumbria LA7 7PY, website: www.ciceronepress.co.uk, or to n.o.m.a.d.s., Greenman's Farm, Greenfield, Oldham, Lancashire OL3 7HA, website: www.nomadstravel.co.uk

Grading of walks and treks

Easy walk No difficulties such as scrambling on rock or scree, no exposure to heights, no steep ascents or descents and no serious route-finding problems. Probably not more than half a day.

Moderate trek Altitude differences may be considerable, though more often than not in a downhill direction! Some easy scrambling may be necessary and experience in route finding is required. Usually not more than one day, but could be combined with other routes to make a multi-day trek.

Serious trek These routes pass through remote areas, sometimes with unreliable water sources, and require a degree of self-sufficiency and experience in wilderness terrain. There could be considerable ascent and descent, and route-finding experience is essential. Inexperienced parties should take a guide. Although mostly described in stages between water sources, the complete routes generally take two or more days.

Grading of canyons

Easy canyon Ascents or descents where the water is usually shallow. There may be a little scrambling, but otherwise the route should be straightforward. As always in canyons, flooding must be borne in mind. Less than a day.

Moderate canyon Ascents or descents with normally flooded sections, possibly waist-deep;

The Thamudic Route, climbing grade 2 rock out of the canyon (Route 124)

scrambling over boulders is likely and the possibility of flash floods should be considered. Some route finding may be necessary. Not more than one day unless combined with other routes.

Serious canyon Technical 'canyoning' routes with long sections of flooded canyon and waterfalls that must be passed using abseil techniques. Swimming also necessary and flash floods a serious risk. Inexperienced groups will need a qualified guide. Less than a day (unless access restrictions are eased on the whole Hidan Gorge–Mujib Siq combination).

For safety and canyoning techniques see *Canyoning in Southern Europe* (see Appendix 2).

Caving in Jordan
To date few true caves in Jordan have been found – and none is technically difficult – but caving can be a dangerous occupation and care should always be taken, particularly as there are no cave rescue teams in the country. Heed this sound advice from a British caving guide: 'When planning a caving trip think of the return journey and remember that caving grades only apply to fit, competent and properly equipped parties; novices in particular will find caves harder than indicated and for most systems there must be sufficient and competent cavers in the party.'

For information on safety see the *Complete Caving Manual* (see Appendix 2).

Grading of caves
There are no caves in Jordan harder than grade 2 on a commonly used British scale (1–5) for grading difficulty and seriousness. However, none should be taken lightly (especially considering the lack of specialist rescue services). A brief résumé of cave grades follows:

Easy cave – grade 1 No ropework or technical difficulties. Route finding may present problems for the uninitiated.

Moderate cave – grade 2 Includes small potholes. Ropes may be required for ascent and descent. Possibly quite long.

Serious cave – grade 3 or more Definitely for experienced cavers only.

Be aware that if you enter an 'active cave' – one which still has (or could have) water running through it – it will be subject to flood hazard. If in doubt, don't go there!

Rock climbing in Jordan
When the 1st edition of this guidebook was written in 1999, the only well-developed climbing area was Wadi Rum, which we discovered in 1984. Outside Rum, only Sami's Cliff (Thôr Motlagh) at Ajloun had any known climbs, found by Sami Sabat in 1998. Since then numerous other cliffs have been discovered and climbed on, some by us, many by Wilf Colonna and friends from France and Wadi Rum. This guidebook offers the first introduction to climbing areas throughout Jordan, some of which have already been equipped with fixed gear by Wilfried.

Grading of scrambles and rock climbs
Using the French system (as in Wadi Rum), modern rock-climbing grades run from 1–9, increasing in difficulty. The hardest Bedouin routes were originally climbed without ropes or equipment and have some moves of grade 5. The rock scrambles covered here, as outlined above, are mostly up Bedouin routes or through rocky canyons with moves of up to grade 3. These routes can be serious undertakings since big falls are possible. Where relevant, rock-climbing grades are noted both in the route introduction as well as in the description and are shown in brackets, for example (grade 3).

Other than some selected 'world-class' Bedouin routes in Wadi Rum not exceeding grade 3 in difficulty, the only rock climbs described are on cliffs outside Rum. Climbing in Rum is covered in *Treks and Climbs in Wadi Rum* (see Appendix 2).

For further information on mountaineering safety see *The Hillwalker's Guide to Mountaineering* and *Rock Climbing, Essential Skills and Techniques* (see Appendix 2).

Grading of scrambles
Easy scramble Otherwise straightforward, the route has quite a lot of ascent or descent, sometimes on scree or grade 1 rock. Probably less than half a day.

Moderate scramble Generally scrambles through rocky canyons or to summits requiring a head for heights and some confidence on easy rock up to Grade 2. Safety rope and associated equipment sometimes advisable, plus the knowledge to use it for ascent and descent. Not more than one day.

Using this Guide

An exposed grade 2 descent through Rakabat Canyon (Route 129)

Serious scramble Serious mountaineering challenges involving a considerable amount of scrambling, as well as rock climbing up to grade 3 (possible for any fit person). Route-finding ability, ropes and other equipment are necessary; a thorough knowledge of rope safety techniques or a qualified guide will be essential for anyone not familiar with rock climbing and mountaineering. Not more than one day (though the routes on Jebel Rum could be extended to two.)

Grading of climbs

Grade 1 The point at which hands are required for balance or safety.

Grade 2 Generally friction slabs or steeper rock with good holds.

Grade 3 The point where the climbing becomes more technical.

Grade 4 Apart from the descent of Hammad's Route on Jebel Rum – which has grade 4 options – there are no scrambles with moves above grade 3. Climbs of grade 4 and above are for experienced rock climbers only and require special equipment.

Grade 5 and above The only routes in this book with moves above grade 5 are on cliffs outside Wadi Rum.

Each grade is divided into three categories in increasing order of difficulty, for example, 5a, 5b, 5c or 5-, 5, 5+. Full details of comparative international rock-climbing grading systems are covered in *Treks and Climbs in Wadi Rum* (Appendix 2).

Do not attempt any routes in this book without either adequate experience and equipment or a qualified guide.

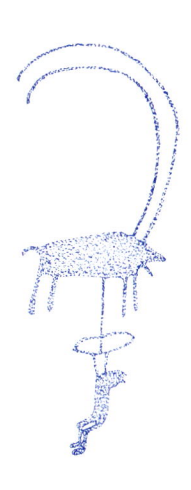

Descending Wadi Yabis (Route 5)

NORTH JORDAN

For the purposes of this guidebook this is the area north of and including Amman. It is described in a clockwise direction, first heading north out of Amman to the Jordan Valley Hills (starting at the rolling hills and deep valleys north of Jerash and extending to the Yarmuk Gorge on the Syrian border), then to the North Eastern Desert including the Azraq Reserve, and finally the Capital Area, which covers the region between the Dibeen Forest Reserve down to the northern end of the Dead Sea, both within easy reach of Amman.

Accommodation and transport
Using private transport you can visit anywhere in the north from Amman and return the same day, and that's usually the best way to do it. Getting around via local public transport services from Amman is not so easy (but it is cheap – you can get to most places in the north for less than 6JD, and there are direct services to Jerash and Ajloun).

There is an abundance of hotels in Amman from five-star luxury to downtown 'backpacker' hotels such as the Venicia, the Cliff and the Farah, all of which charge less than 20JD for a double room. Other hotels near the King Hussein mosque are even cheaper, and there are some pleasant hotels uptown around 30JD per double. The Remal at Abdali charges 20JD per double and is convenient for JETT buses and other bus and service taxis heading out of Amman (although through proposed redevelopment the location of these services may well change).

The only accommodation we know of in the Jordan Valley is at Pella where the Countryside Hotel has some pleasant rooms in an olive grove not far from the Rest House, costing 30JD per double with evening meal and breakfast (less for self-catering): ask the Rest House manager (see Appendix 1). Otherwise you have to go to Irbid or Um Qais where doubles are around 15–20JD; in Ajloun prices are dearer (though possibly negotiable) with a couple of hotels at around 30–40JD per double (the Castle Hotel, up a side road from the approach to Ajloun Castle, has a nice outdoor patio with an excellent view and seems the cleanest). Just north of Ajloun the RSCN Woodland Reserve Camp charges 45JD per double including entrance fee and breakfast. Ajloun has recently been designated as an area for tourism development, so improved amenities may soon be available, although they may be targeted towards the top end of the market. Of course, in places like Yabis you could camp for free away from villages. Out in the eastern desert accommodation in the Azraq oasis is around 20JD per double, or the RSCN Eco-Lodge has camping at 20JD per double and rooms at around 45JD per double.

Guides
This area has not yet really been developed for adventure tourism, so some Jordanian guides and trekking companies are currently unaware of the routes (some are suggested in Appendix 1). The RSCN provides guides for the trails in their Reserves at Dibeen, Ajloun and Azraq; for details on RSCN and other guides and travel companies see Appendix 1.

Maps
The following 1:50,000 topographical K737 series maps cover the Jordan Valley Hills and Capital Area. You are unlikely to be able to get hold of these, but enquire at the Jordanian Royal Geographical Centre in Amman (see 'Maps' in the Introduction).

- 3155–111, 3155–11: Um Qais & Yarmuk
- 3154–1V, 3154–1: Ajloun, Yabis & Pella
- 3154–111, 3154–11: Salt & Talal Dam
- 3153–1V, 3153–1: Amman, South Jordan Valley & Mount Nebo

4. Jordan Valley and the Northern Highlands

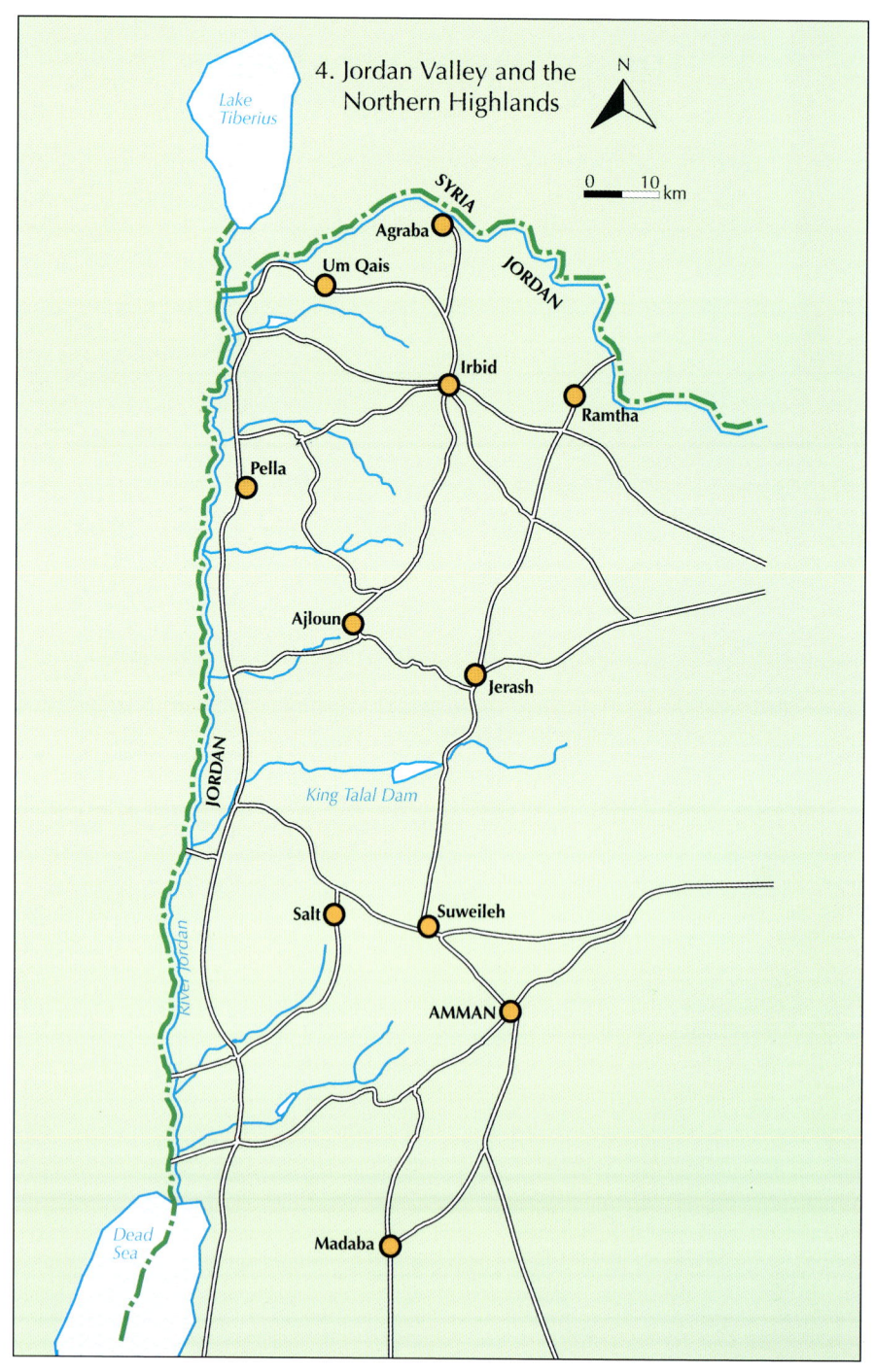

THE JORDAN VALLEY HILLS

Archaeological surveys have identified Stone Age flint tools, hunter-gatherer camps and small settlements in the foothills immediately above the valley floor, indicating a human presence in the foothills for the past half a million years.

Antiquities of the Jordan Rift Valley Rami G. Khouri (1988)

The Jordan Valley is the northern end of the Jordanian Rift Valley. It connects the Dead Sea with Lake Tiberius (Sea of Galilee) and descends from 200m below sea level at its northern end to 400m below at the Dead Sea, the river forming the border between Jordan and the Occupied West Bank. This is a politically sensitive area and there are frequent checkpoints, so you should always carry your passport.

A new RSCN Nature Reserve is to be created at the northern end of the valley in the Yarmuk River basin as part of the Rift Valley Project, which also includes the Dead Sea and Wadi Araba in the south. In addition, seven special conservation areas will be established along the Jordan Valley to promote environmental tourism. The project is targeted for completion in 2013 and will no doubt include eco-lodge style accommodation.

The routes are described heading north from Amman, either via Jerash with its vast Roman city, or up the Jordan Valley. Either way, if you are driving leave Amman at the 7th Circle (where you can go left for the Dead Sea), and continue on to the 8th. Turn right there to Suweileh, which is reached in 9km. **For the Jordan Valley** turn left at the roundabout and continue towards Salt. Ignore the Salt exit (20km from the 6th Circle), and continue down to the valley, passing a checkpoint after another 21km. Turn right

Hollyhock

Ajloun Castle from Routes 1 and 2

49

1km beyond, at the Deir 'Alla junction, close to which the Zerqa River reaches the valley. The 3500-year-old tell or mound of Deir 'Alla stands above the north end of the town. Pottery shards from the nearby Chalcolithic settlement date back 6500 years.

For those heading north for routes in the hills around Ajloun, continue north from Suweileh towards Jerash, which is about 35km from Amman. Turn left at the roundabout near Hadrian's Gate, and continue over scenic hill country to reach Ajloun with its prominent hilltop castle after a further 24km. If travelling by bus there are direct services to both Jerash and Ajloun from Amman.

THE AJLOUN AREA

Passing on to Ajloun we pitched our tents in a grove of fine old olive trees just above a beautiful clear stream, and all the population came out to sit in rows in front of our tents and enjoy a hearty stare at us.

With the Bedouins Gray Hill (1890)

Jordan's finest Islamic fortress Qal'at er Rabad, or Ajloun Castle, dominates the area. It was built in 1184 by Izz ad Din, the nephew of Sal ad Din, as a bastion against the Crusaders. The location – on a high hilltop with fine views in all directions – was well chosen. The rock is karst limestone and there is both rock climbing and caving in the area (see later chapters). The hills and valleys also provide two great treks starting from the castle, Routes 1 and 2.

Route 1
Ajloun Castle to Kureiyima in the Jordan Valley

Grade	Moderate trek
Details	18km, descending from almost 1000m above sea level to 200m below, with c300m of ascent (sometimes quite steep). It's well worth sleeping out on the 740m summit just over halfway for the memorable views of the sunset over Palestine and the lights of the Jordan Valley by night. If you intend to camp leave Ajloun after midday, and walk down to Kureiyima the next morning.
Time	6–7hrs

See alternative start to this route, below.

A splendid walk in great mountain scenery, commencing high in the hills at Ajloun Castle and descending to the Jordan Valley, across which there are magnificent views to Eastern Palestine (alias the West Bank). In springtime the oak-forested hills and fertile green valleys with their orchards and olive groves are full of wild flowers. Apart from crossing a couple of country lanes the route keeps to the hills. See map 5.

NORTH JORDAN – THE JORDAN VALLEY HILLS – ROUTE 1

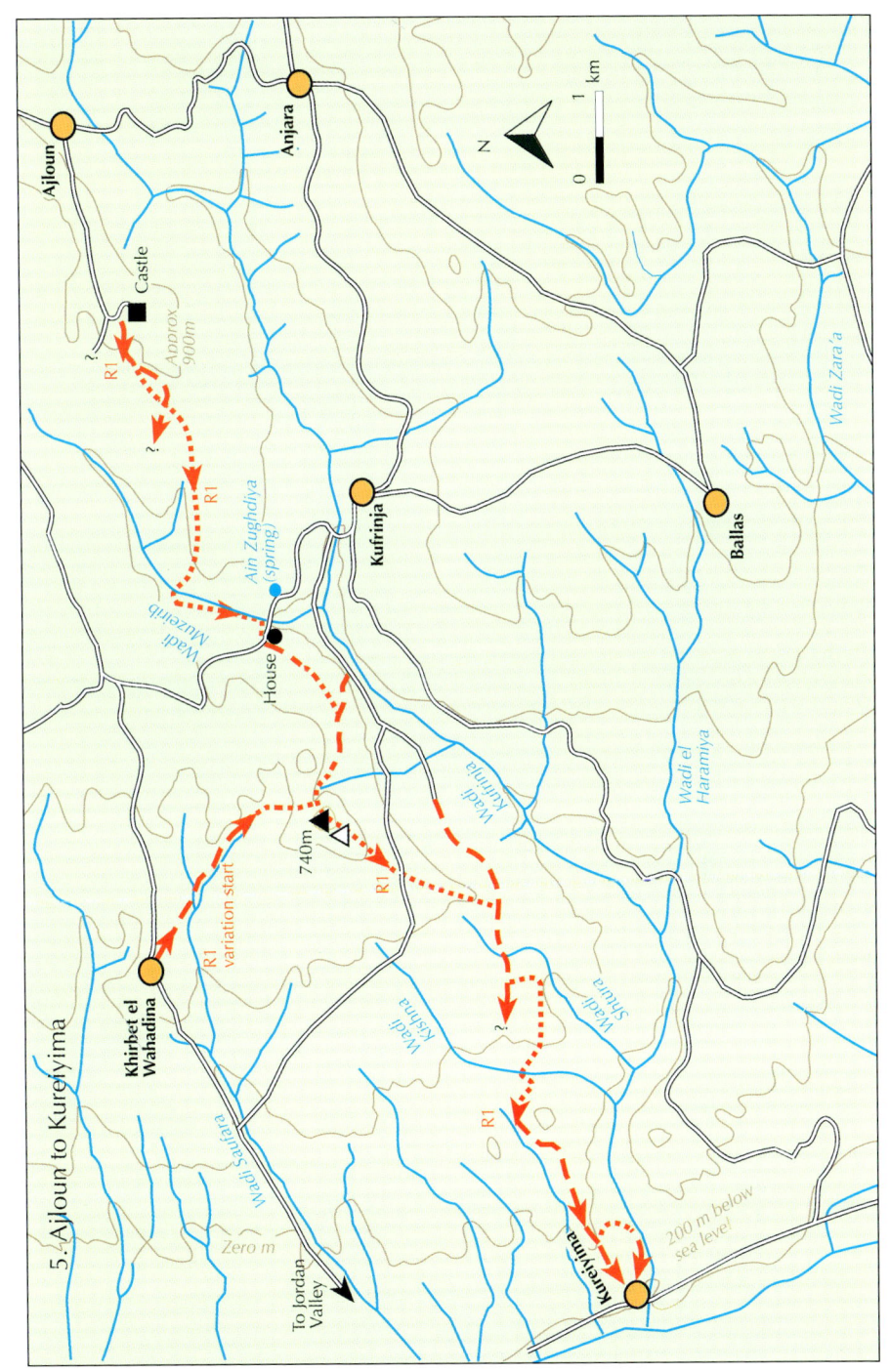

5. Ajloun to Kureiyima

- Ajloun
- Anjara
- Castle (Approx 900m)
- R1
- Ain Zughdiya (spring)
- Kufrinja
- Ballas
- Wadi Muzerib
- House
- Wadi Kufrinja
- Wadi el Haramiya
- 740m
- R1 variation start
- Khirbet el Wahadina
- Wadi Kisina
- Wadi Shuia
- Wadi Shuafara
- Zero m
- To Jordan Valley
- Kureiyima
- 200 m below sea level

0 — 1 km

51

Special requirements Route finding is not always obvious, so take care at key points.

Approach Arriving at the Ajloun roundabout from Jerash (café on right and others just a short way back up the road), turn left and walk or take a taxi up the road for about 2km to the castle. The walk starts along a small track just below its N side (GPS alt. 920m N32° 19.609' E35° 43.575'), not the big track that leaves the road at the bend lower down.

The route

Follow the track W as it descends the hillside beyond. After about 0.5km it's more pleasant to leave the track and follow the ridge to the SW (at this point there are a couple of big farm buildings down to the right).

The ridge goes pleasantly through trees and karst boulders, crossing the track again at a small saddle (840m). Continue, still generally SW, along a path on the ridge past a small farmhouse (where you may be offered tea, goat's milk and cheese, and superb wafer-thin Bedouin bread called *shrak*). The farm dogs may also give you a noisy welcome! Beyond, the ridge rises slowly up, turning W to a small top at 870m.

It is now necessary to descend into Wadi el Muzeirib. Bear right (N) rather than left as there is a 30m-high overhanging limestone cliff to the left (Thôr Motlagh, 'Sami's Cliff', the first climbing area to be found in Jordan outside Wadi Rum – see the chapter on Climbing in Jordan). Head diagonally down until you find a path going N through trees towards a limestone cliff on the opposite side of the valley. Where it meets the wadi, cross to the W bank and follow a path down the valley for about 0.5km until opposite and below Thôr Motlagh (alt. 550m). Continue on the path through the woods down Wadi el Muzeirib to the little country road near a farmhouse (total approx 6km, GPS alt. 480m N32° 18.648' E35° 41.271'). The clear spring of Ain ez Zughdiya emerges about 300m down the road to the left (E).

Go right to the farmhouse, asking permission if anyone is around, before following a good track along its right side into olive groves and fields, ending after about 0.5km. An indistinct path then continues in the same direction first across the top of an olive grove, then descending slightly through a field

Sunset over the hills of Nablus in Palestine from the camp

(identified by a boulder-strewn hillside above to the right, and two white houses across Wadi Kufrinja to the left). It ends at another good, wide track, the key to the route.

Turn right up the track which rises up the hillside for about 0.5km, levelling out briefly to the W, then going over a small hill past well-tended olive groves with new walls. (A small road can be seen very close and just below to the left.) Continue steeply up the same good track, which comes to an abrupt end in an oak forest just below an extensive escarpment of steep limestone cliffs, about 20m high with caves at the right end (Wahadina Cliff, with some climbing possibilities – about 3km from the farmhouse, 9km from the start – see Climbing in Jordan).

Shepherds' paths now continue up through the oaks and rocks to the foot of the cliffs, which are cut by a narrow rocky gorge (GPS alt. 630m N32° 18.229' E35° 40.065'). Scramble up rocky ledges on the right (E) side of the ravine, following goat tracks, to reach the pleasant, open, hanging valley above, then go left (W) to reach the rounded summit of a hill (740m), with superb views W across the Jordan Valley, SW down Wadi Kufrinja and NE to Ajloun Castle. This is about 10km from the start – a great place to spend the night.

From the hill, a ridge will be seen rolling down the right side of Wadi Kufrinja. Follow it down, keeping to its left side, sometimes near cliffs with great views into the valley, to reach a little road after 1km (houses with wells). Cross the road and continue on a track past the second house and out along the ridge, then down past more old houses in an idyllic rural setting. (If anyone is home you will almost certainly be offered *shai* (tea) and perhaps something to eat.)

After going over a small rise on the ridge, continue down, passing left of fields and a final house and crossing a small track which leads to it. Still going down, another track will be reached almost 3km from the 740m summit. This is another key point: go right on the track, which forks almost immediately. Take the left fork, which curves left and leads down to fields, above which the track goes left and ends. Walk round the left side of the fields on small paths, just above the cliffs on the upper edge of Wadi Kufrinja, in the side valley of Wadi Shtura. Still heading for what appears to be the final bare, rocky hill at the end of the ridge, continue down slightly rightwards and cross a side wadi just S of a large flat area of fields. (There is said to be a well, or *bir*, about 5m deep, a short way up the wadi.)

Follow sheep tracks out of the wadi and up left towards the hill, keeping left of the fields, then contour rightwards round the hill on a path, with the fields just below to the right. The path continues to wind round the hill, turning left above a narrow valley and eventually rising up on the far side of the hill to meet the ridge again, once more above Wadi Kufrinja (about 6km from the 740m summit, with excellent views all round).

Still following the same good track, continue down the ridge until the track splits below another top. Take the left fork, down to a saddle. The track continues up and over the final top, and down to Kureiyima and looks straightforward, but we went down into Wadi Kufrinja where a house and gardens can be seen directly below. If you choose this way, to get there from the saddle, follow a little path sharply back left down the hillside, then go right near a little wadi (small cliffs and caves) and scramble down to enter Wadi Kufrinja near the house. From there, a track goes along the side of the stream past orchards and olive groves with cliffs in which there are caves and even a natural rock arch. Kureiyima and the Jordan Valley are just beyond (GPS alt. minus 200m N32° 16.079' E35° 36.040').

Return Regular minibuses go down the Jordan Valley to Deir 'Alla (10km) from where there is a frequent bus service to Amman.

JORDAN

Route 1
Alternative start

Grade	Easy walk, but take care with route finding
Details	10km from the furthest point reached by vehicle (13km from Khirbet Wahadina)
Time	4–5hrs, dependent on start

For those who can be dropped off by a vehicle this start makes the trek easily possible in a day. It eliminates the walk down from Ajloun and up from Wadi Muzeirib to the ravine in Wahadina Cliff (also see *Climbing in Jordan*). Approaching from Khirbet el Wahadina it joins Route 1 at its halfway point, meeting the walk as it emerges from the little ravine. See map 5.

Approach From the village of Khirbet al Wahadina, which is reached from Ajloun via the Ishtafeina turning, then follow signs to Wahadina; about 17km in total from Ajloun.

The route
In Wahadina turn left just beyond the telecom mast and mosque (GPS alt. 570m N32° 19.409' E35° 38.855'), and walk or drive down SE past red-coloured houses into a small valley. Continue for about 3km from the village up the narrow rough track between trees and fields to arrive close to the saddle at the head of the valley; as far as vehicles can go (GPS alt. 710m N32° 18.634' E35° 40.246').

To join Route 1 go about 1km SW, over the shoulder and down right into a small valley; then before it descends into the ravine – which cuts the cliffs below (GPS alt. 630m N32° 18.229' E35° 40.065') – go up the wooded hillside to the 740m high point close to the edge of Wadi Kufrinja. From there it's about 8km to Kureiyima.

The **lower end of Wadi Kufrinja** can also be visited from the Jordan Valley, giving a short but interesting walk. Travelling N up the valley, Kureiyima is 10km from Deir 'Alla (see above). It is nestled in the mouth of the narrow Kufrinja Valley beneath cliffs and caves. If you go E into the old village, the scenic wadi can be seen passing beneath an ancient bridge on its way down from Ajloun Castle, almost 1200m above. In addition to this trek locals say there is also a trail down the valley from Ajloun. Another nearby point of interest is Tell as Sa'idiyyeh, about 2km to the W near the Jordan River.

Next is another trek sharing a common start with Route 1 from Aljoun Castle.

Route 2
Ajloun Castle (Qal'at er Rabad) to Pella (Tabaqat Fahl)

Grade	Moderate trek
Details	36km, descending from 1000m above sea level to 60m below and finishing at 0m, with about 600m of ascent (c430m on Day 1 and 170m on Day 2)
Time	10–12hrs or two days of 5–6hrs

Another springtime floral feast through rolling hills carpeted with multi-coloured flowers including the wild black iris, through forested uplands, green valleys and orchards. There is also plenty of historical interest as the walk goes from an Islamic castle to ancient Pella of Greek origin built on a site with signs of occupation dating back 250,000 years. The route also passes through 'Roman' olive groves, whilst the campsite is an idyllic spot next to abandoned Ottoman ruins. It is not without its wildlife: we saw eagles on the heights and a pair of flashing turquoise rollers near Pella, also two tortoises making a lot of noise doing what comes naturally in spring, as well as a snake and a wolf!

There are a few country lanes along the way, but they don't detract from the ambience of the walk and can be mostly avoided by taking alternative routes. We enjoyed two great two days of easy walking with numerous offers of *shai*, a 'Bedouin breakfast' near Ajloun and a major meal in the small hilltop town of Kufr Abil during the feast of Eid el Adha. See map 6.

Special requirements You're unlikely to find much water en route unless it's very early in the season and the wadis are running (Wadi Yabis should be flowing but the water is not drinkable). There may be water in the wells at the ruins, but you'll need 7m of cord to reach it. Carry plenty of water or get your water bottles topped up at any houses passed en route, especially if the weather is hot. The only other minor problem is finding the best route through the thickly wooded valleys where there is a choice of shepherd's tracks, but this is part of the fun!

Approach As for Route 1. Start GPS alt. 920m N32° 19.609' E35° 43.575'.

The route
Day 1
Follow Route 1 into Wadi Muzeirib until below Thôr Motlagh (Sami's Cliff, alt. 550m). Just beyond, fields will be found above the right side of the path. Go up the right side of the fields, through woodland, trending left above the fields and emerging through trees into another wadi. Just above, on its opposite (S) bank, an old track will be found which follows the wadi W to meet a country road which winds up the hill heading N for 2km to reach first a road on the left then, immediately after, the main road, with a new panorama opening out N down Wadi en Naum (GPS alt. 800m N32° 19.775' E35° 40.891', 3hrs from start). The small hill just SE of the T-junction is Tell Mash-had.

Take the main road right (E) for about 200m, before turning left (N) between fields on the left and a big building on the right. (It may be possible to reach this point directly through the woods from Wadi Muzeirib, missing out the road.) Scramble down into the wooded valley of Wadi en Naum and follow small paths for a short way until the valley floor becomes choked with trees. At this point a path rises out left. Follow it, rising gently across the wooded hillside and heading N above the wadi bed on a series of sheep and cow tracks through clearings in the trees. After about 3km a side wadi enters from the left (W) and a path should be found heading down the shoulder to the main wadi. A ruin is visible to the NE on the opposite side of the valley; this is the objective. Cross the wadi (450m) and rise diagonally

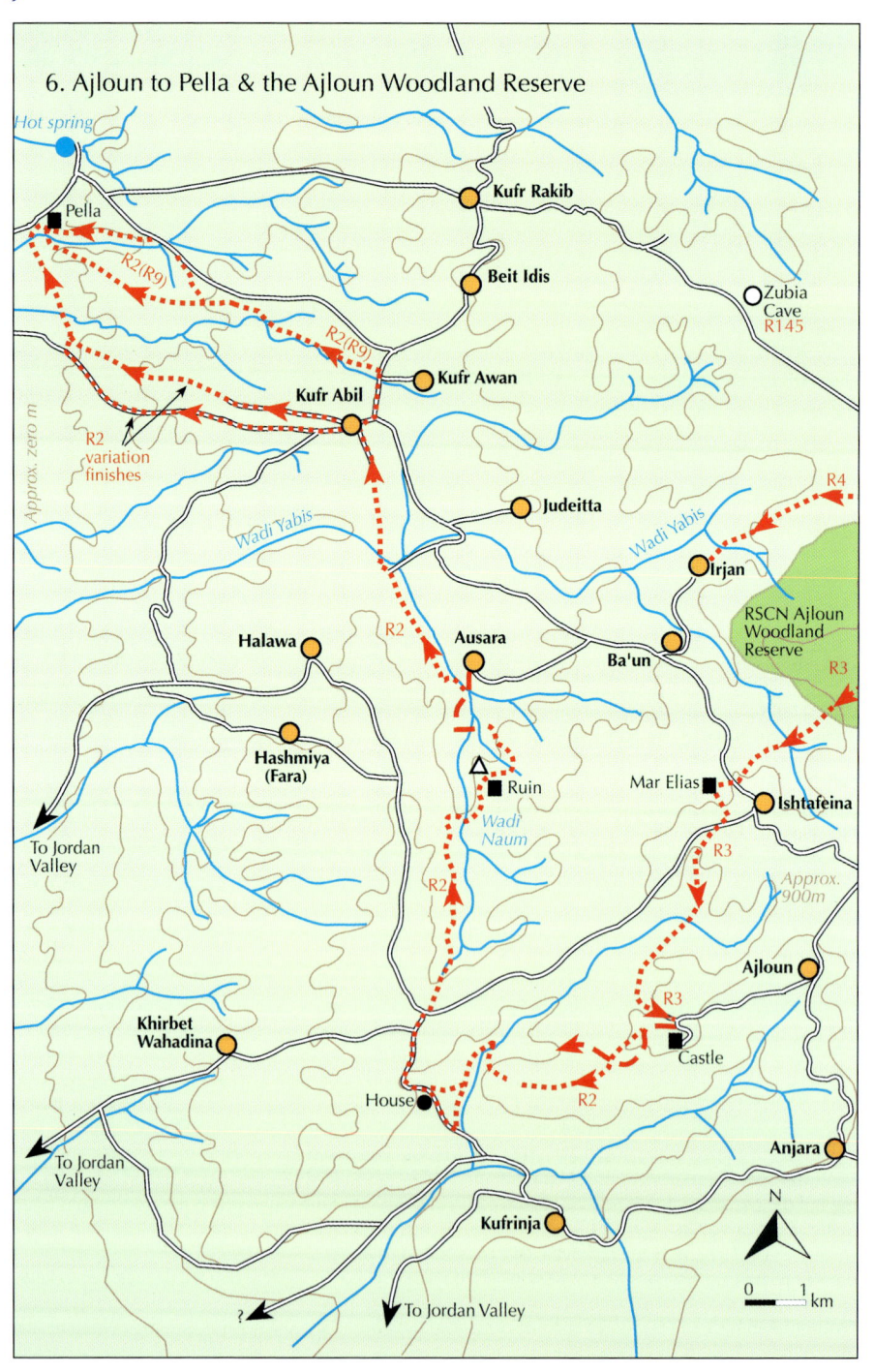

JORDAN

6. Ajloun to Pella & the Ajloun Woodland Reserve

Campsite near Ottoman ruins

NNE up its true right bank to reach the ruin which is probably 17th–18th-century Ottoman in a superb position facing N with excellent views down the valley beyond (550m). There are two old cisterns carved out of solid limestone on the N side of the building, both about 6m deep (both had water in April 1998.) There is also a beautiful camping spot just beyond the walls.

Day 2
Contour round onto the next shoulder to the N and descend it keeping to the left of a wall and fields, then continue down and right until a track is met which winds down to meet a small road in olive groves back in Wadi en Naum (360m). Turn right on the road, which goes across the side wadi, over a bridge. (The road then goes uphill steeply to the small hilltop town of Ausara whose tall minaret is visible from the campsite.)

Leave the road immediately after the bridge and take a track NW through ancient 'Roman' olive groves until that too starts to rise uphill after about 0.5km. Instead go left on a path to meet Wadi en Naum again, and follow the beautiful valley NNW for about 3km. If there is water in the stream this could involve wet feet, as the wadi bed has to be crossed frequently as it descends the narrow valley. It eventually emerges near ruins on the left bank at the confluence with Wadi Yabis which was, in April 1998, a fast stream flowing between orchards from the NE then turning NW to flow down into the Jordan Valley some 12km to the W. This is about 2hrs from the campsite (GPS alt. 290m N32° 23.863' E35° 40.628'). (It is possible to continue down the delightful valley of Yabis from here to reach the Jordan Valley 8km S of Pella; see Route 5.)

Cross the stream about 50m E of the bend where Wadi en Naum joins it. At this point it was about 4m wide and knee-deep on the our first visit in 1998, but only a small stream in spring the following year. Just right of the crossing a path should be found going though orchards and rising directly N then NW across fields to the hilltop town of Kufr Abil (GPS alt. 430m N32° 25.004' E35° 40.059', about 3km from the stream.) A road then runs along the SW side of Kufr Abil, towards the mosque. There are a few small grocery shops nearby if you need some food and drink. There are now a number of possible routes on to Pella.

Option 1 Follow Route 9, probably the most pleasant way from Kufr Abil (checked by the authors in May 2007).

Option 2 The route taken by the authors in 1998. The road past the left side of the small turquoise domed mosque leads W out of town for 4km to a point between two small hills –Tell ez Zeitoun on the left and Khirbat Miryamin on the right. Here the view opens out towards the Jordan Valley and the road trends NW downhill for 2km, to where it passes a small cluster of traditional houses on the left. Scramble N across and down a hillside to cross Wadi en Nuheir in a small gorge (40m below sea level) before scrambling up to meet a track (it is said that there is a Roman bridge nearby). Follow the track NNW for 2km, descending a valley then continuing NE to emerge suddenly at the ruins of Pella (60m below sea level). The Rest House will be seen above.

Option 3 Alternatively, from the cluster of houses (option 2) above, continue on the road for 2km to Wadi en Nuheir, where a track goes N to reach Pella in 2km (not checked by the authors).

Option 4 It may be possible to take a parallel track just to the N (probably from the right of the mosque), leading NNW to the small hilltop of Khirbet Miryamin, then on down the hillside still parallel to the road, meeting option 2 where it crosses the wadi just N of the old houses (not checked by the authors).
The Countryside Hotel at Pella is owned by the Rest House manager and is a pleasant place to relax after the trek, but it's best to book ahead (see Appendix 1).

Return From the village below Pella in the Jordan Valley there is public transport to Amman.

A proposed trek to be called the **Abraham Path** linking some of the finest landscapes, historic sites and holy places of the Middle East will also pass through the Ajloun Hills via Route 3 (below) and Aljoun Castle. Starting in Harran, Turkey, where Abraham reputedly heard 'the call' from God, it will continue through Syria and Jordan into Eastern Palestine (the Occupied West Bank), finishing at Hebron (Al Khalil), believed to be Abraham's burial place, a total distance of 1200km. The Turkish section was opened in November 2007; the Jordanian section should be open for travellers in 2009. The Syrian and West Bank routes will follow later. Volunteers to work on the trail would be welcomed; see website: www.abrahampath.org

Not far from Ajloun is the Ajloun Woodland Reserve.

Nearing Pella on the Option 2 finish

THE RSCN AJLOUN WOODLAND RESERVE

The Reserve is located not far from Ajloun in the Ajloun Highlands and consists of Mediterranean-type hill country, dominated by open woodlands of oak and pistachio. It was established in 1988 in Burqush, where a captive-breeding programme for roe deer was initiated, but was later moved closer to Ishtafeina, northwest of Burqush.

Approach The Reserve is situated on one of the highest hills in the area, at around 1200m, about 9km N of Ajloun. From the roundabout go 5km N up to the top of the hill, then left towards Ishtafeina for about 300m. Here fork right, then after a further 600m fork right again. Then go left after 0.5km up to Um al Yanabi, turning left 1km beyond and follow the road for another 1.5km to the Reserve.

Entrance fee 4JD non-Jordanians, 2JD Jordanians.

Guiding fee 15–39JD, dependent on size of group and choice of trail.

Accommodation Prices vary from 22–30JD/person; camping also possible; for details contact the RSCN (see Appendix 1).

WALKS IN THE AJLOUN RESERVE

There are a number of designated and guided trails in the Reserve including the **Scenic Viewpoint Trail**, an easy 2km round trip, 1–2hrs from the campsite to the summit of a nearby hill overlooking the Reserve. The area surrounding the trail is rich in wildflowers in springtime. The return trip passes the breeding enclosures for the roe deer en route to the Visitor Centre.

The moderate **Rockrose Trail**, an 8km walk, takes 4–5hrs across heavily wooded valleys and ridges both inside and outside the Reserve. This highly scenic trail passes through villages and olive groves and offers beautiful panoramic views to the West Bank and Syria. Steep scrambles en route demand a reasonable level of fitness. Details are available from the RSCN

Two other longer routes (Routes 3 and 4) take the visitor out of the Reserve but still require an RSCN approved guide. Neither of these routes has been checked by the author.

Route 3
The Prophet's Trail

Grade	Easy walk to Mar Elias, moderate trek if the route is followed to Ajloun
Details	8km to Mar Elias rising and falling over hills from the start at 1200m to the hilltop ruins at 900m; a further 9km to Ajloun Castle if desired, descending to almost 700m before climbing to the castle at 1000m; total distance 17km
Time	4hrs to Mar Elias and a further 4hrs to Ajloun; 8hrs all the way

A pleasant trail winding over wooded hills and valleys, this time to the superb viewpoint and beautiful 6th-century church mosaics of Mar Elias, dedicated to the prophet Elijah who was reputedly born and lived in this area around 900BC (also see Route 5); then an option either to return or continue to the dramatic Ajloun Castle. See map 6.

Special requirements RSCN approved guide necessary; donkey available to carry provisions!

The route
The first part of the trail from the Reserve is very gentle, winding along a road between orchards shaded by fig and pear trees. Once in Wadi Shiteau (Winter Valley), you plunge into a dense forest of oak and oriental strawberry trees, heading down a fairly steep bank to Mehna Valley, crisscrossed with stone walls guarding farmers' crops from both winter rains and wild boar. This is also where a local farmer joins you with his donkey carrying water, tea and your homemade snack boxes. The route continues past rock walls pocked with caves and, especially in spring, meadows filled with flowers, to reach the intersection of the two valleys Mehna and al-Alaqa. Beyond, the route climbs to the ridge, then along the road and across the plateau to Mar Elias, the hilltop ruin of two of Jordan's oldest churches.

Mar Elias is thought to be dedicated to the Prophet Elias, also known as Elijah, who appears in both the Bible and the Koran. He is referred to as 'Master Elias' in the Greek inscription in the larger of the two churches on this site, which was discovered in 1999 and boasts beautiful mosaics. It appears to date from the late 6th–early 7th century whereas the smaller chapel, uncovered in 2001, seems to have been built even earlier. Mar Elias provides sweeping views of the surrounding area, including the ruins of an ancient mosque not far from the site.

For those who wish to continue it's a further 9km to the SE to Ajloun Castle, crossing some steep hills: walking towards the Al-Jubb Valley you pass by small farms and their adjacent orchards from where

Ajloun Castle

the West Bank and southern Syria can be seen. From the bottom of Al-Jubb the route climbs through rugged forest that eventually gives way to more orchards holding one of the oldest pistachio trees in the area. Beyond is a small road that provides a challenging walk uphill to Ajloun Castle. Built between 1184 and 1188 and with commanding views, it makes a dramatic end to a demanding walk.

Return By RSCN transport to the Reserve from either Mar Elias or Ajloun.

Route 4
The Orchards Trail

Grade	Easy walk
Details	12km, descending from 1200–540m with a slight ascent to the 'Eagle's Viewpoint' at 1100m
Time	6hrs, including time to visit the soapmakers and to stop for lunch

Another varied and interesting walk, first over high forested hills to reach villages, one with a soap workshop using raw materials from nearby orchards and olive groves. Beyond is an opportunity for a lunch of local produce in an orchard before meeting RSCN transport back to the Reserve. See map 6.

Special requirements RSCN approved guide necessary.

The route
Starting from the Reserve the walk goes through oak, pistachio and oriental strawberry trees, eventually passing stone mounds that were formerly Roman watchtowers and huts; there is also a ruined wine press nearby. Beyond, as you descend to the valley, is one of the oldest oriental strawberry trees in the Reserve.

Walking along the rocky valley floor you may be able to see the snow-capped Sheikh Mountain in southern Syria or, close by, eagles gliding on the breeze. The forest gives way to agriculture at the boundary of the Reserve where you start to climb to the eagle's habitat at 1100m with fabulous views overlooking the villages of Rasun and Irjan (also spelt Orjan), and back towards the Reserve.

The inhabitants of the six surrounding villages work with the Reserve and its supportive programmess for the community such as the new soap workshop in Rasun, which you will reach via a quick hike downhill; the workshop depends on local produce to manufacture floral and fruit soaps such as olive oil, lavender and pomegranate.

After a cup of tea the route continues through orchards of plum, peach, fig, and apple to reach the valley and a local spring at 600m, its water flowing along an aqueduct lined with silver poplars. With the chatter of water in your ears, this stage contrasts with the drier mountains above. The orchards are punctuated with dramatic rock walls and old watermills, once used to grind seeds. Here there is an opportunity to enjoy a delicious local meal in an orchard. The route then continues through more orchards including majestic olive trees dating back – as the locals believe – to the time of the Roman Empire. Beyond, after crossing the stream several times, you finally reach the end of the hike.

Return By RSCN transport to the Reserve (it would also be possible to join Route 5, options 2 or 3a, down to Wadi Yabis and on to the Jordan Valley, see below).

JORDAN

THE YABIS AND PELLA AREA

YABIS

Beyond the Reserve comes the next varied and very enjoyable trek, which follows Wadi Yabis, the headwaters of which were crossed on Route 2 from Ajloun to Pella. Yabis is believed to be the Biblical Yabesh of Gilead where the Prophet Elijah was reputedly born around 900BC (see Route 4). It is a truly beautiful valley descending 20km from the forested uplands to the warmth of the Jordan Valley, where nearby is an ancient tell from that period.

Route 5
Wadi Yabis

The valley is commonly held to be the ancient Valley of Achor (affliction) where Joshua caused Achan to be stoned because at the capture of Jericho he disobeyed the orders of the Lord (Joshua 7.10)... it was also identified with the Torrent of Carith (or Cherith) (I Kings 17.3), where the prophet Elias was fed by ravens. It was here that St Joachim had hidden himself to bewail the sterility of his wife, Anne, when in a vision he saw the angel that announced to him the birth of a daughter, Mary.

Guide to the Holy Land Eugene Hoade (1946)

Grade	Moderate trek
Details	12km, descending from 500m above sea level to 180m below with almost no ascent
Time	4hrs from the Ishtafeina road (option 3b) or from the end of the track through Halawa; 5–6hrs from the centre of Halawa all the way out to the Jordan Valley road at 250m below sea level

A botanical banquet and downhill walker's dream! One of the prettiest and most varied walks in Jordan, especially in springtime. There are optional starts and the walk can be split into two sections, the easier and more pastoral upper valley with its gardens, orchards and ancient olive groves, but also some dramatic rock scenery; then the lower ravine plunging down to the Jordan Valley where the going gets rougher and the precise route is sometimes less obvious. Birdlife is plentiful with eagles in the higher reaches; the olive groves and gardens are full of birdsong; and you may see sunbirds in the pomegranate trees and egrets in the lower valley. See map 7.

Approach Wadi Yabis descends into the Jordan Valley about 80km N of Amman (see Route 6), with access to its headwaters possible by road from the Jordan Valley via Halawa or Kufr Abil,

NORTH JORDAN – THE JORDAN VALLEY HILLS – ROUTE 5

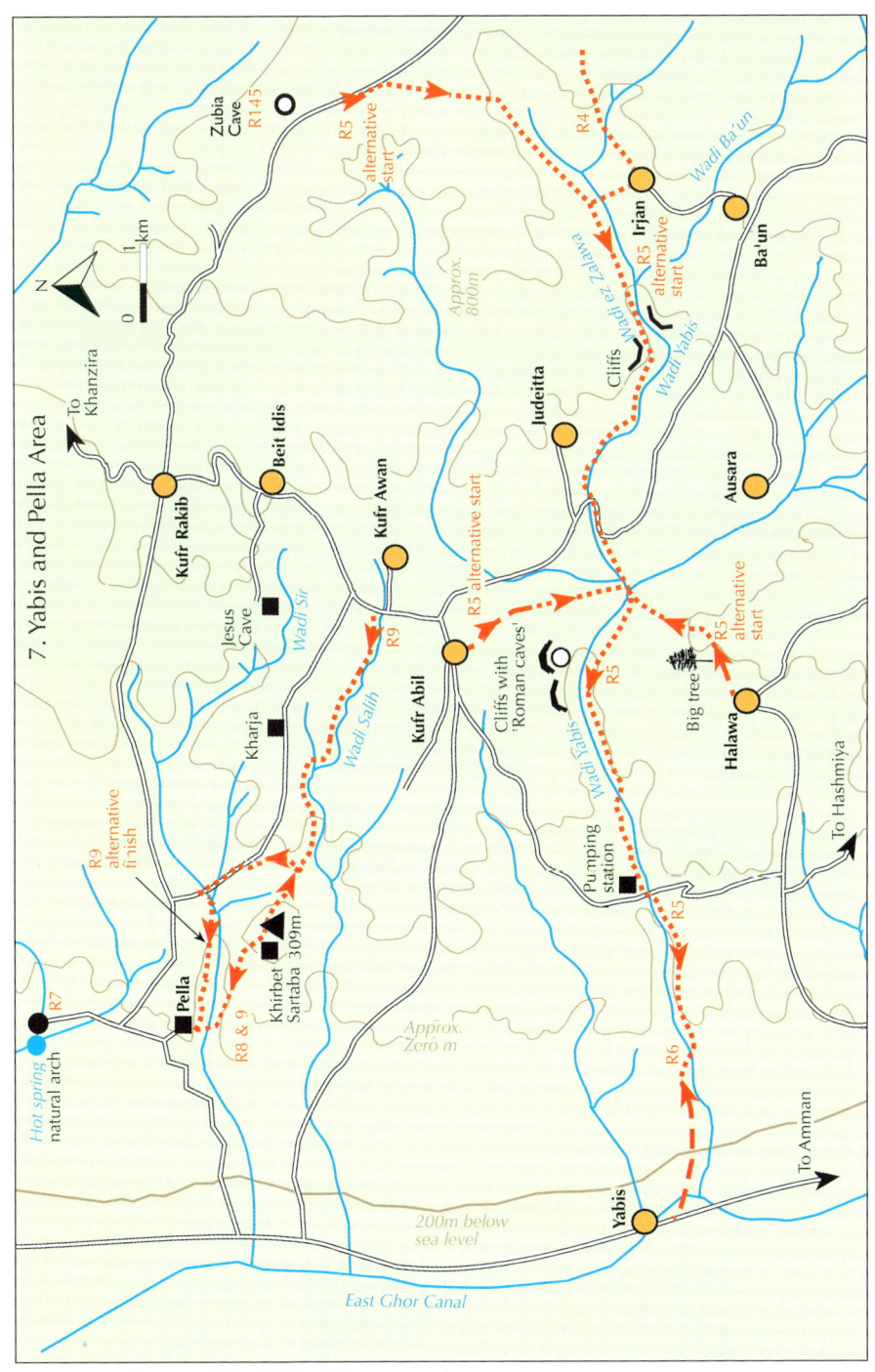

63

or from Amman via Ajloun and Ishtafeina (dependent on the chosen starting point for the descent).

Option 1 Drive up from the Jordan Valley and park in Kufr Abil (GPS alt. 430m N32° 25.004' E35° 40.059'). If you have two cars, leave one at the foot of Yabis in the Jordan Valley.

Option 2 From the road near Zubia Cave (Route 145; GPS alt. 830m N32° 26.171' E35° 44.506'), or follow the Orchards Trail (Route 4) from the Ajloun Woodlands Reserve.

Option 3 From Ajloun, from where there are two routes:
a Take the road N then NW from Ajloun for about 5km to Ishtafeina, then down the hilltop ridge road leading NW towards Kufr Abil, but turn right after 4km at Ba'un and go NE for 2km to Irjan (passed by Route 4 from the Ajloun Reserve).
b Alternatively continue along the road from Ishtafeina, descending to reach Wadi Yabis and its orchards, 5km after Ba'un (GPS alt. 300m N32° 24.075' E35° 41.535').

Option 4 From Halawa, to which there are two approaches:
a From Ajloun via Ishtafeina, then turn left (SW) and follow the road for about 15km to the village, which is on a hilltop 2km above Wadi Yabis on its S side.
b From Deir 'Alla in the Jordan Valley it's about 21km N to the Halawa turn-off, or 26km to the lower end of Wadi Yabis. If you have two vehicles it's best to leave one here first, at the lower end of the wadi (see Route 6), from where it is necessary to go 5km back S down the Jordan Valley to the Halawa junction passed earlier. This small road goes NE up into the hills arriving at Halawa after 10km.

Once in Halawa, go 2km NE up a small road passing right of the mosque and up a hill between houses towards a very tall, slender tree prominent on the hill beyond. The small road becomes a track and stops after 2km on a saddle just S of the tree, at about 500m.

For those wanting a shorter walk there is a fifth option:

Option 5 Approaching Halawa from the Jordan Valley, a sign is passed on the right to Hashmiya at about 7km; next, a small road signed Wadi Ezgig goes left (GPS alt. 250m N32° 23.095' E35° 38.357'). This goes down a couple of hairpin bends to cross Wadi Yabis after 1km at a bridge adjacent to the

Descending lower Wadi Yabis

pumping station (car park; GPS alt. 105m N32° 23.779' E35° 38.280'). From there the road winds up NE to enter Kufr Abil on its S side, so for those with two cars it's easy to leave one at the pumping station and continue with the other down from Kufr Abil to the bridge by the orchards (option 3b).

The route
Dependent on the start chosen, there are various initial stages:

Option 1 From Kufr Abil walk down the good track to Wadi Yabis, reversing that part of Route 2. Approx 3km.

Options 2 and 3a From the Zubia road GPS point (Route 145) go back E along the road for 1km then head S along a W-facing hillside and through a little saddle to descend S into Wadi ez Zalana. Follow the wadi SW, passing below Irjan after 2km. This point can also be reached directly from Irjan by descending W down a side valley.
Continue down Wadi ez Zalana, which joins Wadi Ba'un after 2km to become Wadi Yabis; at this point the valley bottom is choked with trees and there are cliffs on the hilltops above with climbing possibilities (visible from the road at GPS alt. 490m N32° 23.365' E35° 42.431'). Small paths continue along both sides above the treeline and descend to Wadi Yabis for 4km to reach the Ishtafeina–Kufr Abil road; 12km from Zubia, 7km from Irjan (these options only visually checked by the authors, but look good).

Option 3b From the point where the road crosses Wadi Yabis take a narrow lane SSW on the left bank of the stream and through well-tended gardens and orchards of figs and pomegranates (their beautiful red flowers in blossom in mid-May). After about 2km the lane turns into a path that descends to meet the confluence of the Yabis with Wadi Naum near some ruins and ancient olive trees (see Route 2; GPS alt. 290m N32° 23.863' E35° 40.628'). This point can also be reached from Halawa, which is on a hilltop to the SW (see below).

Option 4 From the end of the drivable track in Halawa, a donkey track continues down the hill to some olive groves from where the orchards in the upper reaches of Wadi Yabis can be seen below. Go through the groves on small paths to find a path that continues down slightly left (N) towards the gardens, passing a well-concealed Bedouin house built into a small cliff. Wadi Yabis with its olive groves and gardens 300m above sea level are reached in less than ½hr, 1km from the start of the donkey track. Here are the ruins at the junction of Wadi Naum and Yabis (see Route 2, map 6).

Option 5 A very pleasant 6km walk between the orchards and the pumping station.

The most accessible are options 1, 3b and 4, the latter two being the most popular, whist option 5 is perfect for a short walk if you have two vehicles.

The way on
From the confluence of wadis Naum and Yabis (GPS alt. 290m N32° 23.863' E35° 40.628') the way is obvious and easy. Follow a good path initially down the left side of the river through ancient olives groves – some trees have trunks in excess of 6m and are reputed to date back to Roman times which may well be so. The orchards and gardens are across the river to the right, and the area is particularly pretty.
Continue following the river (cross to the right side as the gardens end; it's easier going for a while). After 15mins some cliffs will be seen above on the right (N), riddled with caves; one in particular is huge. These are known locally as the 'Roman caves', but this is not confirmed. (The cliff with the big cave is about 20m high and has been visited by climbers who found nothing of interest.)
After a while change over to the track on the left bank for the easiest progress and continue down past ancient olives and small cliffs in a truly beautiful valley reminiscent of England's renowned Derbyshire Dales. In less than 1hr from the confluence of the rivers another wadi enters from the left (4km from the start of the walk). Immediately beyond the river enters a scenic canyon. Follow the path down to emerge after 20mins into a *siq* with more 'Roman caves' to the left. Beyond is a pumping station and bridge (see option 5). (Less than 2hrs from the start, 6km, alt. 105m above sea level.)

From the building continue the walk down the valley, having crossed the bridge to the left bank. The river now flows between bamboo and pomegranate trees in full bloom in mid-May, their scarlet flowers attracting sunbirds. There are also many butterflies in the area at that time. The river passes between white cliffs then, after about 1km, starts to descend between more cliffs into a *siq*. At this point the track rises up the left bank to a rocky shoulder above the gorge with the first view of the Jordan Valley beyond. Follow the path along precariously above the deep gorge to the next shoulder; just beyond the path splits. Take the right fork, descending the rocky hillside above the river, which can be seen plunging over a big waterfall where it descends cliffs at the head of the valley.

The track continues along the left side, sometimes quite steeply above the chasm, at one stage supported by an ancient wall as it skirts beneath a small cliff. Now becoming less evident, the track continues past a lone tree and above small crags (don't go too low), eventually descending across easier terrain to reach the river at a point opposite the obvious good path on the right bank where the valley opens out (1½hrs/3km from the building, 3½hrs/9km from the start).

The rest of the way is easy, following the track along the right side of the river for about 1km to reach the 4WD track in the valley bottom (where you can be met by car). Otherwise continue along the track for another 3km to reach the Jordan Valley road.

Return If you don't have a vehicle there are bus services down the Jordan Valley to Deir 'Alla, then on to Amman, or N up the valley passing close to Pella with its Countryside Hotel (see below) and to N Shuna and Irbid or Um Qais.

Wadi Yabis also provides a pleasant walk up its lower reaches, starting from the Jordan Valley 16km N of Kureiyima past one of the frequent checkpoints (26km from Deir 'Alla and 72km from the 6th Circle, Amman, signed '80km Amman' on the opposite side of the road.) The entrance to the valley is found just after crossing the East Ghor Canal.

Route 6
Lower Wadi Yabis from the Jordan Valley

Grade	Easy walk
Details	Distance optional, say 1–2km
Time	½–1hr for return journey

If you don't get the opportunity to walk down this particularly scenic valley from its source high in the mountains (Route 5), it's worth walking up a short way from the Jordan Valley, especially in spring. Flowers are everywhere and there's plenty of birdlife with many large white egrets. See map 7.

Approach Follow a small road on the NE side of the East Ghor Canal for less than 0.5km, leaving it to drive up a track into Wadi Yabis. The track ends at the river 3km from the Jordan Valley road.

The route
Simply follow the river upstream, crossing as and when necessary to finish eventually on the true right (N) side. You should be able to see the cliffs that conceal the waterfall at the head of the valley.

Return Follow your footsteps back, or scramble to the top of the small hill on the right (N) for a view of the Jordan Valley.

Moving on again, a further 5km up the Jordan Valley brings you to the turning for one of the valley's most important archaeological sites, Pella.

PELLA

Pella may prove to be the richest archaeological site in all Jordan... work shows that the Pella area has been the scene of human activity for nearly a million years and the main tell itself has been inhabited almost without interruption for the past 6000 years.

Antiquities of the Jordan Rift Valley Rami G. Khouri (1988)

At the Pella (Tabaqat Fahl) sign, turn right for 3km to reach Pella in the mouth of Wadi Jirm with the Rest House visible above, from where there is an excellent view of the site (GPS alt. zero m N32° 27.027' E35° 37.062').
 Sitting on the balcony with a cool drink is a pleasure not to be missed. The manager Dib Hussein (Abu Bassem) knows the area extremely well. He is also the owner of the Countryside Hotel in the olive groves below (for reservations see Appendix 1).
 Because of the presence of a natural spring (see below) primitive hunters, neolithic and chalcolithic farmers have all lived here, and during the Bronze Age there was a large settlement. However, it was the Greeks and Romans in the 1st and 2nd centuries BC who truly left their mark, particularly the latter during the Byzantine period. Sadly an earthquake in AD749 destroyed most of the site, though much is still being revealed.
 There are some very enjoyable walks in this beautiful part of Jordan, as well as nearby small antiquity sites. There is also an excellent two-day trek to Pella from Ajloun (see Route 2). Apart from Pella itself there are some nearby natural features worth a visit (Route 7).

Route 7
The Natural Bridge and Hot Springs of Pella

Near Fahil [Pella] there is a remarkable natural bridge and a hot spring with a temperature of 103°F. The bridge is thirty feet wide and about a hundred feet high and nearly three hundred feet long; its single arch is thirty feet high formed by the rock itself.

Palestine Past and Present L. Valentine (c1918)

Approach These natural features are 2km N of the Rest House (GPS alt. minus 30m N32° 27.936' E35° 37.225'). Go up the main road from the Rest House then, where the road turns uphill to the E, continue N. See map 7.

The route
The bridge is a huge natural arch spanning Wadi Hamma. There was once an old road crossing it, now unusable for vehicles, but crossable on foot without problem. A dirt track made by bulldozers descends into the wadi E of the bridge. Bulldozers also attacked the hillside opposite in a fruitless 'goldrush' a few years ago, destroying the scenic beauty of the area.
 Though no longer very impressive, the hot spring is directly under the bridge and there is a *hammam* or bath in a small building by the wadi 100m to its W.

Return By the same route.

Just upstream a 4WD track winds NE for 3–4km to Juffein and Deir abu Said, en route to Um Qais. The valley of Wadi abu Salih descends 10km to here from the villages of Kufr Rakib and Khanzira 500m above and may offer a nice trek. Neither route has been checked, but there are some pleasant walks near the bridge and in other, smaller valleys in the area, including the pretty little valley of Wadi Khusheiba about 0.5km before the bridge at a winding hairpin bend in the road. We visited some wadis briefly with the Rest House owner, who pointed out palaeolithic caves on the valley sides. Birdlife was plentiful, with hoopoes, rollers, pigeons and blackbirds darting amongst the foliage.

Route 8
Jebel Sartaba from Pella

Grade	Easy walk
Details	4km up and down, climbing 300m
Time	2hrs including the return trip; more to enjoy the site and summit views; or return via Wadi Jirm, about 5.5km, 3hrs in total; circuit can be done in either direction

This oak-covered hill lies ESE of Tell Hism, the small hill just S of Pella, across Wadi Jirm. The ruined Hellenistic fortress of Khirbet Satarba is on its summit (309m) and can be visited from Pella or via the very enjoyable walk from near Kufr Abil in the hills above (Route 9) or included in the Ajloun–Pella Trek (Route 2, Day 2, Option 1). This summit is particularly pretty in the spring when the hollyhocks and yellow-flowered mimosa are in bloom. Ajloun Castle is visible to the SE and also Mount Tabor rising from the Jezreel Valley to the W. See map 7.

The route
From Pella Rest House (GPS alt. 0m N32° 27.027' E35° 37.062') take Route 9 in reverse up the obvious wide path S from the ruins of Pella to the col between Tell Hism and Jebel Sartaba. From there continue uphill to reach the upper slopes, which are dotted with pine and oak trees; ascend by various tracks (best on the left) to reach the W summit (GPS alt. 309m N32° 26.392' E35° 38.208').

Descent is by the same route; or for a round trip go down the E side (reversing that part of Route 9) to the saddle (GPS 200m N32° 26.202' E35° 38.336') then follow Route 9 variation finish descending N to the small road and down the path on the right side of Wadi Jirm back W to the Rest House.

There are other sites of antiquity in the hills above Pella all known to the Rest House manager (see map 7). These include:

Kahf el Messih (the Jesus Cave) This is W of Beit Idis along a lane for 300m to where an oak stands above tombs cut in the limestone. It is claimed by locals that Jesus stayed here before being baptised in the Jordan River by John the Baptist. A nearby flat area with channels and pools cut in the rock to collect the juice is used for treading grapes. The oak is considered sacred and there is a new mosque nearby with a view W to Sartaba. GPS alt. 510m N32° 26.509' E35° 40.867'.

NORTH JORDAN – THE JORDAN VALLEY HILLS – ROUTE 8

The delightful walk to Pella through the shaded pine woods of Wadi Salih (Route 9)

Khanzira Hellenistic temple A few remains can be found in the village of Khanzira. GPS alt. 540m N32° 28.010′ E35° 42.389′.

The Byzantine ruins of Al Kharja Located on a wooded hilltop just N of Wadi Salih and adjacent to the road but concealed by large cacti and (in spring) hollyhocks. GPS alt. 430m N32° 26.279′ E35° 39.578′.

This road passing Al Kharja (see box above) is the direct route down to Pella and these three locations could be visited on the way from Pella to the start of Route 9.

Route 9
Wadi Salih to Pella

Grade	Easy walk
Details	The route descends 210m from just N of Kufr Abil to where it leaves the wadi. It then climbs 130m to the summit of Sartaba at 309m before descending to Wadi Jirm and climbing up to Pella Rest House at sea level, a total of 180m of ascent and 520m of descent over 8km.
Time	An easy 3hrs

A delightful descent through unexpected pine forests and pretty valleys amongst rolling hills following a fairly well-used path alongside the streambed of Wadi Salih leads down to the foot of Jebel Sartaba. Its summit and the Hellenistic ruins of Khirbet Sartaba are reached by more paths, giving an easy ascent. The ruins are exactly that, with little more than foundations to be seen, but the views in all directions are superb, particularly W across the Jordan Valley to the hills of Gilboa in Palestine with the great open valley of Jezreel to their N and Mount Tabor in the distance.

The valley and its pine forest are unique amongst the walks in this book. On our springtime descent we spotted buzzards, an owl, egrets, Persian squirrels and a tortoise, as well as the unusual sight of Friesian cattle grazing contently in rich wild pasture in the shade of oaks and pine trees. Flowers covered the lower meadows and the hum of bees and other insects filled the air. See maps 6 and 7.

Approach There are two ways of reaching the start (GPS alt. 390m N32° 25.818′ E35° 40.803′).

Option 1 By the Ajloun–Pella trek to Kufr Abil (Route 2). In Kufr Abil turn right in front of the mosque and follow the road round and down through the village for just over 1km to the junction with the main road, or (shorter) turn right where the track up from Wadi Yabis reaches the road on the S side of Kufr Abil and then instead of going left (for 300m to the village centre with the mosque and small shops) go right for less than 1km to reach the main road at almost the same point. From there it's about 0.5km to the start of the trek down Wadi Salih. The wadi is shallow and not obvious at this point, but is in a small olive grove on the left, opposite a wide road going right (unsigned) to Kufr 'Awan.

Option 2 Drive up from Pella Rest House – the manager can arrange transport. It's about 7km by direct road, or 11km via Kufr Rakib (worth the extra distance as there is a baker of excellent Palestinian style *taboun* bread at the crossroads with the decorative arches).

The direct road leaves the Kufr Rakib road about 3km from Pella, turning down right at a checkpoint (passport required). It then reaches the main road about 5km further on; the entrance to Wadi Salih is about 0.5km down it to the right. If you decide to go via Kufr Rakib continue uphill through the checkpoint to reach the aforementioned arches and crossroads about 6km further on. Turn right and go about 4km to reach Wadi Salih opposite the unsigned Kufr 'Awan junction.

The route
From the main road go W for 50m on a dirt track with a small olive grove to your left. To reach the streambed (usually dry) walk left alongside the W side of the grove for 50m, then follow the line of the stream down, soon picking up a small but well-used path on its left. The valley soon becomes deeper and more pronounced and filled with pines through which the path makes its shaded way.

Continuing down the twisting course of the streambed, a shallow cave is passed on your right and eventually the pines on the left thin out, being replaced by more open terrain with a scattering of ancient oaks.

After about 3km the pine-topped hill of Sartaba can be seen 2km ahead. To reach it, leave the wadi where it sweeps round the corner to the left, and go diagonally up across the right side of the valley towards the right shoulder of Sartaba following small paths up through ploughed land and along the edge of an olive grove to reach a dirt track. (There may be a Bedouin camp on the slopes above the point you leave the wadi.) Follow the track right for 100m or so to where it abruptly turns right. Also at this point another faint path goes left (about 5km from start; GPS alt. 200m N32° 26.202' E35° 38.336'). Follow the path left, up onto the shoulder of Sartaba and all the way to an obvious mound of stone on its summit. This is the first of the ruins; others are on the W side of the top from where there are great views (GPS alt. 309m N32° 26.392' E35° 38.208').

The descent to Pella – which is hidden in Wadi Jirm – follows the right shoulder of Sartaba down through scattered trees with the impressive rocky chasm of Wadi Jirm 250m below to the right. At about

Starting the pleasant climb up from Wadi Salih to Jebel Sartaba above Pella

200m altitude a track is reached which winds round the left side of a small top to a little plateau from where an improving track descends the right side of the ridge to a saddle below the final small hill of Tell Hism with an archaeological site visible on its summit. The path continues down right from the saddle to reach Wadi Jirm and the antiquity site of Pella, where fortunately the fence is cut away in two places enabling a direct approach to the Rest House through the site (less than 1hr from the summit). Enjoy the view and hospitality after a wonderful day in the hills!

Return See Route 2.

Shorter alternative finish via Wadi Jirm From the path on the lower shoulder above Wadi Salih on the approach to Sartaba (GPS alt. 200m N32° 26.202' E35° 38.336') descend N for about 300m to meet the road. Follow this N for just over 0.5km, crossing two wadis, the second being Wadi Sir. These merge and plunge into the narrow ravine of Wadi Jirm just W of the road. About 100m beyond, up the hill, a track goes left above this wadi. Follow it down for just over 1.5km. Avoid losing unnecessary height at the end to arrive directly at the Rest House. Less then 3km, descending from 200m on the shoulder, to sea level at the Rest House, allow 1hr.

Heading N again along the Jordan Valley from the Pella junction, the road continues 23km to N Shuna where the road to Irbid forks right. It is then another 19km up to Um Qais, the last section of the road being above the impressive Yarmuk Gorge, which forms the border with Syria.

The 2000-year-old ruins of Pella, with the trail from Jebel Sartaba in the background

THE YARMUK AREA

North Jordan is a great area to spend a few days with a car and a tent or, if you prefer, there are the hotels mentioned at the start of this chapter. There are numerous opportunities for short walks near antiquity sites and no doubt longer treks will be found.

THE YARMUK GORGE

...we pass to the plain of the Yarmuk. This plain has been the scene of great historic battles.
Here, Chedorlaomer defeated the giants; here Israel conquered Og, King of Bashan.
Across it marched the armies of the Assyrians; and on the banks of the Yarmuk
was fought in AD636, a most desperate battle, between the Greeks and Moslems...
the Battle of Yarmuk decided the fate of Palestine; for it was only retained by the Crusaders
for a period of a hundred years, and it was never, even then, wholly free from these
earlier conquerors, who left their faith in Mahomet firmly established among the people...
...The Yarmuk is the dividing river between Bashan and Gilead. It flows through a magnificent
gorge, and is called by the Arabs Sheriat el-Mandhur, from the tribe of Arabs who pasture
in its valley. It falls in a series of cascades into the immense gorges through which it winds, till it
enters the Jordan below Gadara.

Palestine Past and Present L. Valentine (c1918)

At some future date this may well make a good canyon trip, but right now it's politically out of the question! Overlooking it is Um Quais.

UM QAIS

Located 150km from Amman and 30km NW of Irbid, Um Qais is the site of Gadara, a city of the Decapolis, flourishing around the time of Christ but dating from at least 300BC. It is situated on a headland with superb views N and W over the Yarmuk Gorge to the Golan Heights, the Sea of Galilee, Tiberius and Mount Tabor on the far side of the Jordan Valley. The site is well documented in all the travel guides, though it seems that few people wander far beyond the old town and Rest House.

Route 10
Walks near Um Qais

To escape the visitors walk W from the Rest House along the old Roman road, the Decumanus Maximus, to find an ancient mausoleum below ground level on your left. The road continues through the old West Gate and out onto the headland beyond, above the Jordan Valley, its original destination being Tiberius.

Below the car park on the S side of the antiquity site is the head of Wadi um Qais. We have not had time to explore it, but a track is marked on a 40-year-old map going SW down the valley for 5km to the head of the Wadi el Arab Dam, 2km E of N Shuna in the Jordan Valley. Its S side is a popular picnic site

JORDAN

A timeless scene in the hills of Um Qais, with the Jordan Valley below

with a small restaurant and is easily reached by road from N Shuna. If there is still a path down from Um Qais to here it could make a pleasant 7km walk.

About 20km NE of Um Qais the Yarmuk passes below Route 11.

Route 11
The Crusader Caves of Al Habis Jaldak

Grade	Easy walk (with a little scrambling)
Details	2km for the return journey
Time	Allow 1hr (or more if you climb up to the caves)

Reputedly one of the strangest Crusader sites in the Middle East, these man-made caves known as Cava de Suet by the Crusaders are well worth a visit if you're in the area. The walk to them is enhanced by some great views of the Yarmuk Gorge and a big waterfall up a side valley on the Syrian side. See map 8.

Approach The caves are 25km N of Irbid (120km N of Amman). Take the road N out of Irbid (signed Um Qais) for 8km, to where the Um Qais road forks left (NW). Continue straight on for about another 7km past Khureiba to a crossroads with a mosque (GPS alt. 470m N32° 40.185' E35° 52.326').

Take the left road down hairpins past the spring in the pretty little valley of Quweiliba, which is filled with pomegranate and olive trees (See Route 12). Just beyond, up the hill, take

74

the signed turn right to Harta, which is reached in 3km. Continue through Harta to the roundabout. (There is a small café about 100m before the roundabout, on the right.) Continue across the roundabout towards Agraba, with the scenic Wadi um Irsheid below to the left (W). After 4km the road descends into a dip. Turn off the road here and park next to a small olive grove (possible Bedouin tent; GPS alt. 360m N32° 43.364' E35° 49.868'). If you miss this point the road runs up on the left side of a small hill, then up a longer hill to Agraba high on a shoulder overlooking the Yarmuk Gorge.

Just beyond the olive grove an old military observation post on a rocky mound gives fine views of the Yarmuk and Syria to the N and Wadi Habis to the SE. The Crusader Caves are visible 1km away in the cliff at the head of this wadi.

The route
To reach the caves either scramble down right, into the gap, or go left (N) down rock and contour back right to reach the small paths which can be seen contouring round the valley SE to the cliff; in the spring this hillside is carpeted with flowers and falcons skim the crag.

Once at the cliff, the going becomes rather less pleasant as the flat area at its foot is covered in goat muck! The shepherd who lives nearby will be pleased to tell you about the 'Christians' who lived in the caves and may well invite you for tea in his own cave just up the hill.

It is possible to climb up to the caves (which are about 10m above) through what appears to be a natural chimney in the cliff at the left end of the goat ledge, though when we were there in mid-March 1998 the goat muck was soaked by three days of rain and snow and clung thickly to footwear, making climbing impossible. (Steve Cassidy, who visited here in 2002, says the climb is about grade 3 and gives access to the left upper cave and a small side room – a rope might be advisable.)

Return By the same route.

Just 3km E of the caves is Route 12.

Walking to the Crusader Caves of Al Hadis Jaldak, high above the Yarmuk Gorge

Route 12
Wadi Quweiliba, Abila and Wadi es Sijn

Grade	Easy walk
Details	Anything from 2.5–11km
Time	1–4hrs

This very pleasant area is 2km E of Harta (see Route 11) and has relaxing walking to an interesting and seldom-visited archaeological site dating from the time of the Decapolis. See map 8.

Approach Take the road N from Irbid for 15km turning left into Wadi Quweiliba (see Route 11). Here you have two choices:

Option 1 Drive another 2km towards Harta and take the track back right for 2km to the ruins of Abila (the track is rough towards the end).

Option 2 Leave the car at the spring of Ain Quweiliba where the road crosses the valley bottom.

The route
Taking option 2, walk down either side of the valley, first alongside the pomegranate groves then passing some tombs, best on the left (W), for 1.5km to the ruins of Abila which are on the hill to the left (W).

The Decapolis ruins of Abila in seldom-visited hills near the Yarmuk Gorge

NORTH JORDAN – THE JORDAN VALLEY HILLS – ROUTE 12

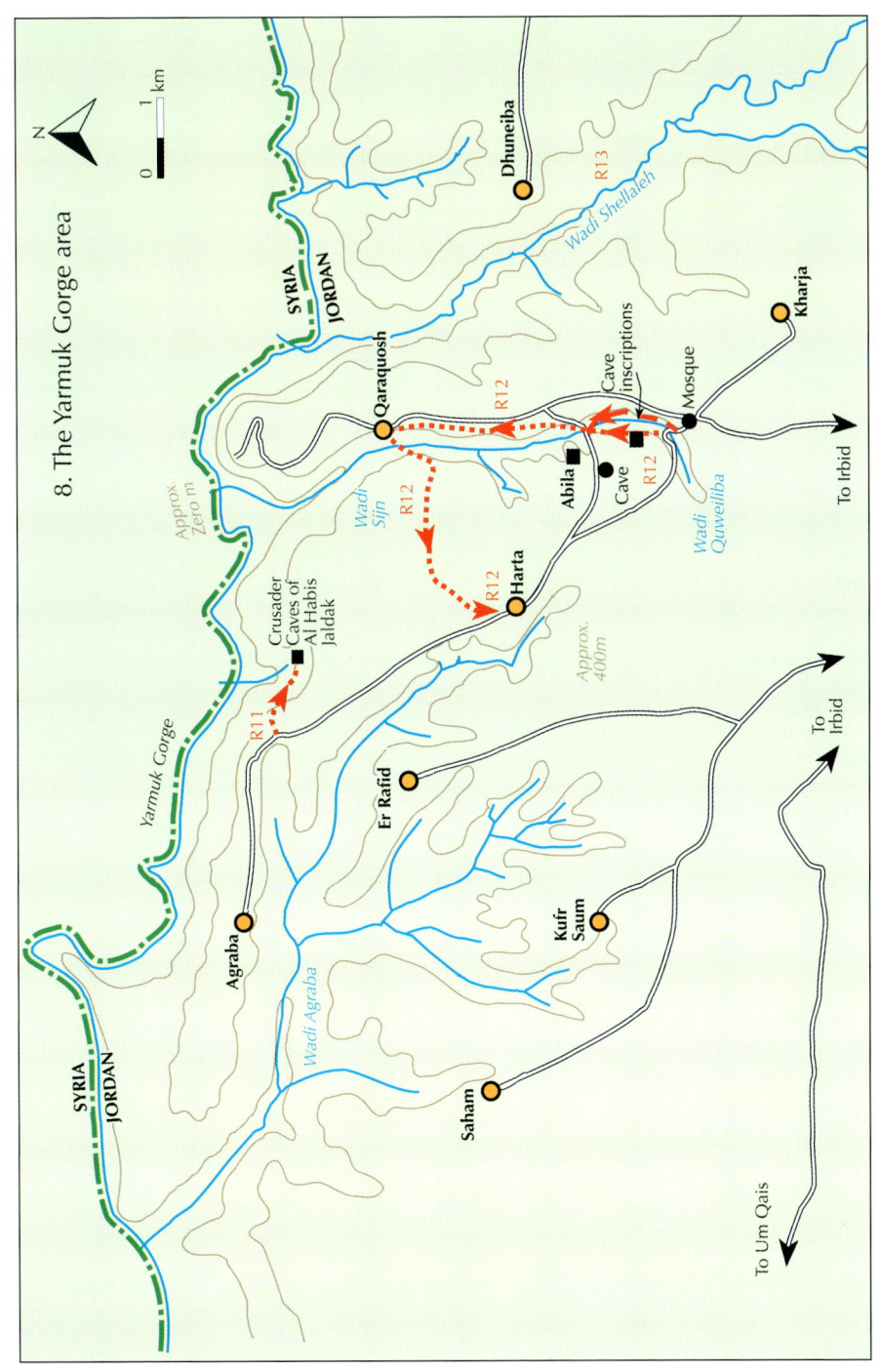

8. The Yarmuk Gorge area

There are two mounds; the most southern has many standing columns hence its name Um el Amad 'mother of columns' (GPS alt. 450m N32° 40.792' E35° 52.087').

From Abila it is possible to continue the walk N down the wadi on paths in the bottom or on a 4WD track on its E side for another 2.5km rising up E to Qaraquosh, beyond which there is a checkpoint closing the road. A patterned red-brown snake almost 2m long (and non-poisonous) seen by us near Abila was identified by the RSCN as *malpolon Monspessulanus* – its common name is Montpellier snake.

If you were to continue a further 3km down Wadi Sijn you would reach the road in the bottom of the Yarmuk Valley. This may be off-limits, and there would certainly be military checkpoints down there. Ask before going. Alternatively there are tracks rising SW from the wadi, passing through the olive groves and orchards of Zawiyya, reaching Harta after 3km.

Return From Harta or Qaraquosh you would need to return to your car at Ain Quweiliba by road – either way about 4km. It would certainly be possible to arrange a lift back from Harta. Ask at the café.

If you have your own transport, it is easy to continue 3km N from Qaraquosh to the viewpoint above the Yarmuk Gorge on a peninsula between Wadi Sijn and Wadi Shellaleh.

Route 13
Wadi Shellaleh to the Yarmuk Gorge

It is also worth driving out further E via Kharja, first 2km SE through orchards on the narrow road from the Quweiliba crossroads (see Route 11), then E for another 2km to the lip of Wadi Shellaleh. This huge river gorge extends 20km S from the Yarmuk, with numerous villages along its upper edges and 4WD tracks descending and rising between them as well as following the gorge itself – it looks like good mountain bike country! There are also rumoured to be caves here. See map 8.

The whole area is particularly beautiful in the spring when the hillsides and orchards are fully in bloom, in contrast to the next area, the North Eastern Desert which is altogether different terrain.

THE NORTH EASTERN DESERT

This vast region of flat basalt desert known as the Badia extends north and east to the borders of Syria, Iraq and Saudi Arabia. Here are the desert castles and ancient caravanserais of Um el Jimal, Jawa, Qasr Burqu and Azraq, the latter two now being the location for RSCN Nature Reserves.

RSCN NATURE RESERVES IN THE NORTHEAST

The next two Reserves are in and adjacent to the Azraq oasis, whilst the third is much further east along the road to Iraq.

THE RSCN AZRAQ WETLAND NATURE RESERVE

Azraq is a unique wetland oasis located in the heart of the arid North Eastern Desert. It contains several pools, a seasonally flooded marshland, and a large mudflat known as Qa' al Azraq. A variety of birds stop here for a short rest on their migration routes each year, staying within the protected areas. At the Ramsar Convention of 1977 the Azraq oasis was declared an internationally important wetland. A small wetland reserve (12sq km) was established in the southern part of the oasis, and at that time contained large areas of permanent marshland and several deep spring-fed pools. Unfortunately, since 1980, because of massive extraction of ground water for Amman, many of these areas – including the main spring – have dried up. Fossil water is being pumped in but replaces barely 3 percent of the extracted water. This can only be a short-term 'solution', and the future of the Azraq oasis – that has made life possible here for 250,000 years – is consequently in doubt.

The best time to visit Azraq is in winter or early spring. Winter rains often create pools and shallow marshes which continue to attract many seasonal species of birds, though only a small fraction of those that visited over 20 years ago. The success of a birdwatching

The Roman castle at Azraq, used by Lawrence in 1917

JORDAN

visit depends largely on the amount of water that has accumulated. Full information will be found in the Visitor Centre with its helpful displays and friendly staff. Location, see maps 1 and 2.

Approach 100km east of Amman by road.
Entrance fee 2JD non-Jordanians, 0.5JD Jordanians.
Guiding fee See below.
Accommodation Camping is not permitted inside the Reserve, but there is a small campsite at the nearby Shaumari Reserve and an RSCN Eco-Lodge near South Azraq. Camping costs from 5–9JD upwards for Jordanians/non-Jordanians. Hotel costs are from 36–45JD per double B&B. For details contact the RSCN (see Appendix 1). There is also accommodation in Azraq.

Route 14
Azraq Marsh Trail

Grade	Easy walk
Details	Short 1.5km walking trail around the marshes (details from RSCN)
Time	1hr for the round trip

Guide No guide necessary for the marked trail with information boards and birdwatching hide.

THE RSCN SHAUMARI RESERVE

Almost adjacent to Azraq, the 22sq km Shaumari Reserve (map 1) was created in 1975 as a breeding centre for endangered or locally extinct wildlife. It is home to some of the rarest animals in the Middle East: the Arabian oryx, ostriches, gazelles and onagers. These animals are rebuilding their populations in a safe haven, protected from hunting and habitat destruction that has nearly wiped them out.

Shaumari represents one of the greatest success stories in the international fight against wildlife extinction. Many different countries have shown their support by donating wildlife species, conducting breeding programmes, and helping to establish Shaumari as a suitable new home for their animals. Visitors to Shaumari have an opportunity to see the living results of this global co-operation.

The oryx can be seen roaming freely in the desert grassland, and the ostriches, gazelles, and onagers can be observed in their enclosures. Shaumari's breeding enclosures provide a small 'zoo' for visitors, making the Reserve popular with children and for school outings. The observation tower is a good place from which to spot oryx, particularly in the early morning, whilst safari tours through the oryx enclosure are available aboard the RSCN shuttle bus.

Approach In the desert S of Azraq and accessible from there by taxi (about 4JD – more if you want the driver to return).

Entrance fee 2JD non-Jordanians, 0.5JD Jordanians. Shaumari's Visitor Centre contains a small museum with a variety of interactive materials, slide shows and videos on the history and wildlife of the Reserve. Outside there is a playground and picnic area.

Oryx safari This 4WD journey into the desert can be arranged at 10JD per trip for up to 10 people; allow 2–4hrs.

Accommodation Camping is permitted in RSCN tents near the Visitor Centre (see the Azraq Reserve for prices), where you will also find drinking water and toilets. Camping permits are required for all overnight camping in the Reserve. Permits and rental tents can be obtained at the RSCN headquarters in Amman or on site at Shaumari. There is also an RSCN Eco-Lodge located near South Azraq. Bookings can be made at RSCN headquarters in Amman or on site at the RSCN lodge.

Outside the Reserve and N of Azraq is a lava tube, formed during a period of lava flow (see Route 149). Heading NE the road continues across the interminable basalt stone desert for another 200km to Iraq. About 40km along this road and 8km before Safawi down a signed gravel track to the S is another curiosity, the lone Begaaweyeh Tree, where the Prophet Mohammed is reputed to have rested in the shade. Nowadays visitors and local Bedouin tie bits of clothing to the branches for luck. Not far from the tree there is a newly made pool where waterfowl can sometimes be seen (we also saw an owl and an eagle – the latter no doubt on the look-out for one of the local pigeons!). About 120km along this road from Azraq (80km after Safawi) is a sign to the ruins of the 'Palace of Burqu', which are in the RSCN Qasr Burqu Reserve.

THE RSCN QASR BURQU RESERVE

Think, in this battered caravanserai
Whose portals are alternate Night and Day,
How Sultan after Sultan with his Pomp
Abode his destined Hour, and went his way.

The Rubaijat of Omar Khayyam E. Fitzgerald (1859)

The ruins of the caravanserai of Burqu about which the above lines could well have been written are 18km into the desert NNW of Muqat at the side of a 2km-long Roman reservoir only accessible by 4WD (location, map 3).

Route 15
Burqu Lakeside Walk

After driving 250km past the hot and inhospitable rock-strewn basalt desert from Amman, Burqu is a refreshing place for a walk by the waterside. Obviously birds think so too as this is the only large expanse of water in this area, so you can expect to see ducks, waders and raptors. (Not worth a special visit unless you are interested in birds or passing that way en route to or from Iraq!)

The ruins of Roman Burqu in the remote North Eastern Desert – the lake attracts migratory birds (Route 15)

AROUND AZRAQ

Returning to the Azraq area, there are three small 'peaks' mentioned in Lawrence's *Seven Pillars of Wisdom*. Adam Messer kindly visited here at our request and supplied the information on these hills and on a meteor crater to the west (Route 17). He wondered if the peaks and the depression in which they stand were created by a small piece of the meteorite that made the larger crater.

T. E. Lawrence passed through the Azraq oasis on a number of occasions. Once, having rested two days there, he 'marched past Ammari, across Jesha to near the Thlaithukwat...'

Route 16
Thlaithukhwat

> *A steep old pathway took us out of Wadi Bair. Near the crest of a ridge we found the others camped for the night round a fire, but there passed no talk of coffee-making for this time. We lay close together, hushed and straining the ears to catch the throbbing of Allenby's guns. They spoke eloquently: and sheet lightning in the west made gun flashes of them. Next day we passed to the left of the Thlaithukwat, the 'Three Sisters' whose clean white peaks were landmarks on their lofty watershed for a day's journey all about; and went down the soft rolling slopes beyond them.*

Seven Pillars of Wisdom T. E. Lawrence (1922)

Grade	Easy scramble
Details	60m to and from any of the summits
Time	½hr will get you up and down

These hills are just E of the Azraq–Ma'an road. E to W their summits are 945m, 964m and 953m, whist the flinty desert in their immediate vicinity is 897m making them only about 60m above their base; not much, but sufficient to provide a great vantage point. Strangely, the desert floor inside the area contained by the three peaks is actually about 10m lower than that outside the peaks. More driving than walking!

Approach 2½hrs from Amman; about 80km, 1hr, S of Azraq. The turn-off from the Azraq–Ma'an highway is not critical but if you have a GPS it's in the region of N31° 00.152' E36° 33.042'. There are many tracks in the desert but the peaks are clearly visible from the highway; 4WD useful. Location of the base of the peaks GPS N30° 58.424' E36° 39.808'.

The route
Steep scrambling on sharp flinty scree. The summits are an ideal lookout point with good views of the desert as far as the Saudi border to the E.

Route 17
The Meteorite Crater

Another novelty that makes an unusual destination for an easy and interesting desert drive. You would think that a feature such as this – which is 6km in diameter – would be well known and easily found, but it was located by Adam Messer using radar elevation data from NASA's Shuttle Radar Topography Mission (see Introduction). He says 'Although we don't have any dates on the crater, it's ancient. The site is heavily weathered. Large red rocks were formed when the iron-rich meteor fused the surrounding soil and rocks. From the dispersion pattern of the fragments, you can see clearly which direction the meteorite fell from. The difference between the rocks at the crater edge and the surrounding flint desert is striking.'

The route
Adam's description: 'The crater is 30–40km SE of the archaeological site of Qasr Tuba. The drive to it was unusually simple. A new road links the main Aqaba highway to the Azraq-Ma'an highway. About 12km S towards Ma'an we left the road (GPS N36° 38.021' E31° 02.827') to head roughly ESE for about 20km. There are many tracks going through the desert and we largely navigated by sight. As it's 6km across, the crater (GPS N36° 46.871' E31° 01880') is hard to miss but seeing pictures first helped. The surrounding desert is flat and undulating, alt. 790m. We drove to the centre of the crater, and walked to the top of the primary impact site, GPS alt. 830m N36° 47.907' E31° 02773'. Total time, a leisurely 2hrs from Amman.'

JORDAN

THE CAPITAL AREA

The rapidly growing city of Amman is on the site of ancient Philadelphia. There are numerous important historic sites within the city, which is built on rolling limestone hills giving pleasant walks within easy reach. This section covers the hills and wadis from Jerash to the north of Amman down to the north end of the Dead Sea, which is only a short drive southwest of the city and is covered in the next chapter (The Dead Sea Hills).

JERASH

This excellently preserved Roman city dating from 170BC is one of Jordan's best-known antiquity sites, and is located 24km SE of Ajloun and 50km N of Amman. If you get the urge to head for the hills after half a day walking its main street, or Cardo, and seeing the sights, try the RSCN Dibeen Forest Reserve.

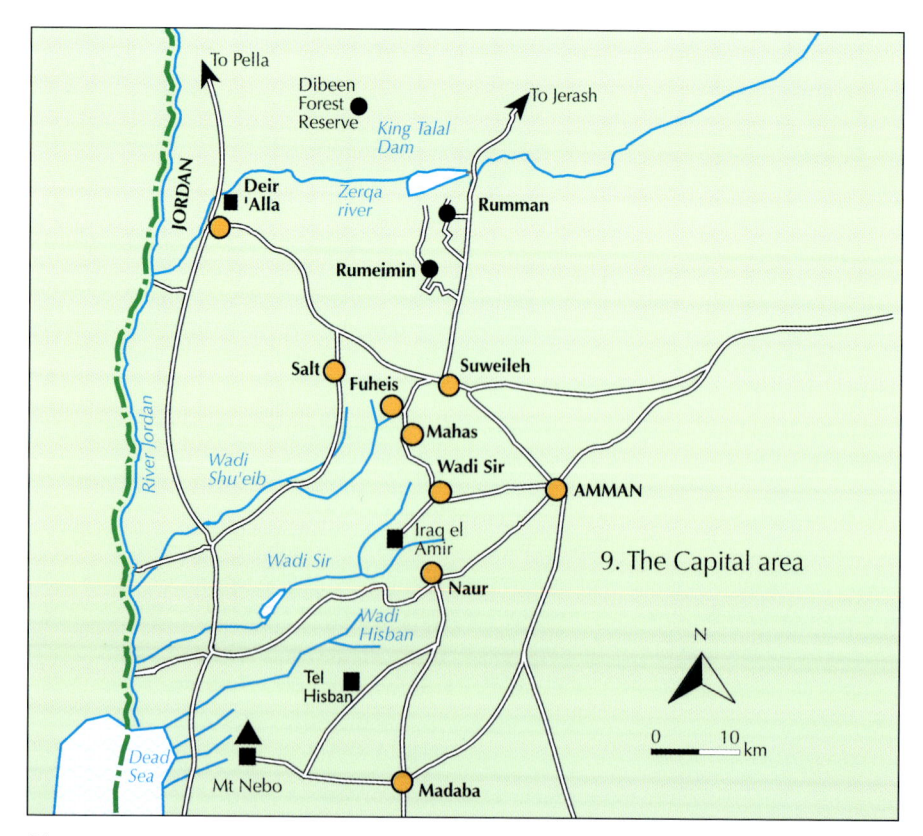

9. The Capital area

84

RSCN DIBEEN FOREST RESERVE

This is a pretty forested hilltop area with a Rest House and accommodation 14km south-southwest of Jerash by road and 7km north of the King Talal Dam (from where a new road may be built). It is best avoided on Fridays when it can be full of people from Amman. There is a privately run hotel and it's sometimes possible to hire horses (Location, map 9).

We were pleased to see that the pinewoods which flourish at 700–1000m were as beautiful as ever and carpeted with flowers when we visited in April 2006, but disappointed that the area was still suffering badly from litter. It's hardly surprising: 700 vehicles were there the previous weekend, which probably means about 2000 visitors from Amman and elsewhere were picnicking and some leaving rubbish. Dibeen Nature Reserve was established in 2004 and the RSCN is working hard to improve the situation and educate visitors about environmental awaremess, but there's a long way to go. Don't be put off!

Wildlife Despite being fragmented and covering only 8sq km, 96 species of birds have been reported in spring, plus jackals, hyenas and wolves as well as Persian squirrels and wild boar. Amongst the pine and oaks the smaller, smooth red-barked trees are strawberry trees and in spring there are flowers in abundance almost everywhere.

Approach Follow the signed road from the south Jerash roundabout (near Hadrian's Gate) for about 14km, passing by Ghazah refugee camp, then El Hadadeh and Jamlah villages, beyond which it's 4km to the Reserve. At the entrance kiosk a small charge per vehicle is made towards improving the site and creating employment for local people. The hotel and parking area is higher up in the forest.

Some useful GPS points
Monastery of Virgin Mary, near Dibeen alt. 750m N32°15.356' E35°49.474'
Dibeen Hotel (at car park area) alt. 690m N32°14.421' E35°49.901'
View to E, on road from Reserve to Saqeb alt. 1050m N32°15.528' E35°48.643'

Route 18
Dibeen Forest Walks

The RSCN has designated two trails, 'long' and 'short' (neither taking more than half a day, fee dependent on the number of people). Their guides are very knowledgeable, and the views over the surrounding area are excellent; rumour has it there are also some caves.

Immediately S of Dibeen and W of the Amman–Jerash highway is the King Talal Dam.

THE KING TALAL DAM AREA

The next day we travelled to 'Ain Roman, a most delightful ride over beautiful country of hills and dales strewn with scarlet anemones. 'Ain Roman is a spring which trickles down a gorge and joins the River Zerka – the Old Testament Jabbok – an important tributary of Jordan. Near this place is a settlement of Turcomans. In the evening we walked down the gorge, through which the stream runs. Oleanders fringed its banks, big rocks were strewn about on each side, it is a very picturesque place, and reminded us of a Dartmoor glen. Here were many of the large blue pigeons of Gilead, and other birds.

With the Bedouins Gray Hill (1890)

Only about 40km – or little more than 30mins – from Amman, the Zerqa River was once the boundary between the land of Og, a fierce giant and the King of Bashan, and Sihon, King of the Amorites. It is a beautiful area of rolling hills and forests, with small villages, orchards and olive groves set above the picturesque – though polluted – lake formed by the King Talal Dam. The area is popular with birdwatchers and is ideal for a half day or more for those with a car, with many possibilities for short walks on the hilltops or in the wadis. Below are some possibilities.

Approach Head out of town following Jerash signs through Suweileh. About 9km further on the road passes to the right of some telecommunication dishes. Turn left (signed Rumeimin and Jalad) almost level with the dishes and then immediately right to pass to the right of them. Another 9km on, along a winding country lane, the road reaches the village of Rumeimin. See map 9.

The King Talal Dam; the Dibeen Forest and Roman Jerash are in the hills beyond

Route 19
Rumeimin Waterfall

Turn right and descend a narrow lane to a small café. Park here and walk for 5mins up the side of the wadi to a pool below a waterfall, spouting 10m over an overhanging limestone escarpment into a pool. If it isn't full of local children you may like to have a swim, though women should remain clothed.

To get to the start of Route 20 return to the road and continue for 2km from Rumeimin, then turn right at the junction and keep right on the main road for about 6km. Here take the left fork. (There are many small roads, villages and wadis, so it could be easy to get on the wrong track; basically, from Rumeimin head generally NW for 4km, then N.) From the left fork the road deteriorates and eventually becomes a rough track going N for 6km along the ridge of Sumiya to a hilltop at 348m overlooking the dam about 170m below.

Route 20
Walks in the Sumiya Hills

The surrounding hills and wadis offer shorts walks in beautiful scenery with forests and the lake to the N and E. The Jordan Valley can be seen in the haze to the W, and there are numerous antiquity sites near the confluence of the rivers such as Tulul edh Dhahab, Tell Hammeh, Tell Damieh and Tell Deir 'Alla. It is not known whether or not there is a path or way down along the Zerqa River (the Biblical Jabbok) to reach the Jordan Valley, but the lower river is supposed to be 'a nice picnic site'.

Other alternatives Instead of turning off the Jerash road at the telecom dishes, continue N another 2km and take the old Jerash road to Er Rumman 7km to the N (or continue on the main Jerash road for 8km from the dishes and turn left for 2km to Rumman).

Route 21
The King Talal Dam Lakeside Walk

2km N of Er Rumman the old road enters a Forestry Reserve at which point the vehicle can be left and permission obtained to walk down to the lake where the old road disappears into the flooded valley of Zerqa. The walk can be continued generally E through oleanders and woodland near the shoreline to the Zerqa bridge on the Jerash road (information from Sami Sabat, not checked by the authors). Location, map 9.

There are also possibilities for short walks outside the Reserve and on the hilltops of Jebel esh Shubeil S of Er Rumman and between the old and new Jerash roads.

AROUND AMMAN

Moving south again into the suburbs of Amman there are some very nice places for short walks.

WADI ES SIR

The ride from Ain Mahis to Arak el Amir was more beautiful than anything we had yet seen in Gilead, though from the first, the scenery of the country had so far surpassed our expectations that we ceased to be surprised at anything. Except where now and then a gorge commenced, where the combination of rock and wood was most picturesque, and where the ground was carpeted with anemones, cyclamens, asphodels, iris and many flowering shrubs, we rode knee-deep through the long, rich, sweet grass, abundantly stubbed with oak and terebinth trees.

Land of the Gilead Laurence Oliphant (c1887)

The suburb of Wadi es Sir is 7km W of Amman. To its SW are the caves and antiquity site of Iraq el Amir, which can be reached by taxi from Amman. It is possible to walk along the hillside past the caves before continuing on and down to the ruins. There is a Queen Noor Foundation Centre here producing craftwork, and a café. Despite being so close to town the whole area is particularly beautiful with small farms, olive groves and orchards, which are especially pretty when the almond trees are in bloom. The many valleys can be walked or sometimes driven through with 4WD. Location, map 9.

Route 22
Walks in Wadi es Sir

This valley runs down to the S for about 7km from Iraq el Amir and the pre-Roman villa of Qasr el Abd. Tracks can be taken from there up to the road coming from the Jordan Valley to Naur and Amman, and there are some very impressive ancient cave-tombs high in a cliff near the lower end. It is also reputedly possible to carry on down the wadi on foot to the Jordan Valley (neither way checked by the authors).

About 7km NW of Wadi es Sir suburb is the small hillside town of Mahas (Mahis), 3km N of which is the Christian village of Old Fuheis.

Lioness at the pre-Roman Qasr el Abd, above Wadi es Sir on the outskirts of Amman

OLD FUHEIS

Despite its proximity to Amman, just 10km W of Suweileh in N Amman, Old Fuheis has so far retained an aura of peace and quiet.

Approach To reach it from the modern suburb of Fuheis (green signs to Old Fuheis), head down the hill to the N, then W. It is nicely situated to the E of Wadi Shu'eib (Route 24) in pleasant rural surroundings, with two old churches and a shrine to St George. There are some craft shops in the old buildings selling pottery, embroidery, weaving, metalwork and the like, and two very pleasant restaurants (at European prices), the Zuwwadeh and the Al Hosh. The shops are open from around 3pm until about 9pm and the restaurants from 10am until midnight. Location, map 9.

Route 23
Walks near Old Fuheis

If you follow the small road down past the lower church it becomes a narrow lane descending into the wadi. The wadi has rocky sides, and a path in the bottom can be reached by following the road down for 1km. The path can then be taken back up to the NE side of Old Fuheis (2km), or it would be possible to scramble up the rocky limestone slopes on its W side to reach the top of Jebel el Khandaq (720m), just 100m or so above, from where there are views down the small Wadi Azraq to Wadi Shu'eib and the Jordan Valley.

Directly across the deep valley to the NW is Salt, another old suburb of Amman, which is also easily accessible from Amman via Suweileh. Close by are the Jal'al and Zai Hills.

THE JAL'AL AND ZAI HILLS

These forested hill 'parks' overlooking the Jordan Valley are a favourite escape for citizens of Amman, being less than an hour's drive away. Access is via Salt from the scenic road that descends Wadi Shu'eib for 30km to S Shunah in the Jordan Valley, beyond which the King Hussein bridge spans the river to the West Bank.

Route 24
Walks in Wadi Shu'eib

Numerous short walks can be done either in the valley, adjacent to the river, near orchards and gardens, or on the hillside above on the opposite side to the road. The valley is also accessible by tracks down from Mahas and Fuheis (see Route 23.) There are a couple of picnic spots with soft drink shops towards the lower end of the valley, the last being on the edge of a dam just before S Shunah. This area is particularly busy on Fridays. Location, map 9.

Moving over to the SW side of Amman we come to the antiquity site of Tell Hisban.

TELL HISBAN

The huge mound of Tell Hisban dates back to around 1000BC and was described in the Book of Numbers as the city of Sihon, King of the Amorites, capital of the country he had captured from Moab. It is close to the old Moabite, Nabataean, Roman road about 25km SW of Amman.

Approach From Amman go first along the airport road from the 7th Circle, then the Dead Sea road towards the suburb of Naur, then SE along a road signed to Madaba. A few km along here are signs to Tell Hisban. Location, map 9.

Route 25
Walks near Tell Hisban

The surrounding area is very rural despite its proximity to town with pretty valleys winding down towards the Jordan Valley and the N end of the Dead Sea, giving both a pleasant drive and nice walks. Wadi Hisban passes 2km to the N of the tell and has an intriguing cave in the cliffs of its S side just below its start at Um el Qanatid, 6km N of Hisban.

THE NORTHERN DEAD SEA

Down to the west of Amman, the north end of the Dead Sea is less than 1hr away. Four modern international hotels have been built there in recent years: the Mövenpick Resort and Spa, the Jordan Valley Marriott Resort and Spa, the Kempinski Hotel Ishtar and the Dead Sea Spa. The Mövenpick and Marriott are as good and pricey as it gets (at around $160 for a double room – these hotels charge in dollars – with possible reductions at the time of booking), whilst the Ishtar and the Dead Sea Spa (which was the original resort) are also in the upper bracket. At least three more hotels are in the process of construction and more are planned.

Nearby three wadis descend from the Dead Sea Hills. Despite the barren appearance of these mountains, their lower reaches provide opportunities for pleasant short walks up perennial streams in sometimes tropical surroundings and usually to the sound of running water, a real pleasure in a desert land. Anyone wanting to explore these canyons further should refer to *Trekking and Canyoning in the Jordanian Rift Valley* (see Appendix 2). We have not had the opportunity to do the following routes, but information on them has kindly been supplied by Mark Khano of Arabian Escape (see Appendix 1) and Brian Hodgkinson.

Route 26 starts opposite the Mövenpick Hotel.

NORTH JORDAN – THE CAPITAL AREA

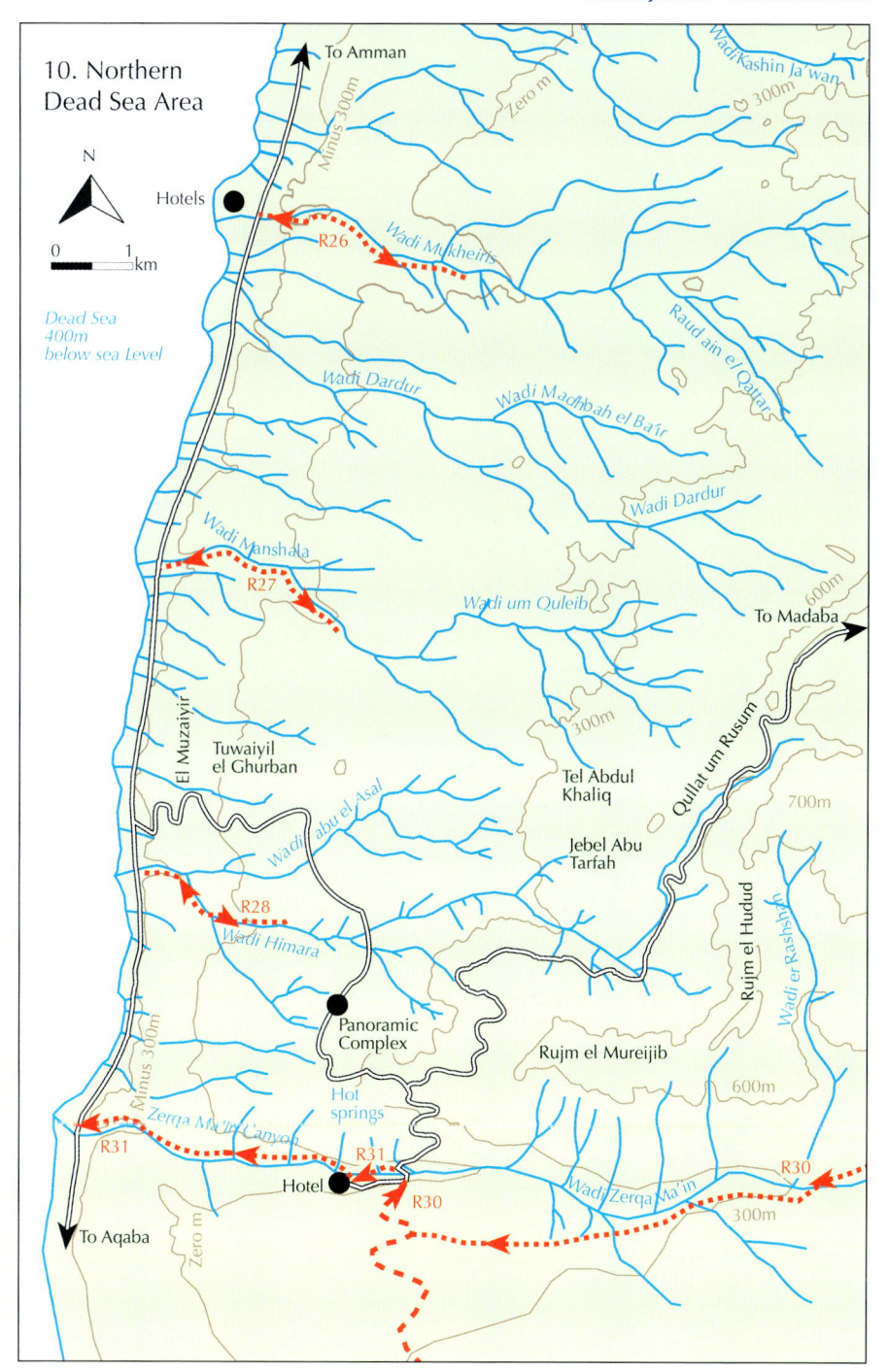

10. Northern Dead Sea Area

91

Route 26
Wadi Mukheiris

Grade	Easy canyon
Details	Over 2km each way, about 250m of ascent and descent (double if you go to the end); beware of floods in the rainy months
Time	About 4hrs for the round trip

An easily accessible 'escape to nature' for city dwellers, providing surprisingly watery fun. The canyon can be followed for almost 5km, but most will be happy to spend a pleasant half day in its lower reaches. See map 10.

Approach Easy – just across the road from the Mövenpick (GPS alt. minus 360m N31° 43.049' E35° 35.398').

The route
Follow the stream up, reaching a 5m waterfall in less than 1hr. Pass this on its left (N) to reach more small waterfalls and pools, which provide an entertaining hour until a 20m waterfall is reached. It is possible to continue up beyond here with increasing difficulty to reach more waterfalls and a cave-like grotto.

Return By the same route.

Route 27
Wadi Manshala

Grade	Easy canyon
Details	About 2km each way, about 250m of ascent and descent (double if you go to the end); beware of floods in the rainy months
Time	About 4hrs for the round trip

The second of the three canyons, found a short way S; another exotic and watery walk. See map 10.

Approach 4km down the road, S of the Mövenpick Hotel to the W end of the wadi, opposite a grey concrete military lookout building (GPS alt. minus 390m N31° 40.486' E35° 34.524'). (The area on the seaward side of the road for around 100m each side of the building is currently screened off for the construction of a beach resort.)

The route
Follow the initially dry wadi up E into an area of oleanders where the stream will be met. Continue up past pools and small waterfalls to an igneous intrusion with a large waterfall beyond. After about 1hr the wadi narrows but paths continue on the right (S) side. Continue past two small groups of palms, sometimes on scree, then follow vague paths back into the canyon to more palms at a 30m waterfall.

Return Return along the same route or, if you need more adventure, scramble up the waterfasll and continue with more difficulty through the upper palm-filled ravine for another 2km past more pools into the final ravine from where small paths should be found on the S side, returning to the road by a parallel route.

Still moving S, the last of the three wadis is S of the turning for the new Dead Sea Parkway road (GPS alt. minus 360m N31° 39.165′ E35° 34.430′). This passes over the wadi about 4km higher up in the hills at GPS alt. 140m N31° 38.292′ E35° 36.073′, at the Al Wadi bridge on its way to the Panoramic Complex.

Route 28
Wadi Himara

Grade	Easy canyon
Details	Easy walk along the wadi bottom to a small waterfall; beware of floods in the rainy months
Time	2–4hrs dependent on turn-round point

Another fun canyon walk. The wadi can also be descended from its start high in the hills, which requires a full day, or probably also from the upper Himara bridge. The route described is the enjoyable option of a round trip from the Dead Sea. See map 10.

Approach 8km down the road, S of the Dead Sea hotels and 0.7km past the road to the Dead Sea Museum (GPS alt. minus 370m N31° 38.785′ E35° 34.438′).

The route
Head up the wadi all the way to a small waterfall. If you wish to continue further you will need to backtrack; watch out for a path going up on the S side of the wadi that rises to a small plateau. Heading SE you will catch sight of the 80m waterfall, the highest in Jordan.

Return By the same route back to the Dead Sea road.

Next stop is Madaba on the northern edge of the Dead Sea Hills.

Entering the Mujib Siq (Route 50)

THE DEAD SEA HILLS

Moab howleth over Nebo and Madaba.

Book of Isaiah

The Old Testament land of Moab extends from the hills immediately north of the Mujib Gorge, near the northern end of the Dead Sea, all the way south to the next great natural barrier: Wadi Hasa at the southern end of the Dead Sea. These hills – the Dead Sea Hills – are described in three sections: the Madaba Area, the RSCN Mujib Nature Reserve and the Karak Area.

Accommodation and transport

At the northern end of the Dead Sea you can enjoy the undoubted luxury of four international-class hotel resorts and spas – the Mövenpick, Marriott, Kempinski Hotel Ishtar and Dead Sea Spa – with double rooms at around $160. The short wadi walks near here are described in the previous chapter. A short way south, at the Dead Sea end of the Mujib Gorge, there are RSCN chalets at 75JD per double. Alternatively, it would be possible to camp in or near some of the gorges, but beware of flash floods and stay well above the high-water mark.

Horned Poppy

Back on the hilltops the routes to the north of this section are easily accessible from Amman, or from Madaba where there are a number of pleasant mid-range hotels including the extremely popular Mariam at 25JD per double including breakfast; further down to the southwest the road culminates at the Ashtar Hotel and

On the shore of the Dead Sea, the lowest point on earth, 400m below sea level and still going down

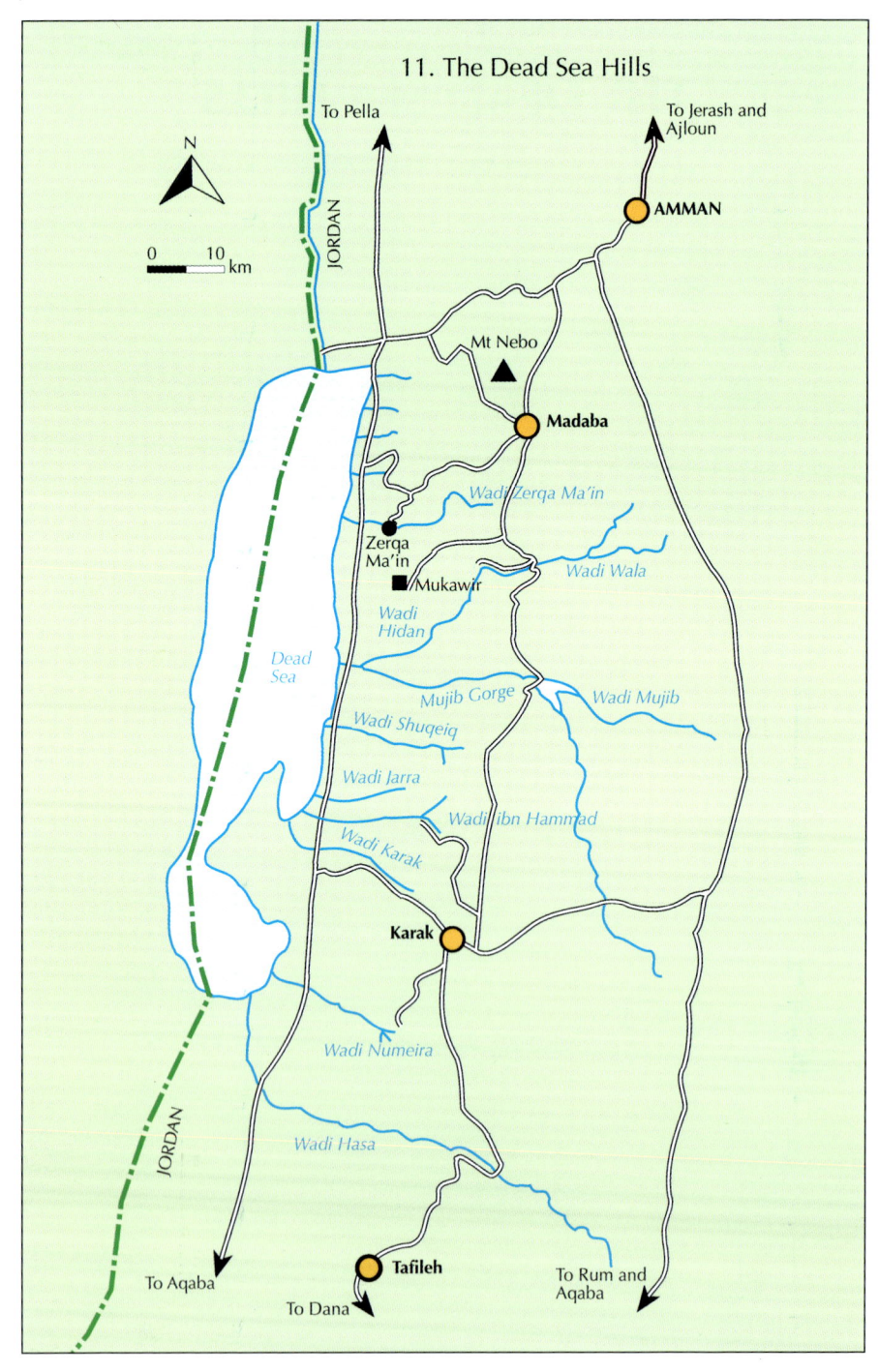

Jordan

11. The Dead Sea Hills

THE DEAD SEA HILLS

Spa at the Zerqa Ma'in hot springs. Karak is conveniently placed in the south and has hotel rooms costing between 15 and 50JD per double such as at The Towers and Rest House respectively, both near the castle gates. Public transport anywhere in this area should not cost more than 3JD, but ideally you're going to need a taxi, hire car or private transport to reach many of the walks. Hiring a guide solves this problem.

Guides
Much of the Mujib area is within the Mujib Reserve so, where relevant, you will need permission and sometimes guides from the RSCN. Otherwise – should you need them – there are guides and adventure travel operators in Amman, Madaba and South Jordan who are familiar with at least some of these routes (see Appendix 1).

Maps
The following 1:50,000 topographical K737 series maps cover this area. You are unlikely to be able to get hold of these, but enquire at the Jordanian Royal Geographical Centre in Amman (see 'Maps' in the Introduction).

- 3153–111, 3153–11: Wadi Zerqa Ma'in & Madaba/Hidan area
- 3152–1V, 3152–1: Wadis Mujib, Hidan & ibn Hammad
- 3152–111, 3152–11: Karak/Numeira area
- 3151–1V, 3151–1: Wadi Hasa

Jordanians enjoying the medicinal Dead Sea mud before a bath in the Zara hot springs (Routes 37, 38)

Trekking down the hills from Mukawir to the Zara hot springs and the Dead Sea (Route 38)

# THE MADABA AREA

Madaba is about 30km southwest of Amman so easily accessible for day trips. It is a bustling town with churches, mosaics, the Bani Hamida weaving centre and Queen Noor Foundation craft centre and restaurant. Nearby is the hilltop of Mount Nebo high above the northern end of the Dead Sea where Moses is reputed to have died, having seen the 'Promised Land'. Location, map 11.

Route 29
Walks near Mount Nebo

> *From the summit of Mount Nebo you can see the whole of Palestine. You see the mountains above Hebron to the south, the highlands of Judea and Samaria, and the Jordan Valley to Hermon. It is one of the finest views in the world and there is no sound on Mount Nebo but the eerie sough of the west wind coming up over the edge of the mountain.*
>
> In the Steps of The Master H. V. Morton (1934)

Approach To reach Mount Nebo (known in Arabic as Jebel Siyagha) drive or take the bus 30km S from Amman to Madaba then take the signed road to Mount Nebo 10km beyond. About 1km before reaching the site there are a few shops selling carpets and souvenirs near the Siyagha restaurant. Just beyond, a track goes left into rolling hills.

This area offers nice walking country with superb views of the Dead Sea and Jordan Valley and is undisturbed by the tourists attracted to Mount Nebo. Sunsets can be memorable. It should be possible to walk S for 10km along these hilltops above the Dead Sea to Ma'in and then down a 4WD track for 10km to join the Libb–Hammamat Zerqa Ma'in walk (Route 30). There are also short walks on Mount Nebo itself including one down to the Springs of Moses (Ain Musa).

A new **Pilgrimage Trail** is being developed from Mount Nebo to the site on the Jordan River where Jesus was reputedly baptised by John the Baptist.

Just beyond Madaba and the three wadis described in the previous chapter at the N end of the Dead Sea, the next big valley S and the first of the gorges to cleave its way completely through the mountains to the Dead Sea is Wadi Zerqa Ma'in.

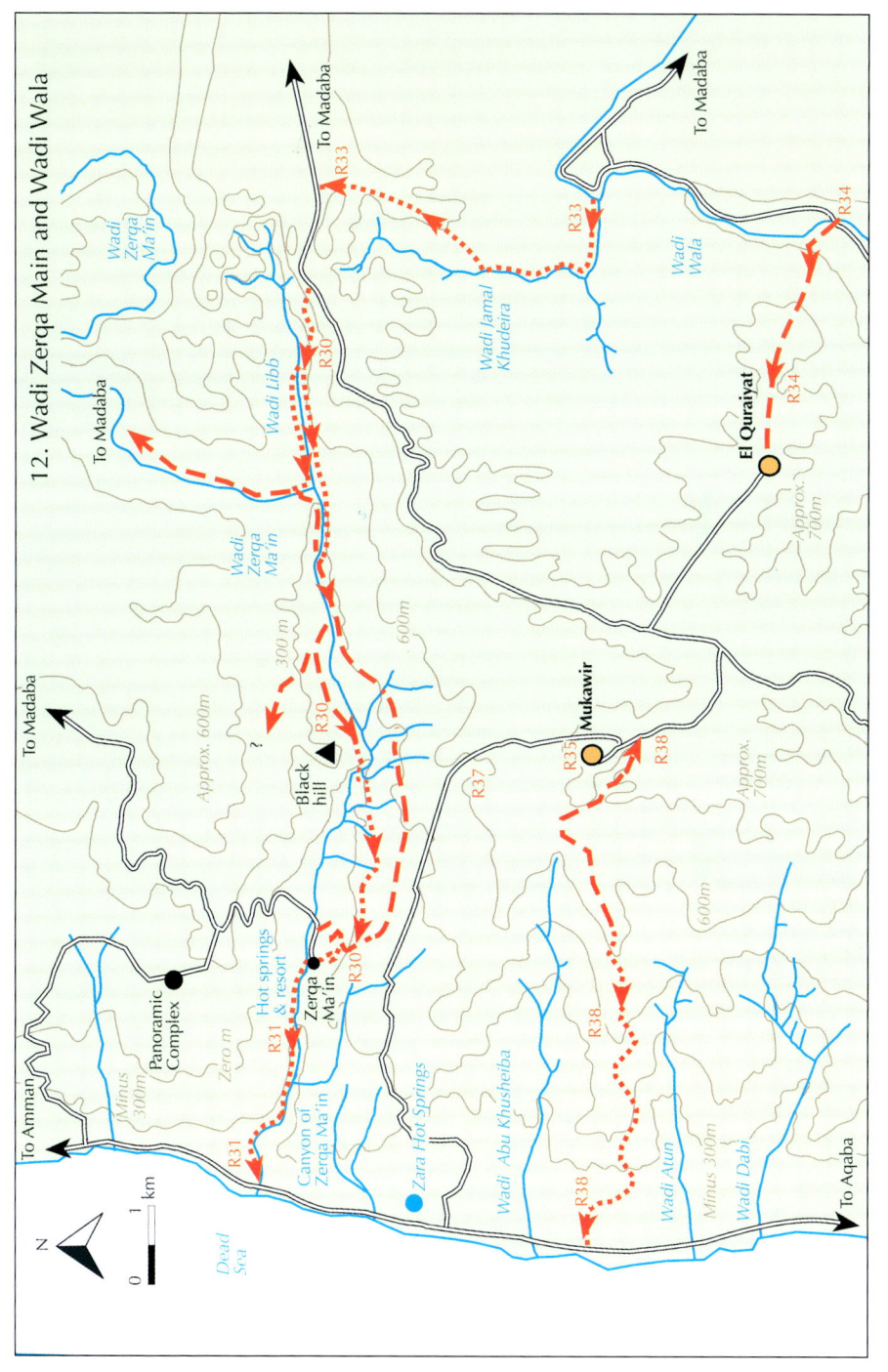

THE DEAD SEA HILLS – THE MADABA AREA – ROUTE 29

99

WADI ZERQA MA'IN

In the time of the Maccabees [Madaba] was a strong fortress. A Roman road leads hence to Ma'in, another spot full of ruins covering the hillsides. Towards the southwest is the Wady Zerqa Ma'in – a magnificent gorge; but there are only tombs to be seen in it. Thence a steep and difficult path leads to the hot springs of Callirhoe. The top of the cliffs in this valley is two thousand five hundred feet above the Dead Sea, and the sides are precipitous. The scenery is extremely picturesque. The south cliff is of black basalt and brown limestone, whilst the north cliff is broken into precipices of red, pink, purple, and yellow sandstone, contrasting with gleaming chalk above and the rich green of palm groves below. Wady Zerka Ma'in is supposed to be the 'Valley of God' Nahaliel mentioned in the Bible as a camping place of the tribes; and by others it is thought to be 'the valley in the land of Moab over against Beth-Peor', where Moses was buried; for the ridge of Minyeh (identified with Beth Peor) is just north of the gorge. The springs are said to be for rheumatism. The bottom of the ravine is full of canes, and palms rise in tufts on the hillside. It was at these springs that Herod the Great sought the health and life he would never possess again. Major Conder tells us that the Arabs have a legend that a demon slave of Solomon found this spring.

Palestine Past and Present L. Valentine (c1919)

The wadi runs from Ma'in 50km S of Amman all the way to the Dead Sea, passing by the Ashtar Hotel and hot springs at Hammamat Ma'in, the therapeutic waters having been used since Herod's time. Its descent is described in two sections, each of a totally different nature.

Route 30
Libb to Hammamat Zerqa Ma'in

Grade	Moderate trek, but easy for its grade
Details	14km, descending 940m to finish 200m below sea level
Time	3½–4hrs

Yet another gravitational luxury! Hardly an uphill step following initially vague donkey tracks now abandoned by all but Bedouin and shepherds down from the Madaba–Mukawir road into the hanging valley of upper Zerqa Main, then continuing by a mixture of 4WD tracks and almost lost Roman roads down to the hot springs in the dramatic lower gorge.

Easily accessible from Amman, easy walking and route finding in peaceful, sometimes beautiful and sometimes wild surroundings; as always, particularly pretty in springtime when wild black irises bloom along the Mukawir road. Numerous Beni Hamada Bedouin camps may be seen en route, offering opportunities to meet local people at their invitation. See map 12.

Approach From Madaba take the King's Highway S passing through the traffic lights by the Apostle's Church on the E side of town. From there it is 13km to the village of Libb, previously Roman Libona. Just beyond signs will be seen pointing right to the Beni Hamida weaving co-operative and Mukawir where John the Baptist reputedly had his head served up on a plate at the request of Salome the dancing girl.

Take this road W. After about 5km the road rises over a small shoulder between two small rounded hills to arrive abruptly high on the edge of the S side of Wadi Libb at 740m (another 15km to Mukawir). Walk a short way down the slopes of the wadi for an excellent view all the way to the black basalt rocks of the gorge that hides the hot springs.

If you don't have transport there are buses from Amman to Madaba and Madaba to Mukawir.

The route

The starting point of an initially vague path will be found 100m below the road (GPS alt. 700m N31° 36.438' E35° 43.093'). Leave the road and head W diagonally down the side of the wadi, picking up the trail almost immediately just below some rocks and following it past some small areas of ploughed land for 20–25mins. It then drops more steeply, zigzagging down to ploughed land just above the wadi bed and opposite some cave shelters on the true right bank, used by Bedouin (½hr from start). Here the track becomes more obvious again, crossing a small side wadi and following the true left bank of the main wadi about 20m above its bed (dry in April 1998). There is a parallel path on the right bank from the lower of the cave shelters (alt. 450m).

Continue along easily until the wadi bed ahead is seen to narrow into a small gorge (about 1hr from the start). Here, there are two options: either cross the wadi to join the path on its right bank (possibly difficult if the river is running), or continue along paths on the left bank, rising up slightly over a shoulder. If the right bank is followed, the path goes over a rocky shoulder above the gorge and descends right to join a 4WD track entering from the N down the winding valley of Wadi Zerqa Ma'in (coming from Ma'in 10km away and providing an alternative start for those with a suitable vehicle). There is likely to be running water in the wadi, which irrigates some farmland and small orchards at the junction of the two valleys (alt. 300m; about 4km from the start).

Follow the track, first along the right (N) side of the valley then over the wadi to its S side where the path coming from the left bank of Wadi Libb joins it without having crossed any rivers. Continue along

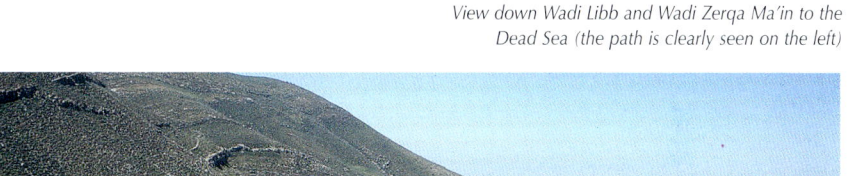

View down Wadi Libb and Wadi Zerqa Ma'in to the Dead Sea (the path is clearly seen on the left)

JORDAN

the left bank to where the track forks just before the wadi drops into a basalt ravine (about 2km from the confluence of the Libb and Zerqa Ma'in wadis). Here again there are two choices: continue by the track on the left or, as previously – with more interest and water levels permitting – take the way to the right.

Cross the wadi where the old Roman road used to cross and follow the track along its right shoulder on fairly flat land (possibility of many Bedouin camps and offers of tea), keeping left at any major forks in the track, more or less parallel to the wadi, and heading towards a black basalt hill. The track then passes through agricultural land (more potential offers of tea from farmworkers!).

Eventually the track bears left, passing between the basalt ravine and the black hill. Ignore the track visible in the bottom of the ravine and continue above the cliffs and across flat stony ground. The track deteriorates to a donkey track and eventually descends by zigzags into the ravine (where there was a pool of clear running water in April 1998). You are now just over 2km from the previous river crossing and about 1hr from the junction with Wadi Zerqa Ma'in (alt. 160m).

A 4WD track enters the wadi from its true left (S) side. Go up it, but about 100m or so after the first hairpin bend close inspection reveals the donkey path going diagonally up out of the wadi up the rocky hillside and heading W. Follow it onto the shoulder of flat land above the cliffs (alt. 220m) where you will get your first views out across the still concealed lower ravine to the Dead Sea. (It's possible to make two 50m abseils straight down the cliffs near the waterfall and then follow the stream to the hotel at the hot springs.)

From here follow the old track S along the stony plateau, possibly passing more Bedouin encampments. (Further back and going in the same direction a 4WD track can be seen, which you would be on if you had stayed on the left bank earlier.) Follow the ill-defined paths W for about 3km across two or three small wadis until it meets an old S–N road coming from the 4WD track directly to the edge of the Zerqa Ma'in Canyon on your right. (The spectacular road that winds down into the canyon on its N side is easily seen directly opposite.)

Follow the road down into the canyon of Zerqa Ma'in. It rapidly deteriorates before it reaches the first hairpin. About 200m beyond it the donkey track will be found again if you look closely. Follow it W across a flat area and down the steepening hillside, the waterfalls of the hot springs coming into view in the bottom of the canyon on the opposite side. Eventually the track narrows to a small path and zigzags ever more steeply down to arrive directly at the Ashtar Hotel (200m below sea level).

Return There are taxis for the 20km journey back up to Ma'in, and also to Madaba, and a late afternoon JETT bus to Amman. Alternatively, you can continue down to the Dead Sea by Route 31.

HAMMAMAT ZERQA MA'IN

The hot streams of Callirhoe flow from the northern slopes; they are ten in number, and their temperature varies from 110° to 140°F; they are strong of sulphur. There is a main stream which forms occasionally pools covered with underwood, in which are numbers of fish; this stream flows from springs higher up the valley, and is of cold water.

Palestine Past and Present L. Valentine (c1919)

The hot springs – to which there is an entry charge of 10JD – now have a couple of hotels, the Ashtar and the Janna Spa and Resort with its modern health facilities (doubles about 90JD, but cheaper in the smaller hotel). There are a number of natural pools beneath waterfalls from the hot springs where bathing is popular – if you don't like crowds avoid holidays and Fridays!

Route 31 starts here.

Route 31
The Canyon of Zerqa Ma'in

Grade	Moderate canyon
Details	4km, with some ascent and scrambling, but mostly in the river
Time	Allow 4–6hrs to descend from 200m to 400m below sea level

You can't get lower than this! An excellent and popular trip down to the Dead Sea in wild scenery. There used to be a lot of litter down the valley from the hot springs and resort, though apparently it has much improved. See map 12.

Special requirements Rope and slings, sufficient for two 5m descents, and ability to downclimb easy rock and/or abseil. Harnesses are not really needed, though could be useful for the less experienced. It may also be necessary to swim in a few places.

Approach Drive from Madaba down to the hot springs in the bottom of the gorge (10JD per person entrance fee). Most people stop well before the gate and walk down the hillside to the W (it's cheaper!).

The route
If you approached by Route 30, walk down under the hotel bridge to the end of the road and follow the path across the river bridge. Steps go up the hillside ('sauna cave' nearby) but it is probably easiest to enter the river here rather than make a tricky descent from the hillside beyond the steps. (If coming from Madaba, you can reach this point directly from the road – see above.)

Follow the river down through magnificent scenery (and hopefully less litter than we encountered – polythene, plastic bottles, tin cans, old shoes, half-eaten chickens – all the way down the canyon, a tragedy in such a beautiful place. However, things are said to have improved, so continue in hope and enjoy the natural majesty of your surroundings rather than dwelling on what may be in the river.)

After a couple of hours the gorge begins to narrow as the river plunges

Descending the Canyon of Zerqa Ma'in

down through a series of cascades between cliffs. A path can be seen going diagonally up the scree-covered hill to the right. It does not return to the river – maybe it goes over the hill and down to the Dead Sea?
Instead, cross the river above the lowest waterfall and continue on the left bank, up which a small path rises gently to cross a shoulder below cliffs. It continues by scrambling along and down exposed ledges (grade 1) and down steep, loose scree and a small cliff (grade 1) to regain the river. (It should be possible to avoid this section and stay in the riverbed by climbing or abseiling down the last 5m waterfall in the cascades, but a rope would be required and there were no obvious belays when we were there.)
The river is now confined between overhanging cliffs and passes over more cascades, some into quite deep pools. Follow it down (a little swimming may be necessary) until stopped by a larger waterfall. This is bypassed by scrambling right between boulders and down a hole (grade 3–4) to regain the beach at the riverside. Not far beyond here the next waterfall has to be descended directly. Fasten 5m of rope to the boulders on the left and climb or abseil down into the pool.
There are no serious obstacles beyond here, but the surrounding cliffs are high and very impressive. The river cascades between them, passing through green areas of oleander and fragmites before emerging abruptly at the bridge on the Dead Sea Highway (GPS alt. minus 380m N31° 37.137' E35° 34.047').

Return There is limited public transport along the Dead Sea Highway, so ideally you need to arrange to be met, or will have to hitch out. From the Zerqa Ma'in bridge it's about 12km up the road (N) to the three hotels on the shores of the Dead Sea, then another 8km to the S Shouneh road junction in the Jordan Valley, where you go right for Amman. The total journey takes 1hr with your own transport (it took us under 2hrs hitching). You could also return directly to Madaba via the new Dead Sea Parkway road that leaves the Dead Sea Highway 4km N of the Zerqa Ma'in bridge, just past Wadi Himara (see Route 28). This goes back up through the hills to meet the Madaba–Zerqa Ma'in road past the RSCN Dead Sea Panoramic Complex with its restaurant and museum (opened in 2006 and well worth a visit).

For anyone wanting a quick water-walk from the Dead Sea the canyon can also be ascended a short way from the bridge. Route 32 also starts not far from the Dead Sea.

Route 32
The Roman Road from the Jordan Valley to Wadi Mujib

The remains of this long stretch of Roman road can still be found starting from the ruins of Tuleilat Ghasul 5km N of the N end of the Dead Sea. It goes SE then SW across a plateau at an altitude of around 350m (750m above the Dead Sea), before turning E above the chasm of Zerqa Ma'in to a high point of around 700m (1100m above the Dead Sea) at Rijm al Mureijib. It then descends into the upper valley of Zerqa Ma'in at a point above the falls at the head of the canyon. This is a distance of around 30km and was considered as a day's march.
From there, the road climbs again to the S to the ruins of Boz al Mushelle, previously a Bronze Age Moabite stronghold. It then goes SE to cross Wadi Wala (see Route 33) and on to Dhiban and so to the Mujib Gorge about 2km E of the present crossing point of the King's Highway. This is another 30km and another day's march (not checked by the authors).

Before entering the Mujib Reserve on our journey S, the headwaters of the beautiful valleys of Wadi Wala and Wadi Hidan are reached.

THE WADI WALA AND WADI HIDAN AREA

I think the richest and greenest region we had come upon since we left Egypt was the Wadi Waleh... the stream cascaded clear and cold through thickets of reed and oleander, laurel and willow herb. The smell of it was English.

In the Steps of Moses the Conqueror Louis Golding (1938)

The wadis of Wala and Hidan form a green and fertile valley whose perennial river passes through minor but nevertheless impressive canyons for about 20km before disappearing into the jaws of the ominous black basalt canyon of the Upper Hidan Gorge (Route 39). This impressive canyon winds tortuously down to reach the awe-inspiring Hidan Falls beyond which the river continues through the chasm of the Lower Hidan Gorge and Hidan Siq to meet the Mujib Gorge just above the Mujib Siq. The Upper Hidan is outside the RSCN Reserve, but the whole of the Lower Hidan Gorge and *siq* are in a totally protected wildlife zone with no access permitted (see Routes 40 and 41).

Wadi Wala, which is easily reached from Amman, has beautiful scenery and is well worth a visit. It is a popular area for weekend picnickers from Amman (though people have drowned swimming in the pools of Wala in springtime). A number of obvious short walks are possible both E and W of the King's Highway, Route 33 being on the line of the old Roman road.

Route 33
Wadi Wala to Wadi Libb and Zerqa Ma'in

... [the Israelites] marched to Mattanah which is the Wadi Waleh, where there is a brook and rude stone heaps. From [thence] they went to Nahaliel (the valley of God), where are the hot and cold springs of Callirhoe. This valley, called the valley of Zerqa, is one of the most lovely and picturesque places in the Holy Land.

Palestine Past and Present L. Valentine (c1918)

Marked on old maps (not checked by the authors). See maps 12 and 14.

Approach Go S on the King's Highway from Amman to Madaba (30km) and continue for about 26km until about 8km N of Dhiban a signed road goes W down the left bank of Wadi Wala. After 6km Wadi Kirdah enters from the W and the two wadis continue S as Wadi Hidan. About 4km down the road from the King's Highway the road splits and meets again 1km further on by the side of the river. Opposite, on the W side, is Wadi Jamal Khudeira.

The route
It would appear possible to walk this wadi for 5km, following a track on the line of the old Roman road, which reaches the road from Libb to Mukawir just 2km E of the track which goes down into Wadi Zerqa Ma'in (Route 30). 7km in total.

Still outside the Mujib Reserve there is another section of Roman road.

Route 34
Wadi Wala to Mukawir

Most of this route may now be on modern roads. See maps 12 and 14.

Approach About 5km downstream from the above (10km from the King's Highway), the road down Wadi Wala crosses a bridge onto its W bank.

The route
A track is marked on the old map going W from here up the side of the valley for 4km to El Quraiyat village, then NW for 4km to meet the road from Libb. About 1km S of there a road forks right and goes for 4km to Mukawir. 13km in total (not checked by the authors).

Next is the site of one of Herod's hilltop citadels, Mukawir.

Route 35
A Short Walk to Mukawir

> *Machaerus or El Mashnaka 'the hanging place' as the Arabs call it, lies on the top of one of the wildest mountains of Moab on the eastern side of the Dead Sea. No roads lead to it and the hills are full of armed nomads.*
>
> In the Steps of The Master H. V. Morton (1934)

A short and easy path up to Mukawir, an ancient and infamous Old Testament site. Location, maps 12 and 14.

Approach Machaerus or Mukawir is 16km S of Libb by road, then 4km W. The reputed ancient hilltop citadel of Herod is in a splendid location on a small isolated hill at 700m, surrounded on all sides by wadis that descend through the Mujib Reserve to the Zara hot springs and the Dead Sea 1100m below (see Route 38).

Back on the King's Highway and travelling S again for 8km the road passes through **Dhiban**, which was once the Moabite capital and the site of the famous stone on which Mesha, King of Moab, had engraved 'I built Aroer, and made the highway by the Arnon'. The Arnon is the ancient name for the Mujib Gorge and Aroer is an Iron Age settlement on its N rim 4km E of the King's Highway which reaches the canyon rim 3km S of Dhiban.

Close by Aroer is another ancient site, Lahoun.

View to the Mujib Gorge from the Iron Age site of Lahoun

Route 36
Lahoun

Grade	Easy walk
Details	1–1.5km
Time	Allow 1hr to enjoy the views and see the excavations

A short stroll around and across an Iron Age site with dramatic views of the Mujib Gorge. Location, map 15.

Approach Lahoun is about 10km by road to the ESE of Dhiban, on the N rim of Wadi Mujib. It is reached by driving on narrow roads until the mound of the old ruined settlement is seen to the S with a sign indicating 'Belgian Excavations'. It can be reached directly from the road, which is about 200–300m away or, more enjoyably, from the E side of Wadi Lahoun, which is immediately E of the ruins. Park by the 'Dig House', destined to become a museum.

The route
Walk W, descending to the dry limestone bed of Wadi Lahoun. From the lip of the waterfall continue W just below the upper edge of the Mujib Gorge with fine views, rising up on a small path to a better path

under huge overhangs just below the plateau. Here there are old sheep and goat pens. Follow the overhangs round until the path rises up to the ruins above.

Return Directly, crossing the head of the wadi just below the road, and back up to the 'Dig House'.

Water levels in Wadi Wala, the Hidan and Mujib Gorges, and the Mujib Siq
Before going down into the RSCN Mujib Reserve and its canyons you should be prepared for the ever-changing scenery caused by flash floods.
  Due to floods that annually inundate these valleys, the riverbed and pools can and do change year to year. In 1993, for example, it was necessary to swim to enter the final Mujib Siq, whereas in spring 1998 it was possible to walk in as the water had fallen to less than waist-high. In October of that year it was even shallower.
  The lower reaches of the Hidan and Mujib – the Hidan Siq and the Mujib Siq – are, geologically speaking, comparatively new features. To the south of these awesome earthquake cracks – and over 200m above the present water level – are the alluvial remains of the old riverbeds. These rise in ghostly pale mounds of dried mud and silt left behind when the rivers gushed into the great cracks that now offer such splendid canyons. (You drive through the old Mujib riverbed when you come up from the Dead Sea to reach the start of the *siq*.) Don't be surprised if you find the situation to be other than that described here!
  Additionally, the RSCN advises visitors that the Mujib Gorge can be extremely hot in the summer months, though that is usually a safe time to experience the excitements of the final *siq*. During the winter (and to a lesser degree in spring and autumn) there is risk of high water and floods, especially since the construction of the Mujib Dam, which sometimes releases excessive water. Check out the situation first with the RSCN Mujib Reserve office (mob 0777 422125) as they have all up-to-date information on the water release plans of the dam operators. You should also book your trip into the Mujib Reserve early – visitor numbers are limited.

THE RSCN MUJIB NATURE RESERVE

One looks down into horrible precipices and deep, khaki-coloured chasms where the foot of man has never reached. Below is the Dead Sea.

In the Steps of the Master H. V. Morton (1934)

The Reserve was created in 1987 and is the second largest in Jordan, extending over 212sq km. It centres on Wadi Mujib, a deep and magnificent canyon which cuts through rugged highlands down to the Dead Sea, and contains a large enclosure used for breeding Nubian ibex for eventual reintroduction into the wild. Most of the Reserve consists of rocky ravines and cliffs with sparse, desert vegetation, but seasonal streams flow through many of the wadis, supporting luxuriant aquatic plants in the riverbeds. A great variety of flora and fauna flourishes around the permanent rivers.

The Reserve lies about 18km downstream of the King's Highway and extends for roughly another 18km to the shores of the Dead Sea. Its northern boundary lies along the edge of Wadi Zerqa Ma'in, including the region around Herod's hilltop fortress of Mukawir and the Dead Sea hot springs of Zara, whilst to the south it extends across wild hills to the edge of the canyon of Wadi Shuqeiq, west of Faqua. See map 13.

Approach The RSCN entrances to the Reserve are at Mukawir and Faqua near the Kings's Highway, and down at the Mujib bridge (some of the routes start elsewhere and access the Reserve directly).

Entrance fee 3JD non-Jordanians, 1JD Jordanians.

Guiding fee From 5JD for short trails, up to 30JD for a full day.

Accommodation There are no campsites but in July 2007 some chalets were opened on the Dead Sea coast near the Mujib bridge; B&B rates 75JD non-Jordanians per double, 65JD Jordanians per double, plus usual tax and service charges. The chalets are open year round, and there is a restaurant.

The trek down the whole Mujib Gorge is possible without needing to camp in the Reserve, whilst the descent of the *siq* is a day trip and can be done using RSCN vehicles to access the Reserve from the Dead Sea.

The following route, which can be driven, starts near to Machaerus, or Mukawir, reputedly a fortified palace of 'Herod the Great' and descends to the edge of the Zara hot springs on the shore of the Dead Sea.

Route 37
The Roman Road from Mukawir to Zerqa Ma'in and Zara

This minor road is approximately on the route of the old Roman road and winds its way down for about 15km from near the hilltop fortress of Mukawir to pass above Zerqa Ma'in before reaching the hot springs of Zara just above the shore of the Dead Sea. It's partially surfaced and accesses land used for agriculture, and is the only drivable road between Madaba and Karak connecting the plateau to

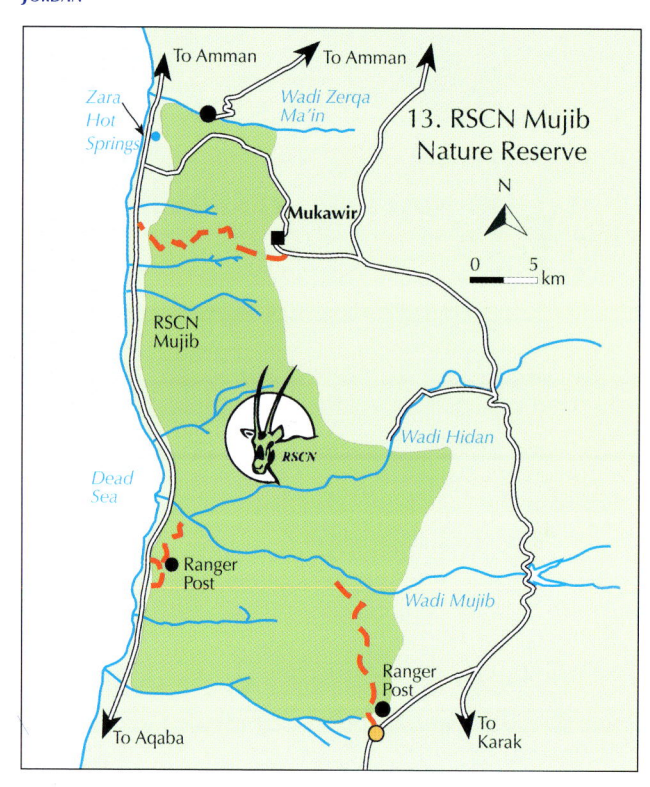

JORDAN

13. RSCN Mujib Nature Reserve

The route
Starting just N of Mukawir at GPS alt. 640m N31° 34.116' E35° 38.270', the road follows the ridge down generally N then NW before splitting at GPS alt. 230m N31° 35.923' E35° 37.058' to go to Zara and Zerqa Ma'in. The track to Zara descends generally W past a military checkpoint. It has old tarmac and is drivable by car but is not suitable for larger vehicles (and has not been checked by the authors). The road down to Zerqa Ma'in was washed out many years ago but forms the end of Route 30. (Information supplied by Brian Hodgkinson and Mark Khano.)

ZARA HOT SPRINGS

There are at least 38 separate thermal springs at Zara ranging in temperature from 45–64°, and rich in mineral salts. The ruins are 200 metres east of the Dead Sea Highway and about 1.5km south of Zerqa Main Gorge. The old port of Zara is 200 metres to the south of here, 35 metres above the present water line. It is believed these are the 'hot baths of Callhirhoe' referred to by Pliny and Josephus in the 1stC. AD. If this is the case, the springs at Zerqa Ma'in are those called Baris by Josephus, and indeed, a Roman road linked the two, and continues south to Machaerus (Mukawir), the site of Herod's hilltop fort.

The Antiquities of the Jordan Rift Valley Rami G. Khouri (1988)

The hot spring pools are 2km S of the Zerqa Ma'in bridge on the Dead Sea Highway (GPS alt. minus 380m N31° 36.086' E35° 33.736') and best avoided at weekends when packed with people from Amman and other nearby towns. Sadly the general public frequently fill the place with litter, but if it's not crowded you can take a hot bath and/or scramble down to the Dead Sea for a swim. There's a shallow pool just before the point at which the stream from the hot springs enters the Dead Sea, where you can wash the salt off after your swim. See maps 12 and 13.

Another track descends more directly to Zara from the S side of the fortress (Route 38).

Route 38
Mukawir to the Dead Sea

Grade	Easy walk
Details	5km, descending from above 700m to minus 400m at the Dead Sea; no route-finding problems except one fork in the road – just keep right
Time	2hrs plus the drive time down from the Visitor Centre, an easy 3hrs max

An easy downhill walk on a disused 4WD track amidst barren hills, starting from the Visitor Centre adjacent to the conical hill of Machaerus. The walk finishes close to the Zara hot springs, site of Herod's baths (at which time it was a Dead Sea port, though little remains today). Other than linking these places of antiquity, there is little of special interest along the walk (although despite the apparently barren hills our RSCN guide said he had once seen a hyena). On the plus side the hills have an almost 'Grand Canyon' feel, descending for 1100m to the Dead Sea, across which there are excellent views as far as the hazy blue hills of Palestine. See map 12.

Special requirements The lower half of the route passes through the Dead Sea Reserve, for which permission has to be obtained from the RSCN who, for a fee, will provide a guide and a vehicle to take you down to the edge of the Reserve. They can also meet you at the Dead Sea and drive you back up.

Guide RSCN approved guide necessary.

Approach From Amman follow Route 30 to the start of that route then continue for approx 17km along the road until reaching the new Visitor Centre on the left, about 1km before Mukawir (GPS alt. 720m N31° 33.730' E35° 38.325'). You will meet your RSCN guide here (see below). After visiting Machaerus (Route 35) – from where much of the walk is visible – you will be driven about 5km down the rough road beneath the S side of the hill to the start of the trek (GPS alt. 490m N31° 33.799' E35° 35.916').

The route

The way down to the Dead Sea is then continued on foot, winding down a ridge. Wadi Atun is on the left (S) across which some prehistoric stone circles of unknown purpose are visible. The wadis to the N lead down to the hot springs. All around are wild, barren hills of black, red and ochre igneous rocks, contrasting with the steamy blue of the Dead Sea far below. After about 3km a shelter is reached, as incongruous as a bus stop in the barren landscape, but giving welcome shade for a lunch break before continuing down the trail and avoiding the left fork. The track emerges just S of fields to the S of Zara, where it turns briefly N to pass irrigation pools too hot to touch and through the greenery before descending to the Dead Sea (GPS alt. minus 320m N31° 34.111' E35° 33.391').

Return If required, via pre-arranged RSCN driver and vehicle.

Continuing S we re-enter Wadi Wala and Wadi Hidan (see Routes 33 and 34), the junction for which is about 56km from Amman down the King's Highway, where a signed road goes W down the left bank of Wadi Wala. After 6km Wadi Kirdah enters from the W and the two wadis unite and continue S as Wadi Hidan.

WADI HIDAN

About 5km downstream of the above the road crosses a bridge onto its W bank.
Continuing down the valley for another 6–7km from the bridge (16km from the King's Highway), the wadi, which is now next to the road, plunges over some small falls into pools then into a narrow gorge with black cliffs of basalt columns. On the hillside about 0.5km to the NW is a huge cave entrance, though unfortunately the cave doesn't fulfil its promise (see Route 150). About 2km further on the track makes a hairpin bend and winds up the hill to the N away from the gorge. If you have a 4WD it can be followed up to the Mukawir road.

Important The upper section of the Hidan is outside the Mujib Reserve, whilst after the Hidan Falls the river passes through a totally protected zone of the Reserve with no access allowed (see below); a great shame, as the whole trip down to the Dead Sea is a formidable feast of fun.

Route 39
The Upper Hidan Gorge

Grade	Moderate canyon
Details	9km (6km in the canyon), descending 200m to 100m below sea level before returning to the start
Time	Allow 5–6hrs

Mega! This is a superb canyon, much of the route being actually in the river, which winds between frequently inescapable vertical black basalt cliffs for 5km to the upper edge of the impressive Hidan Falls over which the river plunges into the Lower Hidan Gorge. From that point on the river and surrounding hills are in a totally protected Wildlife Reserve, which is part of the Mujib Reserve. Access beyond this point is forbidden so a return journey must be made back upriver for 1km then across the N slopes of the Upper Hidan back to the starting point.
There are reputedly ibex and other large mammals in the area though all we saw were eagles, kestrels and other raptors, small fish, some amazingly noisy frogs, and a lot of extremely large oleander hawk moth caterpillars. In early spring you can't miss them – green, blue and orange with light-coloured dotted striations and large eyespots. They are 7–10cm long and about 2cm thick and seem attracted to the warmth of sleeping bags, so don't be too surprised if you sleep near any oleanders and wake up in the night with these rather large creatures exploring your body! The moths – which are up to 12cm in wingspan and can fly at 50kph – may be seen at night. See map 14.

Special requirements Although the river was never more than chest-high when we went down (March 1998), it would be useful to be able to swim in an emergency; otherwise a buoyancy jacket is recommended. Ropes and abseil gear are required to descend the 10m falls, but these can be bypassed which saves carrying extra kit. A waterproof bag would be useful for camera gear.
Guide Required for inexperienced groups.
Approach Turn off the King's Highway at Wadi Wala, as above. (There should be little or no water in the river at this point if the gorge is to be passable.) Drive down for about 18km, passing the

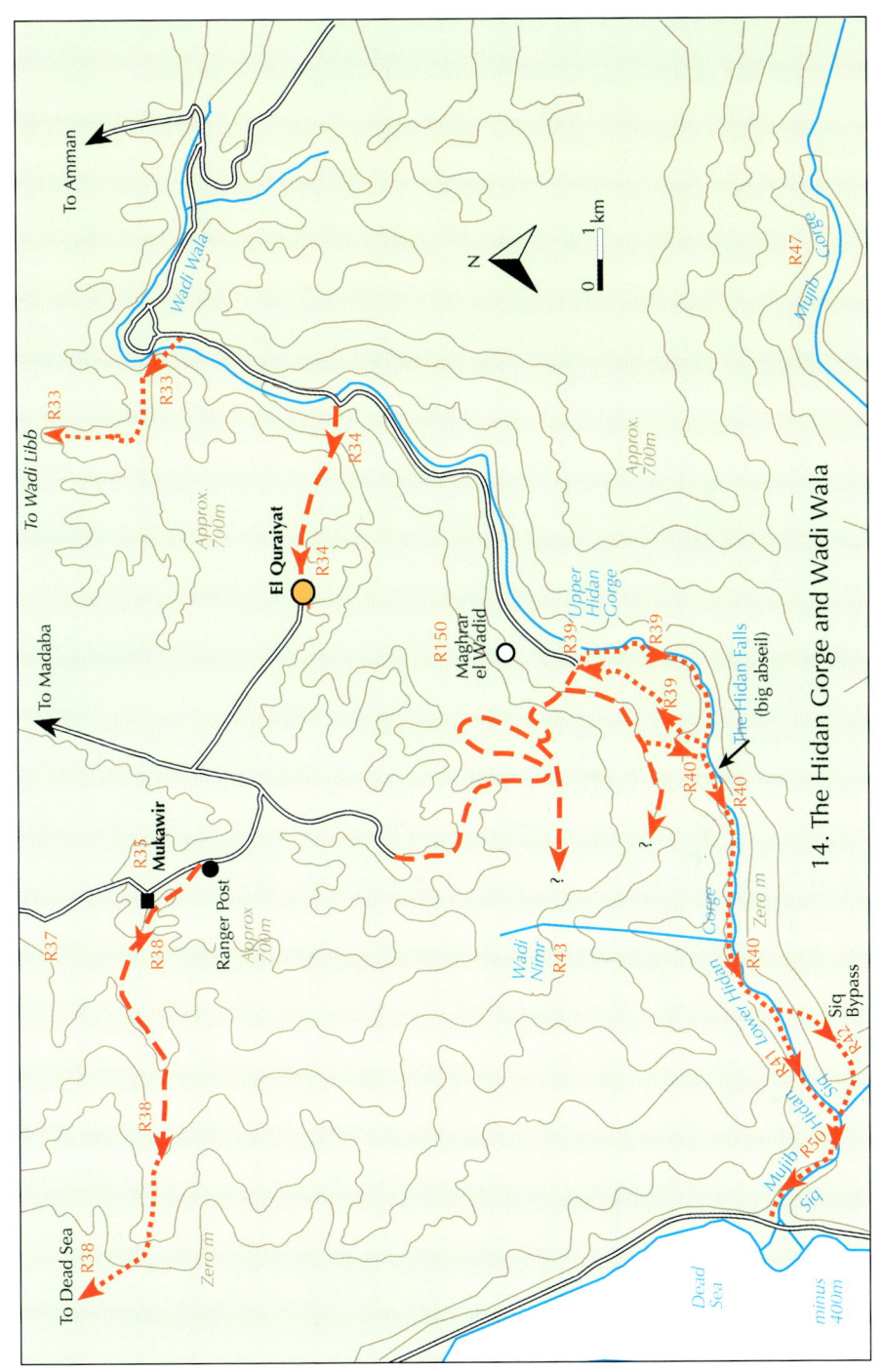

The Dead Sea Hills – The RSCN Nature Reserve – Route 39

14. The Hidan Gorge and Wadi Wala

JORDAN

point where the black basalt canyon starts, to where the road makes a hairpin bend and starts to rise away from the river. There is a small pool and orchard just beyond the bend with a white painted cairn visible to the E on the headland and a small wadi a few metres away to the S (alt. 100m).

The route
Descend the line of the small side wadi to where it drops over a cliff. Pass the cliff on its right (S) and scramble down to reach the basalt gorge just below a small waterfall and large pool.

Follow the gorge down through a series of impressive basalt and sandstone canyons, frequently walking waist-deep in the river. After about 3km a waterfall drops about 10m into a pool. With equipment it would be possible to rappel and swim, or it can be bypassed by scrambling out up the true right bank (grade 2) and back down the gully beyond.

Continue downstream, alternating between rocky beaches and dramatic gorges for a further 2km to the upper edge of the Hidan Falls which plunge around 60m over the projecting igneous rock into a deep pool in a huge sandstone bowl. Here the river enters the Lower Hidan Gorge and Wildlife Reserve where entry is currently forbidden (see Route 40), so it is necessary to return.

Return Backtrack up the canyon for about 1km to an open area where escape is possible on either side of the river (there are Bedouin shepherds' paths if you search carefully, the one on the S side being the most obvious.) Take the one to the N, zigzagging up the right (E) side of a side wadi, then follow the path right through a small pass to the next wadi. Go up this for 1km to reach a 4WD track. Follow this E (2km) to meet the original track just above the hairpin bend where the route started.

Alternatively go easily upstream a short way to the next narrowing of the canyon. Scramble out N here up the line of a gully onto the hillside above the cliffs. The starting point is now about 3km away to the NNE. To reach it continue to rise slightly up the hill, first generally NE then contouring more N, following the approximate line of the river but about 0.5km above it to its W, to reach the road again.

When researching the first edition of this book the RSCN kindly gave us permission to enter the **Lower Hidan Gorge** even though it was off-limits. At their request we gave no details in that edition but since then others have been through the canyon and described the route, so the secret is out. It is, however, still in a closed part of the Mujib Reserve (although we saw empty bullet cartridges and hides constructed by hunters so despite best efforts the wildlife was not being protected). Maybe the passage of a few people through this unique canyon would be beneficial as they could report back to the RSCN on any 'crime scenes' and interesting wildlife. So here's our plea: relax your restrictions, let people in, see how it goes and put any income into patrolling the area – a flash flood can do more damage in an hour than an untold number of visitors in a year!

Route 40
The Lower Hidan Gorge

Grade	Serious canyon
Details	16km
Time	Allow at least 8hrs if starting by walking directly to the big abseil, continuing through the Hidan Siq (Route 41) and finishing by walking out to the Dead Sea; 10–11hrs or more if exiting by the Mujib Siq; 13–14hrs if the Upper Hidan Gorge (Route 39) is included (as it really should be). Really a two-day trip (unless you're extremely fast!).

All the fun of the fair – an unforgettable *tour de force*. Commences with a breathtaking overhanging abseil into the cauldron of the Hidan Falls, continues through a chasm, then a 'jungle' and exits through the Hidan Siq in stunning rock scenery into the exquisite Malagi Pools before meeting the lower Mujib Gorge just before the Mujib Siq.
As with the Mujib there are said to be hyenas, wolves and cobras here. Birdlife is plentiful and varied and the river is full of frogs and fish, not to mention water snakes. (We saw one close by, swallowing a frog, and almost stood on a viper whilst making our way through head-high reeds where there were plentiful signs of hunting.) Maps 14 and 15.

Special requirements There should be two bolts *in situ* at the top of the Hidan Falls, but you will probably need an abseil sling. (We left a sling and maillon but these may have been removed; it's possible the bolts may have gone as well.) The sling should be replaced anyway, due to UV degradation. The total abseil height is between 50m and 60m (opinions differ). If a double 50m rope doesn't reach the pool it should be possible to gain the ledge below the roof and fix a big sling (10m?) round a huge basalt block to make a second abseil of around 25–30m into the pool.
You will need harnesses, abseil and prusik equipment; it may also be worth carrying a hammer, a few pegs and wire chocks in case the bolts are missing here or further down the gorge, as well as additional cord for abseil slings. You may also need some gear for use in the Mujib Siq if you are continuing that way (see Route 50).
Waterproof bags for kit are essential and buoyancy jackets worth considering (there has been a death in a waterfall in the Mujib Gorge), as well as some equipment for a bivouac (it will probably be warm down there below sea level, so you shouldn't need much).
You should also be aware that this river may flood or be impassable, particularly in the Hidan Siq at certain times of the year, especially winter and early spring. (We did the trip in October 1998 when there was still considerable water in the siq after the dry summer.)

Guide Permission from the RSCN is essential as the Hidan Gorge is in a totally protected zone of the Mujib Wildlife Reserve. You will need to have an approved guide, or satisfy the RSCN of your credentials and ability; even then permission may not be granted due to the sensitive nature of the area (see above).

Approach As for Route 39 to the hairpin bend in the road. Continue up the road just round the next bend where an old 4WD track forks left but is washed out almost immediately. Walk along it for just over 2km until it is possible to see a small path on the opposite side of the valley, descending into the gorge after appearing from behind a small rounded hill to the W.
At this point, head towards it, down on open wadi, eventually finding a Bedouin path on its right side. Follow this as it goes right above the gorge then zigzags down into it on the left shoulder of the next valley W. Once at the river follow it down in spectacular scenery for less than 1km to emerge abruptly at the edge of the Hidan Falls (1hr; 4hrs if approached by Route 39).

The route
Close inspection should reveal two bolts about 5m above and right of the streambed, the location of the big abseil. The first part of the abseil goes down basalt columns undercut by a 10m overhang with a free fall of about 30m to the outer edge of a ledge where the abseil could be split if the ropes were not long enough.
The abseil then continues for maybe another 30m down smooth rock washed by a hot spring into the pool below. The main Hidan Falls plunge into the pool just at the side of the abseil. The situation is unique with palms hanging out of the surrounding sandstone cliffs that form this huge water-worn basin. Swim out across the deep pool to a 'beach' at the back of the bowl.

Hot springs drip into the chasm beyond the abseil into the Lower Hidan Gorge

The route then immediately enters a chasm between high overhanging walls where it is necessary to wade or sometimes swim. There is one awkward little section of downclimbing (5m, grade 3) in a slippery chimney on the right, to pass a waterfall.

Emerging from the confines of the canyon the river enters an area of 'jungle' terrain, with thickly tangled beds of fragmites reeds and sometimes fallen palms through which a way has to be forced, often waist-deep in water – watch out for snakes. After a total distance of about 3km (3hrs) the vegetation reduces in density and the going becomes easier. There are hot springs here, and beaches. The side stream of Wadi Nimr (Tiger Valley) enters from the right (N). There are numerous bivouac sites along this stretch of the river, which can also be reached by descending Wadi Nimr (Route 43).

Continuing downstream the going is mostly easier though still with some thickets of fragmites (in October – perhaps easier in spring?). After another 3–4km a deep pool is reached at the entrance to the Hidan Siq.

To continue There is no realistic way back from here, but there are two ways to continue: either bypass the *siq* by swimming across the pool and detouring over hills on the S side (see Route 42), or continue by Route 41.

Route 41
The Hidan Siq

Grade	Serious canyon
Details	1.5km
Time	Allow 1–2hrs to enjoy the trip fully and reach the Mujib, then additional time to get down to the Dead Sea via the Mujib Siq (Route 50), plus time to get there by your chosen route (see below).

The Dead Sea Hills – The RSCN Nature Reserve – Route 41

A splendid and extremely narrow *siq*, best accessed directly down the Hidan Gorge (see above), but to come up the track from the Dead Sea and through the bypass (Route 42) to do both this and the Mujib Siq would be a great day out. See maps 14 and 15.

Special requirements At least one 45m rope, abseil and prusik kit, pegs and hammer for emergency, and waterproof bags; buoyancy jackets should be considered. Be aware of flood hazard.

Guide Permission from the RSCN is essential as the entrance to the Hidan Siq is in a totally protected zone of Wildlife Reserve. You will need to have an approved guide, or reassure the RSCN of your credentials and ability; even then permission may not be granted.

Approach Either down the Hidan Gorge (Routes 39 and 40) or up the 'bypass' (Route 42), which takes 3–4hrs from the Dead Sea.

The route

Once in the *siq* the cliffs close in immediately, and soon it's necessary to downclimb for 5m (grade 3) just right of a waterfall. (A sling can be fixed on an old piton or small jammed wire in a crack, to thread a safety rope though.) Continue downstream in dramatic surroundings until the water shoots down a narrow 15m-long 'millrace'. An extremely old bolt and sling should be found on the right to fix a rope (ideally, the bolt needs replacing). Go down the chute to more small waterfalls and pools and continue to a bend, after which the narrow canyon continues in a similar manner with more waterfalls and pools. After a 5m waterfall you arrive at the area of the once-exquisite Malagi Pools (Route 44) where we once saw a water snake eating a frog in a wonderland of striated multi-coloured rock and luxuriously warm

Swimming in the Hidan Siq

117

green water. Unfortunately the Malagi Pools are, at the time of writing (July 2007) almost dry due to debris swept down by flash floods, but this has happened before and the pools may well return. For up-to-date information ask the RSCN.

To continue From the pools at the lower end of the Hidan Siq it's a short walk out to the junction with the Mujib Gorge, then less than ½hr down to the Mujib Siq (Route 50). Continue down this, or escape out to the left up the track taken by Route 49.

Route 42
The Hidan Siq Bypass

Grade	Serious trek
Details	Part of a longer journey and requiring route-finding ability; 1.5km between the 'ends' of the Hidan Siq
Time	1½–2hrs, plus 1½–2hrs to approach or exit down the Mujib Trail (Route 49), unless you have arranged to be met or dropped off by an RSCN vehicle near the Mujib Siq

This route gives direct access from the Dead Sea to the lower section of one of Jordan's best adventures. It provides an enjoyable way into (or, in emergency, out of) the lower end of the Hidan Gorge passing through bizarre scenery along the upper edge of the long-abandoned Hidan riverbed, which was left high and dry in the hills by an ancient earthquake. The way follows an old Bedouin trail marked by cairns. Using this approach both the Hidan and Mujib *siqs* can be done in one day. See map 14.

Guide Permission from the RSCN is essential as the upper entrance to the Hidan Siq is in a totally protected zone of Wildlife Reserve. You will need to have an approved guide, or satisfy the RSCN of your credentials and ability; even then permission may not be given.

Approach Enter from the Dead Sea via the approach for the Mujib Siq (Route 50). Having walked down to the river, follow it up for about 1km to the confluence of the Mujib and Hidan rivers then follow the latter up left a short way to an area of huge boulders at the exit of the Hidan Siq.

The route
From the lower end of the Hidan Siq scramble SE up the rocky hillside to reach the dividing ridge between the Hidan and Mujib gorges (cairn, good views). A bigger cliff (approx 10m) now blocks the way. Scramble right for 100m or so and ascend the cliff by traversing left on a ledge level with the tops of the alluvial deposits of the old Mujib and Hidan riverbeds which are easily distinguishable on the S side of both the *siqs* as weird sandy mounds in otherwise harsh rocky terrain.

Now contour NE below a barrier of cliffs and across the upper edge of the Hidan alluvial mounds for almost 1km until they end abruptly, with a shallow valley to their right (E). Go down this with increasing care as it narrows to a gully filled with driftwood and river debris from floods (watch out for snakes). Below is the deep pool at the upper entrance to the Hidan Siq (Route 41).

If you are coming down the Hidan Gorge and the *siq* is too flooded for safety, the 'bypass' can be followed in reverse as a useful escape.

Route 43
Wadi Nimr to the Dead Sea

Grade	Serious canyon
Details	About 14km descending almost 1200m from 800m; all requirements of the Hidan and Mujib routes apply, and RSCN permission is essential
Time	Probably 5–6hrs (although no firm information available)

The curiously named 'Tiger Valley' provides a direct approach to the Lower Hidan Gorge and has been used to avoid the big entry abseil, chasm and 'jungle', arriving at the bivouac area of that route, thereby providing a less serious approach to the Hidan Siq (Route 41) and the Mujib Siq (Route 50). See map 14.

Approach A track branches left (S) off the road to Mukawir (see Route 38) about 3km before reaching the site. Wadi Nimr is below, to its W, about 4km further on, past Judaiyida.

The route
Not checked by the authors, but done by others. No details available.

Route 44
The Malagi Pools

Magical Malagi! Now you see it... now you don't!

First the good news: these exquisite warm, green pools enclosed by towering cliffs brightly streaked with orange and green mineral seepages are a delight to experience. 'Malagi' means 'confluence' and the pools occur at the end of the Hidan Gorge where the Hidan Siq emerges close to the confluence of the Hidan with the Mujib Gorge. As well as the natural splendour of the place, watch out for a variety of birdlife as well as ibex, fishes, frogs and snakes!

Now the bad news: the pools come and go with flash floods which either fill the canyon with silt or remove silt from it, thus creating the pools. When we were first there in the mid-1980s the water level was much higher than it is today as the exit from the *siq* was blocked by rocks over which the river emerged as a 10m waterfall into a pool beyond the canyon mouth. The rocks and waterfall disappeared years ago leaving a series of warm green pools, but recently these have silted up and vanished. (If the pools return and you want to visit them for what used to be a very pleasurable half-day experience, contact the RSCN.)

Heading S again, the King's Highway begins its long and tortuous descent into Jordan's 'Grand Canyon', the Mujib Gorge.

THE MUJIB GORGE

The view which the Mojib presents is very striking; from the bottom, where the river runs through a narrow strip of verdant level about forty yards across, the steep barren banks rise to a great height, covered with immense blocks of stone, which have rolled down from the upper strata, so that when viewed from above, the valley looks like a deep chasm formed by some tremendous convulsion of the earth, into which there seems no possibility of descending to the bottom.

Travels in Syria Burckhardt (c1812)

The Mujib Gorge – which extends for over 50km from the desert uplands 800m above sea level to the Dead Sea 400m below – is one of Jordan's most spectacular features, and is often referred to as 'the Grand Canyon' of Jordan. In Old Testament times it was known as the Arnon, and the King's Highway or 'Royal Road' referred to in the Book of Numbers passes through its upper reaches. The modern King's Highway crosses the gorge at much the same point, winding a tortuous 18km to descend and ascend the canyon, which at this point is over 600m deep and 5km wide.

There are Iron Age remains along its crest at places like the above-mentioned Aroer and Lahoun (see Route 36), and though the Mujib formed an obvious natural boundary between the Kingdoms of Moab to the S and Ammon to the N the Moabites actually held the N side as far as Madaba for a considerable time: a line of old beacons can still be seen which served the purposes of the Moabites and later the Nabataeans and Romans. After the Romans modernised the old highway, creating the Via Nova Traiana, Eusebius described the Mujib as 'a very treacherous place with ravines... in which the garrisons of soldiers keep guard everywhere due to the terrifying nature of the region.'

When Louis Golding looked down on the gorge from Aroer in the 1930s he described it perfectly, capturing the springtime essence of this wild and majestic valley: 'Far down twinkles interruptedly the silver thread of the torrent, the "sounding" torrent (as the Hebrew word announces) so soundless here, eased over with the dark green of laurel and arbutus and the paler green of oleander. Along the less steep slopes hurry currents of springtime flowers, the yellow daisies, marigolds and purple irises, and the guttering red anemones. But for the most part the slopes are too grim for flowers, with cliffs of limestone, sharp swirls of gravel and loam.'

For trekkers, the *pièce de résistance* is the superb Mujib Gorge.

SHORT RSCN GUIDED WALKS IN THE RESERVE

Route 45
Qaser Riyash Trail

Grade	Easy walk
Details	4km
Time	2 hrs for round trip

Route 46
Mujib Circuit Trail

Grade	Easy walk
Details	8km
Time	4–5hrs for round trip

Route 47
Mujib Gorge Trek

Grade	Moderate trek and canyon
Details	36km descending from 150m above sea level to 400m below at the Dead Sea, with some ascent on both days to bypass obstacles
Time	2 days

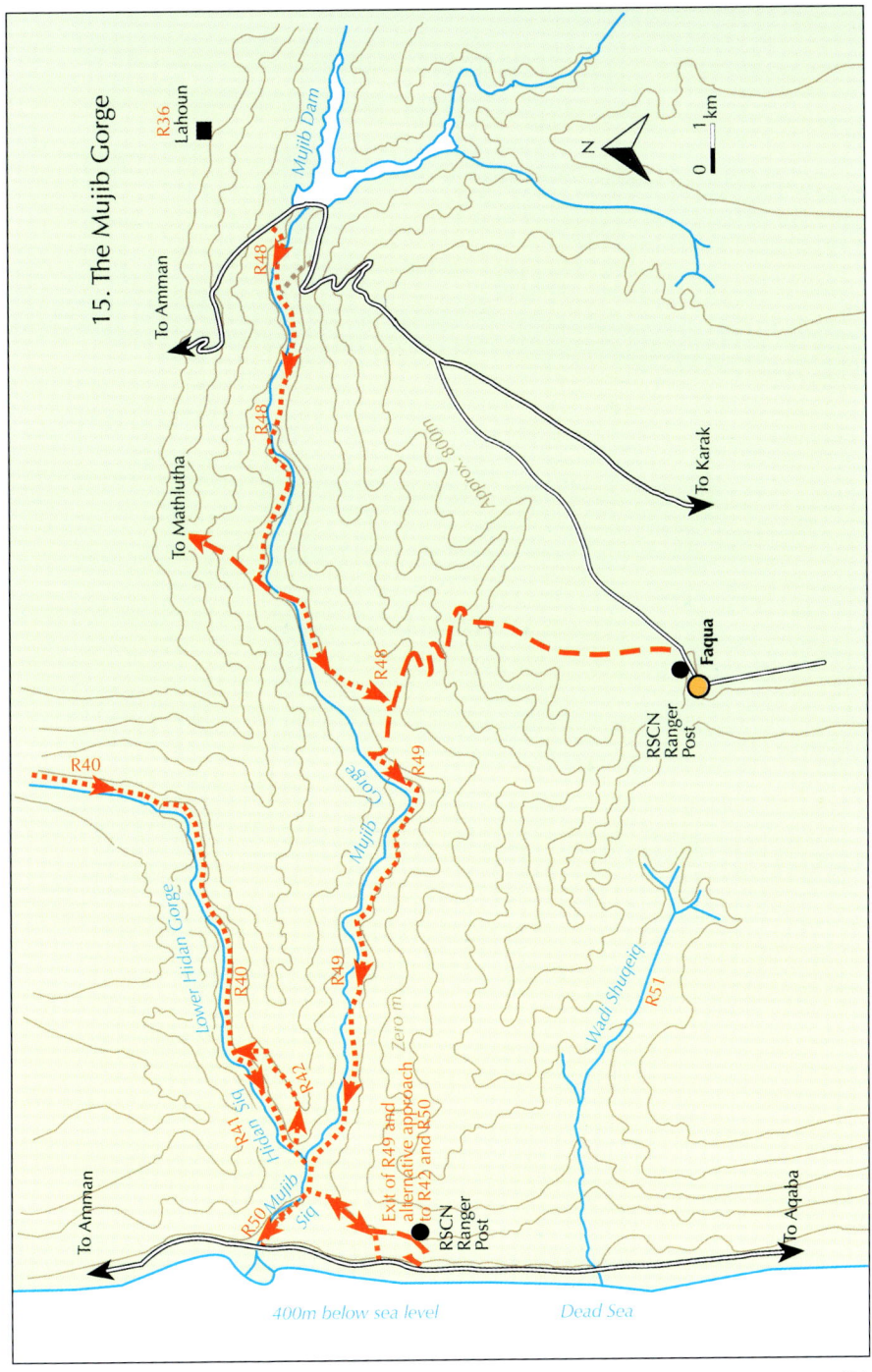

The Dead Sea Hills – The RSCN Nature Reserve – Route 47

15. The Mujib Gorge

121

A magnificent two-day trek starting from the King's Highway 37km S of Dhiban, and going through continuously interesting, beautiful and varied country, always close to the sound of water (and often in it!). There is an abundance of wildlife: porcupine, mongoose, snakes, fish, crabs, frogs of various colours and croaking abilities and, of course, birds including kingfishers, peregrines, eagles and vultures as well as small reptiles (and numerous flies with a nasty bite!). There are also said to be hyenas as well as wolves and cobras in the Mujib area, while ibex can be seen in the RSCN breeding station and on the surrounding hills.

The last section of the gorge goes through the Mujib Siq (Route 50), requiring abseil equipment. As there are long sections of the *siq* where swimming is necessary, buoyancy jackets are required if you are carrying rucksacks with camping gear. The Mujib Siq is therefore described separately, the trek ending by an 'escape route' to the S of the *siq*.

If you intend to walk the whole gorge notify the RSCN well in advance. At the end of Day 1 you should camp just before entering the Reserve. See Routes 48 and 49, map 15.

Guide RSCN approved guide required after the first day.

The first day of the trek – which is outside the Reserve – goes through the Upper Mujib Gorge.

Route 48
The Upper Mujib Gorge

Grade	Moderate trek
Details	18km, descending from 150m above sea level to 200m below with 150m of ascent over 3km to reach the Faqua track before descending again to the river just outside the RSCN Reserve
Time	8–10hrs (plus 3hrs if you finish by walking out to Faqua instead of camping by the river, rising 800m over 10km; a very long and arduous day and not recommended)

The route passes through some agricultural areas as well as wild country in an increasingly spectacular gorge. You are likely to meet Bedouin shepherds and farmers.

Some route-finding skill is needed to pick the easiest way. The possibility of flooding should be borne in mind (see 'Water Levels in Wadi Wala, the Hidan and Mujib Gorges, and the Mujib Siq' after Route 36). With regard to drinking water the river is considered by some to be polluted with chemicals used in agriculture, or from the villages above. Watch out for small springs of good water along the way. See map 15.

Guide Not essential as outside the Reserve.

Approach From Amman follow the King's Highway S to the dramatic gash of the Mujib Gorge. After a tortuous descent the road crosses the new dam about 1hr from Amman. Start by the tracks just up the road away from the dam and its associated buildings, probably best before the first hairpin on the S side.

The route
Gain the track alongside the left (S) bank of the river and follow it down to a field before crossing over the river, then back again soon after, to another track on the S side. Leave this for paths running parallel to and 50m or so above the river and follow these until after 2hrs a huge horizontal strata of rock forms a large overhang with a little (dry) stream bed below.

Continue, on paths below cliffs, just inside the lower river gorge until eventually another track is met and followed down a short way before continuing under cliffs to yet another track leading down to a field with palms and a water pump. Continue along, close to the river and round a bend eventually rising up a little to meet another track parallel to the river. Follow this down to another pump.

Now it is necessary to follow the river itself, most often by paths on its right (N) side until some huge limestone boulders are reached, where we camped, having started late (about 5hrs including stops). You are now on the zero (sea-level) contour, though it's difficult to believe! (See photo page 25.)

Continue down the true right (N) bank of the river, often in lush vegetation – oleander and fragmites reed beds – to fields and a track in Wadi Aiyanat which rises NE up the steep side of the gorge for 3km to the village of El Mathlutha.

Follow the track briefly downriver with big cliffs on the right with hanging gardens and waterfalls, until it crosses the river just after two bends to the S and back W again. Leave the track and follow paths rising up above the river gorge (or it may be better to follow the gorge?) until an area of fields is reached. Pass below these (a little path through boulders), rising up from the last field to another track which goes over a shoulder to finish at a Bedouin camp (which may or may not be there!). On a path again contour along and into a steep side ravine, to reach a field on the other side. The village of Khirbet es Sahila can be seen approx 6km away, on the N rim of the gorge, just E of N.

From here, rise up to meet a track. (It is possible to **return** from here: this goes up out of the gorge, to the RSCN Faqua ranger post – a 3hr walk.)

To continue the trek go down the track which descends quite

Descending the Upper Mujib Gorge, Day 1

steeply to the river, reaching it at a deep pool on a bend about 5km lower down from the earlier crossing point and just downstream of an impressive canyon; possible campsite before entering the Reserve.

To continue The second day of the trek (or the first if starting from the RSCN post at Faqua) passes through the Lower Mujib Gorge.

Route 49
The Lower Mujib Gorge – the Mujib Trail

Grade	Moderate canyon
Details	18km descending from the Day 1 campsite at 200m below sea level to 400m below, with a short ascent of about 150m over 1km to bypass the Mujib Siq before the final descent to the Dead Sea
Time	7–9hrs from the campsite outside the Reserve

You can't get much lower than this! Now within the Nature Reserve, the route follows the canyon continuously until an escape is forced over low hills above the Dead Sea to avoid the Mujib Siq. The scenery is ever more spectacular as the river rushes through a narrowing gorge between cliffs and boulders. Much of the walking is in the river itself, sometimes knee-deep, so beware of flash floods as the canyon is frequently inescapable (as with the Upper Mujib). Vegetation is sometimes abundant in areas of hot springs, whilst dry, inhospitable mountains loom above. A great day out! Map 15.

Guide RSCN approved guide required.
Approach Either by Route 48 or from Faqua at the RSCN entrance.

The route
Follow the river, walking through thickets of vegetation and steep-walled canyons, passing a valley and waterfall entering from the left on a bend (Wadi Juheira).

If you are still trying to keep your feet dry by 'boulder-hopping' you may as well abandon the idea, as river crossings become more and more frequent and it soon becomes necessary to walk in the river itself for increasing distances. After about 5km the river gets even narrower, passing through a *siq* where the water can be above the knees.

Continue walking down (and usually in) the river through more impressive and winding canyons, reaching the river of Wadi Hidan where it comes in from the right through the narrow canyon of the Hidan Siq past large boulders and the deep Malagi pools (if not silted up: see Route 44). About 1km further downstream the combined waters of the two wadis plunge into a dark high-walled ravine, via a deep pool where it is sometimes necessary to swim. This is the Mujib Siq, which should not be attempted by those without the proper equipment and skills (see Route 50).

Instead: on the S side of the river and just at the side of the barrier of cliffs, a bush-filled sandy and stony wadi descends to the pebble beach. It looks most unpromising, but scramble up its left side and within 100m you will find the remains of an old track. Follow this up for 1km through a wilderness of rubble-sided sandy hills (once the ancient bed of the Mujib before it broke through the chasm of the *siq*), reaching a pass and a view of the Dead Sea after ½hr.

Follow the track along, turning right at a T-junction, but then ignore the next two right turns both of which lead down towards the Dead Sea but are unusable, ending at the top of loose cliffs. The third right

Descending the Lower Mujib Gorge, Day 2

turn leaves the main 4WD track, which continues to the ibex breeding station run by the RSCN. Follow this down to the Dead Sea Highway and walk 2km back N up the highway to reach the Mujib bridge with its dramatic view of the exit from the *siq* which is just 100m upstream.

Return If you made prior arrangements you can be met here by car and be back in Amman in 1hr, otherwise there are occasional buses, or you could hitch.

# Route 50
The Mujib Siq

Grade	Serious canyon
Details	1.5km, descending from 300m below sea level to 350m below at the Mujib bridge
Time	Allow 2–3hrs, including time for photography

Welcome to the lowest adventure on earth: the final ominous chasm of the Mujib is one of the most memorable adventure trips in Jordan! It is a serious undertaking following the combined rivers of Mujib and Hidan as they force their way through a great crack in the earth's crust to the Dead Sea 400m below sea level – the lowest point on earth. The chasm is rarely more than 5 or 6m wide and its 100m-high walls are so steep or overhanging that at times they appear to meet, causing the rushing waters to reverberate continually in its dark depths. About halfway through there is a 20m waterfall – The Falls – which have to be abseiled, making return impossible. These are followed by The Cascades, a series of small falls, boulders and pools, the last of which have to be swum before emerging from the *siq*. See maps 14 and 15.

Special requirements Anyone descending the Mujib Siq should be able to swim (some may prefer to use a buoyancy jacket, especially if carrying equipment). Abseiling competence and equipment is essential. Although the main abseil is only 20m (or two of 10m), two 45m ropes should be carried in case of emergency as well as a prusik system, plus about 15m of spare cord in case *in situ* gear is missing or damaged. At least one fully waterproof sack will be needed for photographic equipment and a first aid kit (canyons are not good places to have an accident – helicopter rescue is extremely difficult).

Guide Required for inexperienced groups, and RSCN approval for access.

Approach Whilst it is possible to include the descent of the *siq* after walking down the Mujib Gorge or descending the Hidan, it is usual to come up from the Dead Sea. Arrangements should be made to meet a member of the RSCN at the Mujib bridge on the Dead Sea Highway (about 90km from Amman; 1hr, GPS alt. minus 350m N 29° 26.406' E35° 25.090').

You can then be driven up a rough 4WD track into the mountains through a barren area of dried mud hills about 200m above the Dead Sea, the remains of the ancient bed of the Mujib. The track passes the Nubian ibex breeding station. On the E side of these hills the track becomes so bad it is necessary to walk the last 5mins down to reach the gorge where it enters the *siq*. Allow ½hr for the journey, 2hrs if you have to walk it.

The route

The dark chasm beckons ahead, and even though harnesses will not be needed until about halfway it's best to put them on now, before plunging into the river. When we went through in the first week of May 1998 the water in the first section of the canyon was never more than waist-high, but on a previous visit in April 1993 (before the Dead Sea Highway was built) the water was so deep that it would have been necessary to swim; this was out of the question as camping gear was being carried. Consequently the alternative walk out had be taken; make sure you only carry the minimum essential gear down the canyon.

Swimming out from the Mujib Siq to the Dead Sea

As you continue down the chasm the walls close in imperceptibly and the noise of the river increases, warning of obstacles to come. Eventually The Falls are reached where two or three abseil options are possible. Perhaps the safest is from a point above and left of the main fall. If the gear is in, this gives a 20m abseil into the deep pool below. Swim out with care, keeping to the left edge and avoiding the crashing volume of water cascading into the pool immediately to your right.

It may also be possible to abseil directly into the pool (20m) from a rope loop high between two boulders just right of the main left-hand fall; or there is a third entertaining option from a rope loop round a small boulder embedded in the river and half hidden underwater between the other two options. A 10m abseil goes through a hole, passing directly through a small waterfall to enter a cave under the giant boulder. A second abseil from a rope loop at the back of the cave (about 10m of rope required to make the loop) then goes over an overhang to descend into the pool on the inside of the two big falls that block out the view beyond. Ahead and to the right the river is a mass of white foam – swim close to the left side to reach a shingle beach about 20m beyond – take care with the ropes in The Falls.

Once down The Falls the crux of the descent is over, but there are still more adventures ahead as the canyon gets even narrower, the walls above appearing to touch so that the river descends into the gloom down The Cascades. This series of short falls down boulders commences with a 5m drop for which the rope is again advisable, looped over a boulder low on the right. Beyond, a series of leaps into pools, or slides down water-worn boulders or through the chicanes of water chutes, takes you on down the river. A palm tree that used to be jammed between the walls of the canyon 20m above indicated the high-water flood mark; if it's still there, it gives you some cause to wonder at the depth and power of the river in flood!

The Cascades finish in the lower reaches of the chasm, much of which is totally flooded so that swimming is frequently necessary before emerging into the sunlight almost at the Mujib bridge. There may be one more obstacle to pass in the form of the RSCN fence that crosses the canyon barring entry from the road (following the deaths of inexperienced people in the river). Make sure you have arranged for the RSCN to unlock the gate.

Return It's 1hr from here to Amman. If you are with the RSCN they can arrange transport, but it should also be easy to hitch a ride.

Moving S along the King's Highway, the next big wadi – Wadi Shuqeiq, which forms the S edge of the Reserve – almost reaches up to Faqua, signposted (in Arabic) 5km S of the S edge of the Mujib Gorge.

Route 51
Wadi Shuqeiq

This wadi descends W for almost 20km from Faqua (alt. 900m) to the Dead Sea at 400m below sea level. It passes through some wild and desolate scenery and seems to be dry throughout its length. There are a couple of *siqs* where there may be small dried-up waterfalls requiring ropes. The valley ends about 5km S of the Mujib Gorge (visually checked from the air by the authors). See map 15.

Moving S again on the King's Highway – and currently outside of the Mujib Reserve boundary (though this may change) – the Karak Area is reached.

# THE KARAK AREA

The next valley down to the Dead Sea, about 10km south, can also be reached by taking the Faqua turning, but then continuing through Faqua and Imra for 23km from the King's Highway to reach the village. Here there are excellent views from the old ruins of Sirfa down into Wadi ibn Hammad, whilst to the west lies Wadi el Jarra.

Route 52
Wadi el Jarra

This wadi provides an 'easy' descent by 4WD from the clifftop village of Sirfa, which is about 85km S of Madaba and 5km S of Faqua. It is possible to descend the wadi on a rapidly deteriorating road for about 17km with the Dead Sea visible ahead. Unfortunately, just 2km from the Dead Sea the already poor track has been completely washed out by floods. (Maybe the situation has changed now; it would be easy to continue on foot.) Map 16.

S again, ending at the Ghor which extends W into the Dead Sea, bisecting it, the next wadi has formed a particularly wild and beautiful valley, the head of which reaches SE for 25km almost to Karak with its great Crusader fortress dominating the hilltop and surrounding country.

Route 53
Wadi ibn Hammad

This popular wadi and canyon are spectacular from almost any viewpoint. Its N clifftop with excellent views can be reached by Route 52. The 'Hammamat' or hot springs are 800m below and 3km away, but not accessible by vehicle from this side due to the cliffs guarding the lower canyon. The road to the hot springs starts from the villages at the E end of the wadi. See map 16.

Approach The usual approach is from Karak (see Route 54), but if coming from the N on the King's Highway head for El Qasr about 15km S of the upper S rim of the Mujib Gorge.

The route
From El Qasr take the small road W for just over 1km past the pretty valley of Wadi Zuquuba with Iron Age sites on its rim. The road then bears SSW for another 1km or so, then turns down the left side of Wadi Yarut with its small limestone escarpments and caves.
 The road eventually crosses the wadi by a bridge in the valley bottom (filled with pink flowering oleanders in May) and continues W and SW along its N side before crossing back through the river. It then goes up over a shoulder towards an area of orchards, before branching right over the side stream of Wadi Manasih, to follow the S side of Wadi ibn Hammad above a canyon filled with large fallen blocks. Another 3 or 4km further on (about 20km from El Qasr) the road, now a narrow track exposed to rock fall from the steep hillside above, descends into the canyon (GPS alt. 130m N31° 18.128' E35° 38.322'). It then crosses the river and ends abruptly at Hammamat ibn Hammad in an area of fragmites, palms, oleanders and other vegetation. The tiled hot pool, which was clean and warm when we visited it, is just across the river in the shade of some trees (popular on Fridays).

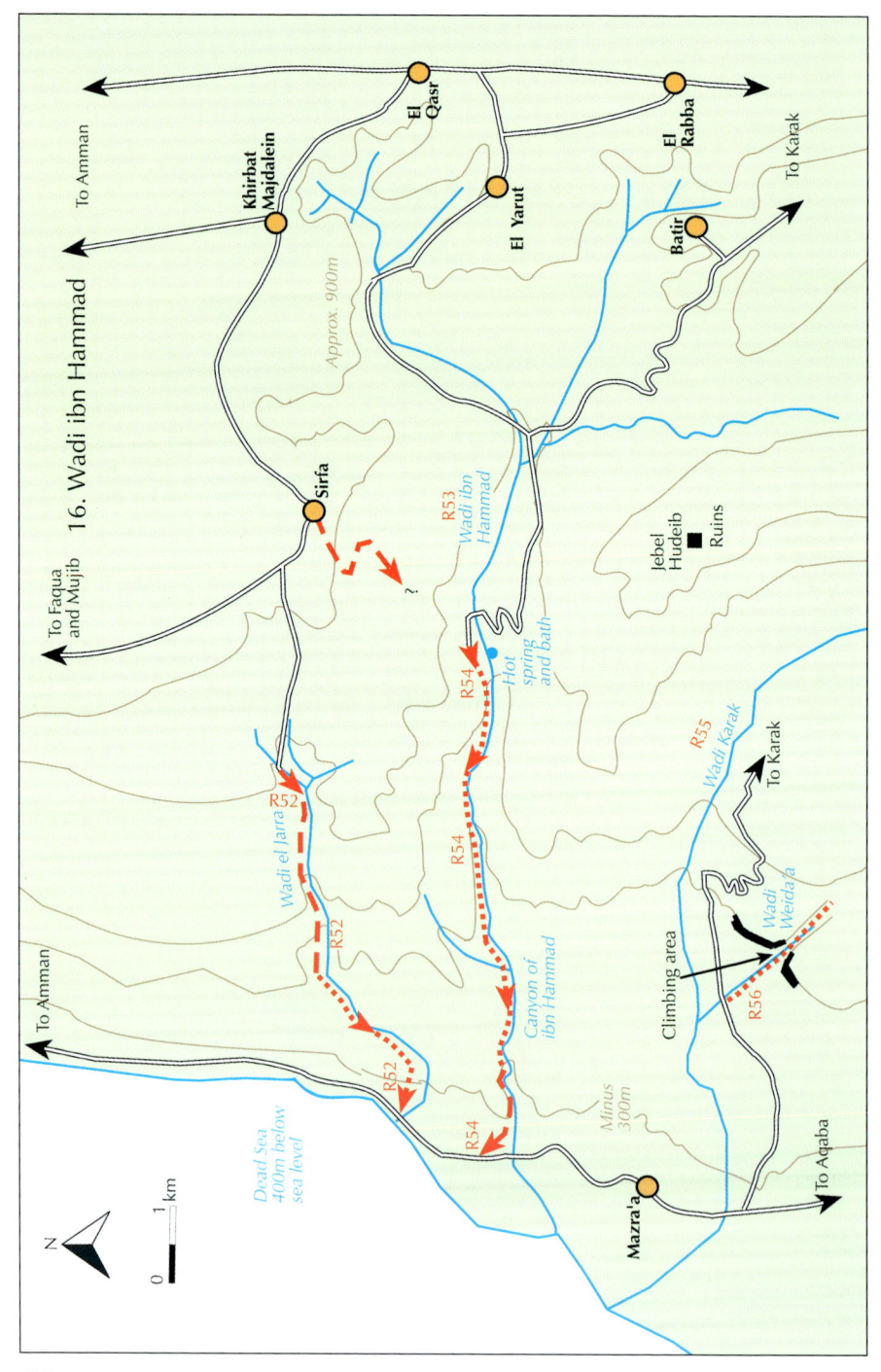

JORDAN

16. Wadi ibn Hammad

THE DEAD SEA HILLS – THE KARAK AREA – ROUTE 54

Storm clouds gathering above Wadi ibn Hammad – beware of flash floods

Beyond, the stream disappears into a sub-tropical ravine festooned with ferns, palms and other foliage with stalactites hanging from the cliffs. If you don't have time to descend the 12km of the canyon to the Dead Sea (Route 54), it's very easy to scramble down for 15mins or so either in the canyon or above on its right bank along paths. Either way, a rocky scramble on the right side of the gorge just before it becomes even narrower permits escape or entry.

Return See above, then follow the road back out.

Route 54
The Canyon of Wadi ibn Hammad

Grade	Easy canyon
Details	10km (12km if you have to walk out to the Dead Sea Highway) descending from about 130m above sea level to 360m below
Time	4hrs

Indiana Jones or what! The route starts at a hot spring and goes downhill all the way through a stunningly beautiful sub-tropical *siq* leading to a wild ravine in the heart of the barren inhospitable lower mountains, yet the walk is always in or alongside a rushing, sparkling river. A superb day out. (Watch out for the climbing fishes and beware of the big bird!)
  In the villages S of the end of the wadi, in springtime, the incredibly beautiful poiensiana (delonix-regia) trees are in full bloom, their blood-red flowers contrasting vividly with the blue skies, the turquoise Dead Sea and the otherwise arid surroundings (see photo page 41). See map 16.

131

JORDAN

Approach As Route 53 to the hot springs or, via the Desert Highway turning W just before the Karak junction to Er Rabba on the King's Highway, then NW into Wadi ibn Hammad to join the small road from El Qasr.

If starting from Karak it may be possible to arrange transport at one of the hotels. If you have your own transport take the King's Highway E then N towards Amman, turning left after 11km towards Batir, then fork right and right again 2km further on, then right again after another 3km to reach Batir. There go left towards Wadi ibn Hammad, meeting the small road from El Qasr (Route 53) after 8km and turning left (W) along the S side of the gorge, finally descending the deteriorating road to reach the hot springs after another 9km (34km from Karak).

The route
Just across the river is the pool of the hot springs – you can have a hot bath to put you in the mood before entering the palm- and fern-festooned chasm beyond. Walking in the river, descend the *siq* for ½hr or so, the walls coming ever closer until you pass through a subterranean passage, its roof encrusted with stalactites and dripping with water.

About ¾hr from the start a pretty side wadi enters from the left via a waterfall between pink-flowering oleanders, fragmites and palms. The wadi then opens out for a while before closing in again through a boulder-filled ravine leading to a waterfall which is bypassed by crossing water-polished limestone slabs on its left.

The scenery then changes again as the river enters a limestone canyon (1½hrs from the start). In places, marine fossils can be seen in the riverside boulders. About ½hr downstream the rushing waters enter new terrain as steep cliffs of solidified sand and mud rise above, opening out briefly then closing in again until 3km from the start the cliffs drop away and a water pumping site is reached.

Beyond, the cliffs close in again almost immediately and soon a huge nest of branches can be seen high on the cliffs on the N side, below an overhang. It looks to be at least 2m wide and 1m high! Just beyond the cliffs close in further and the river plunges 5m into a *siq*. Fortunately a track goes right here on a wide ledge across the cliffs, to descend steeply down rock and scree (take care!) back into the riverbed where we saw small fishes struggling up vertical water-covered rocks in the stream. About 10mins downstream from here is a deep pool and a water pump.

Return If you have arranged to be met by 4WD the car can get to this point by driving up the wadi, otherwise it's a further 2km out to the Dead Sea road where it's possible to hitch to Karak or Amman. If using public transport, there are buses from the nearby Dead Sea village of Mazra'a up to Karak.

To reach the meeting point with 4WD From the junction of the Karak Road with the Dead Sea Highway drive 6km N past Mazra'a to cross the bridge over Wadi ibn Hammad. Continue N until it is possible to go right onto a parallel track, then follow this track back S and onto the gravel riverbed of the wadi. Drive up the wadi for about 1.5km to a pool and water pump. (Don't drive through the pool – it's deep!)

It's then just over 100km from Wadi ibn Hammad back to Amman via the Dead Sea Highway, or about 38km up to the hilltop castle and town of Karak.

Immediately below the N side of this road is Wadi Karak.

Route 55
Wadi Karak

This great chasm descends about 20km NW from Karak to the isthmus of Ghor Mazra'a by the Dead Sea. The Karak road skirts along the top of its S edge. It is now fully equipped and a popular and well-acclaimed canyon trip with six abseils, including a 60m waterfall. We haven't had the chance to do it, but full details can be found in *Trekking & Canyoning in the Jordanian Dead Sea Rift* (see Appendix 2). See map 16.

KARAK

The imposing Crusader castle and town of Karak is 130km S of Amman and accommodation will be found here as a base for exploring the surrounding area. The Towers Hotel and the Rest House, both near the castle, have doubles from 15–50JD respectively; there are others nearby, as well as pleasant street cafés.

Not far away down the road to Mazra'a and the Dead Sea is a pretty little canyon slicing through a tilted shark's-tooth array of brown limestone cliffs, the 250m slabs of which were only recently discovered by climbers, but already provide some quality routes (see chapter on Climbing in Jordan).

Route 56
Wadi Weida'a

Grade	Easy canyon
Details	3km there and back, little more than 100m of ascent
Time	1–2hrs max

A tempting little canyon giving some surprising watery fun in an otherwise arid landscape; there is also a hot spring (more of a warm pool), but the big attraction here is for climbers (see Climbing in Jordan). See map 16.

Approach By taxi, car or bus. The canyon is close to the road, 6km up from the Mazra'a junction at the Dead Sea, or 20km down from Karak, 2km after the checkpoint (passport needed). Big brown slabs of tilted strata rise just above and E of the road, with a wadi cutting deeply through them. If you are in a car, park on the shoulder on its S side, near a pool fed by an irrigation channel from the wadi (GPS alt. minus 20m N31° 14.560' E35° 34.602').

The route
Follow the irrigation channel into the mouth of the canyon, which cuts deeply through the limestone slabs. Follow the stream up, crossing frequently, to reach the hot spring in about 15mins (probably busy on Fridays). Continuing up, the wadi is eventually blocked by a small waterfall in a ravine, which is difficult to pass.

Return By the same route.

Starting from Karak again, and 10km S down the King's Highway, is the small town of **Mouta**. A pleasant side trip from here is to turn right (signposted El Iraq). Drive down to the village of Kathraba (10km, good views of the Dead Sea), or turn left after 5km and go down to **El Iraq** (9km) for more excellent views of the Dead Sea down Wadi Numeira as well as extensive orchards, which look beautiful when covered in their springtime pink blossom. From El Iraq (an area with recent climbing developments) continue round the head of the wadi to **Taibah** (10km) then turn left and drive along a ridge with panoramic views over Wadi Hasa to the S, and down to Wadi Araba in the W. Continue along the ridge top road past **Majra** to rejoin the King's Highway 16km from Taibah, and 7km S of Mouta.

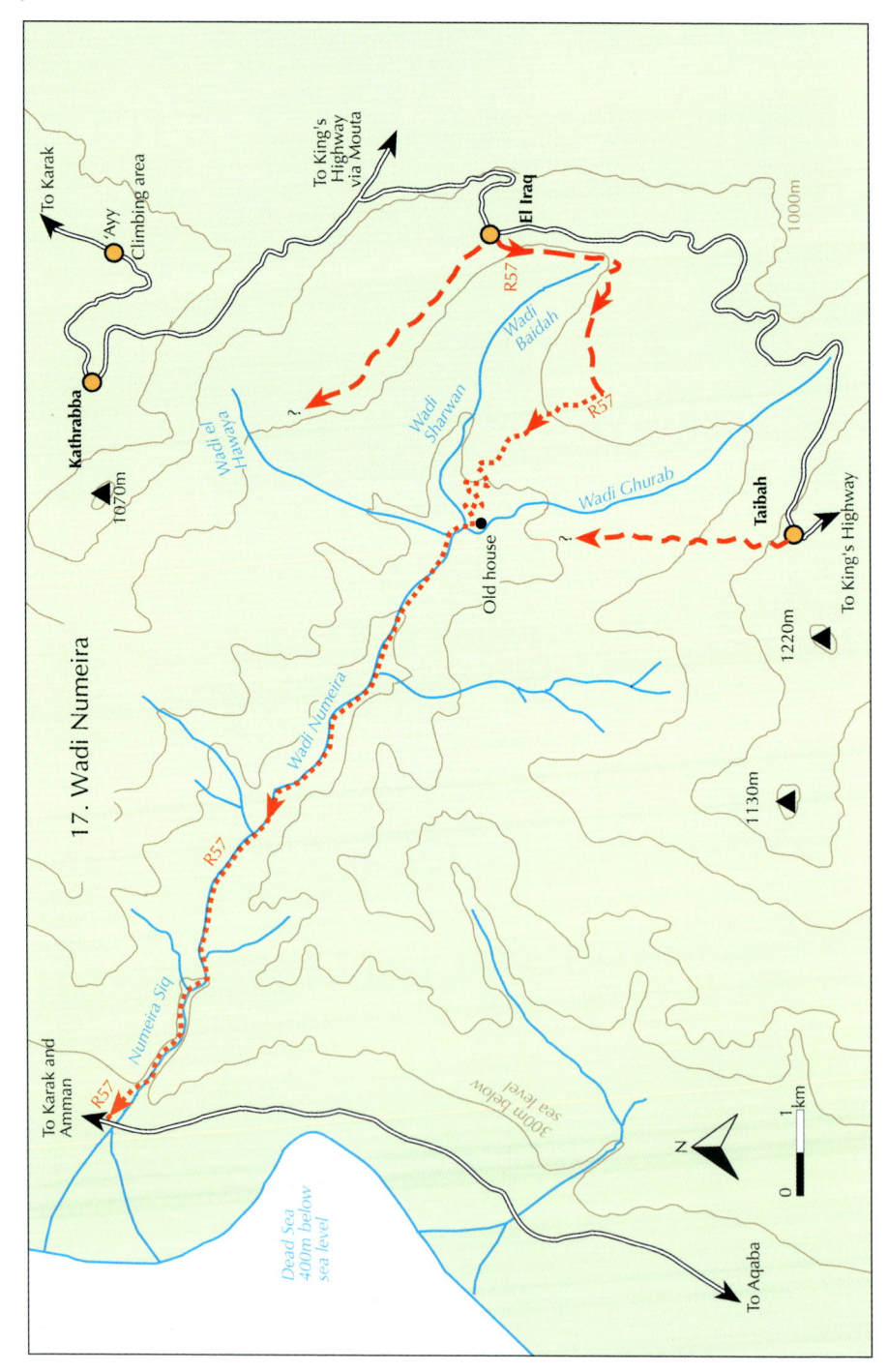

JORDAN

17. Wadi Numeira

The next enjoyable route starts from these villages and finishes with a *siq* and collapsed natural arch. It is possibly the location of 'the Waters of Nimrin' referred to in the Bible, and starts from a fan of smaller tributaries below the pretty villages and orchards of Iraq and Taibah (see above). It emerges in Wadi Araba about 15km S of the junction of the Karak road with the Dead Sea Highway. Its lower end is adjacent to the Early Bronze Age ruins of Numeira on a flat hilltop dating from around 2500BC. It was abandoned following an earthquake about 2350BC, which caused the wadi bed to move, leaving alluvial remains high among the rocks to its N similar to those on the S side of the exits of the Hidan and Mujib gorges.

A bromide production plant has been built on the edge of the Dead Sea just below the exit from the *siq*, which destroys its wilderness aspect when approaching from there; also locals enter the lower *siq* from the highway, leaving a lot of picnic litter.

Route 57
Wadi Numeira (Wadi Hudeira)

Grade	Easy canyon
Details	13km from the end of the 4WD track at 800m or 18km/6–8hrs from El Iraq at 900m, descending to the Dead Sea Highway at Ghor Numeira, 320m below sea level
Time	5–6hrs

Another downhill delight! Very enjoyable, no difficulties or route-finding problems, and a stunning exit, but a 5m drop at one point. See map 17.

Special requirements Carry a short rope and a sling in case they are needed for the 5m descent.

Approach From Karak either approach via Mouta as described above, or take the narrow road behind (S of) the castle, which twists down through Shehabieh and 'Ayy (3km and 14km) to Kathrabba (17km) and so to El Iraq (28km). This is longer than the Mouta route but more scenic.

In El Iraq take a narrow road right (W) down through the village (about 200m before the lowest, most southerly school). Fork left a short way down this road and bear left through orchards to reach a dirt track (visible from the village) which contours S then W above an escarpment, round the head of Wadi Baida to reach the nose of a peninsula of land between Wadi Baida and Wadi Ghurab (5km from El Iraq).

The route
Descend the increasingly steep nose of the hillside, eventually following a well-cairned zigzag path down to the junction of the wadis where there is a small old house with an ancient millstone near a stream and trees (alt. 100m). This area is Seil Jadeira, 2km from the track, 1hr. (A hyena was killed here a few years ago.)

The direct approaches to Seil Jadeira down Wadi Baida (which becomes Wadi Sharwan) or Wadi Ghurab are, apparently, 'very, very, very difficult – you will need ropes and a full day' or, conversely 'not a problem'. We cannot confirm which of these statements is correct – probably the former!

From Seil Jadeira follow the stream of sparkling clear water down Wadi Numeira for about 8km (approx 2hrs), with wild, barren mountains on all sides, but greenery in the valley bottom. A couple of 'dripping springs' on the right bank provide opportunities for delightful cooling showers.

Looking down Wadi Numeira

Walking down to Wadi Numeira

Some small, water-polished canyons hint at more dramatic things to come, and eventually the sides of the valley close in to form the extremely impressive gash of the Numeira Siq. Its 100m cliffs are so steep and close that it is almost a cave for much of the next 2km. At one point there is a 5m-drop needing a rope for its descent. (When we were last there it was only a 2m drop, which could be passed on the right down 'Bedouin steps' – grade 1 – but things may well be different now.)

Just before the end of the canyon a few shallow pools and cascades offer opportunities for a relaxing bath before emerging from the *siq* under a huge arch formed by a fallen rock. (Expect some litter as it is easily accessible from the road.) Round the corner is a view of the Dead Sea.

Return The highway is 0.5km further on, where it should be easy to hitch N to the nearby village of Mazra'a, or up to Karak.

To the S the Biblical site of **Lot's Cave and Monastery** is signed just after Safi. This region 5km S of the Dead Sea is also thought to be the location of Sodom and Gommorah. One of the new RSCN Reserves will be in this area.

Back on top on the King's Highway, about 25km S of Karak the road reaches the edge of the plateau at 1220m and starts its long descent via Wadi Falqa to enter the main ravine of Wadi Hasa (the Biblical Zered) after a further 4km; it then continues down SE to the riverbed.

Route 58
Wadi Hasa

There are many oleanders whence perhaps the ancient name of Zered, the willows. There are hedges of prickly-pear and even a thicket of bananas. On sheltered slopes are shelves of wheat and barley, hanging orchards of silver-grey olives, fig trees just sprouting, almond and pear in thick bloom... Along the valley bottom a stream twinkles under its curtaining of tamarisk and bamboo and laurel into a narrow gorge, then appears again, making for swift asphyxiation in the sulphurous pan of the Dead Sea.

In the Steps of Moses the Conqueror Louis Golding (1938)

Wadi Hasa, the Old Testament Wadi Zered, is almost as impressive a gorge as Wadi Mujib. It descends from the desert plateau over 50km to the E at about 1000m down to the S end of the Dead Sea at 400m below sea level. It measures around 4km from rim to rim and is 600m deep where the King's Highway crosses it. Barren at its E end it is quite verdant in its middle reaches (where there are a couple of hot springs) before it descends again through its lower gorge. The section from the King's Highway to the zero altitude level has good tracks leading to farmland. Location, map 11.

The route
A two-day trek through a beautiful canyon, with hot springs and waterfalls. Not yet checked by the authors – for information see *Trekking and Canyoning in the Jordanian Dead Sea Rift* (Appendix 2). Wilf Colonna has done some climbs here, approached from the Dead Sea (see the chapter Climbing in Jordan).

Above it to the S, and close to the King's Highway, is Route 59.

Route 59
Jebel Tannur

Grade	Easy scramble
Details	4km up and down
Time	1–1½hrs for the round trip, ascending and descending 160m

This is the small pyramidal hill with the Nabataean temple of Khirbet Tannur on its summit. There are the remains of a stone floor, pillars and ruined walls. The isolated hill rises from the S side of Wadi Hasa almost opposite a black basalt hill known to the local Bedouin as 'the mountain of evil'. Its ascent is a pleasant walk and gives good views of the huge gorge of Wadi Hasa as well as an opportunity to visit a quiet antiquity site.

Approach 4km S of the point where the King's Highway crosses Wadi Hasa, the road goes through a small pass (alt. 540m) marked by a stone plinth. About 2km to the right is Jebel Tannur (704m). A dirt track goes off towards it for 0.5km. Park here.

The route
Follow the path to the top, gaining height easily up the ridge of the hill.

Descent By the same route.

Down below, 4km WNW of Khirbet Tannur in Wadi Hasa, are more hot springs, accessed by Route 60.

Route 60
The Hot Springs of Hammamat Borbita and Hammamat Afra

These are signed 2km S of Jebel Tannur, where the road crosses Wadi La'ban. Take this turn then fork right after 7km for Borbita or continue down the poor track for another 6km to a stream. Walk a short way down to reach a little valley, the sides of which are stained by minerals. The sulphurous hot baths of Afra are situated here; the two baths, segregated for the sexes, are currently (2007) being repaired.

The next chapter moves south from here to ancient Edom and the mountains of Dana.

Descending Wadi Adethni from its oasis (Route 72)

THE DANA AREA

O thou that dwellest in the clefts of the rock, thou that holdest the heights of the hill: though thou shouldst make thy nest as high as the eagle, I will bring thee down from thence, said the Lord. Also Edom shall be a desolation: everyone that goeth by it shall be astonished and shall hiss at all the plagues thereof... no man shall abide there, neither shall a son of man dwell in it.

Old Testament (Jeremiah, speaking of the Land of Edom, now southern Jordan)

Well, he certainly got it right! Edom is full of surprises: perennial streams and hidden oases, the forests, valleys and mountains of the Dana Nature Reserve, grim Shaubak Castle standing aloof above its web of palm-decorated canyons, magnificent Petra (where nobody dwells since the Bedouin were moved out 'to preserve the site' in 1985) and, way down south, the unique and colourful deserts and mountains of Rum, then the striated igneous mountains guarding the approaches to the beaches of Aqaba. This chapter deals with the complex arrangement of mountains and canyons in the region of Dana and Shaubak.

Accommodation and transport

The only town of any size immediately north of Dana is Tafileh, which is around 50km south of Karak. Tafileh has nothing much in the way of accommodation, but at Dana there are the RSCN hotel and campsite, both of which need to be booked well in advance. Luckily there are also two small hotels nearby in Dana village, the Dana Hotel run by the local co-operative and supported by the RSCN, and the Towers Hotel whose new upper storey makes an anomalous intrusion into the village skyline. West of Dana, down in Wadi Araba and only accessible on foot or by 4WD, is the award-winning Feynan Eco-Lodge, a luxurious surprise in wild surrounds (for prices and information see the section below on the RSCN Dana Reserve). Moving south en route for Petra there is Abu Seif's campsite at Shaubak, whilst at Beidah there are two Bedouin camps. A little further away in Wadi Musa, the gateway to Petra, there seems to be a hotel on every corner and to suit every pocket (see the following chapter on the Petra area), and there are also two campsites.

Public transport around Tafileh is infrequent, but there are reasonably regular services between Dana (from nearby Qadissiya on the King's Highway) and Petra, none costing more than 3JD.

Guides

In addition to guides and travel companies operating from Amman there are others specialising in trekking and adventure tourism – including local individuals – mentioned in the relevant areas, and others in Wadi Musa (Petra) and Rum (full details in Appendix 1). As elsewhere the RSCN must approve guides operating within its Dana Reserve.

Maps

The following 1:50,000 topographical K737 series maps cover this section of the guidebook. You are unlikely to be able to get hold of these, but enquire at the Jordanian Royal Geographical Centre in Amman (see 'Maps' in the Introduction).

- 3151–1V, 3151–1: Wadi Hasa & Selah area
- 3051–11, 3151–111: Buseira, Dana, Feynan, Shaubak area
- 3050–1: Petra

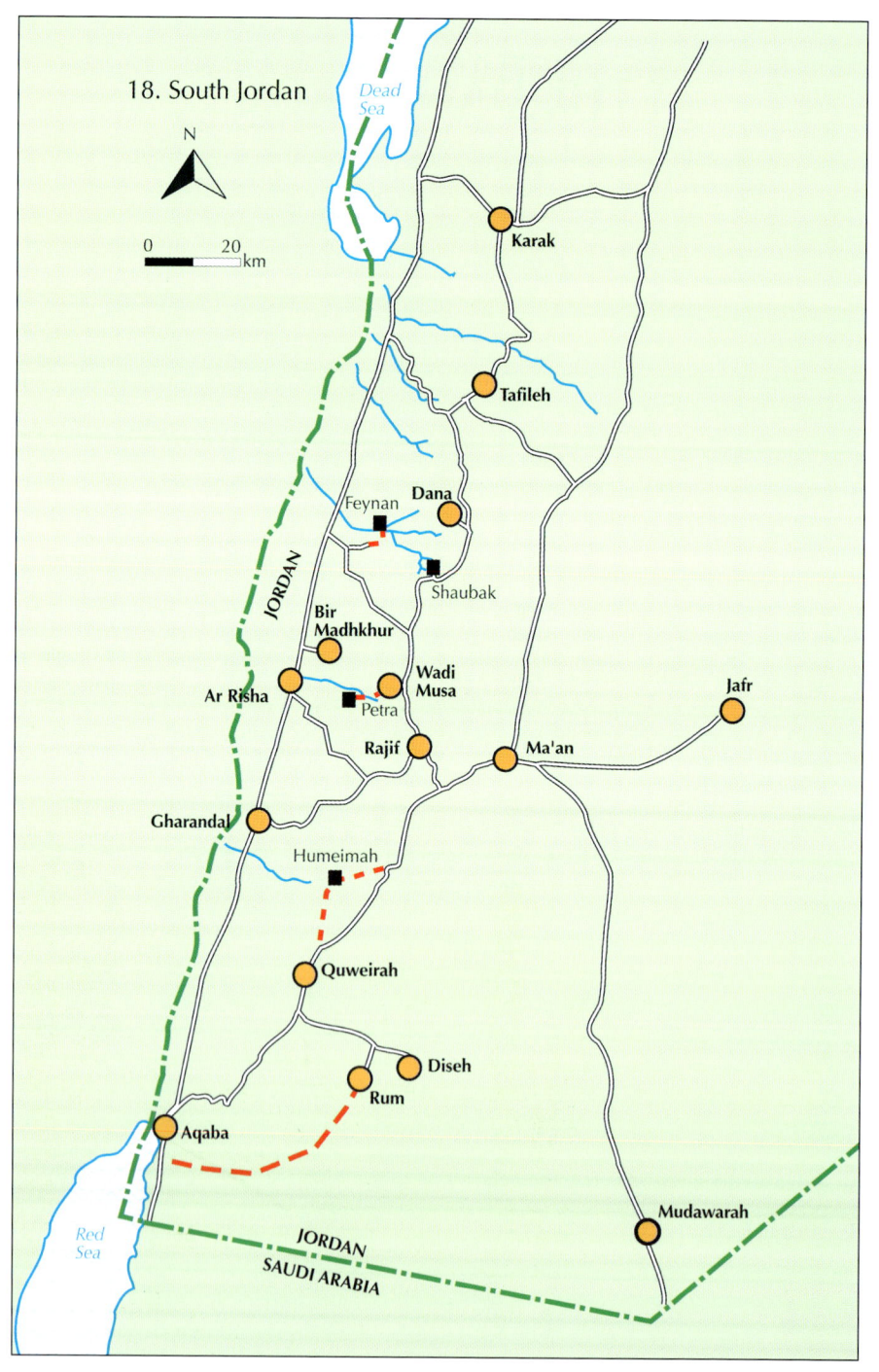

JORDAN

18. South Jordan

THE NORTHERN DANA AREA

We were penned in verminous houses of cold stone; lacking fuel, lacking food; storm-bound in streets like sewers, amid blizzards of sleet and an icy wind: while there in the valley was sunshine among spring grass, deep with flowers, upon flocks in milk and air so warm that men went uncloaked.

Seven Pillars of Wisdom T. E. Lawrence (1926)

The hillside town of Tafileh nestles dramatically in a great bowl of hills at an altitude of 1000m above the upper canyons of Wadi Tubl el Humur, which plunge 20km northwest to the south end of the Dead Sea. It was obviously a much less pleasant place when Lawrence was fighting there than it is today, but there is still little for the traveller other than those waiting for local transport who may need to make use of the few small restaurants and one very basic hotel.

Oleander

THE TAFILEH–WADI ARABA ROAD

Continuing through Tafileh on the King's Highway for 4km SW of the main Tafileh mosque (and about 7km N of Selah, see Route 61), a new road forks right (W) to go out along the hillside for 4km to Sinifha at 1020m. It then winds dramatically down through a particularly beautiful and wild mountain area along the S edge of the Tubl el Humur canyons to reach Fifa in Wadi Araba, S of the Dead Sea at 300m below sea level. There is a superb viewpoint 9km down the road: just go up onto the small hill on the right for an unbeatable panorama of the canyons to the N. Just beyond there are more good views of Wadi

Jordanian hospitality to passing strangers, Ain el Beidah, north of Dana

143

JORDAN

Khnaisser to the S (see Routes 62 and 63; it is also possible to trek into the canyon from here). From the Wadi Araba road junction it's 173km to Aqaba and 157km to Amman.

Going S again on the King's Highway, the next walk goes to Selah.

Route 61
Selah

...a most strange mountain on the further side of a vast and profound ravine, a great flat-topped rock rising from the centre of it like a round tower... the cliffs of it nearly vertical lapped round by a stillness and secrecy... after some time the eye made out that men had the handling of the mountain... squared windows and doorways cut out of solid rock and carved stairways dizzily ascending... the holders of the heights... had made their nest truly as high as an eagle. But it had not been high enough. I will bring thee down from thence saith the Lord. And the carved square windows of its houses stare like the eye-sockets of a skull.

In the Steps of Moses the Conqueror L. Golding (1938)

Grade	Easy scramble
Details	3km
Time	If you drive down allow 1hr each way from and to Es Sil and 1hr to look around Selah (3hrs in total; plus 1hr if you walk from Es Sil and back, descending from 1100m to 700m before climbing up to the summit of Selah (840m), making 540m of ascent/descent

The impressive natural fortress of Selah was a hilltop refuge occupied from the early Bronze Age to medieval times. It is possibly the site where the Judaean King Amaziah threw 10,000 prisoners to their deaths over the cliffs, but for those more upwardly mobile it provides a great little walk in very impressive mountain scenery. See map 19.

Guide A guide is recommended; it is the responsibility of Fahad Shahabat at Ain el Beidah (on the King's Highway above Es Sil) to be aware of and assist tourists going into these hills, or visiting the site of Selah. Contact him first (see Appendix 1); if he cannot accompany you he will find a guide for you.

Approach About 9km beyond Tafileh, towards Petra, the road passes the village of Ain el Beidah on the crest of a hill. Turn right here to the small village of Es Sil on the lip of a deep wadi, a nice site with picturesque old stone flat-roofed houses reminiscent of Dana. If you have 4WD continue down through the village, round a hairpin bend descending steeply to the N until the track curves S and stops in a hollow.

The route
About 100m back from the end of the track there is a cave on the right, and a small pool (Bir K'sair) on the left. Just beyond here a path goes right (W) over rocks through a defile, fairly well defined with some cut steps to a little valley (Khenduk). From there the trail continues in the same W direction into the next obvious defile in the mountain wall, winding up to meet a hewn staircase on the right side of the ravine

THE DANA AREA – THE NORTHERN DANA AREA – ROUTE 61

Descending the hewn rock-steps from the summit of Selah, with its Bronze Age relics

145

JORDAN

and eventually turning left 100m before the top to reach the summit area (20mins from Bir K'sair). There are walls to the left and what are probably observation posts at strategic points along the perimeter, as well as a Babylonian relief near the summit from where there are magnificent views in all directions. There are many water cisterns cut in the summit plateau, with small entrances but large chambers below.

Return By the same route.

Below Selah, snaking a tortuous way NW through rugged mountains, the 17km canyon system of Wadi Jamal leads into Wadi Khnaisser (also known as Khanzira) down which it continues for almost as far again to Wadi Araba. The headwaters are about 6km upstream via Wadi Buseira and Wadi Labun, originating in Buseira (see Route 63). It's a long way, well over 30km in all – and not yet completed. If you do it, let us know.

Route 62
The Canyon of Wadi Jamal and Wadi Khnaisser (Wadi Khanzira)

Grade	Serious trek, moderate canyon
Details	About 30km in total, but we have only done the first 17km (which took 6hrs – and the same to return). Make sure someone knows your intentions. Whilst there is only a gap of around 3km between known routes, there is no information on what problems there may be in that section.
Time	Allow 12hrs for the full descent, maybe more

A long, trek through the heart of lonely mountains. So far only partially explored, with a small blank on the map midway; the route starts on map 19.

Guide Recommended, especially if you want to continue to Wadi Araba (see Route 61 for contact information).

Approach As Route 61 to Es Sil.

The route
There are various routes down from the hilltop village of Es Sil (see Route 65), into Wadi Jamal and its eastern tributary, Wadi Buseira (see Route 63). To find either of the two ways in from the olive groves below and N of Es Sil take a local guide until further details are available (we went down into the canyon with Redwan Al Qararah from Ain el Beidah).

The two routes from the olive groves go down almost due W through white sandstone domes and are difficult to locate (hence the need for a guide). One is a 'hunter's route' taking a direct line and requiring some agility, the other a 'shepherd's route' following a winding donkey track. Either way will bring you in 2hrs to the junction of Wadi Hersh (S of Selah) with Wadi Jamal. This place is Al Faqarah; there was a small, almost stagnant, pool here in mid-October 1998, with an attendant shepherd and a herd of goats. The young guide who took us down to this point said that 'In springtime it is too beautiful to describe; sometimes there is water 3m deep in Wadi Jamal.' (Wadi Jamal is here known as Wadi Sidreh due to the large sidreh tree – the zizyphus tree, or *spinus Christi* – with its edible sweet orange-brown berries, which is just downstream.)

In October the main wadi was dry, but after walking down through the impressive canyon for ½hr or so the Waters of Mushrada are reached, with a few fragmites clusters and oleanders. The *siq* then

Exploring the depths of Wadi Jamal

closes in again dramatically and it is sometimes necessary to jump down small waterfalls and across pools before emerging at a cave-like 'dripping spring' or *nuwatif* on the left. (There is also an old copper mine on its left, at least 10m deep, maybe more; its history not known.)

Continuing down the *siq* the waters disappear again and it is necessary to walk between canyon walls often only 2 or 3m apart, and once through a 'cave' about 50m long under large fallen boulders. Occasional logs jammed across the *siq* indicate floods of 2m depth or more, but driftwood can be seen considerably higher than that, so winter and springtime explorers should beware!

About 2–2½ hrs from the Waters of Mushrada, the Waters of Jameilha 'the beautiful place' commence. Here there were many signs of Bedouin shepherds, also hides for hunters of birds and other wildlife. Downstream of Jameilha the *siq* becomes completely choked with tall fragmites reeds and progress becomes virtually impossible. It's better to take to the hillside, where careful searching reveals a cairned shepherds' path on the right about 50–100m above the *siq*. However, after following this for a short way the cairns disappear and the path becomes less and less evident; and after 1–1½km it's almost non-existent.

We took 6hrs to reach this point and were only about halfway, so reluctantly decided to return to Es Sil by the same way as the rest of the route was unknown and we were expected back that night.

To continue Following the subsequent publication of *Trekking and Canyoning in the Jordanian Dead Sea Rift* (see Appendix 2) it is now apparent that another trek enters the wadi from the Tafileh–Araba road about 3km beyond the low point we reached. From then on the only obstacles are more vegetation and some wading through water, but there is no information available on the 3km gap between the two routes; anyone attempting the full descent needs to be prepared for all eventualities. Beyond our low point it's a further 13km out to Wadi Araba down Wadi Khnaisser, also known as Wadi Khanzira, 'Wild Boar Valley'.

BUSEIRA

About 7km along the King's Highway to Petra from Ain el Beidah turn right to Buseira (about 2.5km). There are Iron Age ruins mentioned in the Bible as 'Bozrah' both in and just beyond the town to the N, with good views down into Wadi Buseira to the NW and on towards Wadi Araba down the aforementioned Wadi Jamal. See map 19.

According to the locals there are ways into Wadi Jamal from Buseira, starting from the E side of the village. In springtime you may well see a big waterfall cascading into Wadi Labun over a 60m cliff – an unusual sight in Jordan. The wadi continues down from there to meet Wadi Za'rura coming from the W side of Buseira, which passes over a waterfall called Gargur. Route 65 from Selah crosses Wadi Labun where it passes through an impressive *siq* 1km E of this junction. Downstream of here the wadi is named Wadi Buseira, until after 4km it meets the two wadis enclosing Selah (see Route 62); at that point the name changes to Wadi el Jamal before becoming Wadi Khnaisser (Route 62).

Route 63
Wadi Labun – Wadi Jamal – Wadi Khnaisser

Grade	Serious trek, easy canyon
Details	About 35km, descending over 1000m
Time	We were told 12hrs, which is just possible but seems unlikely given potential route-finding problems. Allow 2 days and make sure someone knows where you have gone.

A possible upstream extension to the start of Route 62. The whole system is reputed to be an ancient way down to Wadi Araba, though it seems unlikely. See map 19.

View across wild valleys and mountains to Buseira from above the old village of Es Sil near Selah

The route
The only information available is that the route is very scenic, which is certainly true of the section we crossed on Route 65 as well as the very impressive route through Wadi Jamal (Route 62). Apparently the canyon can also be accessed easily down Wadi Za'rura, avoiding Wadi Labun. (Not yet checked by the authors; see Route 62.)

There is said to be another old trail to the W.

Route 64
Wadi Dhalal to Wadi Araba

...the cliffs and the hills drew together so that hardly did the stars shine into its pitchy blackness... We halted a moment while our camels stilled the nervous trembling of their forelegs after the strain of the terrible descent. Then we plashed, fetlock deep, down the swift stream, under a long arch of rustling bamboos, which met so nearly over our heads that fans brushed our faces. The strange echoes of the vaulted passage frightened our camels into a trot.

Seven Pillars of Wisdom T. E. Lawrence (1926)

Grade	Moderate trek
Details	About 30km from Buseira, descending from 1140m to 100m below sea level in Wadi Araba
Time	6–10hrs depending on where you walk from

The route was used by Lawrence on 20 February 1918, but has not been checked by the authors. See map 19.

The route
There are tracks heading out from Buseira, crossing the wadi immediately W (see Route 65), then 8km W along the N edge of Wadi Dhalal headwaters before descending into it on a dirt road that has been destroyed by rain. The wadi is exactly on the N boundary of the Dana Nature Reserve so an RSCN approved guide may be required – ask at Dana. (Information supplied by Tareq abul Hawa of RSCN Dana.)

Another series of old trails once led between Selah and Buseira and on to the S.

Route 65
Selah to Buseira and Dana

Grade	Moderate trek
Details	16km; starting at 700m the route first descends a little, then ascends 350m before descending 360m to Wadi Labun, then a long haul up 500m to Buseira before descending a little to rise another 500m again to Jebel Sarab above Dana; then an easy 200m descent to the Rummana campsite in the Dana Reserve.
Time	7–8hrs

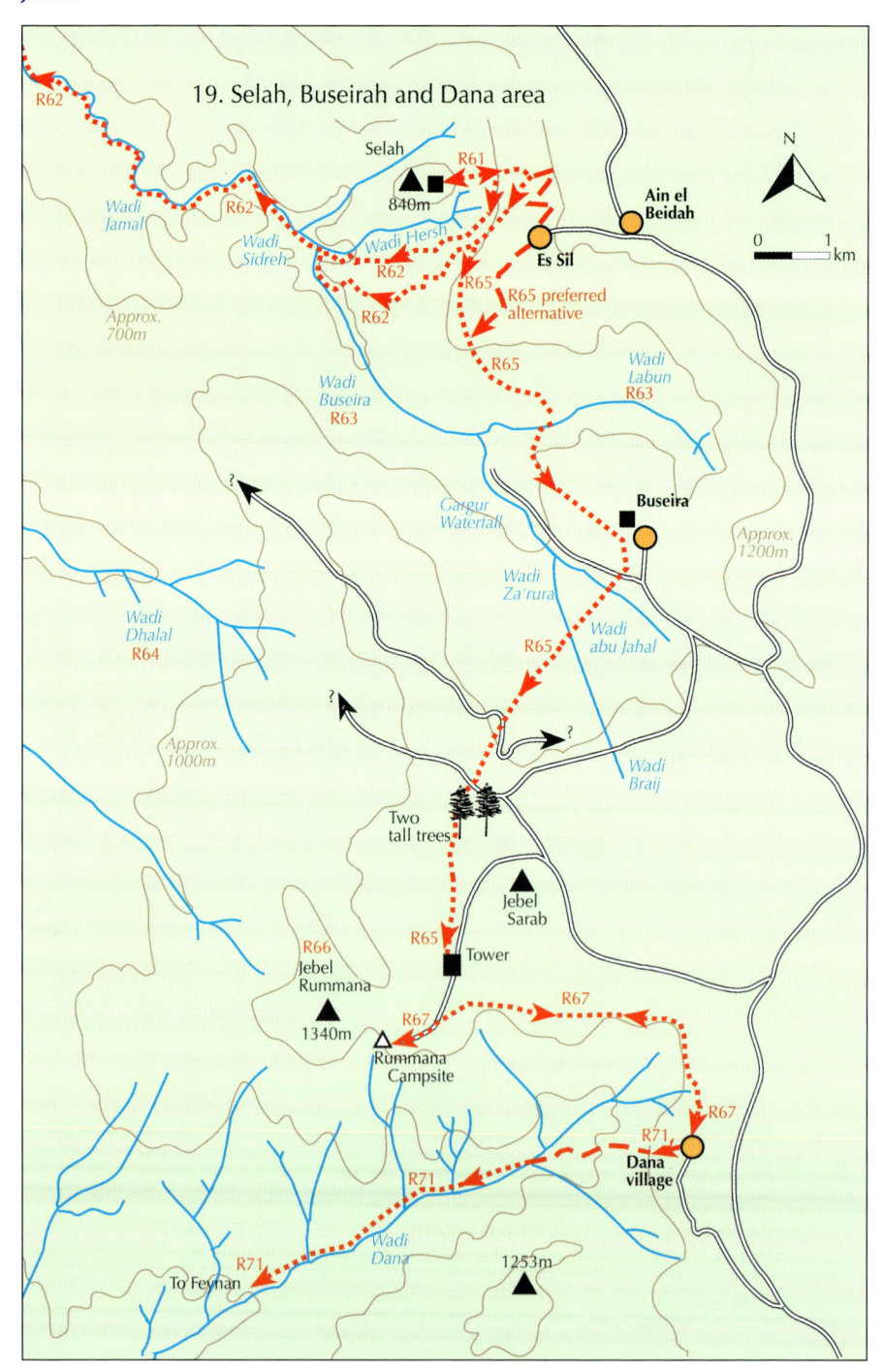

JORDAN

19. Selah, Buseirah and Dana area

THE DANA AREA – THE NORTHERN DANA AREA – ROUTE 65

A considerable amount of descent and ascent links these ancient hilltop sites, each in a commanding position above valleys leading down to Wadi Araba. The original way has been considerably altered by 4WD tracks leading to agricultural areas, so it has lost much of its character and ambience. It nevertheless passes through a variety of interesting country needing route-finding ability and currently forms the first link in a chain of treks that some refer to as the **Nabataean Trail**, which can be extended all the way S to Aqaba. See map 19.

Guide RSCN approved guide required (unless going via the Tower or Dana Village rather than into the Reserve).

Approach As Route 61. Walk (or preferably drive) 2km down from Es Sil (1100m) to the saddle at 700m below the hill of Selah (840m).

The route

About 2km to the S on a shoulder of the hill just SW of Es Sil village a small field (green in springtime) can be seen. This is the first objective; to reach it go S across flat land and small fields to a gap between steep rock towers. Pass between them and carefully scramble down a narrow *siq*, then keep on its left side across the shoulder beyond and descend carefully into the wadi. Now rise diagonally up the hillside, still in the same general line passing through olive groves to reach a good track which contours round past a cave shelter then along the top of the green field on the shoulder at 1000m (about 2km, 1hr). Just beyond is a large cairn and a 4WD track coming down from Es Sil for 0.5km through olive groves. (A direct approach via this track would be very easy and save 1hr or more, and is probably the best way to commence the trek.)

Follow the track down to the SE towards Wadi Labun. After about ½ hr it curves towards the E passing left of a small hill with two small tops. (To the right there are steps cut in the steep slabs, with grooves worn along the sides by Bedouin children sliding down them on stones – these features can also be found in Wadi Rum.) From here pass N of a deep ravine with some cave shelters visible in it below, then continue down the left side of this ravine and go left across a small wadi, then descend again to emerge above the 50m cliffs hiding the canyon of Wadi Labun.

There is only one way in and finding it is the key to the route. The entry point should be a little to your left, where a donkey track winds steeply down into the ravine which is otherwise guarded by cliffs, forming an impressive *siq*. Not so obvious at first, it passes a small juniper tree, becoming more defined as it nears the wadi bed (alt. 640m, 2hrs from the start). The impressive Petra-style *siq* extends both E up to the location of the springtime waterfall at Buseira, and W down to Wadi Araba (see Route 63).

Go about 50m down the wadi to find the donkey track going up the left bank onto the hillside above. Cross a small wadi and go up the shoulder of the hill trending right and eventually reaching a track. Continue up this and the path above to emerge on the ridge directly above and about 0.5km from the springs and waterfall of Gargur, which is to the SW with a road passing it en route from Wadi Labun up to Buseira (½–¾hr from Wadi Labun).

Ignore the road and continue up left of a fenced field above Gargur Falls until, just above a concrete water tank, paths are followed towards a distant shoulder passing through some previously concealed fields and up an improving track to the shoulder and the first view of the houses of Buseira beyond (1hr from Wadi Labun).

Follow the track, which rises easily up to Buseira (1km). The ruins of 2000-year-old Iron Age Bozrah are immediately N of the present village on the end of the promontory between the two wadis but they hardly merit a special visit. If you do go there it's a bit of a slog directly up the hillside from the track (alt. 1140m, 3½–4hrs from Selah).

Otherwise continue along the rising track along the W side of the comparatively new village, passing by some old houses. Just beyond, by a house on the right with a small fruit garden, some steps leave

Trekking from Selah to Buseira (Iron Age Bozrah) and on to the Dana Nature Reserve

the road. Go down these to the road below and take the track forking right that can be seen winding S down into Wadi abu Jahal.

Just before the track reaches the wadi, leave it and descend directly on paths into the wadi (alt. 900m), then across it and up the other side, below then right of a small cliff, to meet another good track. On the far horizon a saddle will be seen between two hills with two large trees on its right side – your next objective. Take the track towards them, eventually following limestone pavements along the left side of Wadi Braij en route, then forking right to cross the wadi (½hr from Buseira).

Immediately beyond leave the track and head up fields past a small juniper, then up through more fields to a path going round the left side of a hill above the top field. Keep going round and up, heading for the saddle and reaching a road about 20mins above Wadi Braij. Go left on the road for 100m or so to just before a walled field with cairns on the left of the road. (Just beyond, the road crosses the wadi at a hairpin bend.) Here go right over a small field and past a tree, heading up towards the saddle again (about ½hr from Wadi Braij).

Ahead you will once again see the saddle and the two large and ancient protected cypress trees that are just inside the N edge of the Dana Reserve. Reach them across fields and over a road (1300m). S of here the Reserve is fenced, beyond which is an area of forest in a protected zone. If you have an RSCN approved guide there is a way through to a track that leads through the woods to the Rummana Camp. If not, it is necessary to head uphill E, on the outside of the fence, eventually contouring S towards Ain Lahdha at 1454m before heading back W to the RSCN gate tower at Jebel Sarab. The RSCN campsite is below at 1180m, 3½hrs from Buseira, see information below. (The last section from the cypress trees has not been checked by the authors, who were permitted through the normally protected area of 'the Forest Trail'.)

Return If required it is possible to return to the start by public transport on the King's Highway.

THE RSCN DANA NATURE RESERVE

Lawrence passed through here on 11 February 1918, as related in *Seven Pillars of Wisdom*: 'Rain came on, and soaked me, and then it blew fine and freezing till I crackled in an armour of white silk, like a theatre knight: or like a bridal cake hard iced.' As the rain turns to snow, Lawrence's camel falls but he continues on foot '...sounding the path in front with my stick, or digging new passes when the drifts were deep... looking down across the chess-board houses of Dana village into sunny Arabeh, fresh and green thousands of feet below.'

The Reserve is comprised of a system of wadis and mountains that extends from the upper edge of the Rift Valley down to the desert lowlands of Wadi Araba. Visitors can experience the beauty of Rummana mountain, the archaeological ruins of Feynan, the tranquillity of Dana village, and the grandeur of the sandstone cliffs of Wadi Dana, as well as visiting the wilderness areas in the company of approved guides.

Dana is home to about 600 plant species, 37 mammal species and 190 species of birds, including 80 percent of the known world population of Tristram's serin. For full information on vegetation and wildlife contact the RSCN (see Appendix 1). See map 20.

Approach From Qadissiya on the King's Highway, 27km S of Tafileh and about 50km N of Petra.
Entrance fee 6JD non-Jordanians, 2JD Jordanians.
Guiding fee 15–85JD dependent on length of trail and size of group.
Accommodation See below.

The Visitor Centre, with displays and information about Dana and the RSCN, is located at the edge of Dana village. The shop sells organically grown produce from the terraced gardens, and silver jewellery and pottery created by the village women. The centre provides refreshments and has an outdoor terrace with a spectacular view of Wadi Dana.

RUMMANA CAMPSITE

The campsite is in a beautiful area about 3km N of Wadi Dana with a superb panorama over orchards, green hills, sandstone domes and savage valleys rising out of Wadi Araba. It is open from 1 March to 31 October (except Tuesdays). Visitors must book in advance and check in before 8pm. Cars must be left at the Tower entrance (see below) from where a shuttle bus provides transportation to and from the campsite at 1hr intervals.

To reach the campsite turn off the King's Highway 1km S of Rashadiya (signed Lahtha) and follow the track for 300m, keeping right at a huge major road leading to a quarry. Leave this to the right after 2km, as the road curves towards the NW and N, then fork left as the road goes W then S, descending slightly to the Tower and gate on Jebel Sarab on the upper edge of the Reserve.

DANA VILLAGE AND GUESTHOUSE

Perched like an eyrie on the edge of Wadi Dana, overlooking the spectacular scenery of the Dana Nature Reserve, Dana is a classic example of one of Jordan's few remaining traditional villages. The

20. The RSCN Dana Nature Reserve

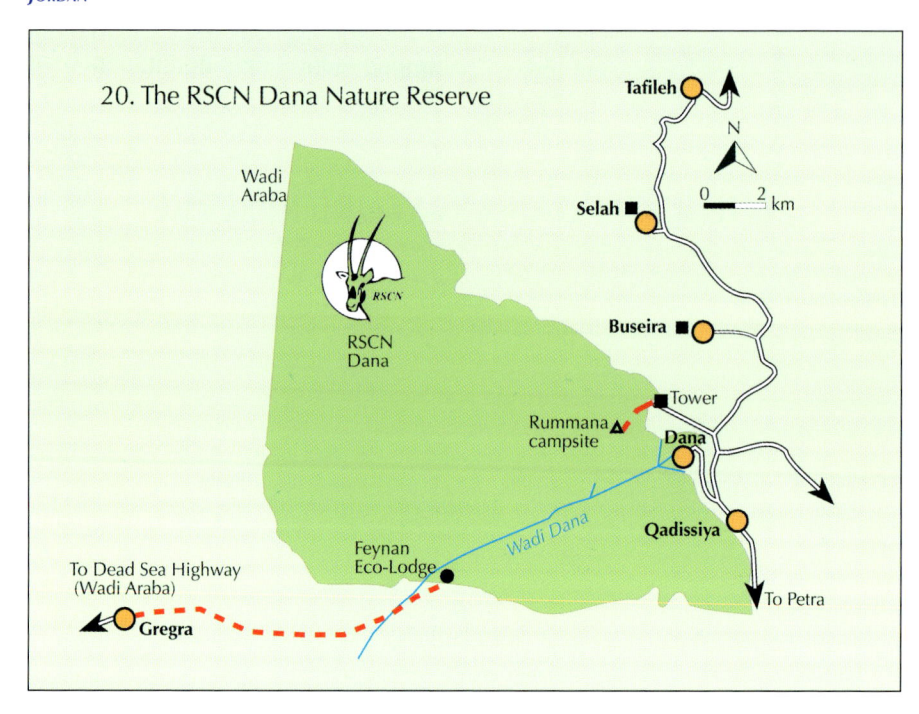

building interiors are divided by stone arches, which support the roofs, large timber beams being unavailable. Alongside –and built in the same harmonious architectural style – is the unique guesthouse and Visitor Centre run by the RSCN. Prices, inclusive of breakfast, vary from 30–40JD per double dependent on season and other requirements. Bookings should be made well in advance. An overnight stay in the small and friendly Dana Hotel run by local people in Dana village and supported by the RSCN costs around 15–20JD per double B&B, whist the nearby Tower Hotel, which protrudes from the village like a sore thumb, costs 24JD per double half-board.

FEYNAN ECO-LODGE

The lodge has received an international commendation under the title 'Best Overseas Tourism Project'. Its unique quality of seclusion is emphasised by its location 8km from the nearest road and the fact that it is only accessible by 4WD, one of the community shuttle services, or a 5hr hike through Wadi Dana. It is managed on proven environmentally friendly principles, with traditional vegetarian cuisine using local herbs and plants prepared by the Bedouin staff. Upon request lamb can be cooked by fire, either in a *zarb* (a hole in the ground) or manually grilled.

The area shows evidence of human habitation stretching back 10,000 years, and was the first place in the world where copper ore was extracted and smelted. The ancient community's most prosperous times were during the Byzantine period when profitable trade – supplying most of the known world with copper products – took place at the nearby Khirbet souk. Remains of this souk, ancient churches and Islamic and Christian graves are accessible on guided hiking tours.

The lodge provides an unparalleled experience with candlelit rooms at night, creating an atmosphere reminiscent of an ancient caravanserai. Prices go from 30–45JD per double B&B, Jordanian/non-Jordanian. There is no camping here, but it would be possible to camp a few kilometres S, beyond the Reserve.

Dana village

RSCN WALKS IN THE DANA RESERVE

Five trails are clearly marked with cairns and some can be hiked independently (but check with the RSCN first), whilst guided hikes offer visitors a unique opportunity to enjoy a stimulating walk and learn about the geology, wildlife, and history of Dana. Guides are available at the Rummana campsite, Dana village and Feynan. See map 19. The trails include the following options.

Route 66
Rummana Mountain Trail

Grade	Moderate walk
Details	2.5km
Time	1–2hrs

A circular walk to Rummana peak for an excellent view of Wadi Araba. Visitors will see an ancient cistern and some magnificent cliffs of sandstone and limestone, observe birds of prey, and view the beauty of the area with its juniper trees and early Islamic ruins.

Guide Not required.

Route 67
The Steppe Trail

Grade	Easy walk
Details	8km
Time	3hrs

The trail contours the huge escarpments of Wadi Dana between Rummana campsite and Dana village. It offers breathtaking views of the canyon-like wadi and passes through the terraced gardens before reaching the Dana guesthouse and Visitor Centre.

Guide Compulsory.

Route 68
Feynan Copper Mine Tour

Grade	Easy walk
Time	1–2hrs

Visit ancient copper mines, Iron Age sites, a Roman tower and the impressive tell of Khirbet Feynan, with its Byzantine churches and Christian and Islamic graves.

Guide Compulsory.

Route 69
Dana Cave Trail

Grade	Easy walk
Details	3km
Time	1½hrs round trip–2hrs

To abandoned cave shelters previously used by Bedouin shepherds and earlier inhabitants.

Route 70
Khirbet Sarab Trail

Grade	Easy walk
Details	2km
Time	1hr round trip

Special one, two- or three-day expeditions – including Routes 71–75 – can be arranged by the RSCN, providing opportunities to discover more about the Reserve and traditional Bedouin life.

Route 71
The Feynan Trail, Dana to Feynan

High over a green valley hangs the red mountain. Straight towards the hazy Arabah thrusts the deep valley, flanked by sheer precipices, enriched by woods and waters... the village of Dana spreads out fanwise on a fan-shaped buttress of rock... it looks so improbable.

In the Steps of Moses the Conqueror L. Golding (1938)

Grade	Moderate trek
Details	15km, descending from 1200m to 200m
Time	About 5hrs

A pleasant walk down the long valley that forms the core of the Dana Reserve. The orchards of Dana give way to wild and mountainous then more barren surroundings as the trail descends through changing ecosystems to ancient Feynan, once the site of notorious copper mines but now the considerably more hospitable location of an RSCN eco-lodge. See maps 19 and 21.

Guide RSCN approved guide required.
Approach The route starts in Dana village (GPS alt. 1230m N30° 40.511' E35° 36.607'); transport provided from the RSCN campsite.

The route
When we first did this trek in 1985, long before the Reserve was created, the route simply followed the old track from the village down steep hairpins for 2km to the floor of the valley, which was followed to what were then the ruins of Feynan. These days the RSCN guides have their own interesting variations on the route, passing some of the copper mines and other points of interest along the way.

The valley route is quite straightforward and most of it is visible from Dana village, from where the sands of Wadi Araba can be seen on the far horizon. The village is left by following the wide zigzag track down to the valley where there are numerous trees, including oak, pistachio, acacia and ziziphus in which the parasitic but pretty red acacia strap flower can be seen in spring.

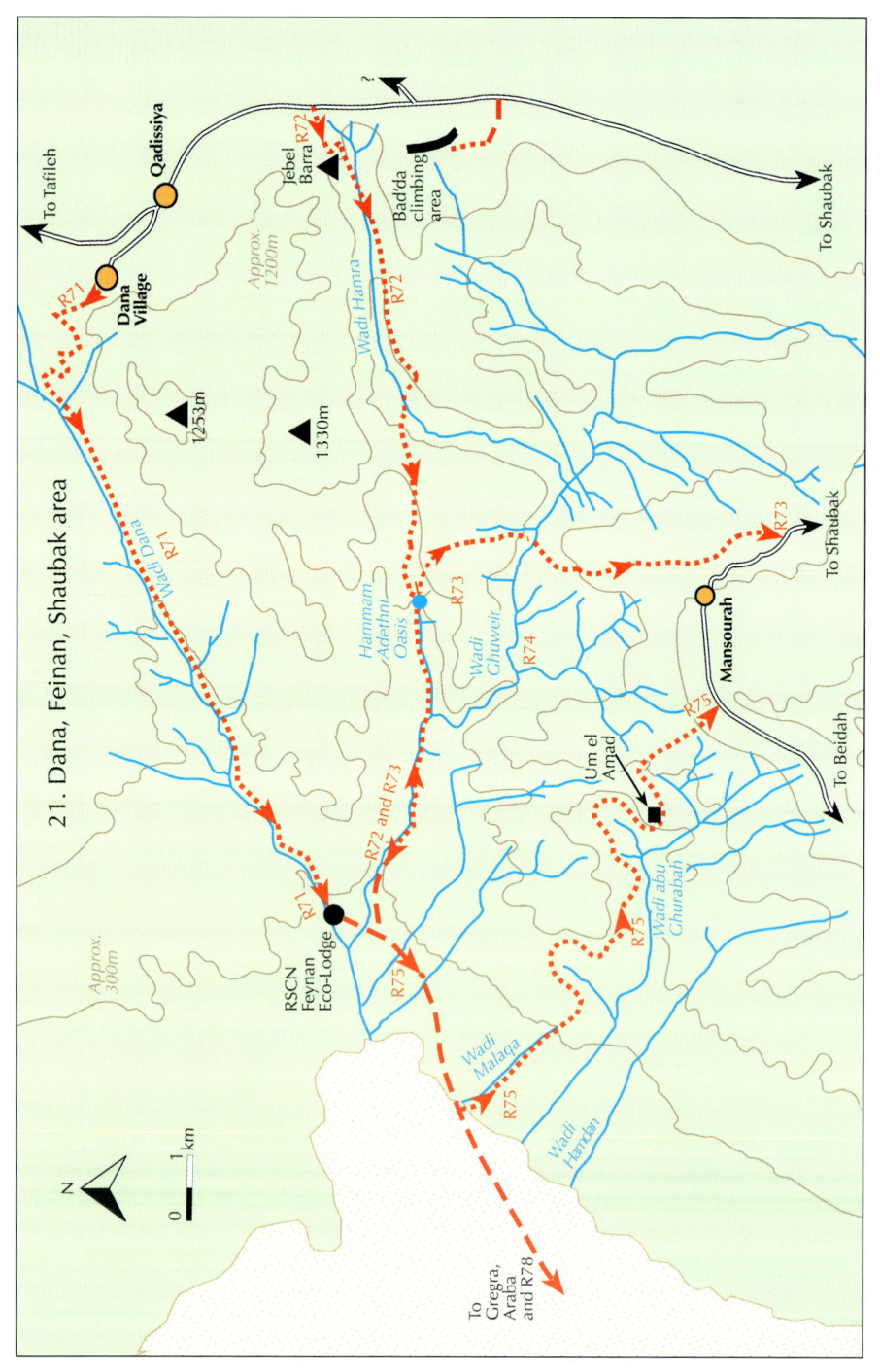

JORDAN

21. Dana, Feinan, Shaubak area

158

Looking down into Wadi Dana from Dana village

The valley continues 13km SW to Feynan Eco-Lodge. Just after reaching the valley floor (at around GPS alt. 760m N30° 40.567' E35° 35.603') leave the track for the riverbed (usually dry). After about 15mins a small path rises left up and out of the wadi, and along a rocky ledge, soon reaching the old track descending the hillside. Follow it down and along the left side of the river, passing a little stream and the halfway point (c2hrs) and eventually continuing opposite Roman copper mines visible high up on the right side (GPS alt. 520m N30° 39.588' E35° 33.336').

When the path divides at an upright stone, descend and cross the dry riverbed through bamboo and oleander, then up onto the right side and along before descending again and crossing a small stream between oleanders to rise up again on the left of the wadi. There may be Bedouin camps just beyond, where you may be asked in for tea. If you have plenty of food why not share it as a gesture of hospitality?

From there follow the main trail down the valley, crossing the river a couple of times before abruptly rounding a bend to arrive at the rather splendid Feynan Eco-Lodge (GPS alt. 320m N30° 38.371' E35° 30.541'). Prepare to be surprised!

Return If you need to return to Dana, RSCN can arrange transport from Feynan; alternatively continue on one of the following treks back up to the top, or to Petra. (Reversing Route 72 is also an option.)

FEYNAN

It had been a city, it had even been a Bishopric, but they had not served Christ here, but copper... Here died the Christian martyrs condemned by the pagan emperors, Maximinus and Diocletian. Here the Catholics were sent to die by the Aryan schismatics. St Sylvanus and thirty-three of his companions were beheaded here. The Egyptian Bishops, St Peleus and St Nile, all of them died, soon and terribly, only copper lived on. And then even that died, and the husks of it only remained, like heaps of blue-green baked rigid for all time in that gross heat.

In the Steps of Moses the Conqueror L. Golding (1938)

JORDAN

There is another excellent and varied trek down to Feynan from Dana along the S edge of the Reserve. To reach it it is usual to go by vehicle from Dana village or campsite, or you can walk. No guide is required for the trail between the campsite and village but an RSCN approved guide is compulsory for the walk from the village to the start of the trek at the head of Wadi Hamra. This approach has not been checked by the authors.

Route 72
Dana to Feynan via Wadi Hamra (the Red Valley)

Grade	Moderate trek
Details	20km, descending 450m before rising 150m to a pass and descending another 900m to the RSCN Eco-Lodge at Feynan, near the ancient copper mines
Time	Allow 7–8hrs

An outstanding trek through ever-changing scenery, descending from pretty sandstone domes and springtime flower-filled meadows past Nabataean tombs to a long valley with red sandstone cliffs. The route leaves this via a pass with good views before descending though juniper trees down to the lush wild oasis of Hammam Adethni beyond which the trek, despite its now barren and rugged surroundings, becomes quite aquatic, continuing in or next to water before emerging into the wilderness of Wadi Araba.

There is a great variety of wildlife due to the different ecosystems, including ibex and very big freshwater crabs. There are also many birds, including lesser kestrels and other raptors and the beautiful Palestinian sunbird. See map 21.

Guide Recommended.

Approach Go by vehicle from Dana campsite or village to a point on the King's Highway about 4–5km S of the Dana village junction, where a track goes right (W) for 1km to the white domes of Jebel Barra which can be seen from the King's Highway. The track ends close to the rocks, at which point Wadi Hamra (also called Wadi Sharir) is just below to the S but guarded by the domes.

Alternatively you can walk to Barra from Dana with an RSCN approved guide – a pleasant 2–3hrs along wooded hills with sandstone towers; this can be arranged at the Visitor Centre. There is yet another alternative start: the RSCN will sometimes drive people along the S side of Wadi Hamra, then enter by the donkey track which descends to its W end down a side valley with natural rock pools (see below). This saves 5 or 6km of walking but misses the nice entry down through the domes of Barra.

The route
To the left of the Jebel Barra domes a little valley will be seen between small white domes, which are left of the higher ones. Descend into it on white rock, and where the valley goes left continue directly W up slabs towards a finger of rock on the skyline. Pass left of the finger and scramble down towards the valley, but then contour left along a rock terrace to emerge at an antiquity site near Nuwatif – the Dripping Spring – and only 20m directly below the starting point. The path then winds down past carved Nabataean caves directly under the traverse ledge. Continue past some more rather 'upmarket' caves,

first on the left then on the right, and on into the valley beyond, which defines the S edge of the Reserve (½hr from start). The valley is full of herbs such as sweet-smelling artemisis (called *shia* by the Bedouin and used for upset stomachs). Here we saw lesser kestrels and the Palestinian sunbird. Eventually the path and valley descend below the white sandstone, reaching the red sandstone strata that gives the valley its name.

Lower down the path crosses the wadi to its left (S) side where numerous sheep tracks contour along the steep, sometimes scree-covered hillside 50–100m above the wadi, which narrows into a *siq* below. The path eventually meets the wadi again beyond the *siq* after about ¾hr in the valley (1¼hrs from the start). A good donkey track then rises up, still on the left side, zigzagging steeply then levelling out onto a shoulder and continuing across a small side wadi just below limestone slabs.

Follow the good path, descending slightly to reach a major side valley (1¾hrs from the start). The path crosses this below natural rock pools (dry in April) and continues as a good trail along and down the hillside to reach the bed of Wadi Hamra again just after passing between two small tops (2hrs from the start). Here is a key stage that must be followed carefully: immediately after the tops the path crosses a small side valley on the left. Leave it just beyond and walk down the actual bed of Wadi Hamra for about 200m, then leave this for a small side wadi on the right (N). Go up this for 50m, then take a good track rising diagonally up the right side of Wadi Hamra. Continue up this over a shoulder on top of the ridge, marked by a few trees on its left. Go through a small rocky pass to see Wadi Silwan and Wadi Hammam Adethni beyond and, in the distance, Wadi Araba (about 7km, 3¼hr from Wadi Hamra, 2¾hrs from the start).

A good track now descends NW between and over tilted limestone pavements and out onto a shoulder above a valley, then down and across small side wadis (a few cairns and small paths). Continue beyond, descending slightly again through an area of dead junipers (½hr from the pass). After another 10mins descend a rocky shoulder to a large cairn (which marks the edge of the Reserve), above the edge of the deep wadi. From here there are good views out W to the tree-filled wadi of Hammam Adethni. Beyond is a black cone-shaped summit, then the arid wastes of Araba (about 1hr from the pass).

Immediately ahead is a small red sandstone top. Descend to its foot and pass it on its left side. The black cone and green wadi are now directly ahead. Follow the crest of the ridge until it ends on a small black top. The palm-filled wadi is now directly below. Descend by a gully just back from the top, then follow the donkey track as it zigzags steeply down the shattered black rock to reach the abrupt edge of the oasis.

Nabataean tomb on the Wadi Hamra trek

Entering Wadi Hamra over the domes of Jebel Barra

Cross the small permanent stream and go though a 'forest' of fragmites reeds on the S bank, just left of a magnificent cluster of date palms. The path then goes W for a short way past oleanders, figs and other trees to reach a clear area and a permanent 'sacred spring' revered by local Bedouin. (The actual source is in a small pool just behind the palm tree where the water can be seen rising up in the bottom of the pool). It should still be a nice place for lunch though it was damaged by a flash flood in winter 2005–6 (about 12km, 1¼hrs from the pass, 4¼hrs from the start). Surprisingly there are freshwater crabs and snails here.

Now follow the path as it descends back to the wadi through the fragmites jungle, then down the thickly vegetated streambed for a short way before gaining the right bank. Follow the stream along on a path just above it, through an area of pink granite boulders, then alongside and finally in the stream until you reach the junction with the fast-flowing Wadi Ghuweir (see Route 74), ¼hr from the spring. Here take some time out to walk up there for 10mins or so to appreciate the magnificent rock scenery of this deep canyon, but watch your toes – there are king-size crabs there!

Back at the junction continue down the river through a long and beautiful black canyon (a lot of river-hopping – expect wet feet) for about 1hr, to reach a weir about 7hrs from the start. If you have made arrangements you can be met here by 4WD, otherwise you must continue either by a short-cut (see Route 74) or, longer, go another 1km down the river to where the valley opens out and the river disappears into the stones. About 2km further down the stony wadi bed a track will be reached. Follow it right (N) for 3km to Feynan (GPS alt. 320m N30° 30.38.371' E35° 30.541') and its striking eco-lodge (it's far better to have a vehicle for the last section!).

Return See Route 71.

THE SHAUBAK AREA

The next route leaves Feynan in the Dana Reserve, returning to the King's Highway via Shaubak Castle, starting up the lower half of Route 72 (it would be possible to start from Dana and combine Routes 72 and 73 without descending the last section to Feynan).

Guides and accommodation
Whilst the RSCN are able to offer guiding services – especially for routes that pass through their Dana Reserve – other guides and adventure travel companies in Jordan, especially in Wadi Musa, also know the area. A good local contact for all the routes in the Shaubak area is Abu Seif (see Appendix 1). He owns a campsite below the fortress (18JD per night half-board) which is handy for local treks. He can also arrange transport to the start of your trek and meet you at the end. Mansourah, at the end of Route 73 and start of Route 74, is about 9km down the road. As an ex-hunter, Abu Seif knows the area extremely well; he has been recommended to us and can also arrange a local guide.

As well as the facilities already mentioned in Dana there are Bedouin tourist camps in Beidah and numerous hotels in Wadi Musa (see the following chapter on Petra). The nearest accommodation to the start of Route 73 is the Feynan Eco-Lodge.

Route 73
Feynan to Shaubak via Wadi Hammam Adethni

Grade	Moderate trek
Details	14km, ascending from 200m to 1200m with an intermediate ascent and descent of about 300m
Time	Allow 5–6hrs

Takes Route 72 in reverse up Wadi Adethni to the oasis, then rises over wild hills to descend S into Wadi Ghuweir (Wadi Shaubak), leaving that almost immediately to climb up to Mansourah, thence by road to Shaubak. (Information supplied by Jalel Bouagga, not checked by the authors.) Map 21.

Guide Recommended.

Approach Best started with 4WD either from the RSCN Eco-Lodge at Feynan, or from Gregra, signed off the highway in Wadi Araba and accessible from Shaubak down the recently surfaced and spectacular road from Beidah to Wadi Araba. Drive up the lower reaches of Wadi Adethni (Route 73 in reverse) until the first signs of water are met as you enter the gorges and canyons and find oleanders and tamarisk.

The route
Now on foot, note the appearance of several springs; the higher you go up the wadi the more abundant the water and vegetation. Continue walking in the wadi (wading through the water) until you find two tributaries, Wadi Ghuweir going straight on (see below) and (to the left) Wadi Hammam Adethni. Go up Wadi Hammam Adethni. At the start the path is not visible, and the vegetation becomes very dense as the oasis is approached, with abundant palm trees, oleanders, tamarisk and fragmites rushes at the sides of the wadi and in the depths of the canyon: a unique forest amidst barren hills. (Much of the lush vegetation was damaged by a flash flood in the winter of 2005–2006, but hopefully it will regenerate.) There is a lot of water in the stream and a hidden spring in the oasis (see Route 73), but no visible spring until you arrive at a small col that dominates the small forest, where a tiny spring flows from a little 'grotto' under a large tree.

From there the view ahead is clear. Route 73 comes down the main valley slightly N of E, whilst another narrow path (hard to see at first) goes E then SE for 1km towards the mountain, reaching a col at about 1000m. Further on descend to cross Wadi Ghuweir where there is an abandoned 4WD track that leads to the village of Mansourah, a small town with terraced fields (alt. 1200m). The asphalt road leads to the castle at Shaubak 9km above.

Return There is local transport available to Wadi Musa or Dana.

The wadi from the Adethni oasis is also passed by Route 74, this time descending from Shaubak Castle down Wadi Ghuweir (see above). This impressive wadi system starts in the hills E of Shaubak and descends through an increasingly deep and impressive canyon to meet Wadi Hammam Adethni about 5km SSE of the RSCN Eco-Lodge at Feynan.

Route 74
Wadi Ghuweir to Feynan

The Lord had announced he would not give [the Israelites] of the Edomite land... because he had given Mount Seir unto Esau for possession. It may have seemed wise to get down to the plain again, perhaps by the Wadi Shobek [Wadi Ghuweir] to Punon [Feynan] and then march northward again.

In the Steps of Moses the Conqueror L. Golding (1938)

Grade	Moderate canyon
Details	16–22km either way, descending 1000m. Possibly some flooded sections, which can be shoulder-deep, but may only be shallow pools in the autumn (take waterproof bags). Some grade 2 scrambles necessary over boulders and down a waterfall.
Time	6–8hrs dependent on choice of route (or camp along the way). If you are not being met by a vehicle allow another ½hr to walk out the extra 2km to Feynan Eco-Lodge (see Route 72).

This is an excellent canyon trip descending from Shaubak to Wadi Araba. It combines stunning canyon scenery with some sections of scrambling and the likelihood of deep pools. (Details supplied by Geraldine Chatelard, not checked by the authors.) See map 21.

Special requirements There are some grade 2 scrambles, so a short safety rope may be useful. Pack your gear in waterproof bags in your rucksack. Beware of flash floods.

Guide Recommended for those without canyoning experience; ask at RSCN Dana, or Abu Seif in Shaubak, or see other contacts in Appendix 1.

Approach Drive down the road from Shaubak to Mansoura; if necessary arrange for the driver to meet you at the end of the route.

The route
Tracks leave the road either at Mansourah or 2km before at El Muqar'iyah, and descend N and NNE respectively reaching Wadi Ghuweir after about 4km, 1hr. The route then descends the wadi, initially wide, flowing between white limestone cliffs and oleanders. It narrows after about 20mins as it descends into red sandstone. Continue easily with some scrambling until, about 1½hrs from the start of the wadi, a 2m waterfall with a pool below is reached (impassable on left). Go right, up rocks, and behind a large boulder before descending past the waterfall (some grade 2).

About 15mins further on there is another 2m waterfall and pool. It is possible to descend the fall by bridging with hands and feet between the walls (safety rope useful) before passing the sacks down. Take care with them in the pool, which can be shoulder-deep for about 20m. (At times the waterfall and pool may be dry and the descent easier.) This is the last difficult section.

About ½hr further on the barren canyon fills with lush vegetation: tall palms, wild figs, huge oleanders, ferns on walls dripping with water. The wadi continues until Wadi Hammam Adethni is met (the hot springs are quite a way upstream) about 5–6 hrs from Mansourah (possible campsite with a 'frog chorus'!).

From the confluence it's 1½hrs through black gorges and another 1hr in the wadi bed to reach a point where a 4WD can be met (arranged in advance).

Alternatively, if you have arranged to overnight at Feynan Eco-Lodge, it's possible to walk there: after the black gorges (see Route 72) cross the low, dark red ridges on the right (NNE) and continue in a similar direction to reach the SW exit of Wadi Dana where the lodge is located (½hr, GPS alt. 320m N30° 30.38.371' E35° 30.541'). If you miss this short cut it's necessary to walk for 45mins down the wadi to reach a sign on the right, then follow the track back N for 3km to Feynan, adding at least another 1hr to the walk.

Return See Route 71, or Route 75 which returns to Shaubak from Feynan, passing a Roman copper mine.

Exploring the lower reaches of Wadi Ghuweir

Route 75
Feynan to Mansourah (And Shaubak) via Um el Amad

...even the hardened criminals who are condemned to the mines of Phaenon, do not survive there many more than a few days... the wretches passing from an outer to an inner hell, from the airless oven of the Arabah in high mid-summer, to the furnace heats of the mine galleries. I saw the yellow faces, and the leathery lips and green copper-dust in the sunken hollows of their eyes. It was a mercy after all, was it not, they did not survive here more than a few days.

In the Steps of Moses the Conqueror Louis Golding (1938)

Grade	Moderate trek
Details	16km, rising from 200m to 1360m
Time	5hrs

Uphill all the way but no less enjoyable for that! The route goes through some wild country with constantly changing scenery and good views out over Wadi Araba. The journey is split halfway by a visit to the Roman copper mines of Um el Amad – Mother of Columns – and finishes on the small road 2km W of Mansourah. See map 21.

Guide Recommended.

Approach Drive about 4km WSW from Feynan Eco-Lodge (or approach from Gregra, GPS alt. 170m N30° 32.410' E35° 24.321') until just past some ruins, where the trek starts (not obvious).

The route
Head SSE up Wadi M'della along its right (true left) bank. At the head of the wadi (½hr) a donkey track zigzags up slightly left to a small gap in a rocky col with good views SW to Wadi Araba. Turn left here and go up the rocky ridge over a small shoulder to gain a broader ridge beyond. Follow this up and take an improving track up its right side to the next shoulder (1hr from the start).

Keep on the track, rising across the right flank again and up to the saddle beyond, ¼hr from the last shoulder. An old 4WD track will be seen below. Descend towards it and go left on a path 50m above it on rock ledges, to descend to the track a little further on round the bend (1½hrs from start). Follow the abandoned track as it descends into a wild mountain valley with a canyon below and cliffs above.

The track makes a big swing round the valley and up the opposite side to reach a pass cut through the ridge with more excellent views S. Continue on the track as it curves E and ends at the mines of Um el Amad (2½hrs from start), above the ravine of Wadi abu Ghurabah. Time to take a rest and contemplate the terrible lives of the copper mine slaves. There is no architectural finesse here, just industrial austerity carved out by slave labour: the rough columns of rock left standing to support the roof and the small recesses in the walls for oil lamps are simply concessions to necessity. This was a place of incessant hammering, dust, darkness and death; you will leave it glad to be alive and free to escape into the mountains beyond.

Back outside, and high above to the left of the wadi (right of Um el Amad looking up), a narrow rocky pass will be seen above a gully with many juniper trees. Scramble up into it to find a donkey track that then zigzags up into a spectacular and beautiful area of white sandstone domes. Continue up to the pass (40mins from Um el Amad) from where the distant flat-topped hills of Shaubak can be seen to the SE.

In the hills above the Roman copper mines of Um el Amad, looking out over the desert of Wadi Araba

Go left up the rocky ridge for 100m or so then right on small paths (a few cairns), descending and ascending but basically contouring along above the upper valley of Wadi abu Ghurabah, 'Valley of the Ravens', and level with a plateau of small domes on its opposite side. Continue on the donkey track, gaining the shoulder up to the left towards the next top, well worn between domes, to reach a summit (just over 1hr from the mines, 3½hrs from the start). From the little top (good views) head directly SE across flat white sandstone forming the divide between two wadi systems to the NE and SW. Head for the high flat summit to the SE. Continue in the same line up a convenient slope and up again to pass the right end of a long limestone encampment (1hr from the domes). At this point the good track goes right a short way before regaining its original SE line which is followed up to meet a good 4WD track (1½hrs from the domes). Mansourah is 2km to the left.

Return Shaubak Castle is another 9km up the road from Mansourah, from where a taxi or small bus can be taken. Otherwise, arrange to be met on the Mansourah road by the RSCN or whoever you have organised the walk with.

MANSOURAH

About 17km S of Dana on the King's Highway there is a junction with a major road leading to the Desert Highway. A further 4km S of this there is a sign to Mansourah on the right. Follow this down for 9km to the end of the road. There are fine views down the wadis towards the ancient site of Feynan at the junction of Wadi Dana and Wadi Ghuweir, and also towards Wadi Araba.

The road also passes through Abu Makhlub 3km from the highway, where there are many old cave dwellings still in use. Just past here, coming back up to the highway, it is possible to turn right and wind up a narrow steep wadi directly to Shaubak Castle. This unusual angle of approach gives a true appreciation of its commanding situation.

SHAUBAK CASTLE

...suddenly the earth fell before us into a great arena where diverse wadis met and swept together... to a breast-like hill commanding all that country. And on top of that hill was a circuit of stout stone walls, embayed, enkeepened and battlemented, and that was Shobek of the Crusaders, of Christian swashbucklers that had captured Jerusalem stretching forth a mailed fist southward towards the unconquered and unconquerable spices of Arabia.

In the Steps of Moses the Conqueror L. Golding (1938)

The classical hilltop Crusader fortress of Shaubak does indeed stand in a commanding position above the complex network of wadis that descend W and NW to Feynan from the edge of the King's Highway. There also used to be a big forest around Shaubak, which Doughty commented on in his classic *Arabia Deserta* in 1888: 'This limestone moorland, of so great altitude resembles Europe, and there are hollows, park-like with evergreen oak timber.' Sadly the timber was mostly used as fuel for the Turkish trains on the Hejaz Railway during World War I, but there are still remnants of these old forests on the rolling hills between Shaubak and Petra, providing pleasant walking country high above the wilderness of Wadi Araba (though now crisscrossed by small roads).

Route 76
Shaubak to Beidah

...suddenly there burst into view a thousand or fifteen hundred feet lower down and not more than three or four miles away, a wonderful mass of castellated peaks, domes, pinnacles and other fantastic shapes, with indescribable colouring, from snow-white at the base, to purple and yellow and crimson higher up, bathed and transformed in the brilliant sunshine till it seemed like an enchanted fairy tale.

The Jordan Valley and Petra Libbey and Hoskins (1905)

Grade	Easy walk
Details	22km
Time	Approx 5hrs

This route is sometimes walked by groups but has not been checked. It is mostly roadwork (information supplied by Jalel Bouagga).

The route
From Shaubak go towards the village at the side of the King's Highway and continue along this for 2km to a sign left to Zaytouna village (radar station behind). Here take a narrow track right for 3–4km. This track becomes a narrow path that leads directly towards a hill. Pass through the village of Huorala then over a small col before arriving in a forest of green oak trees. A narrow road now goes down to Beidah and as far as Siq al Barrid (the Cold Canyon) with excellent views towards Petra. There is accommodation near Beidah (otherwise known as Little Petra) in either of two Bedouin tourist camps: the Ammarin, which belongs to the Beidah co-operative, and the Helali (details in following chapter on Petra, and in Appendix 1).

There is also said to be a very scenic route passing Roman and other sites of antiquity in the valleys below the Mansourah–Beidah road, reaching Beidah via Wadi Hudeith, Wadi Thugra and Siq um el Hiran (see section on Petra, the Northern Approaches; not checked, but it looks like very nice country from above). The ruins of what the Bedouin call 'Al Kutlah Palace' (map 22) are also in this area. Starting in these hills and finishing at Wadi abu Sakakin (see below) is another canyon trip – Route 77 – that French guide, Wilfried Colonna says is excellent.

Route 77
Wadi Feid

A full day descending a remarkable wadi from the hills N of Beidah to Wadi abu Sakakin (Route 78) and Wadi Araba, with 12 waterfalls descended by abseil and equipped by Wilf Colonna in 2007 (max 24m). It was reported in April 2008 that the abseil points have been deliberately smashed part way down, making it impossible to continue or retreat unless you are carrying your own drill and equipment. (Not checked by the authors; see *Trekking and Canyoning in the Jordanian Dead Sea Rift*, Appendix 2.) See map 22.

Finally there are at least two trails that descend from Dana to Feynan before ascending these hills to Petra via the wadis and mountains around Wadi abu Sakakin, just S of Route 75. These trails can be continued to Wadi Rum and Aqaba, forming what some call the **Nabataean Trail**. Route 78 is part of one of these treks, continuing from Beidah to Petra and Wadi Musa via Route 79 (Days 4 and 5). Instead of starting from Dana, the route can also be done as a one-day trek in its own right, driving in from Wadi Araba and finishing at Beidah.

Route 78
Feynan to Beidah via Wadi abu Sakakin and Wadi abu Mahmud

Wadi abu Sakakin, or the Canyon of Knives, was named after the many small basalt stones found there and once used for hunting knives. The campsite at the end of the trek is called Sh'karet M'Said meaning Said's Garden. Said lived there with his family over seventy years ago, growing tomatoes, olives and eggplants. Sadly, none remain after a fight between the Hasanat tribe and M'Saidia tribe, who left to Bir Madhkhur. That was about 1931; my father was there and was 14 years old at the time. He told me this story when I let a man from the M'Saidia tribe put his goats in our land for a night.

Yousef Hasanat, Via Jordan Tours

Grade	Serious trek
Details	13km, climbing up from 200m to 1000m with around 200m of descent, making 1000m of ascent in total; route finding complex due to waterfalls and cliffs blocking the canyon
Time	6–9hrs

A fairly arduous trek and scramble, mostly in savage surroundings, with impressive basalt cliffs rising dramatically above. Whilst the intention is to follow the canyon, numerous unexpected ascents and descents are necessary, sometimes on steep pathless terrain, to avoid cliffs. There is usually water at the start, and a spring higher up, just before rising up into the gentler pastel-hued sandstone hills where the going gets easier and the scenery more open. See map 22.

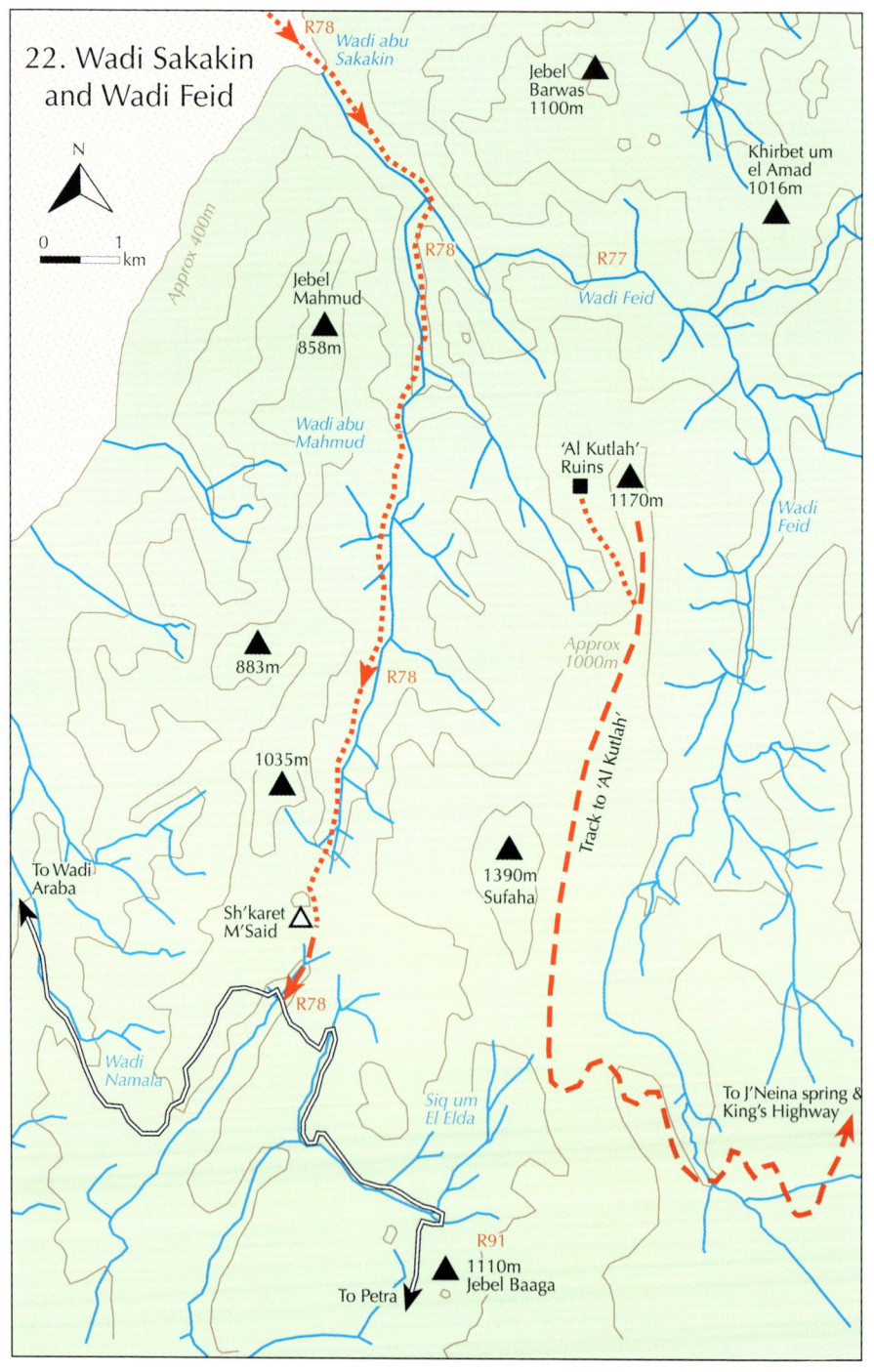

Jordan

22. Wadi Sakakin and Wadi Feid

Special requirements A vehicle is necessary to get you through the rock-strewn desert of Wadi Araba with its savannah-like acacia trees to the start of the canyon, and also to meet you at the end of the trek. For this reason (as well as the complexity of the route) it is usual – if not essential – to organise the trek with a local travel agent who will provide the vehicles and a guide. We did the trek with Jordan Beauty Tours of Wadi Musa, who had a camp and food ready at the end of the trek. Alternatively you could be driven 10km from there to Beidah where the Ammarin Bedouin camp provides excellent facilities. Wadi Musa is not far beyond.

Having no overnight gear to carry meant we had minimal weight and took only a small amount of water, drinking straight from the stream where possible. Others may prefer to carry more water or to use water purifiers.

Guide Required.

Approach If you start by walking down from Dana village (as we did) you will probably spend your first night at the Feynan Eco-Lodge. From there, with any luck, a vehicle will get you to the canyon, probably passing through Gregra, a village in Wadi Araba where water and basic provisions can be bought. From there our driver – who was unfamiliar with the area – failed to find a way through the rough, boulder-strewn terrain to the canyon mouth, necessitating an additional 1hr walk to get to the start of the trek (GPS alt. 230m N30° 32.199' E35° 25.632'). Best to make an early start to allow for problems!

The route

Enter the wadi between canyon cliffs, which close in and rise higher as you follow the stream through oleanders and fragmites reeds to reach a waterfall (GPS alt. 360m N30° 31.309' E35° 25.542') – the first obstacle is just beyond. Jebel Barwas, 1140m (see Route 79) is the mountain to the left (NE), Jebel abu Mahmud, 1121m – otherwise known as the Black Mountain – is to the SW. Climb the left side of the waterfall, cross its top and ascend the right bank steeply on rock and scree for 100m or more to reach a shoulder (GPS alt. 500m N30° 31.156' E35° 26.603') and view up beyond a split in the canyon. Wadi abu Sakakin continues SE to join Wadi Feid (Route 77); Wadi abu Mahmud goes to the S.

Descend steep terrain with equal care to enter Wadi abu Mahmud, only to repeat the experience a little further on (5km from the start), climbing back up to the second col (GPS alt. 500m N30° 30.671' E35° 26.707'). Descend again, still surrounded by impressive cliffs, especially those of Hathbut al Fayuth to the E. After more forced exits to the right – some with small tracks – the way leaves the wadi again, once more rising up to follow a pleasant path in sandstone rocks, again above the right side of the wadi, returning to it to reach a pool and spring at GPS alt. 690m N30° 28.832' E35° 26.593' (about 9km from the start).

You are now reaching the headwaters of the canyon where the trek continues up the S tributary and the sandstone scenery is less savage. A white patch on a cliff is your next marker (GPS alt. 760m N30° 28.445' E35° 26.493'). Pass beneath it and rise gently up, this time on the left side of the wadi (alt. 800m) where there are some impressive old juniper trees. As the hills open out head for a pass on the left side of a prominent dome (GPS alt. 1000m N30° 27.333' E35° 26.242'). Just below, a convenient purple slate ledge forms a pathway contouring south for 1km to the obvious saddle of Sh'karet M'Said, which is behind a rocky tor (GPS alt. 1000m N30° 26.893' E35° 26.282').

This was the location of our campsite. Next day – although the trek to Petra can be continued on foot (see below) – we were driven 2km to the road up Wadi Namala and up it through the pretty Wadi um el Elda (Valley of Oaks) to Beidah, 10km away. With time short – and having missed what would have been the usual third day – the route was then picked up in Beidah and the trek continued to Wadi Musa through Petra via Route 84, giving three very contrasting days.

There is a better-known route – Route 79 – from Dana to Feynan and Petra that has received some promotion from the Jordan Tourism Board (not checked by the authors, but said to be very scenic). Jordan Beauty Tours have supplied the following details.

JORDAN

Route 79
Dana to Petra via Ras Feid

Grade	Serious trek
Details	About 60km (80km in 6 days for the whole route) descending and climbing about 1500m
Time	4 days for the shorter trek, 6 days for the whole route

A four- to six-day trek in varied and wild scenery, starting from the village of Dana. Beyond the Reserve the trek passes through the desert of Wadi Araba before climbing back up through the canyons and savage mountains N and E of Wadi abu Sakakin (Knives Canyon) to the gentler domes of Little Petra, and on to Petra itself if desired, for a triumphal finale. See maps 21, 22 and 23.

Approach As for Route 71.

Special requirements The route between Feynan and Beidah is complex, so it is usual – if not essential (as with the trek through Wadi abu Sakakin) – to organise the trek with a local travel agent or guide who will set up pre-arranged camps to save you carrying excess weight. If desired, the company will also drive you from Feynan to Sakakin and also up the road from the last camp either to Wadi Musa, or to the start of a day's walk through Petra. (Only parts of this trek have been done by the authors.)

The route
Day 1 Dana – Feynan (Route 71) 15km, 5hrs

Day 2 Feynan – Wadi Araba 16km, 6hrs
The route crosses stony desert, with many acacias at 300m with jagged mountains rising up to 1400m to the E. To the NW open desert descends towards the Dead Sea. The morning's route passes several small hills before heading out across open desert towards Wadi Barwaz at the foot of the mountains. From there it's SW into the desert of Wadi Araba, descending across hamada into a region of small sand dunes, giving a true sense of real desert landscape, before camp is reached at 380m for what will almost certainly be a night under amazingly clear starry skies.

Day 3 Wadi Araba – Ras Feid 10km, 6–8hrs
The trek now rises gradually across the desert to Wadi abu Sakakin (Route 78) at the foot of the mountains. From there a steeper ascent across small boulders and rocks reaches the foot of a steep and twisty track going high into the mountains – a particularly challenging section. This is a remote but beautiful region with spectacular views W into Wadi Araba. It continues up to a high saddle (about 800m), reached after 4hrs. Good views into the heart of these wild mountains before descending to the river valley on a small, steep and twisty track. The route then descends back into the impressive Sakakin Canyon (Route 78) for 1km before making camp above the river at Ras Feid at about 800m.

Day 4 Ras Feid – Shkaret M'Said 15km, 8–9hrs
Backtrack up the Sakakin Canyon to an area of reeds. From there the track becomes tougher as it gradually climbs back up into the hills on paths used by Bedouin as they move with their animals from the desert to higher and cooler areas for the summer. The views of the surrounding mountains and down to

the desert below are outstanding. This takes about 2hrs, with some steep climbs and rocky descents, but the rewards are superb. Eventually the route climbs up to a pass with tremendous views across the mountains and desert beyond, and also to the destination and camp at Sh'karet M'Said at 1000m (see Route 78), which is reached by descending and following the wadi up. This is a tough day in some challenging terrain.

Sh'karet M'Said is accessible by 4WD, so the trek can be ended here (Wadi Musa is not far by road through the pretty Wadi um el Elda); alternatively you can miss Day 5 and be driven as far as Beidah then continue on foot (as for Day 6) through Petra to Wadi Musa. For the complete trek, continue as follows.

Day 5 Sh'karet M'Said – Beidah 14km, 5hrs
The scenery now changes from deep wadis to open sandstone hills with a variety of trails and some cut steps, the first signs of Nabataean influence. There may also be some Bedouin camps. The track winds up through the sandstone domes with some short scrambles before an easy descent into Beidah on 4WD tracks.

Day 6 Beidah – Petra – Wadi Musa 10km, 5hrs
Continue via Route 84 past the Monastery, a competitor to the Treasury in magnificence and in an unrivalled setting, then down the well-worn Nabataean steps to Petra (reversing Route 83) and up though the *siq* (Route 81) to Wadi Musa.

Another possible guided route – Route 80 – goes for five days between Dana and Petra through some beautiful and varied country in the hills E of Route 79 (through which Route 75 passes).

Route 80
Dana to Petra via Um el Amad

Day 1 Dana to Wadi Ghuweir (via Route 72). Camp.
Day 2 Wadi Ghuweir – Hammam Adethni – Wadi Abu Nakheel – Mgair'iah. Camp.
Day 3 Mgair'iah – Wadi Ballout – Um el Amad – Sufaha. Camp.
Day 4 Sufaha – Heisha – Beidah. Camp.
Day 5 Beidah – Petra – Wadi Musa (via Routes 84, 83 and 81, Day 6).

For further information on this and other trails in the area contact Jordan Beauty Tours, Wadi Musa, or any of the Wadi Musa or other specialist Jordanian trekking companies (see Appendix 1).

Next is the legendary Petra, which offers numerous excellent walks and treks.

JORDAN

The awesome canyon of Tibn Siq (Routes 110, 112) – note the cliff slides scoured by water to a height of 5m

THE PETRA AREA

Strange and horrible as a pit, in an inhuman deadness of nature, is this site of the Nabataean's metropolis; the eye recoils from that mountainous close of iron cliffs, in which the ghastly waste monuments of a sumptuous barbaric art are from the first glance an eyesore.

Travels in Arabia Deserta Charles M. Doughty (1888)

Despite Doughty's apparent abhorrence of Petra it cannot be denied that this renowned ancient city and World Heritage Site is truly magnificent, a 'must' for anyone visiting Jordan. Hidden in the heart of the Shara Mountains it is one of the most fascinating sites of antiquity in the Middle East, and was declared one of the 'New Seven Wonders of the World' in July 2007 – all of which means it is extremely popular with tourists. However, most visitors don't have the time or inclination to get beyond the old city in the Petra Basin, probably including a visit to the High Place and a pilgrimage to Ed Deir, the Monastery... but there's much more to Petra than that.

Make an early start, stay late, or get off the beaten track and you soon lose the crowds. You could spend weeks in Petra and not see it all. If you go beyond the old city on the Nabataean and Roman trails you can walk for days through unique scenery, passing remnants of civilisations dating back over 10,000 years, without seeing anyone. You can link into mountain treks from the hilltop Nabataean eyrie of Selah, north of Dana, or walk all the way south on ancient caravan routes over mountains and deserts to Wadi Rum, and even to Aqaba.

Basically Petra includes the area between Beidah and Sabra, west of the Petra entrance gates and including the mountains to the west down to the edge of Wadi Araba. Beyond to the east is the desert of the Hisma, whilst the old Nabataean caravanserai of Humeimah is to the south, en route to Wadi Rum and Aqaba (see the following chapter). The best way in for any first-time visitor to Petra is undoubtedly via the famous Siq, the world-famous narrow canyon that emerges at the Treasury. There are, however, numerous other trails into and around Petra. Regardless of the route you take you will need a permit for the requisite number of days, which can be obtained from the Visitor Centre. Information on the Petra Archaeological Park will be found at http://nabataea.net/ppark.html.

FEES AND PERMITS

Petra, entrance fees and permits
- 1 day: 21JD
- 2 Days: 26JD
- 3 Days: 31JD
- Under 15s free

There is no charge for additional days, but your permit should still state the number of days required. The cost for Jordanians is 1JD per day.

The Petra tourist police

The tourist police are there to protect the site and for your safety, and will even be found in remote places such as Jebel Harun. Naturally, some speak only Arabic; the more zealous ones may try to stop you going 'off the beaten track' without a guide. Although guides are usually good company and obviously enhance safety, many experienced trekkers prefer to go it alone. If this is your choice it could be useful to carry a note in Arabic explaining that you are experienced and capable of trekking without a guide, that you are using this book (written with the knowledge and approval of the Petra Authority), and that you have left details of your route and expected time of return at your hotel or with a responsible person.

Walking through 'the Siq' into Petra – possibly the most stunning approach to any city (Route 81)

THE PETRA AREA

Accommodation and transport

Approaching from Dana and Shaubak in the north there is accommodation near Beidah and Siq el Barrid in either of two Bedouin tourist camps: the Helali (25JD B&B) and the Ammarin (which belongs to the Beidah co-operative, 11JD per night or 17JD B&B). Guiding services are also available (see Appendix 1).

In Wadi Musa there is accommodation to suite all pockets and tastes. Prices go from around 16–22JD per double B&B at places like the Musa Spring, the Diamond, Sunset and Al Anbat (where there is also camping at 5JD). Leila and Harun Daqlalah do B&B at their home for around 15JD, as do some other families (see Appendix 1). Going upmarket you can pay $160 or more at international hotels such as the Mövenpick; in between are those such as the Silk Road and Petra Moon at around 27JD and the Edom at 33JD. Further south along the King's Highway there are more new hotels springing up, the furthest away being the award-winning converted village of Taybet Zamman (from 80JD per double B&B).

The Petra area is well served by local and express transport services. The bus from Amman costs 2JD and takes less than 3hrs; buses to Aqaba and Wadi Rum also cost about 2JD (ask at your Wadi Musa hotel or the Rum Rest House if coming from there). There are also service taxis and private taxis, which charge 20–25JD to Aqaba or Wadi Rum.

Guides

If you have sufficient experience you can go without a guide, but you may wish to go by camel or horse (there are treks all the way to Wadi Rum) or simply to enjoy the company of a guide who knows the area well. There are some very good local Bedouin guides in Wadi Musa, B'dul and Beidah, and some good adventure travel companies and guides operating from Amman, Wadi Musa, Wadi Rum and Aqaba. For information call at the Visitor Centre near the entrance to Petra in lower Wadi Musa, or contact any of the companies listed in Appendix 1, three of whose offices are just up the road past the Mövenpick Hotel.

Maps

The following 1:50,000 topographical K737 series map covers this section. You are unlikely to be able to get hold of this, but enquire at the Jordanian Royal Geographical Centre in Amman (see 'Maps' in the Introduction)

- 3050–1, 3050–11, 3049–1: Petra, Sabra, Humeimah areas

There are also a number of quite good maps of the Petra Basin in the various Jordan travel guides and in guidebooks specific to Petra. The Royal Geographical Centre (see Introduction) also produces a good map which is available from hotels and bookshops. None of them, however, go much beyond the old city, which is where the real adventures begin.

RSCN Reserves

A huge new RSCN Nature Reserve is planned in the wild mountains immediately south of Petra. Announced in November 2007 as part of the Rift Valley Project, the northern boundary of the Jebel Mas'uda Reserve will extend westwards from Taybeh on the King's Highway along the line of Wadi Tibn (Route 110) and through Lower Wadi Sabra (Route 115) to the foothills near the Wadi Araba road. Its eastern boundary follows the road from Taybeh south to Rajif then runs southeast to Bir Hamad (Route 118), then on west into Wadi Araba.

As a consequence, Routes 109–115 and the various treks from Petra to Rum (see Route 118) will come within the Reserve, which may make entrance fees, guides and advance booking necessary; it may also limit numbers of people in the area. Hopefully, as these routes are well established, the RSCN will continue – as in Rum – to allow those who are competent enough to do so to experience the true freedom of the hills, to bivouac under the stars and to trek without guides. Check with the RSCN (see Appendix 1).

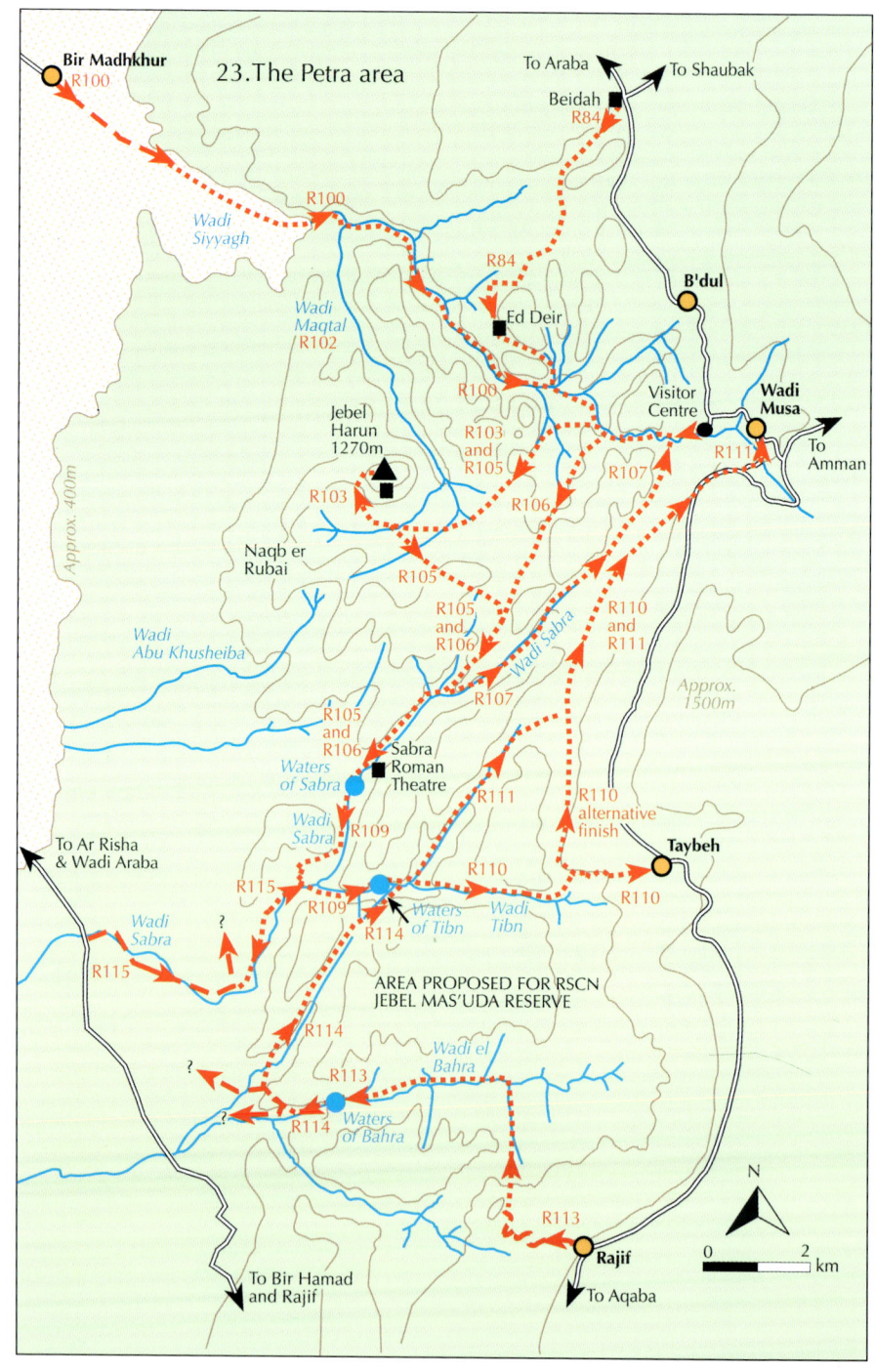

JORDAN

23. The Petra area

PETRA

The green slopes end suddenly and the gnome-like mountains begin, so split and cut by millions of crevices that the whole mass is always filled with small patches and pockets of shadow. In the heart of these grotesque mountains is the mysterious city of Petra. ...I have noticed that some mountains, although fantastic from a distance, are apt to become quite ordinary when you approach them. But that is not true of Petra. In fact the grotesque eruption becomes even more grotesque as you draw nearer to it. The Valley of the Dead at Luxor is a cheerful place in comparison with these mountains, which are like the blue, devil-haunted landscapes which early Italian painters have put behind their saints. They are so weird and ominous I was grateful for the sound of the horses stumbling among the stones.

In the Steps of The Master H. V. Morton (1934)

So it wasn't only the formidable Doughty who found Petra a foreboding place! It's interesting to see how opinions differ: these 'gnome-like' mountains are to most eyes marvellous. Walking into Petra through its world famous Siq – that dramatic chasm splitting the mountains – provides what must be the most remarkable entrance to any city: an unforgettable experience. Once you have become familiar with the main sights of the old city and the view from the High Place, you may wish to spend more days in this beautiful part of Jordan, and look a little further into the quieter, less-frequented parts of Petra.

For example a visit to Ed Deir, 'the Monastery', situated high above Wadi es Siyyagh and the distant Wadi Araba, can be combined with a walk through one of Petra's three northern valleys, or to Beidah, the 9000-year-old Pleistocene settlement and nearby 'Little Petra' in Siq el Barrid, the 'Cold Canyon'.

Purple iris

Jebel Harun, the legendary burial place of Aaron, brother of Moses, is a sacred mountain also well worth visiting. Go there in spring when the area around the white summit tomb is rich in flowers, in stark contrast to the barren mountains and canyons leading to the desert

The Roman road and a backdrop of Nabataean tombs in the Petra basin (Route 81)

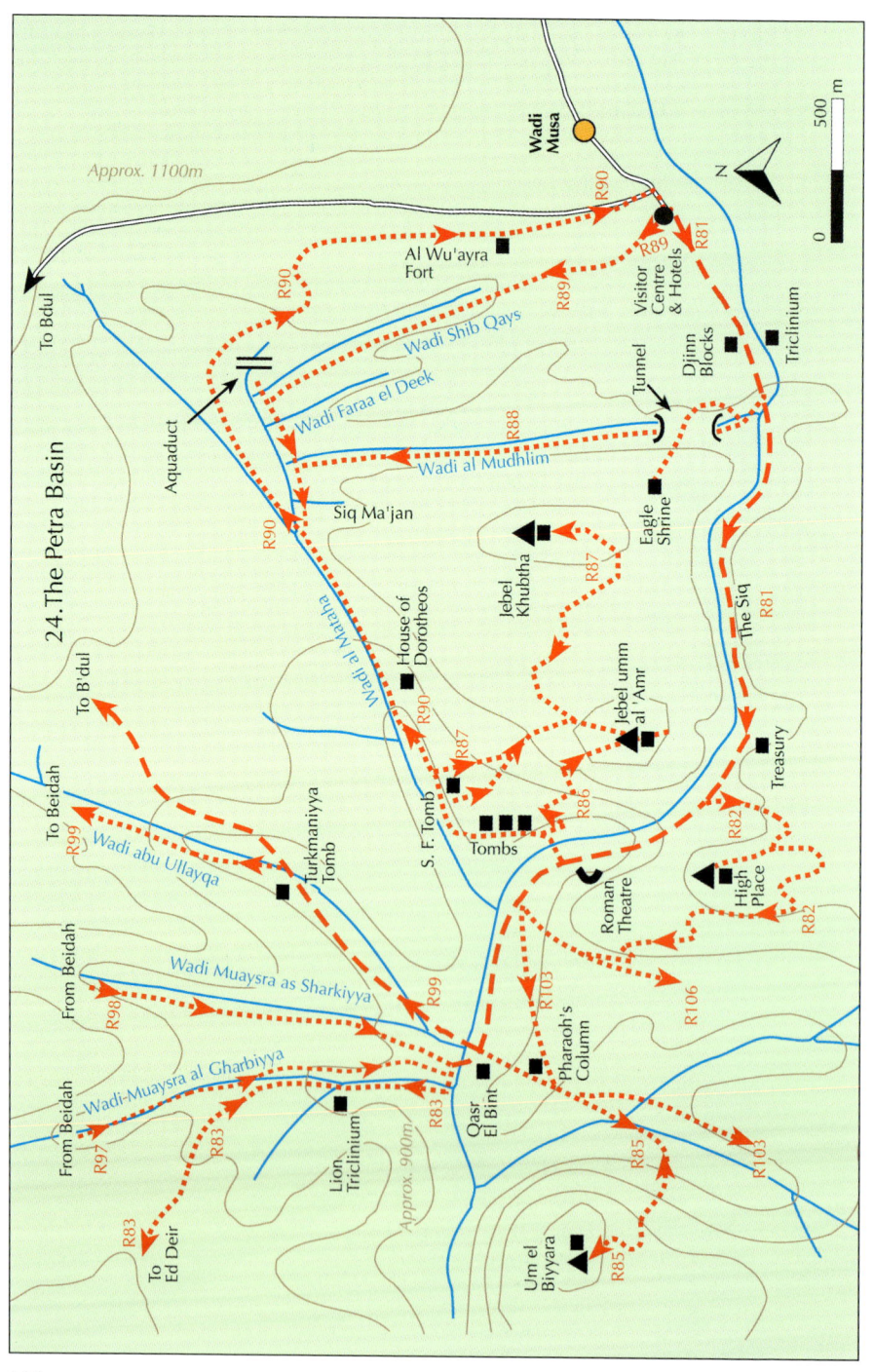

JORDAN

24. The Petra Basin

of Wadi Araba far below. The trek to Jebel Harun can be combined with a journey on foot or by camel to the remote Roman Theatre in Wadi Sabra, a green oasis to the south, from where Nabataean and Roman camel routes lead west to Wadi Araba or south to Wadi Rum and Aqaba. Other Bedouin trails go from Sabra up to Taybeh and Rajif high on the escarpment on the King's Highway.

Yet another old route from Petra descends a canyon close to Jebel Harun down to the windswept village of Bir Madhkhur in Wadi Araba, which can also be reached by a scenic, recently surfaced road that winds down from the beautiful valley of Wadi um Elda, north of Wadi Musa. Once there you can return on foot up the verdant canyon of Wadi es Siyyagh, past waterfalls and pools back into Petra – a long but incredible journey.

These are just some of the walks and scrambles; there are other shorter ones in Petra itself that are less frequented by tourists such as the Nabataean ways to the mountains of Al Khubtha and Um el Biyyara, or to Petra's last aqueduct near the hidden Siq el Ma'jan. There are even guided tours at night under the stars. The choice of routes is endless, and what follows just a selection of the possibilities.

Route 81
The Petra Siq

Grade	Easy walk
Details	3km
Time	2hrs there and back (but allow a full day in Petra)

By far the most popular walk in this guidebook! And why not – it is truly amazing, combining historical interest with majestic surroundings and a breathtaking entrance to Petra at the Treasury (Khazneh). It's unbeatable – and unforgettable! Get there in the early morning to catch the sun on the façade and to avoid the crowds. Spend the rest of the day enjoying Petra, perhaps including some of the other walks. See maps 24, 25 and 26.

The route

Follow the track down from the Visitor Centre past the Petra Gate (ticket required; GPS alt. 1020m N30° 13.444' E35° 28.074') and on down the side of the wadi (taking a horse if you wish, but only as far as the Siq entrance). Almost immediately the walk passes monuments which are all well documented in the various guidebooks, the most striking being the Djinn Blocks, the Obelisk Tomb and the Triclinium.

In about 0.5km you arrive at Bab es Siq – the entrance to the Siq (GPS alt. 1000m N30° 19.274' E35° 27.692'). The tunnel carved out of solid rock by the Nabataeans in AD50 to take any floodwater away from the Siq is to the right (see Route 88). Once in the Siq pass immediately beneath the remains of a monumental arch painted by David Roberts in 1839 (seen on many postcards). Walk down the Siq, marvelling at its proportions, torn between hurrying to see what lies round the next bend and wanting to linger where you are. Along the way are the remains of Nabataean water channels, sections of Roman road and various niches and shrines, but what really impresses most (apart from the Siq itself) is the first view of the Treasury.

After the Treasury the walk continues down the Outer Siq at a more leisurely pace; you're now 'in' Petra and have time to look around, explore and enjoy the sights. As you emerge from this section of canyon about 0.5km from the Treasury, steps leading to the High Place (Route 82) are on your left and the Roman Theatre is just beyond, with the impressive Palace Tomb and Urn Tomb and so on up to the right. The Lower Petra Basin is 1km further on down the Roman road, finishing near Qasr el Bint (GPS alt. 880m N30° 19.832' E35° 26.385'). Beyond are some cafés and a restaurant.

At this point the wadi slips mysteriously and temptingly into the canyon of Wadi Siyyagh through which it passes to Wadi Araba (Route 100) '...beyond the Roman colonnades, the walls of the canyon close again and the well-worn paths of tourists end. The shadows of high mountains with tombs and castles on their tops draw closer as the dry bed of the wadi leaves the city and its ghosts to pass through pink-flowered oleander bushes before disappearing into the gloomy unseen recesses of the final canyon' ('Petra's Secret Canyon' Tony Howard, *Footloose* magazine, 1985).

The trails to Ed Deir (Route 83) and Beidah (Routes 95–99) begin or end here, whilst the ways S to Jebel Harun, Wadi Sabra and beyond also start from this general area. Routes 82–86 all start in the Petra Basin.

Route 82
The High Place or Attuf Ridge

Grade	Easy walk with a bit of scrambling, dependent on exact route
Details	2km up and down, rising from 930m in the Outer Siq to 1070m on the top
Time	Allow 1–1½hrs

This must be the second most popular route in this guidebook, so best to go very early or late to avoid the crowds. The panoramic view of Petra from the top is unbeatable. See map 24.

The route
The way is obvious, starting near the exit from the Outer Siq at a sign on the left. Follow Nabataean steps up the big ravine for 15mins, then go right and up below a quarried wall with Crusader ruins above. From the col go right to reach the High Place with views around the Petra Basin and out towards Jebel Harun and Wadi Sabra (½hr from the Outer Siq).

Descent Return down to the col (Bedu café). On the left are two stone 'Dushara' obelisks. Do not go left back down the ascent path but continue directly ahead to the S for about 150m before turning right (W) through cut passages and down steps and along a sandy path back below the High Place, on the W side of the mountain. Continue by steps over and round domes, eventually descending left again through great mountain scenery and down past the Lion Fountain. Continue down cut stairways in colourful rock to reach the Garden Triclinium and the Roman Soldier Tomb (½hr from the High Place). A further 10mins along the base of the mountain leads to the top end of the Colonnade street or, go down the obvious wadi to the Crusader fort of El Habis and the cafés at the lower end of Petra near Qasr El Bint, which are run by local people.

The Forum Restaurant is just beyond, by the start of Route 83.

Route 83
Ed Deir (the Monastery)

We came out suddenly into unconfined air. Brown Eagles were slowly circling under our feet. Below these unquivering wings, red sandstone peaks and grey limestone flanks tumbled down into the sweltering trough of Arabah, here wider than we had hitherto seen it. Rivers of heat slid sluggishly along its devious channels. Far off, beyond the gulf, the blunt tops of Et Tih extended in phalanx. Only southward the view was checked, where Jebel Harun was blocked against the intense sky, holding up for all Islam to see, the white tomb which houses the bones of the Sheikh Harun.

In the Steps of Moses the Conqueror L. Golding (1938)

Grade	Easy walk in mountainous surroundings
Details	2km for the round trip from Qasr el Bint in the Petra Basin
Time	Allow ½hr to enjoy the ascent, rising over 200m to 1060m, and the same for descent

The way to Ed Deir is probably the third most frequented walk in this book, combining great mountain atmosphere with a walk to a truly majestic site over 2000 years old, with excellent views of Petra along the way as well as awe-inspiring views of Wadi Siyyagh and Wadi Araba from the plateau rim just a short way to the W. See maps 24 and 25.

Approaching the Monastery, above Petra

The route
From the cafés at the lower end of Petra cross the bridge, continue past the Forum Restaurant and go N up the stony wadi with oleanders, and up steps in a little side valley on the left leading to the Lion Triclinium. Continue up the carved stairway, curving left and zigzagging up to the NW. Eventually a cave will be seen in a cliff over to the left. This is the 'Hermitage' and can be reached by an easy scramble.

Return to the main stairway, which eventually becomes a cut passage on the edge of a ravine with spectacular views back down into Petra. After rising through a little pass the track arrives unexpectedly on a plateau with the amazing 'Monastery' on the right and a welcome Bedouin teashop in a cave on the left, run by the Daqlalah family (GPS alt. 1050m N30° 20.269' E35° 25.822'). The family was living here in 1984 when we first visited Petra, but in 1985 the B'dul Bedouin were all moved out of their homes in the tombs and caves into what was then the new B'dul village.

It used to be possible to climb steps on the left of Ed Deir to reach its top, but following a fatal accident the steps have been blocked by a rather unsightly wall (see photo page 21).

Descent By the same route. Allow a similar time; alternatively take Routes 95 or 96 to Beidah, or reverse Route 84.

Whilst at the Monastery it is worth making the 5min walk out W rising slightly up the plateau away from Ed Deir to reach the lip of the huge canyon of **Wadi es Siyyagh** (Routes 100 and 101) and views of wild mountain and desert scenery; a good sunset view if you've made arrangements to stay the night in this inspiring place.

Route 84
Beidah to Ed Deir by the High Route

Grade	Easy walk, but an exposed grade 1 traverse on rock to finish
Details	6km, with less than 100m of ascent and descent. The return from the Monastery by Routes 83, 95 or 96 necessitates an extra 6 or 8km
Time	Allow 2–3hrs from Beidah or 1½hrs if driven down Wadi Ghurab to the 'heads of the Three Valleys'. Allow another 3hrs for any of the return routes.

A superb, varied and scenic trek into Petra along a rock terrace high above Wadi Maruan and Wadi Siyyagh with a few exposed steps at the end to reach the Ed Deir (Monastery) plateau. See maps 23 and 25.

The route
Follow Route 94 through Wadi Ghurab, leaving the Petra–Beidah road at small white domes of sandstone and a roadside information sign to nearby Kharrubat al Fajja, the remains of a Nabataean dam with a carob tree growing in it (GPS alt. 1050m N30° 21.418' E35° 27.158'). Continue on the 4WD trail through meadows between domes to reach the heads of the Three Valleys (GPS alt. 1030m N30° 21.148' E35° 26.266'). Wadi Maruan is directly ahead to the SW, with the entrance to Wadi Muaysra Gharbiyya on its left marked by two rock towers on its skyline.

Follow the track to the head of Wadi Muaysra Gharbiyya and continue along it as it bends away from the valley, passing round some walled fields and the head of a little valley sloping down right into

Wadi Maruan (about 10mins from the head of the valley). Still on the 4WD track walk up to a col then descend to a little valley beyond, now on a well-used path, which contours along between cliffs before descending a steep rocky corridor past cairns and winding up left to a juniper terrace with a yellow overhanging wall above (less than ½hr from the head of the Three Valleys, GPS alt. 1080m N30° 20.754' E35° 25.957').

Continue along the path to the left (W), and follow it out to a terrace above Wadi Maruan. Still contouring along, a magnificently situated natural balcony and viewpoint is soon reached high above the junction of Wadi Maruan and Wadi Siyyagh with a great view down to Wadi Araba 1000m below (less than 1hr from the head of the Three Valleys, GPS alt. 1090m N30° 20.634' E35° 25.747'). From here the terrace curves round left (S) and the white tomb on the top of Jebel Harun comes into view in the distance. A little further along, the terrace narrows, almost disappearing and a few exposed steps have to be made (grade 1) high above Wadi Siyyagh to reach the safety of the continuing ledge.

Once on the little plateau just ahead descend steeply down a well-worn path towards a narrow valley, trending left to just above the ravine in the valley. From there follow rock terraces gently down towards the head of the valley. (The keen observer will see the finial of Ed Deir sticking up behind rock domes just ahead.) Once in the valley walk up to reach the plateau and the magnificent Monastery in its wild mountaintop setting (GPS alt. 1050m N30° 20.269' E35° 25.822').

Walking along the exposed rock balcony from Beidah to the Monastery, with views to Wadi Araba far below

Descent By Route 83 through Petra to Wadi Musa.

Route 85 is a much less travelled and rather more difficult route to a Petra mountaintop.

Route 85
Um el Biyyara

Grade	Easy scramble (grade 1), but quite exposed in places
Details	2km from the Roman Theatre, climbing almost 300m to 1160m at the summit
Time	1–2hrs to the top with ½hr or so of ascent; allow the same for the descent

This is the imposing mountain whose sheer cliffs dominate Petra to the W. The route to it and up it is not always obvious, and is quite steep and exciting in places! There is an excavated Edomite village on the top, with cisterns and inscriptions in Greek and Nabataean, plus excellent views of Petra and the surrounding mountains.

Don't attempt this route without a guide unless you are confident on rock and have a head for heights. At the very least take the advice of the sign at Pharaoh's Column 'Attention – venturing from the regular route on your own is not advisable. It is highly recommended that should you wish to do so beyond this point we strongly advise either a local guide or at least one companion.' Maps 24 and 25.

Guide Recommended.

The route
Follow the broad track W from just beyond the Roman Theatre to Pharaoh's Column and descend into the wadi ahead. About 100m after crossing the wadi go right towards a stony gully 50m left of some tombs. Pass through a rocky defile into a little basin surrounded by caves, then out through the other side and up diagonally left past more small caves and a juniper, then zigzag left and right to enter the gully at a new wall.

Go up the ravine, which presents two majestic incut ramps in corridors to the left or right. Continue up the ravine above the ramps (cairns) and up a defile, moving right into a parallel corridor. Above, steps zigzag up right to a stepped corridor followed by more steps, then left from a large dead juniper and along a cut edge to 'Bedouin steps' (grade 1, exposed). Above more ledges and steps zigzag up the mountain then go left along a cut path into a gully, then right to a terrace. Go immediately left again onto the SW shoulder and up a gully (Bedouin steps) to the top; the end is marked by a cairn so you can relocate it for the descent.

Take some time to wander round the remains of an Edomite settlement, also Nabataean sites and cisterns (particularly on the E side overlooking Petra). To the NW there are some caves and, after a little scramble (grade 1), good views down Wadi es Siyyagh towards Wadi Araba. There is almost no wood, so don't damage the trees to make a fire.

Descent By the same route.

For a shorter and easier scramble to a mountaintop take Route 86.

Ascending the carved Nabataean ramps to the hilltop Edomite ruins of Um el Biyyara

Route 86
Jebel umm al 'Amr

Grade	Easy scramble
Details	Less than 1km from 900m in the valley below the Urn Tomb to the top at 1070m
Time	¾hr for the ascent; slightly less for the descent to the Sextius Florentinus Tomb

Until recently this Petra mountain was seldom visited but it is now more popular, leading to a proliferation of cairns in the summit area that could confuse the unwary; nevertheless it is still an interesting little scramble with excellent views from the top. See map 24.

The route
Start below the Urn Tomb, taking the staircase on the right as you approach from Lower Petra. It's then a ½hr climb. There are four 'high places' on top and a large walled cistern. To the right it is only a short way up domes and steps to fine views over Petra, particularly of the Roman Theatre positioned perfectly below, and the High Place opposite. There is also a scramble down to an unusual view of the Treasury.

The Treasury Viewpoint From the cistern – instead of going back down the gully to the Sextius Florentinus Tomb – go left (S) down a little valley for 5mins to reach a platform above the inner entrance to the Siq and opposite the Treasury. Return the same way. (The loose gully, which continues directly down to reach the Outer Siq just opposite the Treasury, is dangerous and should not be descended.)

Descent Go NW through the steep valley of Wadi Zarnuq with a spectacular section cut through vertical rock on the left side. Follow the gorge down a recently built rock staircase (the way over boulders is sometimes rather difficult in places – see Route 87) until it ends near the Sextius Florentinus Tomb.

Route 87
Jebel Khubtha via Jebel umm al 'Amr

Grade	Moderate scramble, grade 2
Details	1km, climbing from 930m to 1130m
Time	1hr for the ascent, similar for the descent

A more difficult way up, going all the way to the two summits, for those wanting to test their rock-scrambling and route-finding skills. See map 24.

The route
About 10m right of the Sextius Florentinus Tomb large steps lead to an incut corridor gained by a huge step. It is left with greater difficulty (grade 2) up the right wall to regain the steps. Follow these up to the upper reaches of Wadi Zarnuq. (Wadi Zarnuq can be followed all the way up from the left side of the Sextius Florentinus Tomb by scrambling between boulders and bushes – see Route 86; easier, but not as enjoyable or interesting as Route 87.) The gully ends at a wall and above are the remains of a cistern, 20mins from the tomb. To the right it is only a short way up domes and steps to Jebel umm al 'Amr and fine views over Petra, particularly of the Roman Theatre and the High Place opposite.

To the left is the way to the summit of Jebel Khubtha – the big flat-topped mountain behind the Forum Hotel. Go E across the little plateau and left to pass domes, in a cut corridor. Follow steps into and out of a wadi and left round the next domes. Now trend right between domes (some steps) to a little grassy plateau. Here go left up a stony slope towards the flat-topped summit, then right between domes again. (Remember the way: it is a real maze up here!)

At the base of the big summit dome go right to the skyline arête where steps can be seen. Follow these up (quite exposed), to reach the top and fine views all round (½hr from the cistern).

Descent By the same route.

Having spent some time in Petra and entered through the Siq you may decide to enter or return by alternative routes, for example Routes 88–90, or any of the 'Three Valley' routes 97–99, or even via the Monastery to Beidah (Route 84 in reverse).

Route 88
Petra via Wadi al Mudhlim

Grade	Easy canyon; difficulty dependent on the amount of water in the Siq – it could be more than waist-high, or dry
Details	4km
Time	Just over 1hr to the Petra Basin

To appreciate the ingenuity and hard work put in by the Nabataeans in AD50, this 'side entrance' into Petra is worth taking as a variation. Do not enter after rain, or if rain may be imminent here or in the hills to the E. See maps 24 and 25.

The route
Walk down to just before the Bab es Siq (the start of the Siq, GPS alt. 1000m N30° 19.274' E35° 27.692'), then go right and follow the wadi bed N through a tunnel cut by the Nabataeans to divert floodwater. (A detour can be made before entering the tunnel by going over its roof then right as far as the second valley on the left, up which are several niches carved in the rock including the beautiful Eagle Shrine.)

Once through the tunnel the stony riverbed continues for 1km, with many oleander bushes, eventually narrowing to a ravine only 1m wide with smooth twisting walls and pools. Towards the end, near the deepest pool, are small shrines, after which it meets the equally narrow Siq Al Ma'jan at a T-junction. Downstream to the W it is joined by Siq al Ujul before emerging into Wadi Mataha, with tombs on the left and, across the valley, the caves of Mughur an Nasra. About 1km further downstream the Sextius Florentinus Tomb will be found on the left as the whole Petra Basin opens out ahead.

Route 89 exits at the same place.

THE PETRA AREA – PETRA – ROUTE 88

A unique route through a Nabataean tunnel and canyon into Petra

though
Route 89
Petra via Wadi Shib Qays

Grade	Easy canyon with possible pools and grade 2 scrambling; high water levels increase the difficulty
Details	5km
Time	1¼hrs to the Petra Basin (longer with detours)

A route to or from Petra with a rather off-putting start by the waste overflow from the Petra Forum Hotel. Don't worry – it definitely gets better! Although there are often many deep pools – in 1999 some were more than waist-deep, some thigh-deep – the canyon can also be dry; either way it's a delight. It's possible to bridge over some pools, and there are some quite tricky and exposed steps at boulder chokes where caution is needed. (On the other hand the flash floods of 2006 may have changed everything!) Maps 24 and 25.

The route
From the right side of the hotel follow the wadi down easily, passing the start of an incut Nabataean irrigation channel in the right wall, which continues down the wadi. Keeping left continue through bushes and caves and on down the wadi to a T-junction 1km from the start. (Go right to find Petra's last remaining aqueduct, which doesn't look like it will last much longer!)

Go left at the T-junction down Wadi al Ma'jan, a beautiful narrow *siq* polished by water (dangerous if rain is possible; wading through pools required if recent rainfall). There are some awkward steps down jammed boulders (grade 2). After passing Wadi Faraa el Deek another narrow *siq* enters from the left (Wadi Mudhlim, Route 88). A jammed log 10m above reveals the strength and depth of the floodwaters.

Continue down the polished and winding *siq* passing a cluster of votive niches to emerge 50m beyond into Wadi al Mataha where a wall has been built to divert the water away from the left side of the valley. It is now 10mins walk past the House of Dorotheos to the Sextius Florentinus Tomb with the Petra Basin beyond.

Petra's last aqueduct can be visited whist scrambling down the surprising Wadi Shib Qays

Route 90
Wadi al Mataha and Al Wu'ayra Fort from Petra

Grade	Easy scramble
Details	5km
Time	About 1½hrs from Qasr el Bint

This alternative route out of Petra passes by the Sextius Florentinus Tomb and the Crusader fortress of Al Wu'ayra to Wadi Musa. The walk is easy and interesting but route finding a little complex. Andrew Moore did the route in 1999 and comments, 'This attractive route was seriously spoiled by paint marks which were particularly evident on its upper slabs. Whoever put them there deserves to suffer a fate that would be unkind to describe! The paint marks, like the many ambiguous cairns, are superfluous and not only litter easy routes but are also a potential danger to the inexperienced.' Maps 24 and 25.

The route
Walk up the colonnaded Roman road to the Sextius Florentinus Tomb and continue NE up the right side of the valley past many rainbow-coloured rocks and caves until the mountainside meets the wadi. Descend a wall into the riverbed. (The narrow *siq* on the right is the exit of Wadi al Mudhlim – the stream that the Nabataeans diverted from the Siq down through a tunnel – see Route 88.)

Do not enter this, but keep in the main valley and take the next prominent right fork. This rises up a little, then continues in the same direction above the other tributary. Eventually an obvious wadi goes right at 90°. Follow this up into a little flat green valley seemingly surrounded by cliffs. (A cairn on the fort can be seen ahead on the clifftop; if you continue slightly right and up a ravine you will pass below the fortress bridge, but there is no easy way on.)

Instead, go back left up a side entrance and then take an obvious easy ramp of white rock or scree up right until it levels off on rock terraces 100m below the Wadi Musa–B'dul road. Follow the road S keeping below it, passing the entrance of the fort after 5mins. Petra Visitor Centre is 15mins further on.

THE NORTHERN APPROACHES TO PETRA

The Arabs of Petra [were sent] up their hills into the forest towards Shobek. It was an uncaring march in the hoar mist, that of these frozen footed peasants in their sheepskins, up and down sharp valleys and dangerous hill-sides, out of whose snow-drifts, the heavy trunks of junipers, grudging in leaves, jutted like castings in grey iron.

Seven Pillars of Wisdom T. E. Lawrence (1929)

Coming in from the north you can connect with treks from Shaubak and Dana or even as far away as Selah and Buseirah, making a one-week trip to reach Petra (see the Dana chapter). Many of the adventure travel companies mentioned in Appendix 1, especially those from Wadi Musa, have their own favourite variations on this theme; contact them for details.

BEIDAH

There is now a new Bedouin village of Beidah about 8km N of Petra, but the original place of that name is a Natufian (late Pleistocene) site dating back around 10,000 years, used regularly by hunter-gatherers; many flint and chert tools and artefacts were discovered in the excavations. The area is at an altitude of 1050m and is dominated by the steep faces of sandstone from which Petra is carved. The excavated site of Beidah is 10mins walk on a good (drivable) track to the left of the car park. It is drained by the seasonal Wadi el Ghurab 'Valley of the Raven' which originates to the NE on Jebel Shara, named after a Nabataean god, and meets Wadi Slehsil, 'The Place of Steep Cliffs', 1km further on before falling steeply into Wadi el Siyyagh and Wadi Araba.

SIQ EL BARRID (THE COLD SIQ)

Close to old Beidah, just 0.5km to the NE, is the northern caravanserai for Nabataean Petra, often referred to as 'Little Petra'. It is visible in a ravine just beyond the car park, and well worth a visit for its unique carvings. The Helali and Ammarin Bedouin tourist camps are signed nearby.

Approach Walk or drive from the Shaubak area or, more likely, from Wadi Musa – drive down to the lower end of town and follow the road as it turns right just before the Visitor Centre. Continue past the village of B'dul through increasingly pleasant scenery with sandstone domes exhibiting Nabataean steps and caves to arrive after 8km at Siq el Barrid. There is a huge Nabataean water cistern cut into the rock near the car park.

THE BEIDAH–ARABA–FEYNAN ROAD

Coming from Wadi Musa, and just beyond Siq el Barrid, a small, newly surfaced road forks left (NW) from the main road and goes through a very nice area of domes near Siq um el Hiran at 1km and on to

THE PETRA AREA – PETRA

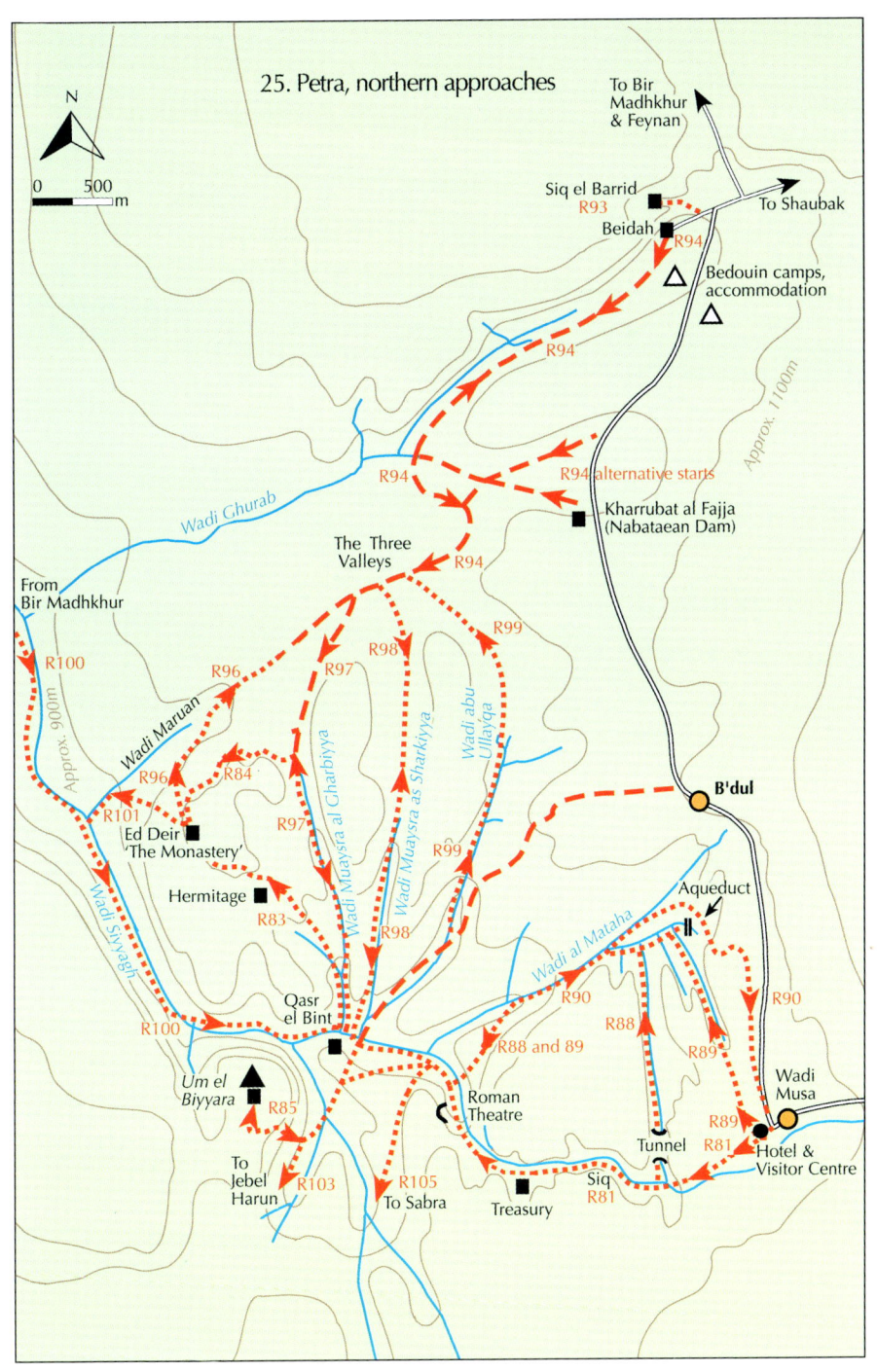

25. Petra, northern approaches

the pretty Siq um el Elda at 6km where it starts the descent to Wadi Araba. Bir Madhkhur (see Route 100) can be reached off this road after about 25km. A further 20km NW across wild country through scattered acacia trees brings you to the Feynan road from where it's either left to the Dead Sea Highway in Wadi Araba, or right to the Feynan Eco-Lodge in the Dana Nature Reserve (see the Dana chapter).

Route 91
Jebel Baaga

Follow the above road for 4km from the main road to where the valley of Wadi Jabu can be followed up E for 2km into Baaga Siq. The small summit of Baaga (1110m) is directly above with a Nabataean trail, cistern and gardens. (Not checked by the authors, but said to be worthwhile; 3km max, 2–3hrs to explore the area.)

Route 92
Beidah to Shaubak or Feynan

Just beyond Wadi Jabu and before Siq um el Elda (map 22) various trails lead up the reputedly scenic and historic valley of Wadi Thugra into Wadi Hudeib and all the way N for almost 20km to meet tracks from Shaubak or Feynan. These offer excellent multi-day treks and canyons with some Roman and Ottoman antiquities. (Not checked by the authors; information provided by Petra Moon Travel, see Appendix 1; they and some of the other local adventure travel companies know the area.)

Route 93 is an entertaining little route from Siq el Barrid (Little Petra) into Wadi Ghurab and 'the Three Valleys', which provide some enjoyable walks into Petra from the N.

Route 93
Siq el Barrid (Little Petra)

Grade	Moderate scramble
Details	Some excellent exposed scrambling which, though relatively short, is sufficiently serious and technical to warrant grade 3
Time	Allow 1hr to enjoy

A useful and enjoyable link from Siq el Barrid with its Nabataean remains to Wadi el Ghurab, making an entertaining round trip from and to Beidah possible, or providing a good start to one of the 'Three Valley' walks (information from Andrew Moore). See map 25.

Special requirements Grade 3 climbing ability essential.

Nabataean tomb in the narrow cleft of Siq el Barrid (Little Petra)

The route
At the W end of Siq el Barrid go up then down Nabataean steps to arrive in a N–S wadi. Turn left and follow the wadi downstream, then round a 90° right-hand bend to the top of a dry cascade with a view into Wadi el Ghurab. Go right onto the rock, on worn steps, and round the rib to downclimb two moves on cut holds to an exposed traverse. Follow this right to descend slabs to the remains of some steps next to a tree. Use the tree (cut holds) to descend to the streambed and cross it to an obvious hewn Nabataean channel on the left. Descend the cascade to enter Wadi el Ghurab (it is possible but scary to traverse the water channel).

The more usual route into the Three Valleys is more straightforward. To do any of the walks from Beidah and Petra it is first necessary to understand this approach – Route 94 – which crosses the valley of Beidah known as Wadi el Ghurab.

Route 94
Beidah to 'the Three Valleys'

Grade	Easy walk
Details	3–4km
Time	1–1½hrs; allow 2–3hrs if you're just going for a stroll and returning perhaps by the track that leads back out towards B'dul village

This is not so much a walk in itself as the key to the walks between Beidah and Petra. It used to be a nice quiet valley 'far from the madding crowd(s)' of Petra, but it has become popular with walking groups who tend to access the starts by 4WD, so the paths down Wadi Ghurab have become well-worn tracks. Nevertheless, a walk here is still a pleasant experience. See map 25.

The route
Coming from Wadi Musa, past B'dul and about 2km before reaching the Beidah junction, take any of the 4WD tracks into Wadi Ghurab, the first being at Kharrubat al Fajja, a Nabataean dam with a carob tree growing in it (GPS alt. 1050m N30° 21.418' E35° 27.158'). Follow the valley down through idyllic surroundings (see Route 84).

Alternatively, if you started from the car park at Siq el Barrid, the wide track becomes a footpath where it crosses the riverbed after about 20mins, near some dunes. A little further on the cliffs close in to the river and, just after, the landscape opens out as the river bends right. Take a wide track up left (small tomb cut into the nose of the mountain just above). Continue on the good track, passing right of an isolated rock lump (about ½hr from the start). There is now extensive ploughed land to the right and, not very obvious, a fan of small but deep sandy wadis. To avoid this area continue about 100m past the rock buttress to where a small track goes right (S) at right angles to the main track, between the fields. It meets the well-used 4WD tracks of the regular approach a little further on, just at the head of the sandy incut wadis.

From here follow the 4WD track past the heads of several more little sandy wadis to a fork. Keep right (small white rocky dome ahead), between fields. The track splits again; this time go straight on, ignoring the right fork and after 100m there is an area of white flat rocks on the left. You are now above the first of the Three Valleys.

Wadi abu Ullayqa (see Route 99) has fields at its mouth and is identified by a view of B'dul village beyond if you descend into it. If you look closely in the small white domes between this valley and the next to the W you will see a few incut steps leading to two small shrines.

The second of the three valleys is **Wadi Muaysra as Sharkiyya** (see Route 98, GPS alt. 1020m N30° 21.278' E35° 26.387'), distinguished by a long straight and high dark-coloured cliff on its right (W) side. To reach it continue from above the first valley on an indistinct path, left across the head of the wadi towards the low point on the far W skyline. Cross a small tributary which descends into the main wadi, go over a small rise and enter the main valley by an obvious little streambed (5–10mins from the first valley).

The third valley is **Wadi Muaysra al Gharbiyya** (see Route 97, GPS alt. 1050m N30° 21.052' E35° 26.234'). To reach this valley continue for another 5–10mins over the next rise (the mountain on the left between the middle and last valleys is split by a big vertical chimney). Go down into the left side of the valley entrance on white rock (two little towers on the crest of the rock wall opposite identify the valley).

Route 84 uses the same route to this point (about 1¼hrs from the car park) but instead of going down into the valleys it continues in the same direction, contouring round the cliffs to the monastery. It makes the start of a nice circuit (Route 95).

Route 95
The Monastery Round Trip

Grade	Easy walk and scramble with a bit of grade 1 to reach the Monastery plateau (see Route 84)
Details	About 100m of ascent and descent
Time	Allow 5hrs

A great day out for those who have already visited Petra by the Siq but who want to experience quieter less 'touristy' surrounds, starting and finishing at Beidah. See map 25.

The route
Follow Route 84 up to the Monastery (Ed Deir), then reverse Route 83 back down the Nabataean steps, but instead of going all the way to the restaurant take a small path left immediately you see the point where the path goes under an arch formed by leaning boulders (just after crossing a small bridge over a dry streambed, about 20mins from Ed Deir).

Follow the path up red rock for about 50m (some Nabataean steps) to a good view over Petra, Qasr el Bint and the tombs on the opposite side of Wadi Muaysra al Gharbiyya. Now descend, still on worn red and purple rock to the streambed of Wadi Muaysra al Gharbiyya, reaching it just before the point where it drops over a 5m cliff down to the Ed Deir track (see Route 97). This point could also be reached from the Forum Restaurant in the Petra Basin in 5mins or so (GPS alt. 890m N30° 20.037' E35° 26.404').

From now on reverse Route 97, following the wadi up through oleanders, then up rightwards and through a small cut defile to reach the ruined Nabataean dam, which is passed on its left. Beyond is the multi-coloured rock. Further up – after another cut ledge – the valley goes left into a ravine. At this point go easily up slabs on the right to enter a defile with two large junipers on the left and two cut tombs on the right.

Continuing up, the 4WD track is reached at the head of the valley (GPS alt. 1050m N30° 21.052' E35° 26.234', less than 1hr from Ed Dier steps or the restaurant).

The walk back to Beidah or the B'dul–Beidah road is another 1–1½hrs on 4WD tracks through meadows. Beidah is hidden behind the dark red mountain to the NE. Do not take the direct way across the fields, but follow the tracks as described in Route 94 in reverse (circuitous but easy, and no damage to agricultural land.) Alternatively, keep on tracks up the right side of the valley to reach the B'dul road directly near the Nabataean dam.

Two other routes can be used to return directly from Ed Deir to Beidah, the first of which is Route 96.

Route 96
Ed Deir to Beidah via Wadi Maruan

Grade	Easy scramble (grade 1), but route finding not always obvious
Details	6km
Time	2½hrs from Ed Deir plus time to get there by your chosen route

From Ed Deir (the Monastery) the walk goes through rugged mountain scenery to the pastoral land above the Three Valleys, and so to Beidah. It involves some scrambling on rock down a small cliff. When included with a walk to Ed Deir from Petra or Beidah it makes a good round trip. See map 25.

Approach From Wadi Musa it's about 1½hrs up to the Monastery via Routes 81 and 83. Once there Bedouin tea and soft drinks are available in a nearby cave.

The route
From the Monastery follow the wide rock plateau N keeping close to the cliff, which has cisterns cut into it. After 200m there is a deep recess on the right. At the back of the bay, just beyond and above a large juniper, there is a cave with carved relief of camels and men right of its entrance.

Back on the main rock plateau a little wadi soon descends through a gap in the rocks, then widens to a small open area, and narrows again to a ravine. At this point do not go down it further (it soon drops steeply over a cliff, see Route 101). Instead go easily up onto the first rock terrace to the right, just below the main cliff and only about 5mins from Ed Deir. (This is directly below the exposed traverse at the end of Route 84, which can be reached by scrambling higher.) Continuing along, the view down into Wadi es Siyyagh (Route 100) soon opens out, and its junction with Wadi Maruan coming SW from Beidah is seen.

Do not go further along the terrace but descend by zigzagging down ledges and chimneys in the cliff (grade 1) to scree slopes below (15mins from Ed Deir). At this point take a poorly defined path NE along the very base of the cliff, contouring round with some scrambling over boulders to reach a long sandy terrace below overhangs. Follow this easily, in wild scenery, passing a little side wadi (about 10mins from the cliff descent) until, just after the point where the tomb on the summit of Jebel Harun is visible behind, it is necessary to go up ledges for about 50m into the mouth of the next side wadi. (There is a small manmade wall here, behind a juniper.) Go up again, past the stump of a felled tree, to the next rock terrace. Follow this past Bedouin cave shelters in a small ravine and continue at the same level as the terrace rapidly opens out, passing another side wadi. Continue on again on rock terraces which wind round above Wadi Maruan, eventually meeting it at a little walled field in its bed (about 1¼hrs from Ed Deir).

Go up the wadi (marked by a small red-black rock tower) past more small walls and fields, then up easy white slabs to emerge above ploughed fields close to the entrances to the Three Valleys. The dark red mountain concealing the valley of Beidah is visible to the NE.

Return Reverse Route 94 to Beidah or, if you started from Wadi Musa, return via Petra through one of the Three Valleys described below for an excellent round trip totalling about 14km, 6–7hrs with about 300m of ascent and descent.

Routes 97–99 explore the Three Valleys.

Route 97
Beidah to Petra via Wadi Muaysra al Gharbiyya

Grade	Easy walk
Details	7km
Time	About 2½hrs

A pleasant walk in verdant surroundings to the Petra Basin. See maps 24 and 25.

The route
Follow Route 94 to the head of the wadi. Descend into the valley entrance down white slabs, cross a little side wadi at its head near a large juniper, and continue down to enter the main valley of Gharbiyya on its left. Continue on the left through small white rock domes and bits of ploughed land to the lip of the wadi and the first view of Petra.

Descend into it through a defile in the rocks and follow it down until a tomb is seen on the left. Continue down on quite well-defined paths. Eventually the track passes a huge split boulder and ruined Nabataean dam and goes left along carved ledges and down purple slabs (some cut steps) to regain the wadi bed.

Continue through oleander bushes that are soon escaped by a rock terrace on the right leading to an area of well-carved tombs on the left. Soon Qasr el Bint comes into sight, and after more oleanders the streambed drops into a rocky ravine at a bend in an area of many tombs. The path to Ed Deir is visible below (GPS alt. 890m N30° 20.037' E35° 26.404'). Do not go down here as there is a vertical drop of 5m; instead follow a path left and out into the Petra Basin and Qasr el Bint (GPS alt. 880m N30° 19.832' E35° 26.385').

Return This route can be followed in reverse; see Route 95, or take any option back out from the Petra Basin.

Route 98
Beidah to Petra via Wadi Muaysra as Sharkiyya

Grade	Easy walk
Details	7km
Time	About 2½hrs

The central of the Three Valleys; a beautiful and constantly interesting valley descending into Petra. See maps 24 and 25.

The route
Follow Route 94 to the head of the valley. A meandering little streambed goes down into the right side of the valley amongst beautiful scenery until it meets the big cliff face on the right. Here the wadi bed drops into a tree-filled cleft but the path – which is carved into the rock – continues along the foot of the cliff with the wadi on its left (some pools in springtime) to a junction with a side valley from the right (nicely carved tomb here; about ½hr from the valley head).

From here the way down follows the wadi bed, sometimes changing sides (more pools here in spring), emerging eventually in an area of tombs on both sides of the valley. Just beyond here cross to the left side and continue down past more tombs, going easily down rocks into Wadi Abu Ullayqa, just before Qasr el Bint in the bottom of the Petra Basin.

Return The route can be followed in reverse, or take any option back out from the Petra Basin.

Route 99
Petra to Beidah via Wadi abu Ullayqa

Grade	Easy scramble, perhaps with pools to pass
Details	7km, rising 150m to 1050m
Time	2hrs

The first and most easterly of the Three Valleys. A road from the B'dul Bedouin village enters Petra down the lower third of this valley, so it makes a fairly quick way back out if you've done one of the other walks and left a car at Beidah. The last two thirds of the valley are nevertheless interesting and may involve wading through one or more pools in springtime. See maps 24 and 25.

The route
From the cafés by Qasr el Bint follow the road to B'dul up Wadi abu Ullayqa passing a new dam and the Turkmaniyya Tomb, at which point the road leaves the wadi to wind up hairpins to the village (about 20mins from Petra).

Nabataean tombs adorn the cliffs at the entrance to Wadi abu Ullayqa

Carry on up the right side of the wadi, on footpaths to where the cliffs close in. Continue in the stony wadi bed through a small gorge almost blocked by a large boulder to a junction of wadis marked by a huge old tree.

Avoid the narrow *siq* to the right and keep straight on. It splits again after 50m, and here the way goes left avoiding the oleander-choked bed by a goat track on the rocks 10m above it. Continue in the same line, crossing the next right junction then descending into the ravine and passing under another huge boulder (possible pool here may need wading through). Continue up the wadi, scrambling up boulders until it levels out into a beautiful secluded upper valley (about 1hr from Petra).

Follow this up until it forks with a juniper in the left fork. Take this (the right side is blocked) and rejoin it again after 50m. Carry straight on along the right side of a rock tower, which divides the wadi ahead, to reach a small ploughed plot of land. Fork left here and continue on white rock between small domes to emerge on the Beidah plateau. B'dul village is still visible behind and there are a couple of little incut shrines up some steps on the left.

Return Reverse Route 94 back from here to Beidah and Siq el Barrid, or keep right to reach the B'dul road.

Now we come to something rather more serious – a great way into Petra from Wadi Araba.

THE WESTERN APPROACHES TO PETRA

The western caravanserais for Nabataean Petra were at the foot of the mountains where the last water sources are found before the onset of the windswept sands of Wadi Araba. One was at Gharandal to the southwest, en route from Sinai and Egypt; another was at Khirbat Taybeh 15km south of Bir Madhkhur, at the mouth of Wadi Taybeh (from the ruins of which an old track goes to Petra). The third was at Bir Madhkhur immediately west of Petra, through which routes from the Negev passed on their way to the ancient city.

From Bir Madhkhur one route then took a detour to the north of the mountain barrier which forms the formidable western wall of the old city, going up through Wadi Namala and Siq um el Elda to reach Petra via Siq el Barrid. This is now a new road. Another took a more direct but steeper way commencing in the lower end of Wadi Siyyagh. This is the continuation of the Wadi Musa stream, which passes through the Petra Basin before disappearing into a chasm in the heart of these rugged mountains. The way up avoided the increasingly difficult canyon by taking the side valley of Wadi Maqtal, reaching the outskirts of Petra on a plateau between Petra and Jebel Harun (see Route 102). The third, Route 100, follows the impressive canyon directly.

Route 100
Wadi es Siyyagh to Petra

It was good, at last, to be off on our own, walking up the early morning canyon, hills striped with dark coloured intrusions of basalt slowly closing in around us and then suddenly, hungrily, swallowing us into the deep recesses of a cool ravine, to be greeted by that most beautiful of desert sounds, running water. Only a hundred metres back down the wadi we had been in bare dust brown hills and now as we rounded the bend, a waterfall cascaded into a pool surrounded by a jungle of tall green fragmites. As we parted the dense undergrowth, startled birds chattered in alarm and a dark green frog plopped into the pool.

'Petra's Secret Canyon' Tony Howard (*Footloose* magazine, 1985)

Grade	Moderate canyon with grade 3–4 climbing
Details	16km, rising from 800m to 1030m at the Visitor Centre
Time	7–10hrs

A great day out, packed full of surprises! Starting from a dry wadi bed near Bir Madhkhur, and heading into what appear to be barren and inhospitable mountains, it is not long before you reach water in a lush green canyon. The way on is continually interesting, first passing Nabataean irrigation systems then scrambling over rocks and round pools. At one stage the route is forced out of the canyon bed by an impassable waterfall in a narrow ravine; higher up some grade 3 climbing is necessary to pass another waterfall, which plunges into a very tempting pool – a great place for a swim. More scrambling is needed beyond before emerging into hidden verdant gardens just below the Petra Basin. See maps 23 and 25.

Special requirements A rope for those without climbing experience.
Guide Recommended.
Approach Coming from Wadi Araba leave the highway at the signposted road about 100km N of Aqaba and drive to the police post and village at Bir Madhkhur, a distance of about 8km. Alternatively drive down to Bir Madhkhur on the newly surfaced road from Beidah (see Route 91). If you have a 4WD vehicle it is then best to drive by desert tracks S then SE from Bir Madhkhur to enter Seil Wadi Musa. Go up this to a point where driving becomes increasingly difficult (10km from Bir Madhkhur), just past an area of high vertical wadi walls above which is a ruin and, a little further on, a concealed burial ground. Just beyond here is a pleasant camping area, from where the trek begins.

The route
Go easily E up the wadi bed for 1km passing Wadi Maqtal, which goes up SE to below Jebel Harun (Route 102). (The tomb of Aaron, brother of Moses, is visible as a small white building on the summit.) Here the going becomes ever more difficult through almost jungle terrain between the canyon walls, with a stream of running water, waterfalls, pools and even frogs and crabs, and many birds. Some scrambling on granite cliffs (grade 2) past incut Nabataean irrigation channels is necessary to pass the deeper pools. After 1km of this terrain the wadi turns abruptly S below a 200m granite and basalt wall, and opens out for a while with a good track high on the E side of the valley below the cliffs, finally narrowing again after 3km and turning SE. The going is still fairly easy in spectacular scenery following the main wadi past other wadis, which enter first on the left, then on the right. (There is a way up E from here to Wadi Ghurab and Beidah, or down from the Monastery, see Route 101.)

Eventually the wadi becomes impossible to follow, entering a vertical walled canyon (Wadi es Siq). Here the water is waist-deep and the way is blocked first by a giant boulder then an 8m waterfall. Tony Howard wrote in 'Petra's Secret Canyon': 'There, in the gloomy recesses, the vertical sides of the canyon plunged directly into a murky pool beyond which the way on was blocked by a giant boulder wedged across the gap, its lower end leaving only a chink of light above the water. Wilfried, the French member of our team, otherwise known affectionately as "Le Frog", was obviously better suited than most to probe the depths of this watery barrier and stepped into the pool, grimacing as the green water rose up to his waist. He prodded cautiously at some slime covered sticks floating, seemingly innocuously, in the gloom but concealing who knows what strange creatures. Satisfied that nothing was lurking in the depths he eventually reached the boulder. Peering through the gap above the waterline he could see nothing so with a struggle he climbed up onto its top. The way on was blocked by yet another boulder more massive than the first, completely barring any progress.'

Forced out of the canyon, continue straight ahead up the hillside on the right and follow a steep goat track beneath the S-facing barrier cliff. Pass through the second col on the left, after which descend a stone shoot on its right, first slightly leftwards then along ledges climbing across basalt columns (grade 2) back rightwards before dropping down to another pool below a waterfall (good swimming spot). To escape from here climb a pink granite rib on its left, going left up a black wall with the help of a jammed 'Bedouin' log. Continue up until it is possible to descend a rock gully to regain the wadi above a second, higher, waterfall and pool. This section involved grade 3 climbing in 1985, but note Andrew Moore's comments from 1999: 'The jammed log wasn't there, making this section fairly serious, especially in wet, sandy trainers on smooth granite! The move felt at least grade 3+. There was a belay peg in place about 15m above the pitch, on the shoulder. Also, the traverse into the wadi above the "second, higher waterfall" looked improbable from the point at which you descend to it, though perhaps it was just that it was almost dark when we did it!'

From there follow the wadi until the walls narrow again and more climbing (still on granite, grade 3) – or wading through a long green pool – give access to the last section of the wadi. Man-made walls are soon seen here, indicating the lower end of a paradise of Bedouin gardens with fruit trees, date palms and vegetable gardens. Continue up with care through these well-irrigated gardens (probably of Nabataean origin but called the Roman Gardens by the Bedouin), eventually climbing above them to a

Scrambling past pools in the canyon of Wadi Siyyagh on the way to Petra

The dramatic view west from the Monastery plateau over the depths of Wadi Siyyagh

track below the cliffs on the N side of the canyon where the first signs of Nabataean quarrying will be seen. A good track will eventually be joined in the wadi bottom, and before long the tombs of Petra appear in the distance. The Bedouin cafés and Forum Restaurant are just round the corner; another 4km through Petra and the Siq leads to the Visitor Centre.

As the logistics of reaching Bir Madhkhur are fairly complicated, Route 101 uses an alternative start, making the upper reaches of the canyon more accessible from Wadi Musa.

Route 101
Ed Deir to Wadi Siyyagh and Petra

Grade	Serious scramble and canyon; grade 3–4 climbing
Details	About 13km to and from Wadi Musa, with around 350m of ascent and descent
Time	Allow 7–8hrs: 3–4 hrs from Ed Deir down to the canyon and back to Qasr el Bint, plus 3hrs from Wadi Musa to Qasr el Bint and back, plus ½hr for the climb to Ed Deir (Routes 81 and 83).

The following information was supplied by Andrew Moore and Tim Pidsley, March 2000. 'Superlatives aren't enough for Wadi Siyyagh [Route 100]... We reached it by an adventurous round trip enabling many of Wadi Siyyagh's delights and challenges to be experienced without having to get to Bir Madhkhur. The descent into the wadi is geologically enthralling – a journey backwards through time.' Map 25.

The canyon of Wadi Siyyagh starts with a walk through pools, reeds and oleanders (Routes 100, 101)

Special requirements The route involves abseils and (returning up Wadi Siyyagh) exposed 3+ scrambling, so a rope and associated equipment are necessary.

The route
From Ed Deir walk along the edge of the plateau overlooking Wadi Siyyagh (see Route 83); near its highest point a well-named 'High Place' can be seen about 10m below. Not far E of this a shallow valley will be found. Follow this past a stone wall through juniper trees. The valley soon steepens and a 10m cliff is descended by abseil from a tree. Follow the left bank of the gully steeply, cross a small col, and go to a rocky island in the middle of the gully. Keeping left, descend rocky islands then scree to where a second abseil down a dry waterfall is necessary. Continue down to above an 8m (dry) water chute where the T-junction with Wadi Maruan can be seen. To reach the wadi there is a fairly obvious line on a cliff above the right bank of the water chute: scramble up then left across the cliff then descend increasingly rotten granite down Wadi Maruan to the confluence with Wadi Siyyagh. From there, follow Route 100 back up to Qasr el Bint and on to Wadi Musa.

A variation of this route descends directly from Wadi Ghurab alongside Wadi Maruan to Wadi Siyyagh; done by Wilf Colonna and Bernard Domenech, but no details available.

Returning to the start of Wadi Siyyagh, Route 102 also leads to Petra.

Route 102
Wadi Maqtal to Petra

This is said to be one of the old camel routes from Bir Madhkhur. It starts in Wadi Siyyagh but leaves it almost immediately, ascending the obvious wadi to the right, just E of a long sandstone ridge and below a prominent black summit, with Jebel Harun and its white summit tomb visible in the distance. From the head of the wadi the route then picks up the tracks between Jebel Harun and Petra to the NE. (Not checked by the authors, but information available from adventure travel companies in Wadi Musa.) See map 23.

JORDAN

JEBEL HARUN AND THE SOUTHERN PETRA AREA

The reputed tomb of Aaron, brother of Moses, overlooks Petra from the summit of Jebel Harun and provided the excuse for Swiss explorer Burkhardt to enter the city in 1812 via the following route.

Route 103
Petra to Jebel Harun

Every step opened out fresh interest and beauty in the wild scenery, immense chasms and vast views over strange boundless desert unfolded themselves at each turn of the winding path up the steep mountain; ...the slow advance chills with a feeling of strange solitude the intruder into the loneliness of this bygone world.

Edward Lear, en route to Jebel Harun (13 April 1858)

Grade	Moderate trek
Details	11km, descending about 100m to the Petra Basin then rising 370m to the summit at 1270m
Time	3½–4hrs; allow almost the same for the return journey – or combine with other treks through Wadi Sabra for a longer trip in this wild and mountainous area

A great mountain walk in the footsteps of the Prophets which was followed by Burkhardt when he 'discovered' Petra back in the early 19th century. The route passes through the heart of Petra then escapes the crowds for the breezy heights of the tomb of Aaron with its superb panoramic views. Camels can be taken to the foot of the mountain. See maps 23 and 26.

Guide Necessary if you want to enter the shrine, or to hire a donkey or camel. If not organised beforehand, arrangements can be made with local Bedouin at the Treasury or Roman Theatre area.

The route

Follow the broad track that leaves Petra just past the bend after the Roman Theatre area and rises W over the hill of Katuta to Pharaoh's Column. Continue along the new, wide track, descending into and crossing Wadi Ras Suleiman below Um el Biyyara (Route 85), and on towards the Snake Monument, which it passes below before curving back above it near the Djinn Block to a plateau.

The broad track stops just ahead, at which point Jebel Harun can be seen again. Three caves on the left here were still occupied by Bedouin in the late 1980s. Carry straight on along footpaths crossing the tributaries of Wadi Maqtal (Route 102) and continuing S, rising up a shoulder, parallel to a branch of the wadi. Carry on, eventually crossing this wadi and following a distinct path round a shoulder and up a

THE PETRA AREA – PETRA – ROUTE 103

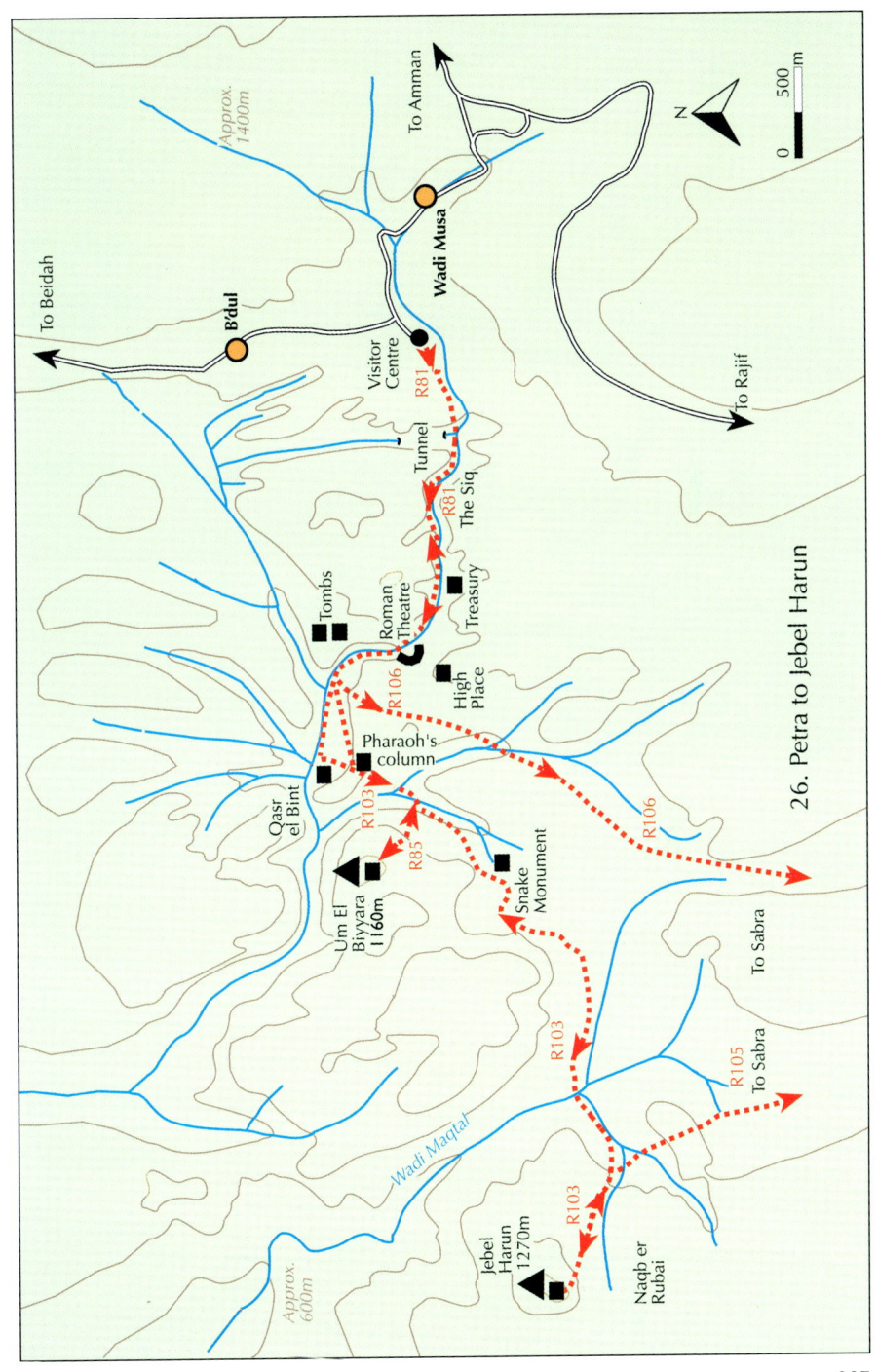

26. Petra to Jebel Harun

Nabataean steps leads up to the summit of Jebel Harun, location of the tomb of Aaron, brother of Moses (Routes 103, 112)

gentle valley, before rising up to the saddle on the far skyline. Zigzag back on a good path winding through cliffs to reach a flat area of land below the S side of the summit.

Continue on (ruins on left), turning right at the end with a great view through the gap of Naqb er Rubai to Wadi Araba (see Route 104). Above is the retaining wall of a huge Nabataean underground cistern with water (Bir Huweimel), well worth seeing. The path goes up some new steps at the front of the cistern and across its roof, then up old steps hewn in the rock to the summit from where the Monastery can be seen (it can also be seen looking N a third of the way up the final steps to the Maqam (Shrine of Aaron). A chance perhaps to meditate on the legendary events that have taken place on this remote mountaintop '...and the children of Israel whom God had forbidden to fight with Edom or to force a way through his land journeyed from Kadesh and came to Mount Hor [Jebel Harun] ...this mountain is of very difficult and steep ascent, rude steps and niches being cut in the rock to help the traveller. Here Moses and Eleazor, by God's command, accompanied Aaron to the top of the mount, where Moses took off his brother's sacerdotal robes to put them on Eleazor his son, for the high priest's service and life were about to close. And Aaron died there on the top of the mount, and Moses and Eleazor came down from it sorrowfully.' L. Valentine, *Palestine Past and Present* 1919 (see Appendix 2)

Return By the same route.

Apart from the route over Naqb er Rubai immediately S of Jebel Harun (see above), the key to the S entrance of Petra is the hidden but beautiful valley of Sabra.

THE JOURNEY OF SULTAN BAIBARS

The trade routes that reached Petra from the S and W were documented by Dr Fawzi Zayadine in *Archaeology of Jordan* (1985).

The Journey of Sultan Baibars, 1276

'Looking for the exact route of Sultan Baibars into Petra in 1276, I was able to walk or trace, with help of the Bedouins, six access roads from Wadi 'Araba. To the south, the route Suez–Ma'an ascends by Wadi Gharandal (Aridella) to Sadaqa (Sadagatta). It was possible to travel by Landrover from the village of Gharandal through Wadi es-Siq, a narrow colourful gorge, strewn with large boulders, and reach Delagha in two hours (30km). At el-Rajef, the explorer can enjoy a most fascinating panorama of the sandstone mountain range of Petra. At 3km from Delagha, a road bifurcates to Sadaqa or descends through Tayyibeh to Wadi Musa. Parallel to the Suez–Ma'an route, runs the Suez–Petra track which can reach the Nabataean capital from Wadi 'Araba by Wadi Sabra, Wadi Abu Khusheibeh or Naqb el-Ruba'i, the latter being the easiest for camels' (Major C. S. Jarvis had problems with his loaded camels in the ascent of Abu Khusheibeh: see below). This caravan road was probably described by Strabo as the track from Babylon to Egypt by Petra.

A fifth outlet to Wadi 'Araba runs through Wadi Musa. A large terraced area, called the Roman Garden by the Bedouin, extends at its mouth, west of Qasr Umm Rattam. A water reservoir at the northern side of the tower is fed by a long channel, which drains the wadi's water. From there a steep and narrow track climbs up to Petra by Wadi el-Siyyagh or to Beida by Sleisel. Finally, an easier outlet to the N crossed to the Negev through Beidah, Siq Um el 'Elda, Namala and Bir Madhkhur [the location of the new road].

Baibars, who was eager to reach Karak in a short time, had travelled by the shortest way (five days from Cairo to Petra). The last segment of his track had certainly impressed the chronicler: 'And thus, at the break of dawn, he ascended the Mountain, and wondrous high it was, cut with tortuous ravines, and these of crumbling stones, resemblance unto hardened sand, changing in their hues from red to azure and white; thither also were defiles in the mountains admitting the horseman riding through, in which are places as though rising steps hewn in the rock. On this mountain is the tomb of Aaron, Prophet of God, the brother of Moses, son of Umrân, peace upon them, on the left of the traveller whose face is unto Damascus.

The description of the itinerary by Nuwairi is accurate. Actually, the road that traverses Naqb el-Ruba'i by Jibal Sumr el-Tayyibeh ascends Wadi Jarret Salman or Jurf Himar and, leaving Jebel Harun to the left, drops down to Petra. In 1940 Major C. S. Jarvis, travelling from the Sinai, organised a caravan expedition by camels and horses from Wadi Abu Khusheibeh into Petra. He identified 'the old made track' which leads to the shoulder of Jebel Harun. 'I followed the same caravan route with a team from Paris, starting from Qasr el Bint, and reached the bed of Wadi Abu Khusheibeh, where extensive ruins are extant, in four hours. Little Nabataean pottery was collected at the ruins called Sayalet Abu Khusheibah, compared to the Late Roman and Byzantine pottery. There is a large water reservoir at the foot of Jebel Harun, known today as Bir Huweimel. At the bottom of Jebal el Farasheh, the slopes are terraced, and barrages built with large boulders extend in Wadi 'Iyal 'Id. No doubt such an agricultural technique was initiated by the Nabataeans. Another rock-cut cistern provided with a drain is at the mouth of the valley. The route passes by Jebal el Barrah, near the Snake Monument where the passage is carved in the sandstone and at the foot of Um el Biyarah where Arabic graffiti dated 723H (1323AD) were recently noticed. Crossing Wadi Farasa the path leads to the Pillar of Pharaoh and Qasr el Bint.'

Many of the adventure travel companies in Wadi Musa and Aqaba can organise treks on these ancient trails at your request, and we have had good reports of Wadi Abu Khusheibeh (see map 23).

Route 104
Ancient Trails to and from Wadi Sabra

Welcome to Sabra where only Allah and the Bedouin live.

Greeting made from a small Bedouin camp in the heart of Sabra when we first trekked through in the 1980s.

Sabra was the southern caravanserai of Petra and still has the remains of a small Roman outpost and theatre near its S end. From there ancient Nabataean trails continue to Humeimah, Rum and Aqaba in the S, and to Gharandal in Wadi Araba in the W en route to Sinai and Egypt. The route to the W starts about 1km after the Sabra Roman Theatre where a trail takes the right bank onto plains, passing eventually through a carved corridor 24m long. The wadis then merge into a sand-filled tongue, enter a gorge preceded by an ancient wall and ending after 70m at basins and cisterns. Beyond here is Ras adh Dhawi and its spring and, on the edge of Araba, the Tower Tomb made famous by David Roberts' sketch in the 19th century, now known as 'Roberts' Rock' (GPS alt. 430m N30° 16.514' E35° 19.084').

Far to the W of Sabra is a Roman copper mine, its chambers supported by columns of rock and called – like its counterpart in the Feynan area – Um el Amad or 'Mother of Columns'. We have checked very little of the area W of Sabra, but it is part of the trek from Petra to Wadi Rum and known to many of the adventure tourism companies.

Sabra is little disturbed by tourism and a great place to wander through or camp in; the Waters of Sabra, just beyond the Roman Theatre (see Routes 105 and 106 below), are usually a reliable source of water. Whether or not this freedom to roam will be curtailed when the region S or Sabra becomes an RSCN Nature Reserve remains to be seen.

Route 105
Petra to Jebel Harun and Wadi Sabra

Grade	Moderate trek
Details	20km, descending about 100m to the Petra Basin, rising 370m to the summit of Jebel Harun at 1270m, then descending almost 500m to the Roman Theatre of Sabra, from where Routes 107–109 continue
Time	Allow 7hrs

A wonderful day in the mountains: pleasant walking, great scenery and lots of historic interest. Go on foot or with camels. See maps 26 and 27.

Guide Necessary if you want to travel by camels or donkeys; recommended if you're going to continue by a different route, rather than return the same way.

The route
Follow Route 103 to the summit of Jebel Harun (3½hrs). Descend the steps from Aaron's Tomb and follow the path down the zigzags and out onto the SW saddle, above Naqb er Rubai, then down again in the direction of Petra, crossing a small wadi.

Following the well-worn trail from Jebel Harun to Wadi Sabra and its Roman Theatre

Here leave the main Petra track and continue down the left (E) side of the wadi across a flat area by a little path and down well-worn zigzags to a bend in the next wadi. Cross this and continue in the same direction into another wadi. Descend this past two juniper trees and cross the next wadi up red sand. Continue still on small paths in the same direction along wadis left of two small domes and up a wadi with terraces and dams to a field. Ahead are small mountains. Continue towards them, following a path through fields and up to a saddle above the N end of Wadi Batahi. There are now two options:

Option 1 Contour round to join the Petra–Wadi Sabra track where it leaves the wadi rim to contour round SE between the wadi and the mountains (Route 106; 1½hrs to here from Jebel Harun, and another 1½hrs down Route 106 to Sabra Roman Theatre).

Option 2 From the saddle take a path contouring right across a sandy slope, then descending a ridge into Wadi Batahi, which leads down to the junction with Wadi Sabra. Continue another 1km to find the Roman Theatre and associated ruins in oleanders and other vegetation.
Springs should be found a little further on down the wadi at the Waters of Sabra. The usual direct way to Sabra is via Route 106.

Route 106
Petra to Wadi Sabra and its Roman Theatre

Grade	Moderate trek
Details	11km to Sabra, descending and ascending about 100m before descending 200m. The trek may be extended to include Jebel Harun (Route 105), or continued through canyons and valleys up to the King's Highway by Routes 107–109, or down to Wadi Araba, or all the way to Wadi Rum (see Route 118).
Time	About 3hrs

> A reasonably easy walk needing careful route finding and combining fascinating history with majestic mountains and wild valleys. If you return to Petra the same day it is quite a long journey – why not make the most of it and sleep out in Sabra? It may be done on foot or with camels or donkeys, which can be hired in Wadi Musa. See maps 26 and 27.

Guide Recommended; essential if you go by camel or donkey.

The route
Go down the Siq into Petra, turning left round the end of the mountain just after the Roman Theatre. Rise up the hillside and then head S about 100m below the cliffs, past caves and across the old city wall. Pass the entrance of the wadi leading to the Soldier's Tomb and carry on until below some tower-like tombs. Below is a wadi in a small rocky ravine.

Descend and cross it, finding a well-trodden path up rainbow-coloured rocks on the opposite side. This path is the key to the route. Follow it along the right side of this ravine and continue S over a little col and, still on the obvious path, cross the next small wadi to its left side and rise above it through more rainbow-red rocks. Immediately after continue rising through bright white flat rocks (the Jebel Harun tomb is obvious to the right), and carry on towards the distant mountains to the S. Don't go left through the first valley.

The path now continues past fields with a wadi on the right (stone dam) to the col above Wadi el Batahi, which plunges directly S to join Wadi Sabra after 2km. (Excellent views, 1½hrs from the Visitor Centre.) It is possible to descend this valley (Route 105, Option 2). Instead the main path descends a few metres before contouring left towards two rocky hills, then out onto the peninsula between Wadis Batahi and Sabra. From here it descends by zigzags (supported by old walls) to a flat area of land above Sabra.

The Roman Theatre in Wadi Sabra, southern gateway to Petra

Cross this by a path on the left side to a rocky promontory where the path goes right along a narrow ridge and up to a small top. From the S end of this little hill descend into Wadi Sabra, close to its junction with Wadi Batahi. Beyond this point Sabra is wide and for a while increasingly lush and fertile with running water in springtime. The Roman Theatre is 1km down on the left side – the Waters of Sabra are beyond.

Return By the same route, or by Routes 107, 108 or 109.

Route 107
Wadi Sabra to Wadi Musa

Grade	Moderate trek
Details	9km, rising 200m (20km for the round trip starting by Route 106)
Time	Allow 3hrs (6hrs if starting by the previous route)

A pleasant and very direct route back to Wadi Musa, finishing on vague paths with a bit of tricky route finding through the eastern limits of Petra before descending terraced gardens between the entrance to the Siq and the Triclinium. See map 27.

The route
From the Roman Theatre follow Wadi Sabra back to the NE for about 5km along paths which occasionally cross the meandering riverbed past old walls, eventually climbing up the slopes at the valley head to arrive at a col (1½hrs). (The Petra road is high above on the hillside to the right, with new hotels and unsightly rubble from roadworks visible.)
   Continue in the same line, descending through a little valley with ploughed land and rising up and along with domes to the left. Continue in the same direction (roughly NE) increasingly close to the domes, rising up to an area with stone walls and crossing a 4WD track (ignore it). Still in the same line descend towards a fairly large white dome split into three by cracks, with a Bedouin shelter below it.
   Go right of this (a few Nabataean steps) and pass through a gap in the domes, then follow a path which rises up past junipers and between white rocks to a ploughed field. Go round the field to reach its far bottom corner and descend a path into and across a valley, then follow the path up and along, still heading in the same general NE direction with domes on the left.
   At the top of the rise note terraces below and tombs on the left. Go down the terraces and trend right to join the road to the Siq, at the side of the Triclinium. The Petra Gate is 5mins up the road (you will need your pass).

The Sabra area is a great place to explore and excellent trekking country. There are various ways on as detailed in Dr Fawzi Zayadine's report 'The Journey of Sultan Baibars' (see page 208). If you have a local guide you can continue on foot or with camels on old caravan routes to Gharandal in Wadi Araba, to 'Roberts' Rock', or all the way to Bir Hamad, Humeimah and Wadi Rum.
   There are other routes – sometimes requiring one or two days – which head out from Sabra towards Taybeh and Rajif on the King's Highway high above, or even alternative ways back to Wadi Musa. Routes 108 and 109 lead to the next water source – the Waters of Tibn.

Route 108
Wadi Sabra to Wadi Tibn via M'zayla Siq

Grade	Serious trek; short but in a remote area and part of a longer journey
Details	4km to the Waters of Tibn, rising from 800m to the pass at 1000m before descending to 800m
Time	1½hrs from Sabra

Short and sweet! A typical Bedouin short cut – straightforward in concept but quite complex in detail, always interesting and in wild mountain scenery – shown to us by Awad Faraj, a Bedouin who spends much of his time in Sabra. Despite its brevity, good route-finding ability is necessary as is confidence in the mountains. See map 27.

Guide Recommended.

The route
From the Roman Theatre in Wadi Sabra go back up the riverbed a short way to where it sweeps over to the SE side after travelling in a fairly straight line from the junction of Wadis Batahi and Sabra 1km to the NE.

A careful search now reveals a little path zigzagging up the E side. High above is the huge rock face of Jebel el Jathum. Follow the path up as it becomes more defined and enters a narrow ravine, which rises up S. Very soon it goes through a small pass to enter a hanging garden. Cross to the right side and go through a gap in the rocks before reaching the end to enter a parallel ravine. (This is the ravine that drops into the Roman Theatre and, so it is said, used to supply water for aquatic games.)

Follow this forested valley up, still heading generally S to SE. When it starts to climb more steeply a big black narrow cleft will be seen on the left. Water will usually be found about 50m inside.

The little-known Bedouin 'short cut' of M'zayla Siq connects Wadi Sabra with Wadi Tibn

THE PETRA AREA – PETRA – ROUTE 108

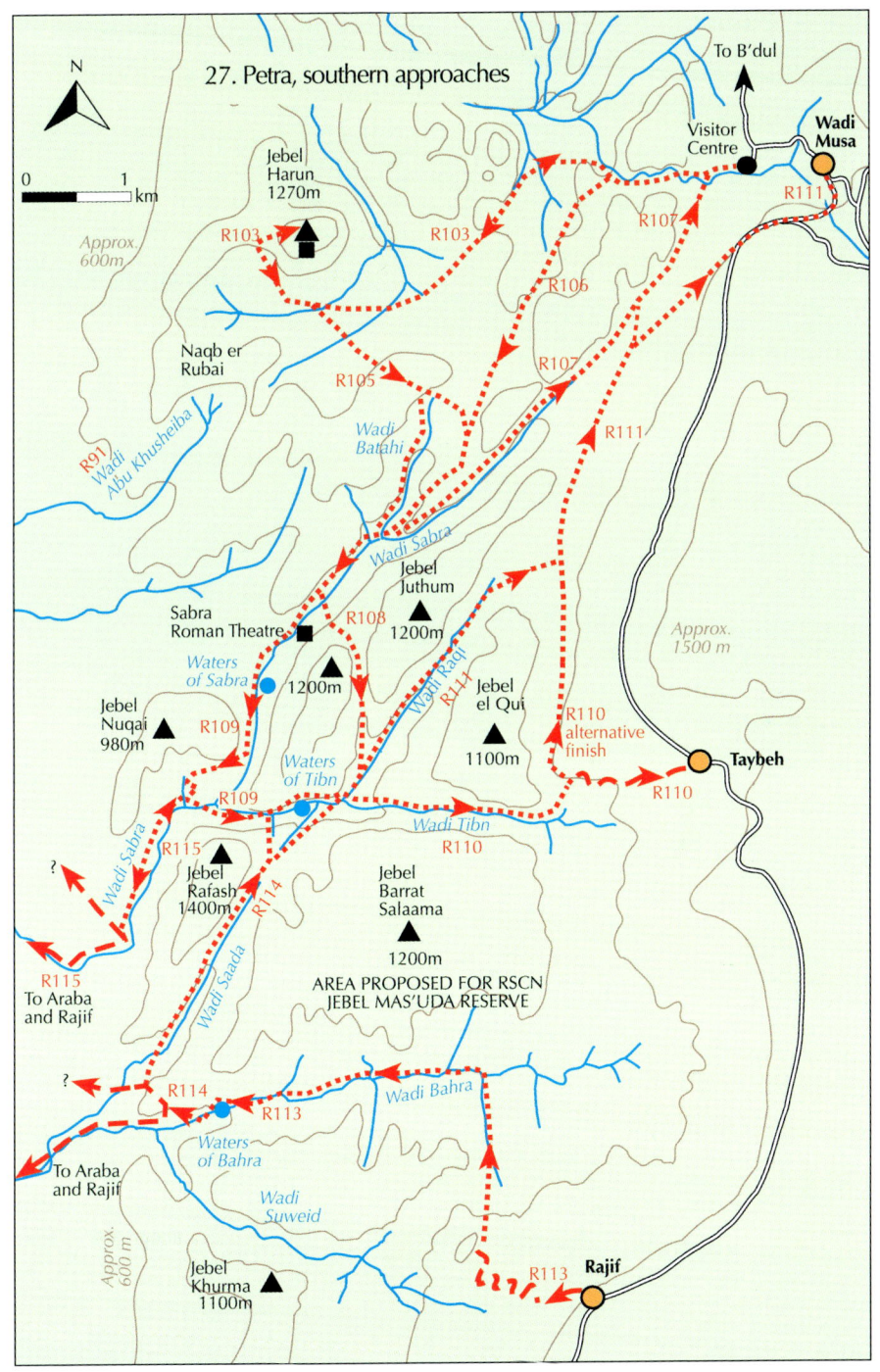

27. Petra, southern approaches

Continue up the steepening ravine to the pass and descend the other side, keeping near the right side and eventually passing close to three Bedouin cave shelters. Just below here the path goes out of the main wadi bed, curving right below a big rock face and passing the head of another wadi. Bedouin steps go down the right side of this and eventually into the bed of the big valley below, Wadi el Raqi. Follow this down to the SW for 1km, where the impressive narrow *siq* of Wadi Tibn will be found gashing the cliffs on the E side, almost hidden by oleanders.

About 100m further down, Wadi Raqi bends sharply to the right (W); a little way past this bend follow a path along the right side of the valley. The Waters of Tibn should be found below some large fallen rocks with a fig tree growing from them. Also at the bend in Wadi Raqi another wadi enters from the S. This leads to Wadi Saada which cuts through Jebel Barrat Salama to meet with Wadi el Bahra leading to Rajif, a small village high above on the edge of the plateau (Routes 113 and 114). There should be a seasonal pool a short distance up this wadi.

Route 109 to Tibn is equally interesting, with some impressive canyon scenery and its own unexpected route-finding problems.

Route 109
The Sabra – Tibn Connection

Grade	Serious trek; short but in a remote area and part of a longer journey
Details	5km, descending 100m to 700m then rising again to 800m
Time	2hrs

Despite the fact these two wadis meet downstream of the Sabra Roman Theatre the way is not quite as straightforward as you might imagine. Like Route 108 it is not so much a route in itself as a way to the next water source. See map 27.

Guide Recommended.

The route
Follow Wadi Sabra down from the Roman Theatre, passing the Waters of Sabra then going though a narrow white twisting canyon. En route, 1300m down from the theatre, a columned building lies in ruins above an S-bend with a prehistoric site above. Continuing down, as the canyon becomes more pronounced about 3.5km from the Roman Theatre, follow a path along its right bank contouring along a steep cliff. Don't follow the stream – it continues to descend for a short way then plunges over a cliff into a box canyon. Follow the path right, along the lip of the canyon for a short distance to where the lower end of Wadi Tibn can be seen below. To reach it, follow the Bedouin shepherds' track as it curves W before descending steeply down the rocky hillside past GPS alt. 730m N30° 15.316′ E35° 23.849´ to the valley.

Now follow Wadi Tibn upstream, passing the box canyon on your left (GPS alt. 670m N30° 15.219′ E35° 23.876′) before entering the Lower Tibn canyon. Scramble up this in rugged surroundings until after 1km it opens out a little into an amphitheatre in the mountains. Continue up the wadi bed passing a wooded valley which goes right (S) to Wadi Saada and eventually Rajif (Route 114, Option 1) until you find the Waters of Tibn seeping out below some large fallen boulders with a fig tree growing from them.

The best is yet to come …

Route 110
The Ascent of the Siq of Tibn to Taybeh or Wadi Musa

Grade	Easy canyon, moderate trek (part of a longer journey)
Details	8km, rising from 800m to 1360m at Taybeh, or 16km to Wadi Musa. The start is reached by Routes 108 and 109 from Sabra, or Route 115 from the Rajif–Araba road.
Time	3hrs to Taybeh, 5hrs to Wadi Musa

The *siq* of Wadi Tibn winds its awe-inspiring narrow way between steep water-polished cliffs, at one point passing below a huge jammed boulder. After rains it may be necessary to wade through pools (or it may be impassable); during rains it would be extremely dangerous. This route is used by Bedouin coming down with loaded donkeys or sheep and goats from the village of Taybeh on the King's Highway to get to Wadi Sabra and beyond. Don't miss it! See photo page 174 and map 27.

Guide Recommended.

The route
From the Waters of Tibn go up the path on the left (true right) bank to reach the upper valley of Wadi Raqi almost immediately. Follow Raqi as it bends left into oleander thickets, which conceal the unexpected and extremely narrow entrance to the Siq of Tibn on the right.

Follow this up generally ESE in very impressive surroundings rivalling – if not exceeding – the Petra Siq to a junction where the main wadi bed curves left and passes between big cliffs. The best path with Bedouin steps for pack animals is always on the right side, and bypasses obstacles in the wadi bed.

Eventually a yellow scree slope appears to bar the way, but the path continues loosely up it to a col, the wadi being in a narrow *siq* below to the left. Continue in the same direction (N) along the line of the wadi, following its true left bank and passing two small sunken Nabataean water cisterns cut into the rock. Just beyond the valley

Approaching the upper end of Tibn Siq

opens out into a pleasant arena surrounded by white rock domes. About 100m above to the left a house will be seen built into the cliff. On its right side is a huge concealed water basin; there should be a bucket here, and a rope, to reach the water a few metres down (2–2½hrs from the start). From here there is a choice of two routes and destinations:

Option 1 (to Taybeh) To the right (E) a 4WD track will be seen descending into the valley. This winds up to Taybeh about 2km away, arriving first at the old village (now tastefully converted into the award-winning hotel of Taybet Zamman). The new village is above on the King's Highway.

Option 2 (to Wadi Musa) Pleasant walking between domes and along the upper edge of the canyon of Wadi Raqi, most interestingly completed by joining Route 107 to the Petra Visitor Centre. Otherwise the route ends by following rather tedious 4WD tracks to Wadi Musa.

Directly ahead from the water basin the main valley of Wadi el Batha continues N. Follow this up, taking the main (right) branch after about 1km, rising up for another 1km to a gap in the cliffs ahead to reach the tops of the white domes and the E rim of Wadi Raqi (the road from Taybeh to Wadi Musa is about 250m above to the E). Follow the path N along the rim with some minor detours up and down to cross or bypass the occasional *siq*, but always keeping close to the canyon rim for about 5km (about 1½hrs from the water basin).

Almost immediately after leaving the end of the canyon rim – where the canyon ends – it should be possible to descend the hillside for 150m to join Route 107 as it emerges from Wadi Sabra. Alternatively the path meets the end of a 4WD track, which rises gradually up the hillside in the same N direction for a further 3.5km to meet the road above. Just before meeting the road (telegraph poles visible 100m above) another 4WD track descends gently to the left, reaching the outskirts of Wadi Musa village after 1km. From there various paths or roads can be taken directly into Wadi Musa or down to the Visitor Centre (1½hrs from the canyon rim).

Route 111
The Waters of Tibn to Wadi Musa via Wadi Raqi

There is an alternative exit up Wadi el Raqi. This has not been checked but local Bedouin talked about a path following the valley to the NE from the lower entrance to Tibn *siq* for about 3km, and finally ascending to the E rim about 1km before reaching the head of the valley, to join the route described above. The distance from Tibn to Wadi Musa is about 13km. See map 27.

Next comes Route 112, a great trip combining some of the best features S of Petra.

Imagine you're driving north along the edge of an escarpment: to your right, rolling green uplands are cut here and there by stony ploughed fields sometimes with a black Bedouin tent on their perimeter. To the left, the hillside plunges steeply down past a village of stone-walled, flat-roofed houses reminiscent of Morocco or the Himalayas, to a petrified cloud sea of pale rock domes split by dark, mysterious canyons. On the summit of the highest and most distant peak the tomb of Aaron, brother of Moses, brightly reflects the morning sun, already high in a clear blue sky. Far beyond, blue hills shimmer in the heat haze rising from the unseen desert valley of Wadi Araba deep below sea level. What's down there in those unknown mountains and canyons? Is it as inhospitable as it looks? Is there any water? The area intrigued and tantalised us for years as we passed by on the local bus between Wadi Rum and Petra.

'Trekking through Tibn' Tony Howard (*The Great Outdoors* magazine, 1990)

Route 112
Taybeh to Wadi Musa via Tibn, Sabra, Jebel Harun and Petra

Grade	Serious trek
Details	33km; the route descends almost 800m to the junction of Lower Tibn with Wadi Sabra, then rises about 600m to the summit of Jebel Harun before descending about 300m and rising 100m to reach Wadi Musa
Time	1 day, but better over 2 days with a bivouac in Sabra

This is a great trek, taking in reverse a selection of the routes described above and detailed here in that direction so the route is more easily followed. See map 27.

Special requirements Competence in route finding is necessary.
Guide Recommended.
Approach From Wadi Musa take a bus or taxi 12km S on the King's Highway to Taybeh and walk down to the converted village hotel complex of Taybet Zamman.

Stage 1 Taybeh to the Waters of Tibn (8km, 3hrs)
Walk down to the lower gate of the hotel and follow the track slightly downhill above an orchard. After 100m take the left fork and follow the gravel road as it winds down the hill. After ½hr it reaches a picturesque basin and wadi between large rock domes. Across the wadi, hidden in the cliffs, are water cisterns. Up the wadi to the N in a red valley is the track to Petra (Route 110, Option 2). Down the wadi to the S is the way to the Siq of Tibn (Route 110). After 100m the streambed disappears into a narrow rock chasm. The path goes over the shoulder on its left from the top of which the view abruptly opens out and down into Wadi Tibn.

Carefully descend the long loose slope into the tree-filled wadi and follow it for 20mins or so from the end of the road to the first wadi junction where Wadi Taybeh enters from the left. Continue straight on down the riverbed, through the increasingly impressive canyon. Wherever there are minor impasses, a donkey track will be found on the left bank. After about ½hr the wadi bends right, and in another 20mins or so it goes right quite sharply with a steep tree-filled valley entering from the left.

Keep going down the streambed, taking the donkey track to right or left wherever convenient. Eventually the walls close in until the last section is sometimes less than 2m wide with smooth cliffs on either side, sometimes passing below large jammed boulders. Suddenly, at the end of the second narrow section, the *siq* emerges into Wadi Raqi and widens out. Follow the valley left (SW) for 100m to where another wadi enters from the SW. There is usually a deep pool of water not far up this wadi, but it is often stagnant, being the remnants of winter rains. This little valley connects with the next side valley of Wadi Saada (Route 114, Option 2) at the T-junction with stone walls (not checked by the authors).

The main riverbed of Tibn now swings W. Follow a path along the right side of the valley and about 200m down, just past a fig tree in some large fallen rocks, there should be (but cannot be guaranteed) a series of water seepages in the riverbed – the Waters of Tibn. Possible overnight stop.

Stage 2 The Waters of Tibn to the Waters of Sabra (5km, 2hrs)
From the Waters of Tibn, descend the wadi bed. (The second valley on the left goes to Wadi Saada and eventually Rajif: Route 114, Option 1.) Continuing down Tibn, the walls close in again impressively after

Crossing a Bedouin bridge in Tibn Siq, built to allow the passage of livestock

which a path will eventually be found on the right side where the wadi changes direction from W to NW. Follow this path along until Wadi Sabra enters through an impressive gash on the right. Don't bother going up it; it's a vertically walled box canyon (GPS alt. 670m N30° 15.219' E35° 23.876'). Instead go down the main valley, which almost immediately widens.

A path will be found on the right at this point, traversing below cliffs across a rocky hillside – the key to entering Sabra. Follow it for about 200m, rising gently into a small side wadi. Scramble up this, often quite steeply (it is a donkey path). Where the angle eases, the Sabra path goes right on ledges. These ledges (well-trodden) emerge directly above the cliffs of the box canyon (GPS alt. 730m N30° 15.316' E35° 23.849'). Follow them round and along above the streambed, which it eventually reaches.

Continue (NE), following the wadi bed for ½hr or so until reaching the little stream of the Waters of Sabra. This cuts its way through some small winding canyons in white rock. Eventually the vegetation in the wadi becomes so dense at an area with a big palm that you are forced onto a track worn into a rocky headland just above. This leads almost directly to the old Roman settlement. The Roman Theatre is a little way further on, cut into the mountain on the opposite side of the wadi. Possible overnight stop.

Stage 3 The Waters of Sabra to Jebel Harun, Petra and Wadi Musa (20km, 7hrs)
Follow Sabra up for 1km to the junction of Wadis Sabra and Batahi, then either go directly up Wadi Batahi or the hillside on its right to find the track of Route 106 on the ridge between the two valleys. Either way you will eventually arrive at the head of Wadi Batahi after about 1½hrs. Jebel Harun with its white tomb is unmistakable to the W. Cross small wadis and fields heading slightly N of W to reach the track going up to Jebel Harun from Petra (Route 103). Follow this to the top and return by this route to Petra and Wadi Musa.

The next village S of Taybeh on the King's Highway is Rajif, below which two deeply incised valleys can be seen descending into the wilderness of mountains. The S one is the narrow steep walled canyon of Wadi Suweid (no details, although there is a route through). The N one is Wadi el Bahra and is a well-used Bedouin route – Route 113 – to the lower valleys.

Route 113
Rajif to the Waters of Bahra

Grade	Moderate trek, which becomes more serious if you continue on other routes rather than returning
Details	10km, descending from 1500m to 600m
Time	About 4hrs from Rajif, 3hrs from the end of the initial 4WD track

A reasonably straightforward yet varied trek through some wild terrain. Having reached the Waters of Bahra you still have to get out again which requires care with route finding if you are continuing by another route. Water supplies are unreliable in late summer, so take plenty if you're planning to stay overnight. See map 27.

Guide Recommended if you are planning to walk out by another route.
Approach Going S from Wadi Musa on the King's Highway Taybeh is reached after 12km and Rajif after another 10km (local bus and taxi services).

Descending the Wadi Bahra in wild surroundings

The route
In Rajif take the first major right (W) turn, then immediately right again, and take the road down through the small village till it becomes a track zigzagging steeply down the hillside for 3km (2km in a direct line WNW if you are walking) to reach some flat ground. This rises gently for a short distance to meet a cliff, which bars further W progress (alt. 1240m). This point can be reached by 4WD. (To the left, a path goes along the foot of the cliff for about 200m to a Nabataean water cistern cut into the narrow ravine above Wadi Suweid.)

To the right (N) is a ploughed field and beyond it a wadi descends towards the hidden valley of Wadi el Bahra. Walk along the left side of the field, below the cliff, to enter the wadi, which goes N between the rocky domes of Jebel el Jilf. After about ½hr the wadi drops steeply over small cliffs.

Bypass the obstacle by going up a Bedouin donkey path on the right side, along a rock ledge below an overhang. (There is a supporting wall on the outside of the path, built by Bedouin to ease access for loaded donkeys.) Follow the ledge round and across a side wadi, then pick your way carefully down the donkey track which descends rocky ledges back into the continuation of the wadi.

After 200m or so the wadi drops over more small cliffs and another path will be found on its right (E) side, contouring along above the wooded ravine and eventually emerging into Wadi el Bahra (approx 1hr from the end of the 4WD track).

(If you are coming up Wadi el Bahra in the opposite direction this wadi can be identified by a massive projecting rock at the top of the opposite cliff, on the N side of Bahra, vaguely reminiscent of the Sphinx's head.)

The wide stony bed of el Bahra is followed easily W for about 4km, passing right of a prominent rock tower beyond which the wadi suddenly narrows, then becomes filled with oleanders. There is some water seepage here (in springtime). Just beyond this point a stone shelter will be found built into the cliff on the left (S) of the wadi. This marks the place where the donkey path leaves the wadi and rises up left (SW) to an obvious shoulder above the deep and narrow ravine. The path then descends again to reach the riverbed at a (probably dry) waterfall with small shelters built into the overhanging cliff below on both sides of the wadi. Beyond are an olive grove and gardens, with pools in the wadi (March 1998), the 'Waters of Bahra'.

From here 4WD tracks continue downstream connecting with routes to Wadi Araba in the W and to Bir Hamad, Humeimah and Rum in the S (not checked by the authors). There is also a cunningly direct Bedouin way through the mountains to the N to reach the Waters of Tibn: Route 114.

Route 114
The Rajif – Tibn Connection

Grade	Serious trek; short but in a remote area and part of a longer journey; some grade 2 scrambling
Details	7km, rising 300m from the Waters of Bahra to 900m then descending 100m to the Waters of Tibn
Time	2½hrs

Another essential part of the maze! The hidden valley and tree-filled ravine of Wadi Saada make a direct link between the two water sources. See map 27.

Guide Recommended.

The route
Above the olive grove at the Waters of Bahra (Route 113) is a concrete water tank and a bulldozed track. Follow this up NW for 0.5km out of the wadi and over a shoulder (alt. 640m), then down into the next little valley. (This valley goes back down to join the main valley of Bahra about 0.5km to the SW, whilst the bulldozed track goes W over the next shoulder to an area of low hills S of Wadi Sabra.)

Go up the valley to the NE for 1km at which point it suddenly enters a narrow ravine filled with oleanders, figs and other trees including white broom with (in springtime) sweet-smelling blossom. This ravine goes directly NNE. Follow it to its end in Wadi Saada, picking the easiest way on small paths through the bushes. The ravine is about 2km long and varies from 5 to 10m wide (1½–2hrs from the olive grove and about 6hrs from Rajif).

Exit from the ravine by scrambling up a water-worn sandstone chimney to the left (grade 2) for 10m in easy steps. Beyond is a rocky slope then the open valley of Wadi Saada, which rises in 1km up to a pass (alt. 900m), the best path being on its right (E) side, past a juniper tree. From the col the valley continues in the same NNE direction for 1km to a hollow with old walls and stone shelters tucked in the small cliffs on either side of the valley. There are now two choices of route: a tree-filled valley to the N, or an open valley rising up to a prominent cairn to the NNE. Either way is less then 0.5km.

Option 1 The tree-filled valley descends quite steeply past a large boulder, which can be passed on either side (most easily on the left). Continue down the left side, through trees and boulders, crossing to the right at the valley mouth to emerge at a large juniper. Descend easily into Lower Wadi Tibn. The Waters of Tibn are 5mins upstream below a huge fallen block on the N side. The way to Wadi Sabra is downstream.

Option 2 The other open valley rising NNE is (according to a local Bedouin) the easiest way to reach Wadi Tibn from the hollow. There is a water basin (seasonal) in the right hand valley 200m before reaching Tibn. The Waters of Tibn are 200m downstream of this junction. This is probably the easiest and therefore the best way if you are continuing straight on to Taybeh up the canyon of Wadi Tibn (not checked by the authors).

Scrambling up the ravine to Wadi Saada, another little-known Bedouin 'short cut', this time connecting Wadi Bahra to Wadi Tibn

It would obviously be possible to pick up the Tibn – Sabra – Petra trek here (Route 112), the whole route being 42km and best spread over two days. It would also be possible to start from Beidah in the N of Petra and continue S by any of these routes making a 50km trek. An alternative start or finish to treks passing through the Sabra–Tibn area is to enter or leave via Route 115.

Route 115
Lower Wadi Sabra

Grade	Easy walk, leading to more serious treks en route to Petra or Taybeh
Details	6km from the Rajif–Araba road to the Sabra–Tibn confluence at the box canyon (see Routes 109 and 112)
Time	2hrs to the box canyon and the same for the return journey if not continuing by other routes to Taybeh or Petra (less if you don't need to walk from the road)

A very pleasant area surrounded by rugged mountains and worth using to start any of the Sabra–Tibn treks (if you can get to the start). It's also part of the **Nabataean Trail** from Dana to Petra and Wadi Rum. See map 27.

Approach Drive down the recently surfaced road that starts 4km S of Rajif, signed to Gharandal and Wadi Araba, passing the well of Bir Hamad (see Route 118) after about 15km to reach the first dramatic view of the cliffs W of Rajif after a further 10km. Continue down hairpins for about 6km to the bridge over Wadi Bahra, W of Bahra Canyon (Route 113). From there it's about 4km to a point just before the Sabra bridge (GPS alt. 580m N30° 14.364' E35° 21.540') where a track heads off E up the wadi. If you haven't got a car, a taxi should be able to get you here from Taybeh or Rajif. A 4WD would be better as it would also save a 3km walk up Wadi Sabra.

The route
Walk or drive the track up Sabra for about 3km to just before it enters the wadi bed for the last time before sweeping up left into the hills and leaving the valley. Here there is a nice sandy sleeping place above the wadi bed with lots of trees and dead wood, but almost certainly no water in the wadi. Up to the left (W) is a cliff of steeply tilted strata, above which is a small summit. Park off the track (GPS alt. 600m N30° 14.045' E35° 22.960').

Walk up the valley on the right of the wadi either by the side of the wadi bed or on the plateau, just above where there are ruins and some fenced-off Bedouin gardens. Beyond the paths merge and continue most often on the left side of the dry riverbed. Eventually a small stream (probably seasonal) may be met in the valley bottom after which the walk continues to the point where the valley narrows to a little canyon. The path is forced up left here. Not much further on the junction of Sabra and Tibn streambeds is reached. Wadi Sabra goes left into a box canyon, which bars access to its upper valley (GPS alt. 670m N30° 15.219' E35° 23.876'). Wadi Tibn continues up to its spring and upper canyon (Route 109).

Unless you are returning the same way, two options are now possible:

Option 1 Continue up Tibn in dramatic rock scenery to reach the access routes to Wadi Bahra or to continue out up the Siq of Tibn (Route 110).

Option 2 Backtrack about 200m along the cliff downstream of the box canyon to find the way into the upper Sabra Valley, its Roman Theatre and routes to Petra (Route 112).

Back at the Rajif–Araba road (see Route 115) and a further 7km NW of the Sabra bridge, the famous **Nabataean Watchtower** or **Tower Tomb** depicted by David Roberts in 1839 (see Route 104) will be seen on the right with its 'lookout post' carved out of the summit. It's in a commanding position, with the open expanse of Wadi Araba to the W and the approaches from there to Petra, and the summit of Jebel Harun to the NE (GPS alt. 430m N30° 16.514' E35° 19.084').

Another 8km further on the road meets the highway from Aqaba to the Dead Sea at a military checkpoint; you may need your passport (GPS alt. 250m N30° 17.588' E35° 15.099'). From there it's about 125km N to the Dead Sea or, after 42km (having passed the turning for Bir Madhkhur – see Route 100 – after about 15km) a small but recently surfaced road can be taken back up to Beidah and Petra (see Route 91), with an option to visit the RSCN Feynan Eco-Lodge below the Dana Reserve. Take the turning signed Feynan Eco-Lodge, 31km, and Little Petra. About 9km up this road there is a turning to the right; either continue up the road to the lodge, or take the right turn, signed 'Namlah' (Wadi Namala), which gives a scenic drive of 34km to the Beidah–Little Petra junction 7km N of Petra, location of the two Bedouin tourist camps (see introductory notes to the Petra chapter).

The Rajif–Araba road also passes the well of Bir Hamad (map 28) on its way down to the Sabra bridge. This is a staging post for treks and safaris from Petra to Wadi Rum via Lower Wadi Sabra (see below and Route 118). For details contact the various adventure travel companies listed in Appendix 1. From Bir Hamad the route continues S for 20km, crossing the curious crevasse of Shaq al Ajous to reach Humeimah, the next point of historic interest.

Ominous clouds gathering above Lower Wadi Sabra

HUMEIMAH

This is the last important caravanserai on the way south from Petra to Wadi Rum or Aqaba. Humeimah is the largest important antiquity site in this comparatively barren area and is famous for its water systems, some of which are still in use. Originally Nabataean, dating from around 80BC, Humeimah was later an important way station on the Roman Via Nova Traiana. An aqueduct brought water down 19km from the Shara Mountains in the northeast and there are various reservoirs, underground cisterns and baths – quite an achievement on the edge of the Hisma and Rum deserts (map 28).

It is most easily accessible from the Desert Highway. Heading south from Ma'an the road soon descends the big hill of Ras Naqb, passing through the new village of Humeimah at its foot before reaching Quweirah and the Wadi Rum junction. A signed track leaves the road near the bottom of its descent from Ras Naqb and heads west for 11km across the desert plateau to reach old Humeimah at an altitude close to 1000m. The extensive ruins of the original Nabataean and later Roman town are at GPS alt. 950m N30° 32.411' E35° 24.321'. Humeimah can also be approached along 4WD tracks heading north for about 8km from Quweirah which is further south along the highway, just before the Rum junction.

A Visitor Centre is being constructed here and it is worthwhile having a look at the remains of the houses, churches, cisterns, dams, hilltop tombs and so on. Beyond, to the northwest, accessible on 4WD tracks, is some truly dramatic scenery where the plateau drops abruptly into the depths of Wadi Araba and is riven by a maze of spectacular sandstone canyons. There is a great viewpoint at the top of Wadi Heimar (GPS alt. 960m N29° 58.261' E35° 20.445').

Route 116
Wadi Heimar

This dramatic canyon system cuts its way W through complex mountains into the sands of Wadi Araba. See map 28.

There are routes both up and down this canyon and through others in the area. Sabbah Eid (see Appendix 1) knows some as, no doubt, do other Bedouin guides from Wadi Rum and Petra. One route is a round trip, returning to the Humeimah plateau further N. The canyon can also be accessed from Wadi Araba via Route 117.

Route 117
Wadi Heimar from Wadi Araba

The wadi, which is visible in the hills, can be followed by 4WD for about 14km up its right (SE branch) ending in a short Petra-like *siq*. From there (as far as we have been) it's less than 15km up Wadi Heimar to the ancient Nabataean/Roman town of Humeimah, probably emerging near GPS alt. 960m N29° 58.261' E35° 20.445'. Location, map 28.

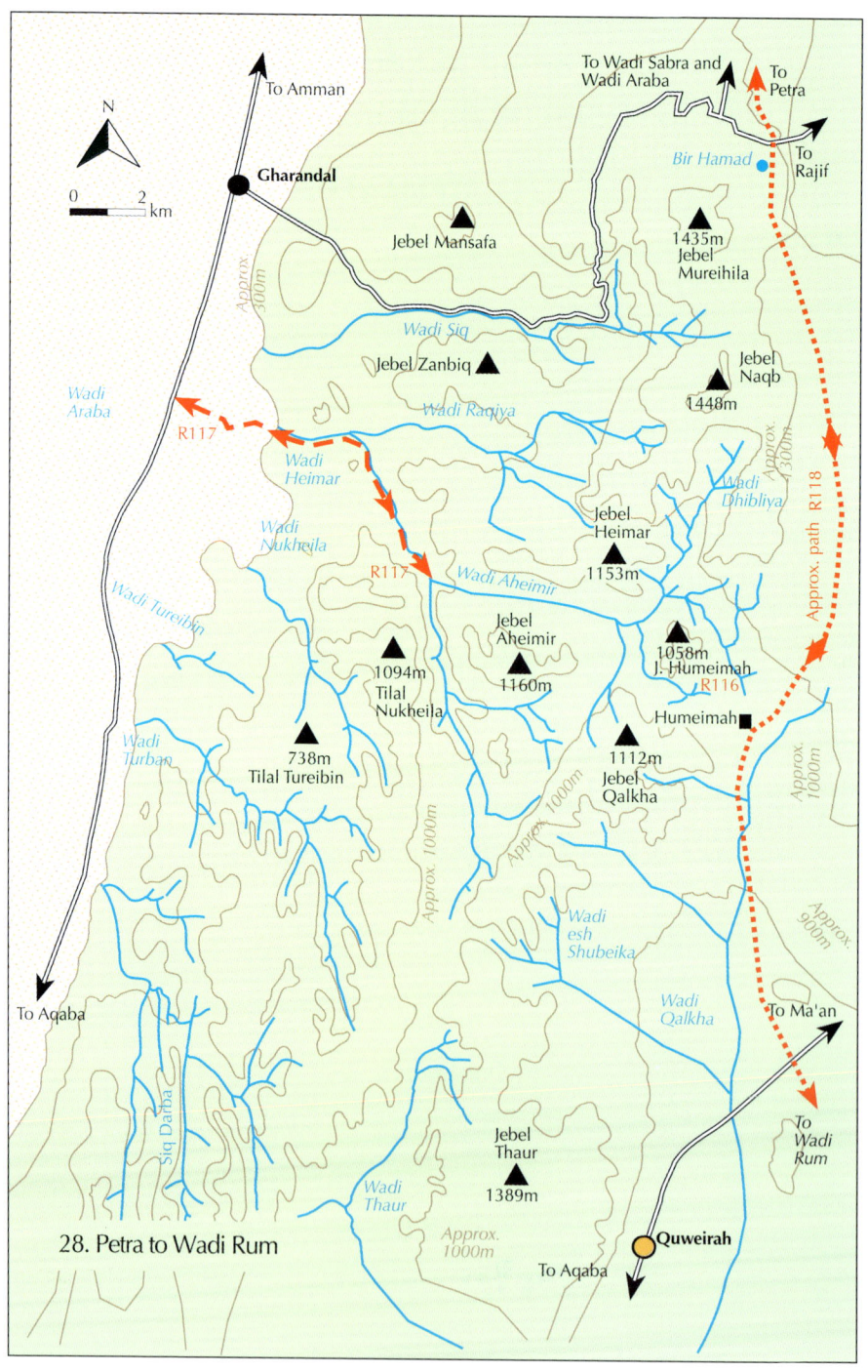

JORDAN

28. Petra to Wadi Rum

Approach Take the Dead Sea Highway N from Aqaba, up Wadi Araba to a checkpoint and 'Military Zone' sign at about 68km. Wadi Heimar is just beyond, in the hills the right. Coming S, it's about 5 or 6km after passing a pagoda built by the Chinese road builders at Gharandal.

Various long-distance trails – see Route 118 – go by a choice of routes S from Dana through Petra to Rum and Aqaba; all pass through or near Humeimah.

Route 118
Trails from Petra to Wadi Rum and Aqaba

A choice of trek, horse or camel safari for about 100km to Rum, or 150km if you go all the way to Aqaba.

The route
Adventure travel companies and guides (mostly in Wadi Musa and Wadi Rum) organise treks, camel and horse safaris (or 4WD trips) along the various routes, taking anything up to two weeks. Petra to Humeimah is about 50km, either down through Wadi Sabra and on past the well of Bir Hamad below Delagha, or up over the high escarpment from Wadi Musa to meet the same route. There are also other ways following abandoned Roman roads and old trade routes previously used for transporting precious goods, spices and incense from the Orient, Yemen and Egypt (see Route 91, information on ancient routes to Petra, and maps 27 and 28).

From Humeimah it's another 50km past the huge natural rock arch of Kharaz and the strange petroglyph of Abu Hawil to Rum, beyond which it's another 50km to Aqaba via Lawrence's Way (Route 142). For information contact the companies listed in Appendix 1; they all have slightly different itineraries or can tailor a trip to suit your requirements.

To the S and E of Humeimah lies the barren terrain of the Hisma desert, an area that includes the remains of a Turkish fort at the border post of Mudawarah. The old Hejaz railway (or what's left of it after the raids of Lawrence and the Arab forces) passes through here and can be visited by crossing the deserts of Rum by 4WD (see Route 141). There are also other desert journeys in this area, though the real desert and mountain experience is to be found in the next chapter, in Wadi Rum.

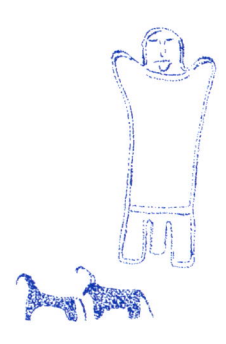

The petroglyphs of Abu Hawil

Camel safari at the mouth of Rakabat Canyon, Wadi um Ishrin (Route 129)

WADI RUM AND THE AQABA MOUNTAINS

'Welcome to Wadi Rum' said Anthony Quinn in the persona of Auda abu Tayi. It was Christmas 1983 and Di Taylor and I were watching David Lean's film, Lawrence of Arabia. It was a pivotal moment in our lives: great cliffs and desert canyons opened out before us as we saw for the first time the awesome valleys of Rum and Um Ishrin. There were more mountains than a climber could dream of – and having been involved in the exploration of desert rock for the previous twenty years I had a shrewd suspicion they were unknown to the climbing community.

'Climbing in Jordan' Tony Howard (*Climber* magazine, 1984)

Accommodation

South of Petra the next accommodation is found in and around Wadi Rum. The first possibility is the tourist camp of Bait Ali, signed off the highway over the railway track just before Salhiyeh village; camping starts at 14JD per person per night, dependent on season, with chalets and meals extra; there is also a swimming pool, and guiding services available (see Appendix 1). Just beyond, after the road forks at a police checkpoint, the new Visitor Centre at the entrance to the Rum Protected Area is directly ahead (entrance fee 2JD). The village of Diseh is down the road to the left and has a number of tourist camps popular at weekends.

Wadi Rum is ideally situated for desert and mountain activities. The campsite most popular with climbers and trekkers is at the Rest House close to Rum village. It's nice to camp just beyond the Rest House periphery in Wadi S'bach, away from the tourists, but still with access to the showers, toilets and other Rest House facilities for 2JD per person or 3–5JD for hire of tent, mattress and so on. Buffet meals at the Rest House vary from 6–10JD depending on what you choose, or you can select from the menu. A beer costs 3.5JD. There are also friendly Bedouin cafés in the village serving Arabic food at local prices. There is a campsite at Abu Aina 2km down the valley (run by the Rest House) as well as other Bedouin tourist camps even deeper into the desert (the Teva camp near Khazali is 25JD full board), or you can camp or sleep for free in the desert. If you have to use wood for fuel, use it sparingly: it is the sole fuel source for the Bedouin and is a precious and fast-disappearing resource. It's far better to bring your own stove (for camping contacts see Appendix 1).

It is now also possible to stay in Bedouin homes in Rum village either on a B&B (for example with Mohammad Sabbah) or self-catering basis (ask local Bedouin guides). You may also get the opportunity to stay with a Bedouin family in their *beit es sha'ar* (the ubiquitous black goat hair tent of the desert nomad), which should not be missed (see Appendix 1).

Stop press! In February 2008 we were told that whilst the Rest House is expected to remain as it is for the foreseeable future, it may eventually be put to other use. However, the Rum Cooperative Society plans to open a campsite near the old Arab Legion fort in the village (information supplied by Atieq Ali and Geraldine Chatelard). Any further news will be posted on www.nomadstravel.co.uk/Jordan.update.html

Finally, an hour to the south, Aqaba has numerous hotels. 'Bottom-end' places like the Petra, Jerusalem and Jordan Flower, all near the market, cost around 10–15JD per double room, whilst the hotels near the post office and mosque such as The Amira and Nairoukh are slightly pricier, but cleaner and less basic. Mid-range hotels like the friendly Alcazar with its private pool and diving centre have a long history of catering for the needs of the adventure tourist; doubles are 25–45JD including breakfast, dependent on season, whilst the sky's the limit for the new five-star beach hotels such as the Mövenpick and Intercontinental.

Transport and hire of camels and 4WD

The area is well served by local transport services, daily buses between Wadi Rum and Aqaba costing no more than 3JD; departure time from Rum is around 7am and from Aqaba around midday. (Go up

WADI RUM

29. Wadi Rum central area

1. Jebel Hubeira
2. Jebel Leyyah
3. Jebel Rumman
4. Jebel Makhras
5. Jebel Kharazeh
6. Jebel um Ejil
7. North Nassrani
8. South Nassrani
9. Draif al Muragh
10. J. Anafishiyyah
11. Jebel um Kharg
12. Jebel al Hasaani
13. Jebel um Anfus
14. Jebel Rashraasha
15. Jebel Barrah
16. Al Riddah al Baida
17. South Barrah
18. Jebel abu Judaidah
19. Jebel er Raqa
20. Jebel um Harag
21. J. Khush Khashah
22. Jebel Qabr Amra
23. Jebel Ikhnaisser
24. J. abu Khashaba
25. J. abu Khsheibah
26. Al Maghrar

the road from the post office and across the road at the top to find the bus station.) The bus belongs to the Rum community and is sometimes filled with local people, mostly women, going shopping. If you arrive before the seats are full it's polite to let them on and make alternative arrangements for your journey (especially if travelling from Aqaba to Rum, as the local people come down in the morning and the bus is their only way back home). If the bus is full, or if you miss it from Aqaba, catch one to Rashdiyeh at the Rum junction on the Desert Highway, then hitch to Rum – it's usually easy, but may cost you a couple of JD. Coming from Rum, hitch to Rashdiyeh then catch the bus, or take a taxi, which will cost about 20JD to Aqaba or Petra. In the tourist season the Rum–Petra bus leaves most days around midday.

The entrance fee to the Rum Protected Area is 2JD, payable at the Visitor Centre. Once in Wadi Rum you can hire 4WD vehicles with a Bedouin driver, or hire camels or even horses to get out into the desert. Horses and camels can also be hired for journeys into the surrounding area or all the way from Petra to Rum, or vice versa (see Appendix 1). Either book in advance, or ask a local guide. Tour prices vary from 20–60JD depending on the length of tour and whether or not 4WD, camels or horses are needed. If you are going climbing or trekking ask to be met later at a specific time and place.

Guides

If you want a guide in Rum you should, if possible, book ahead by phone, fax or e-mail (see Appendix 1) and inform the Visitor Centre on arrival. Failing that, the Visitor Centre can make arrangements. If you don't need a guide tell the receptionist that a guide is not required and that you are going to the Rum campsite. Hopefully you will be able to continue your journey by bus; if not there are numerous Bedouin taxis outside to take you to Rum (or Diseh if that is your destination). You will inevitably meet local Bedouin on arrival at the Rum Rest House if you prefer to make arrangements there.

If you have sufficient experience you can go anywhere in Rum without a guide, but you will inevitably need 4WD transport into the desert or to your chosen climb on some days, when a driver or guide will be essential. You may wish to stay at a Bedouin camp, or go by camel or horse, or simply to enjoy the company of a guide who knows the area well. For these reasons it's worth finding a guide/driver early so you can discuss your plans with him.

For routes involving scrambling or climbing – such as that to the top of Jebel Rum – visitors without sufficient experience will need a mountain guide with equipment. At the moment there are only three residents of Jordan who have been on training courses for mountain guiding and rescue in the UK: Sabbah Atieq, Sabbah Eid and Atieq Auda, all of whom live in Wadi Rum. Other local Bedouin are now also very familiar with guiding in Rum's mountains, such as Talal Awad who seems to know every Bedouin hunting route, M'sallim Atieq (son of Sabbah Atieq, Rum's first mountain guide) and Mohammad Hammad (son of Hammad Hamdan, an excellent mountaineer and grandson of Sheikh Hamdan who guided the Alpine Club ladies up Jebel Rum in 1952). A mountain guide will cost from about 100JD per day dependent on the number in the group and the difficulty and complexity of the route; this price includes any transport necessary.

All Jordanian adventure travel companies take tours into Rum, on foot, with camels (or sometimes horses) and 4WD (all contact details in Appendix 1). Many European mountain guides and trekking companies also visit Rum.

Maps

The following 1:50,000 topographical K737 series maps cover this section of the guide. You are unlikely to be able to get hold of these, but enquire at the Jordanian Royal Geographical Centre in Amman (see 'Maps' in the Introduction).

- 3049–11, 3149–111, 3048–1, 3148–1V: Wadi Rum area
- 3050–11, 3049–1V, 3049–111, 3048–1V: Wadi Araba

The four Wadi Rum maps are dislayed on the wall of the Rest House, which is very useful when planning trips. If the Rest House closes we have asked (February 2008) if the maps can be transferred, together with the climbers' new routes books (which are also kept in the Rest House), to the proposed Rum Cooperative campsite, or a similar location.

View south from the Thamudic Route, Bedouin mountain guide Sabbah Eid in the foreground (Route 124)

WADI RUM

History
This area – one of the world's most colourful and unique landscapes of desert and mountain – has long been inhabited by man. Petroglyphs mark the passage of ancient tribes in prehistoric times. Thamudic inscriptions, burial mounds, ancient megaliths and ruined buildings abound and Nabataean dams, temples and carved stairways are still to be found throughout the area. Rum is mentioned in Greek and Roman literature; there were once 'vineyards and pine trees' here. There are still relict olive trees growing in remote corners of the desert and large ancient junipers close to the summit of Jebel Rum and the other high summits where ibex roam.

The following routes – which were shown to us by the Bedouin of Rum – are a selection of their many traditional ways through the labyrinths of canyons, passing from one desert valley to the next, or up into the mountains – even to the highest summit – in pursuit of ibex or collecting edible plants and medicinal herbs. They are amongst the most fascinating walks, scrambles and climbs anywhere in the world. Some have been described as being 'amongst the world's best mountain adventures'. Others, as evidenced by the inscriptions high on Jebel Rum's Thamudic Route (Route 124), date back over 2000 years and must be amongst the world's oldest known rock climbs.

Calotrapsis

These routes have been known to the Bedouin for generations, but it was not until the late 1940s that 'outsiders' began to explore these mountains. The first known non-Bedouin ascent of Jebel Rum was in 1947 by Major Henry Coombe-Tennant, Welsh Guards, and Lance Corporal 'Havabash' Butler, Royal Signals, with Major St John Armitage (who did not complete the ascent). All were members of the British military mission to Saudi Arabia, who were travelling with the Jaish al Badia in Jordan by kindness of its commander and Glubb Pasha. They started their ascent from Wadi Shelaali (Route 119), though the precise route they took to the top is not clear – it appears to have taken a similar line to an excellent Bedouin climb, Rijm Assaf (see *Treks and Climbs in Wadi Rum* in Appendix 2).

The next non-Bedouin party to explore Rum's mountains was Sylvia Branford and Charmian Longstaff, members of a cartographic team who made an ascent of Jebel Rum from the 'back' of the mountain, up the west side via the impressive Great Siq, guided by Sheikh Hamdan Amad in November 1952 (Route 125). (Sheikh Hamdan Amad was the father of Hammad, and the combination of their eponymous routes has become the classic traverse of the mountain, see Route 126.) Although other Europeans – usually with military connections – visited the mountains of Rum intermittently over the following years, no effort seems to have been made to record the Bedouin climbs or to further explore these unique mountains until our arrival in 1984. We have been captivated by Rum and its people ever since.

Don't miss the opportunity to follow the superb Bedouin routes described below, either up into the mountains, through the canyons, on foot or with camels or 4WD across the desert. Travel and spend some time with the Bedouin – they have given us unforgettable memories and will no doubt do the same for you.

Weather
A word about the weather: it's not always hot and sunny in Rum. Spring and autumn are the best time to visit, but climbers and trekkers are active in the area from late September through to mid-May. Nevertheless, in recent years it has snowed around Christmas time, and winter sometimes brings heavy rainfall leading to flash floods. The following is an extract from an article entitled 'Desert Storm' written by Tony Howard for *Adventure Travel* magazine: 'Where only a few days previously we had been

The 1984 team of Al Baker, the authors, Defallah and Sabbah Atieq (two sons of Sheikh Atieq) and Mick Shaw, who opened up Wadi Rum for climbing and trekking

climbing on Jebel Rum's east face up pink, lavender and purple rock, a roaring river of water now burst from a ravine high above and careered down the wall in a breathtaking crescendo of violence. All across the five-kilometre-long wall of the mountain countless other waterfalls crashed from concealed canyons, many falling free for three hundred metres. Suddenly, water from the largest cleft of all, the Great Siq, burst out of the centre of the face in a foaming brown flood, gathered from canyons cutting through the very heart of the massif as far as the summit itself. Roaring down the overhanging wall the waters plunged into the wadi bed below, surging over giant boulders in their rush towards the desert.' Take care!

THE PEOPLE OF RUM

*Three easy marches... up Wadi Yitm [from Aqaba] and behind
the range El Sharra, one day south of El-Ma'an...
The fountains flow in winter, in summer the wells are never dry;
the people, especially the Huwaytat, are kind and hospitable.*

The Land of Midian Richard F. Burton (1879)

Early days

The majority of the Rum Bedouin are from the Zalabia family or clan, a sub-group of the Huweitat tribe which has links with the great Anaiza tribal confederation of northern Arabia through the Bani Atiya. As their numbers increased the Huweitat spread out from the Aqaba region in various directions, one branch even emigrating to Egypt. Their black *bait es sha'ar* tents have been in Rum longer than anyone can remember. Tribal pride is very strong as a legend told by one of the ancestral Huweitat sheikhs, Suleiman ibn Jad, illustrates: 'The human race was divided at the beginning into three classes: the tent makers, the agriculturalists and the Huweitat!'

When we first arrived in the area in 1984 the Rum Bedouin were semi-nomadic, but are now mostly based in the rapidly growing villages of Rum in the heart of Wadi Rum and the more recent outliers of Salhiyeh and Shakriyeh, whilst the Zuweida Bedouin are in Diseh some 20km to the northeast. These people – their lifestyle, black tents and wild desert homeland – were brought to the world's attention in T. E. Lawrence's book *Seven Pillars of Wisdom*, in which he described the area as 'Rumm the magnificent... vast, echoing and godlike.'

During World War 1 the Huweitat fought against the Turks. They were led by their paramount sheikh, Auda Abu Taiyy, who – already a famous fighting man in Arabia – became internationally known through the writings of Lawrence of Arabia. The Huweitat also fought in World War II as soldiers in the Arab Legion with Glubb Pasha in the Syrian campaign against the Vichy French. A number of the tribe, led by Sheikh Zaal bin Mutlaq (who had been at Auda's side in World War I) joined in the fighting as irregulars. On one occasion –whilst most of them sought cover in trenches with the regular troops – Zaal stood on a hilltop in the open, firing at French aircraft which were strafing them. He afterwards complained that war was not as good as it had been in the old days! This typically bold, relaxed and highly confident approach is mirrored in the attitude of many locals to climbing, enabling them to become totally intimate with every detail of the mountains of Rum during their hunting exploits.

The hospitality of the Bedouin is also legendary, as is their anger when crossed. We were advised from the beginning: 'If you are soft with us, we will squeeze you; if you are hard with us, we will break you; if you are straight, we will be your friends.' Treat them honestly and openly and you will be welcomed into their homes and desert camps and enjoy a unique experience.

We have become close friends with this tightly knit community and also with Geraldine Chatelard, a social anthropologist who has spent considerable time in their company. She has kindly contributed the following information.

The Wadi Rum Bedouin

Wadi Rum's vast semi-arid pasturelands, combined with several tiny perennial springs in the mountains, have drawn human attention through the ages. Ancient rock carvings depicting animals and human or God-like figures are attributed to neolithic village communities as early as the 5th millennium BC. More recently, around the beginning of our era, nomadic tribes left their signatures in ancient Arabian scripts, drew camels, ibex, ostriches and hunting scenes on the rocks and built water-collecting systems. Caravan routes from Arabia to the Mediterranean and to Syria passed through the valley (*wadi* in Arabic) of Rum

A Bedouin of Wadi Rum

where pre-Islamic shrines and a Nabataean outpost and temple are located at the very place where the modern village of Rum stands. The tradition of caravans endured until the early 20th century in the form of caravans of pilgrims to the Muslim holy places that were crossing the region slightly to the east of Rum. They came to a halt with the opening of the Hejaz railway in 1908 that connected Damascus to Medina.

In the 20th century Wadi Rum became famous as the setting for the movie *Lawrence of Arabia*. T. E. Lawrence had indeed passed through the region in 1916, at the time of the Great Arab Revolt against Ottoman rule that paved the way for the independence of modern Jordan. Lawrence spoke very highly of Wadi Rum's natural beauty in his masterpiece the *Seven Pillars of Wisdom*. Today new place-names developed in the context of tourism, like the ones connected to the story of T. E. Lawrence, usually co-exist with other more ancient names still used by the Bedouin. In 1934, 13 years after the creation of modern Jordan – and long before the first Bedouin families started building houses on the same location in the 1970s – a fort of the Desert Police was built in Wadi Rum below the main spring of Ain-Shelaali (which T. E. Lawrence described and which is described in this guidebook as Route 119). This was the place where tribespeople gathered for water supply and events. The Desert Police are Bedouin recruits patrolling the borders of desert areas on camels and, these days, in motor vehicles.

Origins and traditional lifestyle

Bedouin are not a separate ethnic group. They are Arabs who practise nomadic livestock herding, or pastoralism, as their main form of livelihood. They speak Arabic and are Muslim. The English term 'Bedouin' derives from the Arabic word *bedu*, meaning those who live in the *badia*, the semi-arid and arid ecological zone of sands and rocks that stretches across the eastern part of Jordan and extends south into Saudi Arabia, east into Iraq and north into Syria. The Bedouin themselves have another explanation for their name. They like to say that it comes from *badaa*, the origin, the beginning, because the way of life of the Bedouin has not changed since the beginning of human history.

The Bedouin of Wadi Rum used to specialise in camel husbandry but also bred some goats and sheep. As there are no springs in the southern part of Wadi Rum, the Bedouin continued a tradition of rainwater harvesting that dates back to antiquity by constructing dams and reservoirs in the mouths of rock crevasses or *siqs* to collect the rainfall. Many of these reservoirs contain a surprising quantity of water in the spring, and remain in regular use.

Women used to weave animal hair for the tent, the *beit es sha'ar* (literally 'house of hair'), and almost everything they needed: rugs, purses, cushion covers, storage bags for foodstuff, saddlebags and other animal gear. Livestock also provided meat and milk products. Meat was only eaten on special occasions (such as feasts, weddings and visits from guests). Should a visitor of some standing arrive the Bedouin host was obliged to slaughter a sheep or a goat and honour his guest with the classic Arab feast: *zarb* (meat cooked in a hole in the ground), *mensef* (trays heaped high with rice, succulent meat and yoghurt) and flat rounds of unleavened bread.

Contrary to a commonly held view, agriculture was an important component of the traditional Bedouin economy. On a good rainy year wheat, barley and lentils were produced, while on a dry year the land was not cultivated. With excess livestock and animal products as a source of income, Bedouin could purchase the agricultural products they needed: mainly dates, rice, flour, sugar, tea and coffee.

Hospitality and reciprocity as a means of survival were essential features of Bedouin society in a land where people were few, distances between encampments great and where there was little to sustain life. On being welcomed into the tent a visitor knew that he would enjoy the immediate benefit of food and somewhere to sleep. He was also guaranteed the protection of his host for the duration of his stay, and for another three days thereafter. This code was called the bond of salt, since even if a visitor carried only the salt of his host in his stomach he could call on his protection.

The elaborate yet sincere show of hospitality and generosity that still takes place today under the tent is never complete without the ritual of preparation and offering of coffee (see photo page 285). Coffee is always poured with the pot in the left hand and the cup or cups in the right, the 'clean hand'. The host should offer three complete rounds of coffee. The first is *finjan al-dayf*, the 'guest cup', to welcome the visitor and establish trust. The second is *finjan al-sayf*, the 'sword cup', to honour the courage of the men and/or to mark resolution of any pending conflict. The third round is *finjan al-kayf*, 'the pleasure cup', purely for enjoyment. After three helpings it is polite to indicate that one has had sufficient by shaking the cup when handing it back to the host.

Hammad Hamdan, son of Sheikh Hamdan, Rum's earliest mountain guides

Although Bedouin society was mostly illiterate, extremely elaborate oral traditions were the vehicles for popular medical and environmental knowledge, customary law, tribal genealogies, a very rich oral literature and other aspects of knowledge and artistic expressions.

Adapting traditions to the modern world
The lifestyle and cultural heritage of purely nomadic Bedouin have undergone substantial changes due to settlement in villages, widespread schooling and literacy and technological advances such as the use of motor vehicles that have replaced the camel or modern means of communication. Yet because of the extraordinary adaptability and flexibility of their lifestyle Bedouin communities are modernising without fundamentally changing the social structure and ethical values of their society: the cohesion of the household, the strength of kinship ties, spatial mobility (if not strict nomadism), the knowledge and know-how about the essentials aspects of Bedouin culture (rituals of hospitality, customary law and so on) and the centrality of eloquence and oral cultural expressions such as poetry and music.

Today most Bedouin communities have switched from camel to mainly goat and sheep husbandry and are seasonally mobile, circulating between village and encampment (or cave dwelling) in the pasturelands, or sharing economic and social roles between several generations of a same household. Those who appear to spend more time living the 'traditional' life of the nomads are the elders. Young adults, for their part, are much more likely to stay in village houses or in encampments near settlements where they can access other economic opportunities and where their children attend school. This generation nevertheless retains strong connections to the desert by keeping smaller herds and moving out to distant pasturelands whenever the school calendar permits.

Bedouin pastoral communities can also diversify their economic activities and intelligently recycle elements of their material and intangible culture and their knowledge about the environment in the framework of tourism development projects and nature conservation efforts. This has been the case specifically with the tribes in Wadi Rum and in the nearby villages of Diseh, Shakriyeh and Salhiyeh.

Weaving

Manufacturing handicrafts to be sold as souvenirs provides new economic and social opportunities for Bedouin women who live in these villages. Tribesmen work as desert guides, cameleers, Jeep drivers or rangers. They also maintain Bedouin-style campsites for tourists and are developing services for visitors based on their traditions. Crucially, desert tourism offers Bedouin communities in Wadi Rum the possibility to maintain their organic relationship with the desert and with the camel, the breeding of which is once again on the increase.

Literally following in the footsteps of their fathers, from whom they learnt the skills of hunting ibex and collecting wild honey on the steep cliffs where the bees make their hives, a number of men in the area of Wadi Rum have developed outstanding rock-limbing abilities. Now, however, Rum has been declared a Protected Area and hunting has been banned so fewer young men have the opportunity to develop this capacity. Luckily the authors of this book arrived in Rum in 1984 when these skills were still in use and – thanks initially to them and their Bedouin mentors – Wadi Rum is now acknowledged by the international climbing community as 'one of the world's best desert climbing areas'. The Bedouin hunting routes also have a reputation as 'amongst the world's best adventure climbs' often involving grade 4 and 5 moves, so it's all the more remarkable that they were originally climbed solo by the Bedouin hunters. These days, they and their sons are guiding visiting climbers and trekkers and making a massive contribution to the economy of the community.

In conclusion your visit to Rum – whilst perhaps being primarily to climb or trek – should also include some time with the Bedouin. Whether you chose to hire them as desert guides, on foot or camel or in a vehicle, or to climb with them or spend some time in their desert camps, it is a unique opportunity not to be missed.

Geraldine Chatelard, social anthropologist

THE RUM PROTECTED AREA

The 'Protected Area' is controlled by the Aqaba Authority (ASEZA) and was designated by the RSCN who remain on the steering committee along with the Bedouin Co-operatives of Rum and Diseh. The area covers approx 500sq km centred on the Rum valley and includes the distinctive sheer-sided 'jebels' along with some of the typically sandy and vegetated wadis including Wadi Rumman to the west. Elevation ranges from 800m to 1754m above sea level (map 30).

The mountains were formed millions of years ago when an enormous upheaval thrust Rum's granite and sandstone outcrops through the earth's surface. Looking at the cliffs one sees the colourful phenomenon of ever-changing hues, depending on the hour of day. Human habitation dates back 8000 years as evidenced by numerous sites and rock drawings. Ruins of a Nabataean temple at the foot of the great massif of Jebel Rum identify Wadi Rum as an important centre for Nabataeans in early times, and it was also on one of the frankincense routes from the Yemen.

The Protected Area is one of the few remaining places harbouring remnant populations of large animals such as ibex and goitered gazelle. Efforts are being made to reintroduce the oryx, which have been almost decimated recently in their main reserve in Oman where numbers have fallen from 450 to 60. In addition there are hedgehogs, striped hyena, wolves, hare, red fox, rock hyrax, porcupine and various snakes including Palestinian and horned vipers as well as the ubiquitous scorpions. Resident birds include mourning wheatear, white-crowned black wheatear, Sinai rose finch, brown-necked raven, Tristram's grackle, griffon vulture, the rare Verreaux's eagle and many more. A move to declare Wadi Rum an IUCN World Heritage Site would give the area additional status and protection.

As Wadi Rum already had a well-established tourism business thanks to the early development of climbing, trekking and safari by the local Bedouin, access to and camping in the area is not restricted

Traversing to the second col, Jebel Mayeen, with a view east across Wadi Rum

WADI RUM AND THE AQABA MOUNTAINS – WADI RUM

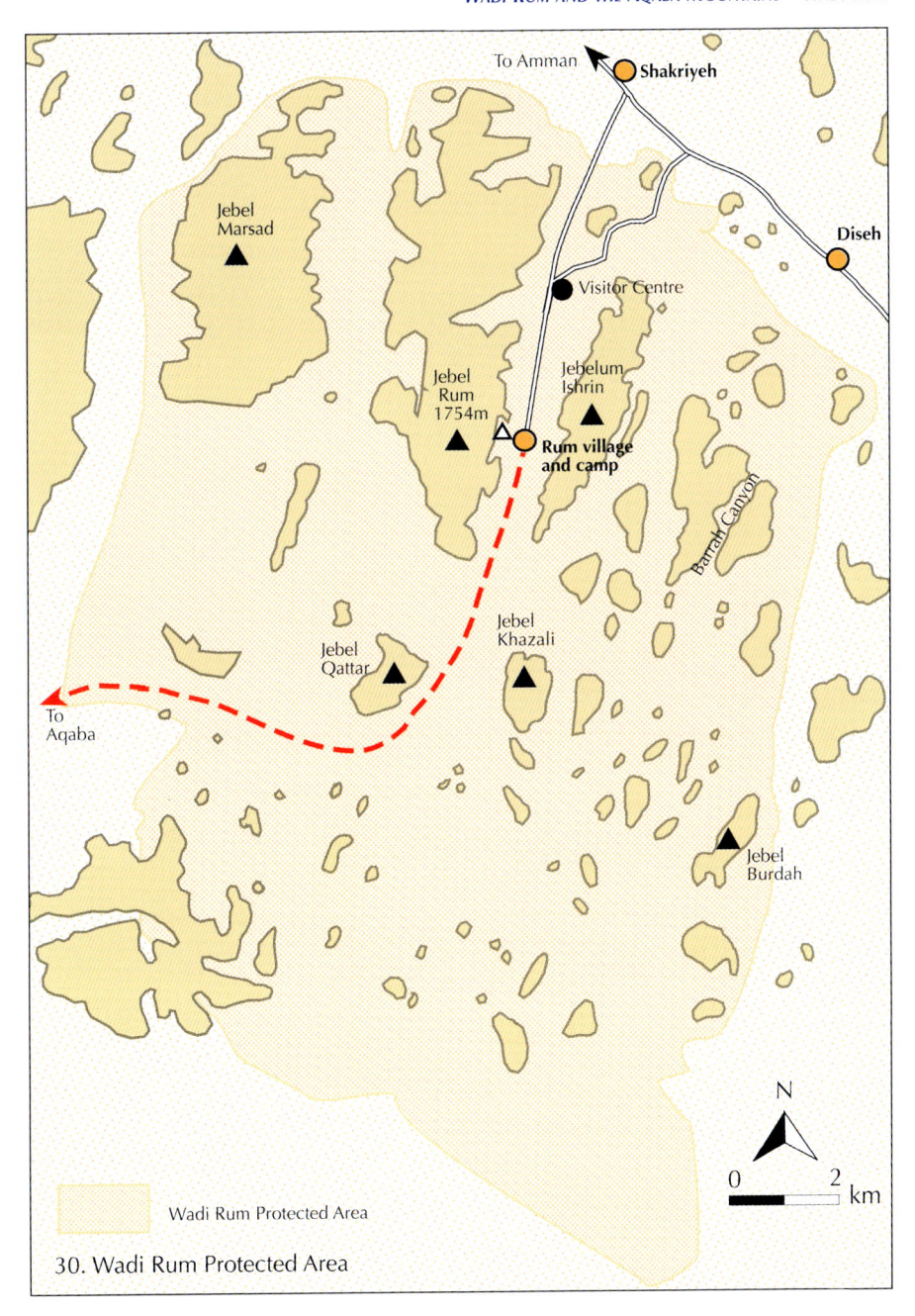

30. Wadi Rum Protected Area

as in RSCN Reserves, and the position of the local community and its desert and mountain guides are respected. The regulations and compulsory guiding service applicable in RSCN Reserves was also modified to suit the traditions of Rum and other climbing areas worldwide.

THE REST HOUSE AREA

There are some enjoyable walks and scrambles easily accessible from the Rest House campsite adjacent to Rum village (GPS alt. 950m N29° 34.630' E35° 25.195') and dominated by the 500m cliffs of Jordan's most famous mountain, Jebel Rum. Beneath these cliffs is the spring of Wadi Shelaali, one of the best-known sites in the valley (not to be confused with the well at Abu Aina 3km away at the south end of Jebel Rum which is erroneously called 'Lawrence's Well' and consequently on the 'tourist trail').

The following is an extract from Lawrence's description of his visit on 11 September 1917:

The sun had sunk behind the western wall leaving the pit in shadow; but its dying glare flooded with startling red the wings each side of the entry, and the fiery bulk of the further wall across the great valley. The pit-floor was of damp sand, darkly wooded with shrubs; while about the feet of all the cliffs lay boulders greater than houses, sometimes, indeed, like fortresses which had crashed down from the heights above. In front of us a path, pale with use, zigzagged up the cliff-plinth to the point from which the main face rose, and there it turned precariously southward along a shallow ledge outlined by occasional leafy trees. From between these trees, in hidden crannies of the rock, issued strange cries; the echoes, turned into music, of the voices of the Arabs watering camels at the springs which there flowed out three hundred feet above ground.

On another visit Lawrence bathed in one of these springs:

Its rushing noise came from my left, by a jutting bastion of cliff over whose crimson face trailed long falling runners of green leaves. The path skirted it in an undercut ledge. On the rock-bulge above were clear-cut Nabataean inscriptions and a sunk panel incised with a monogram or symbol. Around and about were Arab scratches, including tribe-marks, some of which were witnesses of forgotten migrations: but my attention was only for the splashing of water in a crevice under the shadow of the overhanging rock.

From this rock a silver runlet issued into the sunlight. I looked in to see the spout, a little thinner than my wrist, jetting out firmly from a fissure in the roof and falling with that clean sound into a shallow, frothing pool, behind the step which served as entrance. The walls and roof of the crevice dripped with moisture. Thick ferns and grasses of the finest green made it a paradise just five feet square.

Upon the water-cleansed and fragrant ledge I undressed my soiled body, and stepped onto the little basin, to taste at last a freshness of moving air and water against my tired skin. It was deliciously cool. I lay there quietly letting the clear, dark red water run over me in a ribbly stream, and rub the travel-dirt away.

Route 119
Wadi Shelaali – The Real Lawrence's Spring

Grade	Easy walk
Details	2.5km there and back
Time	Allow 1–1½hrs

WADI RUM AND THE AQABA MOUNTAINS – WADI RUM – ROUTE 119

A pleasant short walk that visits the spring described so evocatively by T. E. Lawrence in *Seven Pillars of Wisdom*. It can be linked with a visit to the Nabataean temple immediately W of the Rest House to make a combined 'pilgrimage'. Wadi Shelaali (Valley of the Waterfall) also has a Nabataean stone water channel – parts of which are in place – which runs from the spring down to a Nabataean site just S of the temple. The spring is in the shade after late morning and is surrounded by greenery, making a pleasant retreat from both the heat of the day and the crowds around the Rest House. See maps 31 and 37.

The route
To visit the spring (SW of the Rest House) cross the desert either directly towards a white water tank right of the valley entrance or, first, visit the Nabataean temple behind the Rest House.

From the tank, a track 'pale with use' zigzags up the hillside to a little flat plateau above the valley entrance. From there it contours round above the valley and just below the cliffs, past the green, minty springs of Abu Shleilieh to arrive at 'Lawrence's Spring'.

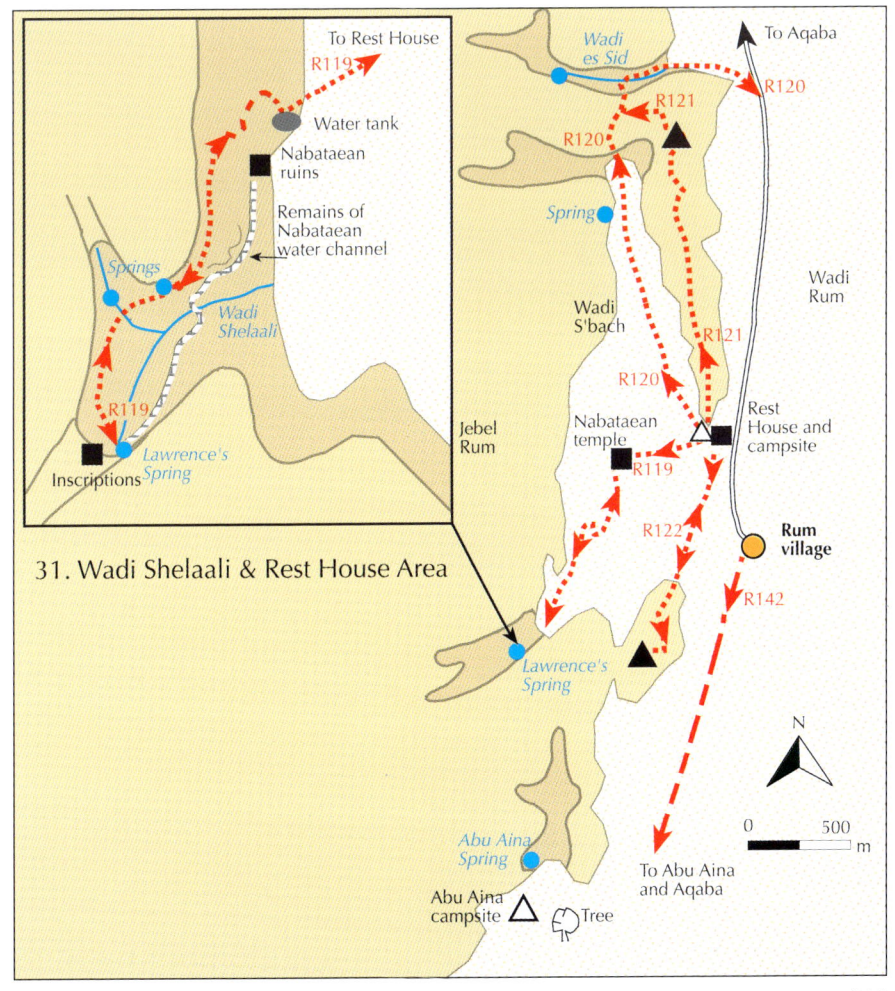

31. Wadi Shelaali & Rest House Area

JORDAN

The canyon of Wadi Shelaali is just above and can be entered from 200m to the right, up easy ledges. It is blocked after a few hundred metres by the steep cliffs of Jebel Rum.

Around the area of the well will be seen the ancient 'tribal markings' described by Lawrence. From here, along the right (E) side of the valley, will also be found the start of the Nabataean water channel. This can be followed back with care (and some detective work) down the true right side of the valley, across the wadi bed above some smooth granite slabs, then along the other side of the wadi to the valley floor.

Return Along the water channel or by the outward route.

Other routes near the Rest House on outliers of Jebel Rum offer slightly more serious scrambles, the first being Route 120.

Route 120
Wadi S'bach to Wadi es Sid

Grade	Easy scramble
Details	5km
Time	Approx 2½hrs round trip from and to the Rest House

A pleasant secluded valley with springs, palm trees and birdlife leads to an easily attained mountain pass and a nice scramble back to the road. See maps 31 and 32.

The route
Wadi S'bach is immediately behind the Rest House, hidden by the S end of the long ridge of Jebel Mayeen (see Route 121). Walk up the valley, with the big cliffs of Jebel Rum's E face on the left. The valley becomes increasingly green, with palm trees at spring locations on its W side, then after passing large boulders the streambed (quite often with a trickle of water) turns to the W. Here continue N, rising up to a col in the ridge at the head of the valley.

It is now essential to go down through a little ravine for 100m, otherwise cliffs will be met. Once through this, scramble easily down into Wadi es Sid. Go E down the streambed to a narrowing where there are often pools. Pass these (some rock scrambling may be necessary) and descend a little cliff (grade 1) to the desert, by escaping to the right. Walk out E to reach the road, and follow it back to the Rest House.

Route 121 climbs the mountain circumnavigated by Route 120.

Route 121
Jebel el Mayeen, 1100m

Grade	Moderate scramble with some grade 2 climbing
Details	3km; a good introduction to route finding on Rum rock
Time	2–2½hrs for the return journey

WADI RUM AND THE AQABA MOUNTAINS – WADI RUM – ROUTE 121

An attractive little peak immediately N of the Rest House, the ascent of which is a nice introduction to the complexities and idiosyncrasies of Rum rock. It provides a pleasant scramble with good views of the Rum Valley and village and the cliffs of Jebel Rum and Jebel um Ishrin, the opposing barrier E of the valley. See maps 31 and 32.

Special requirements A safety rope may be useful.

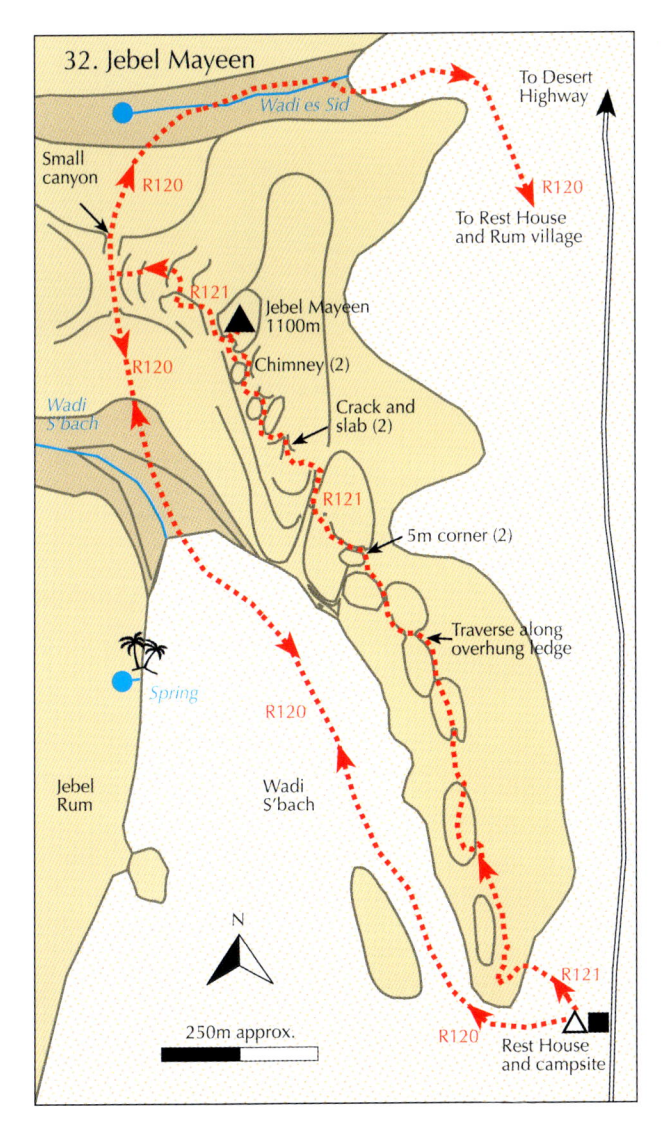

32. Jebel Mayeen

(map labels: To Desert Highway; Wadi es Sid; Small canyon; R120; R120; To Rest House and Rum village; R121; Jebel Mayeen 1100m; Chimney (2); R120; Wadi S'bach; Crack and slab (2); R121; 5m corner (2); Traverse along overhung ledge; Spring; R120; Jebel Rum; Wadi S'bach; R120; R121; Rest House and campsite; 250m approx.; N)

The route
From the Rest House car park scramble leftwards up the hillside to the very end of the S ridge where there is a flat rock ledge with some burial mounds. Go N along the ridge, rising up the right side of the next top to more cairns and mounds and good views. Descend again to the right to the second ledge down and walk round to the ridge beyond (more graves). Descend to a col and up a bushy gully to the R side of the next top. Cross this plateau (more mounds), curving left to just below the next top. Do not go up; instead descend a short bushy gully on the right and contour round left on a rock ledge under overhangs to the next col.

Pass through this and walk along below the left side of the next top and scramble down to a saddle. From here go up a little slab and traverse along on ledges again, now on the right side of the mountain, to the next col. There are good views from all these tops and climbers may sometimes be seen on the smooth walls of the Dark Tower which is immediately opposite to the W, across Wadi S'bach. Beyond here the way starts to become steeper and, for

247

View south from Jebel Mayeen, past Rum village to Jebel Nassrani

walkers, a descent can be made left (W) into Wadi S'bach, down the gully (keep left at the bottom to avoid overhangs above the valley floor).

To reach the summit of Jebel Mayeen continue along on the right side then up rock steps and a steep V-groove (grade 2) to a col below a tower on the ridge. Contour round onto its left side and descend to scree ledges. Walk along these, rising up slabs where easily possible to enter the next gully near a flat rock with camel inscriptions. (Possible descent from here to Wadi S'bach, once again keeping left just above the valley floor, to avoid overhangs.)

Above, the gully goes up a little ravine to the col. From here, cross slabs left, round a nose of rock and up the slabby ridge above it (grade 1). Carry on up to a tree on the skyline. Here go left, all the way round the next tower, to reach the next saddle. Go straight up a bushy gully then pass the next rock bulge up cracks on its left (grade 2). From the ledge at the top go right (not up the gully ahead) onto knobbly slabs and up to a ledge with boulders. Go left through these, to the left side of the mountain again where there is a little corner with a fallen block below. This leads abruptly to the top from where there are excellent views. (The summit boulder can be climbed – grade 3).

Descent Either return the same way, perhaps descending into Wadi S'bach by either of the descent gullies, or take the N ridge: go down the little fallen block corner then right to a bushy hollow with a col just beyond. Continue in the same direction (easiest on the left, down slabs) to the top of a steep section. Descend a chimney (grade 2) to a ledge, then down it again, under a boulder to the next ledge, and down again to a third ledge above a juniper tree. Go down behind this and left behind a boulder, then W along humpback slabs, on the left side of a gully, which is gained by descending a little wall (grade 1). From its foot zigzag right to the next ledge and walk W along this and down a little wall (grade 1) to the shoulder above the saddle between Wadi S'bach and Wadi es Sid (½hr from summit). Return to the Rest House by either of these valleys (see Route 120).

Another scramble at a similar grade, Route 122, starts near the village S of the Rest House.

Route 122
Jebel Ahmar al Shelaali, 1125m

Grade	Moderate scramble; easy apart from the summit rocks (grade 2)
Details	2.5km; a good introduction to route finding on Rum rock
Time	2hrs for the return journey

A pleasant scramble to a good vantage point situated directly above the S end of the village, and E of the entrance to the valley of Wadi Shelaali. See maps 31 and 33.

Special requirements Safety rope advised if not familiar with rock climbing.

The route
From the Rest House cross the desert directly S towards the mountain, passing behind the graveyard, to a ridge of granite boulders that extends a short way N into the desert. Go up this and trend right towards the right side of a large smooth yellow cliff. (There is a flat-topped boulder with inscriptions about 30m below the right end of the wall). Go up left from here to the left edge of the yellow wall and up 3m to a flat ledge (cairn). Go left, and trend up left for about 50m into an easy angled bushy gully. Scramble up past a split, then walk right below a sandy overhang out of the gully and up left onto a plateau. Good view (20mins from Rest House).

Walk S along the ledge a little way, then up rocks on the right to cross the rounded ridge and walk along its right side a short way. Gain the ridge again, and follow its top to the next little plateau and walk S to a prominent gap between the mountain and a tower on the skyline. Through the gap there are good views S down the desert to Jebel Khazali.

To continue to the top go back a few metres and scramble through a little gully, crossing the ridge to its W side, then walk along to the furthest gully. (Across Wadi Shelaali,

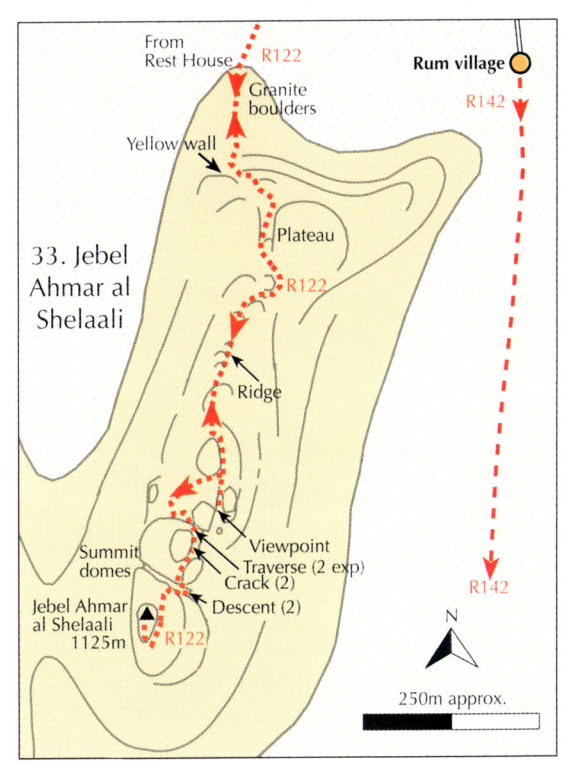

33. Jebel Ahmar al Shelaali

View north from Jebel Ahmar al Shelaali, past Rum village

W of here, small figures of climbers may be visible on the big cliffs of Jebel Rum, which really puts their scale into perspective.)

Go up the gully, then almost immediately left up a slab to avoid vegetation and a steep section of rock. Step onto the next slab and make an exposed traverse left (grade 1) to a corner, which is followed easily back right to regain the top of the gully. Here go through a slot onto the E side of the mountain and traverse a ledge (exposed, grade 1) to a bush in a recess. From there it is possible to reach the top by some very exposed moves (grade 2) after going along the ledge, but it is safer to go directly up the leaning chimney and crack above (also grade 2) to the top of the N summit.

To reach the S summit (which is marginally higher) go S to the edge of the little ravine separating the tops. Walk left 10m on a flat black ledge. Descend 2m (exposed, grade 1) and scramble back right into the ravine, climbing up easily to the next top and the summit rock, which is just beyond. Excellent views.

Descent Return by the same route taking particular care with downclimbing the summit rocks.

It's possible to walk from the village behind Jebel Ahmar al Shelaali and through the hills to the camp at Abu Aina, 3km S, returning by the desert track up the Rum Valley (see *Treks and Climbs in Wadi Rum*, Appendix 2), but more adventurous souls might like to experience a much longer proposition round Rum's most famous summit, Jebel Rum.

JEBEL RUM, 1754m

Route 123
Round Jebel Rum Trek

Grade	Moderate trek, easy scramble; take care with route finding
Details	Approx 22km
Time	9hrs, early start advised

An interesting and varied trek in a clockwise direction round Jebel Rum. See map 34.

The route
Follow the desert track S to Abu Aina springs and Bedouin camp (3km). From here there are two options:

Option 1 Easiest (but longest) continue S 2km more then round the end of the massif and NW into Wadi el Khweimilat (which leads eventually to Wadi Rumman).

Option 2 Take the valley just SW of the Bedouin camp (Rakabat Abu Aina) and follow it over the col pleasantly into the descent valley (Khmeileh – small place of trees) and so to Wadi el Khweimelat, on the W side of Jebel Rum.

Now follow the edge of the desert and go N below the W face screes, where there may be some Bedouin camps, into a cirque leading to the col between Jebel Rum and its outlier, Jebel Rumman on the NW.

Here it is best to keep close to the side of Jebel Rum up granite scree to a small pass (not in the larger valley which is immediately W; 3hrs from the Rest House). From the pass descend into Wadi um Hassa to where a big valley enters from the R (E). This is the canyon taken by Sheikh Hamdan's Route (Route 125) to the summit of Jebel Rum. Here there is a well and springs (1hr from the pass). At this point the valley narrows through a polished granite riverbed, which is descended with some scrambling. Where the valley eventually opens there is a stone with some Thamudic inscriptions; there may also be a Bedouin camp.

Continue N along the E side of the cirque until in the N end where three valleys enter; take the central (E) one and follow this up to a pass with a huge cairn, with a mountain basin just ahead (1½hrs from the spring in Wadi um Hassa). Go along the right side of the basin ascending a little until a big valley is seen going down and winding left into Wadi Leyyah, through bushes and trees (1hr to descend). Follow this wide valley E for 2km to the road, then down the Wadi Rum road back to the Rest House (1½hrs).

Now for something considerably more serious; Routes 124–126 have been described by visiting European mountain guides as being of Dolomitic or even Alpine proportions. They should be undertaken with a guide (except by experienced mountaineers).

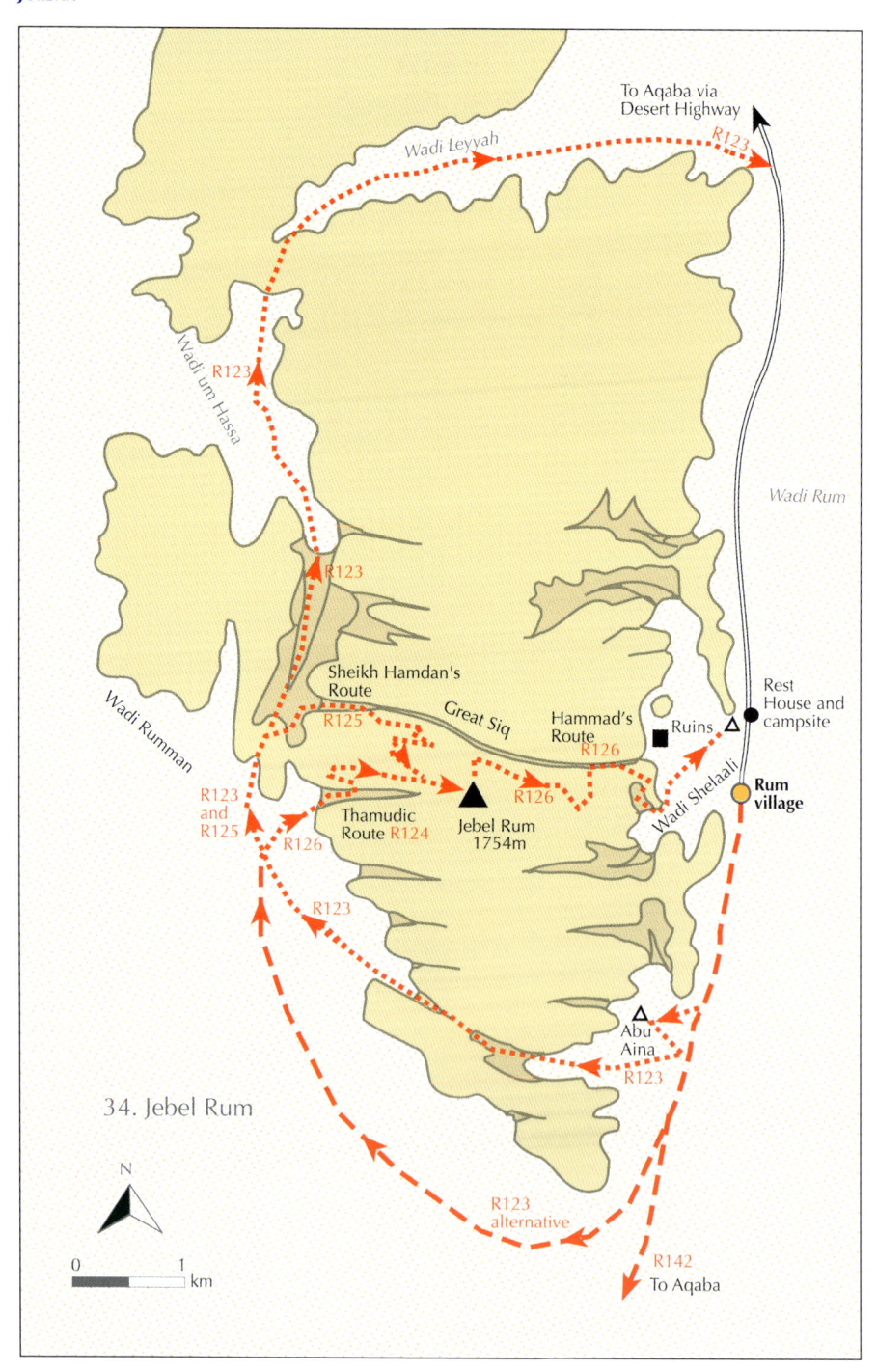

JORDAN

34. Jebel Rum

Route 124
Jebel Rum, The Thamudic Route

Grade	Serious scramble; don't underestimate
Details	About 2km to the summit, 750m of ascent
Time	Allow 2½–4hrs for the ascent, maybe more, and the same to return

One of the world's oldest known rock climbs; a truly magnificent day out in wild and beautiful scenery reaching the remote summit of Jordan's best-known mountain. The Thamudic inscriptions in the 'cave' (see below) are names: 'By Kharajat, son of Sa'adan' seems to have been inscribed first, then at a later date, 'By Jahfal, brother of Taym' on the left. These inscriptions would seem to indicate that these people climbed to the summit plateau over 2000 years ago to hunt the ibex depicted in so many Rum petroglyphs. These animals are hunted there to this day, but hopefully the newly designated Protected Area and the increasing awareness amongst Bedouin hunters of the endangered nature of the species and their value to tourism will protect them for future generations.

Also known locally as the Nabataean Route, the climb demands the ability to climb grade 2–3 rock comfortably, the key section crossing steep rock where an unroped fall would be fatal. Nevertheless the ledges are large and the holds are big so a competent team can climb without ropes, but remember: this is Rum sandstone so route finding is not straightforward and holds should never be trusted implicitly. The route is a serious undertaking for someone not familiar with climbing. If in any doubt, hire a qualified local Bedouin mountain guide.

The plateau below the summit domes is a great place to spend the night and watch the sun set over the distant mountains of Sinai. See maps 34, 35 and 36.

Special requirements Climbing equipment, lightweight boots or trainers and confidence to climb grade 2–3 in exposed terrain are all necessary, as are route-finding skills and the ability to abseil in descent (though competent climbers can downclimb both this route and the alternative Sheikh Hamdan's Route). If staying the night you will need sleeping bags, food and water. Any fire should be minimal as wood is increasingly scarce – better to use a stove.

Guide Required for inexperienced groups.

Approach The day before the trip arrange for a vehicle and an early start. It is ½hr by 4WD from Wadi Rum village, first to the S end of Jebel Rum then back N up Wadi Rumman to below the entrance to the hanging canyon that leads to the summit. (The Bedouin driver should know the location, but check when making arrangements.)

The route
Scramble up scree and easy granite slabs to flat ledges on the right (S) side of the entrance to the big canyon (½hr).

Now on rocky ledges keep going left with the occasional 2m steep rock step (grade 2–3) rising diagonally into the canyon across its right (true left) side; a confusion of cairns! (Ignore the ones that continue to rise up the canyon wall; they are on another superb but considerably more difficult Bedouin climbing route, Sabbah's Route – see *Treks and Climbs in Wadi Rum*, Appendix 2.)

The route then goes up through the cliff close to where the wadi drops down from the upper canyon floor, by easy ledges on its right. The upper wadi floor has a few water basins in it; passing the last one

JORDAN

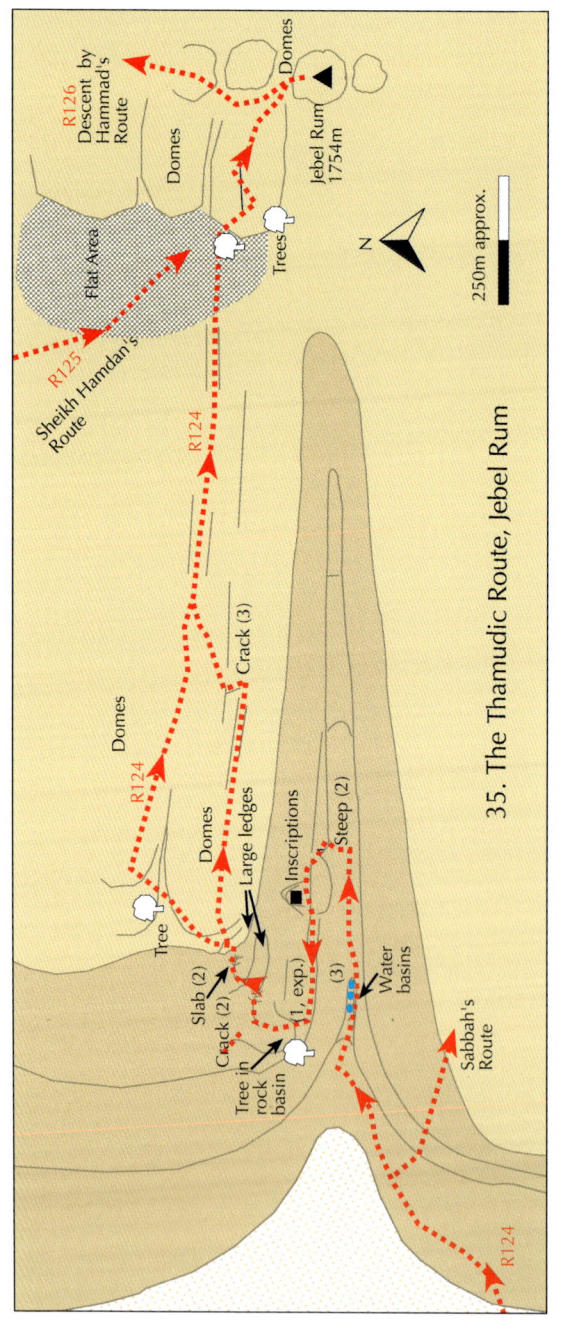

is awkward (grade 3) to reach the next level of the canyon 2m above. Continue along the canyon floor with cliffs rising over 200m on each side. A rocky depression is passed on the left (N) side in less than 100m and a short distance beyond that another larger depression with scree, also on the left, will be found.

Go up the scree a short way, then climb rocks above and on the right (good holds and ledges, grade 2) to just below a hollow with a scree-covered ledge. Go left (large cairn), across the gully and out onto ledges. Scramble easily up to the right end of a long ledge with steeper rock above. The wide ledge leads back W along the steep canyon wall. Follow it with care, walking in a superb position to a 'cave' overhang with Thamudic inscriptions (about 1hr from the desert) – see page 325. Step down a little and continue along the lower ledge until it narrows, then move back up easily to the next level where an exposed bulge has to be passed with care (grade 2) before entering a huge rock basin with a juniper tree high above the canyon mouth.

From the back of the basin climb a crack (grade 2–3) then up slabs and an easy gully to a big flat ledge. From the ledge rise diagonally left up pocketed slabs (grade 2) to another gully line trending right to reach the white rock of the domes.

Go left here and keep rising diagonally left to cross behind a previously hidden but large juniper tree onto the next line of domes to the N. If the correct way is found, the route to the summit is then almost a direct line. (If the tree is missed and a route is taken too far right, it will eventually be necessary to go back left up a short steep crack – 10m grade 3 – which will be found on the left, just after emerging from a little *siq* between domes.)

Back on route, continue heading directly E towards a saddle with a dead V-shaped tree in it, just left of the highest point. The way rises and falls over domes and through sandy areas until the final domes

A flash flood from the Great Siq, which forms part of Hammad's Route, thunders down Jebel Rum's east face into the valley of Rum

The Thamudic Route, the exposed grade 2 traverse

are reached leading to the saddle; the correct ridge of domes is identified by two small juniper trees just left of the foot, where Sheikh Hamdan's Route (Route 125) joins it from the N. (There are also junipers in a hollow to its right.) The way then goes up a shallow curving groove in the slabs, eventually moving left at the top of the groove then, higher, stepping back right to continue up to the saddle. The summit is directly above up a 20m ramp (grade 1) in its N face. Please don't add to the increasing profusion of painted and inscribed graffiti on the top.

Descent Allow at least the same time as for the ascent. Unless you are very sure of your route-finding and climbing abilities, it's best to take the same way back. You will need to have made arrangements to be met at the bottom to be driven back to Rum. If not it's a long walk round the S end of the mountain!
    For competent groups or those with a guide it is possible to return by other Bedouin climbing routes, namely Sheikh Hamdan's Route (Route 125) back to Wadi Rumman, or by descending Hammad's Route (Route 126); the latter requires five abseils and finishes in Wadi Rum, thereby completing the unique and magnificent W–E traverse of the mountain, 'one of the best adventure trips in Jordan'. (For the ascent of Hammad's Route – grade 5 – see *Treks and Climbs in Wadi Rum*, Appendix 2.)

Route 125 is an equally splendid historic route to the top.

Route 125
Jebel Rum, Sheikh Hamdan's Route

Grade	Serious scramble; don't underestimate
Details	About 3km to the summit, 750m of ascent
Time	3–4hrs for ascent, and the same for descent, possibly more

A Bedouin classic! A fascinating way to the top of Jebel Rum, with few difficulties and nothing more than grade 3, but nevertheless requiring a head for heights. The route takes the shaded N-facing wall of the Great Siq, utilising a long ledge which rises all the way to the domes from where – with some Bedouin cunning – all major obstacles are passed by a circuitous but enjoyable bit of route finding which arrives at the col immediately N of the top. For non-climbers this is a route well worth doing with a guide, perhaps spending the night up in the flat area in the domes just below the summit, before returning by the same route. See maps 34, 35 and 36.

FIRST REPORTED ASCENT

Although a traditional Bedouin route, the first reported ascent was by Sheikh Hamdan Amad, Sylvia Branford and Charmian Longstaff in November 1952. The following excerpt is from Charmian Longstaff's article in the Ladies Alpine Journal 1953, which gives the first description of a climb in Wadi Rum:

We started off up broken scree to enter a wide gully leading into the heart of the mountain. Usually these gullies, so promising at first, end, as my husband put it, inhospitably, but we circumvented this by taking to cliff ledges on our right and traversed along always making height until we reached a narrow cleft which led us still further into the mountain along a level gravelly bed. I remember a few bushes beside which we had our first rest. To the right of us was vertical cliff and to the left, broken rock leading upwards to a red palisade a thousand feet high.

Hamdan climbed with bare feet as surely as a mountain goat. We had gym shoes and were glad of them. I suppose really that it was very easy climbing but it was very exposed. Sometimes holding one or both of us by the hand, Hamdan led us along horizontal ledges in the cliff face. There always came a time when we had to climb from one ledge to the one above. Once we did this up a small gully that held two tall trees; we found afterwards that they were a kind of juniper. Then there were two vertical pitches and suddenly we were among the gleaming white of the summit domes. 'The top!' cried Hamdan.

We looked round us and saw that although we were indeed on the summit plateau we were a long way from its highest point. 'We must go there,' we said, pointing towards it. 'If you go there,' replied Hamdan, 'you will be very tired,' but by now the spirit of the intrepid woman explorers was in us and it must be the top and nothing but the top.

'You English women,' said Hamdan, 'are as strong as men.' 'You should see our husbands,' we replied.

It had taken us about two hours up to the plateau and it took us another hour up and down the complication of white domes to reach the summit. Between the domes were beds of gravel and these must hold moisture after the rare rains, or perhaps dew, because to our surprise we found junipers growing in them up to two or three times the height of a man.

Special requirements Climbing and abseil equipment will be needed by most parties as well as route-finding skill, ability to climb grade 3 and a 'head for heights'.

Guide Required for inexperienced groups.

Approach As for Route 124 round to Wadi Rumman on the W side of the mountain, to a point immediately W of the summit and below the big canyon.

The route
Scramble N up a wadi to a col between Jebel Rum and Jebel Rumman. The entrance to the Great Siq up which the route goes will then be seen across the head of the little valley of Wadi Hassa to the NE. The route enters the *siq* and, from its end, ascends its right (S) side in pleasant shade first by steep zigzags then along a perfectly situated gradually rising rock ledge to the domes, with some short sections of climbing including a steep chimney (grade 2 and 3).

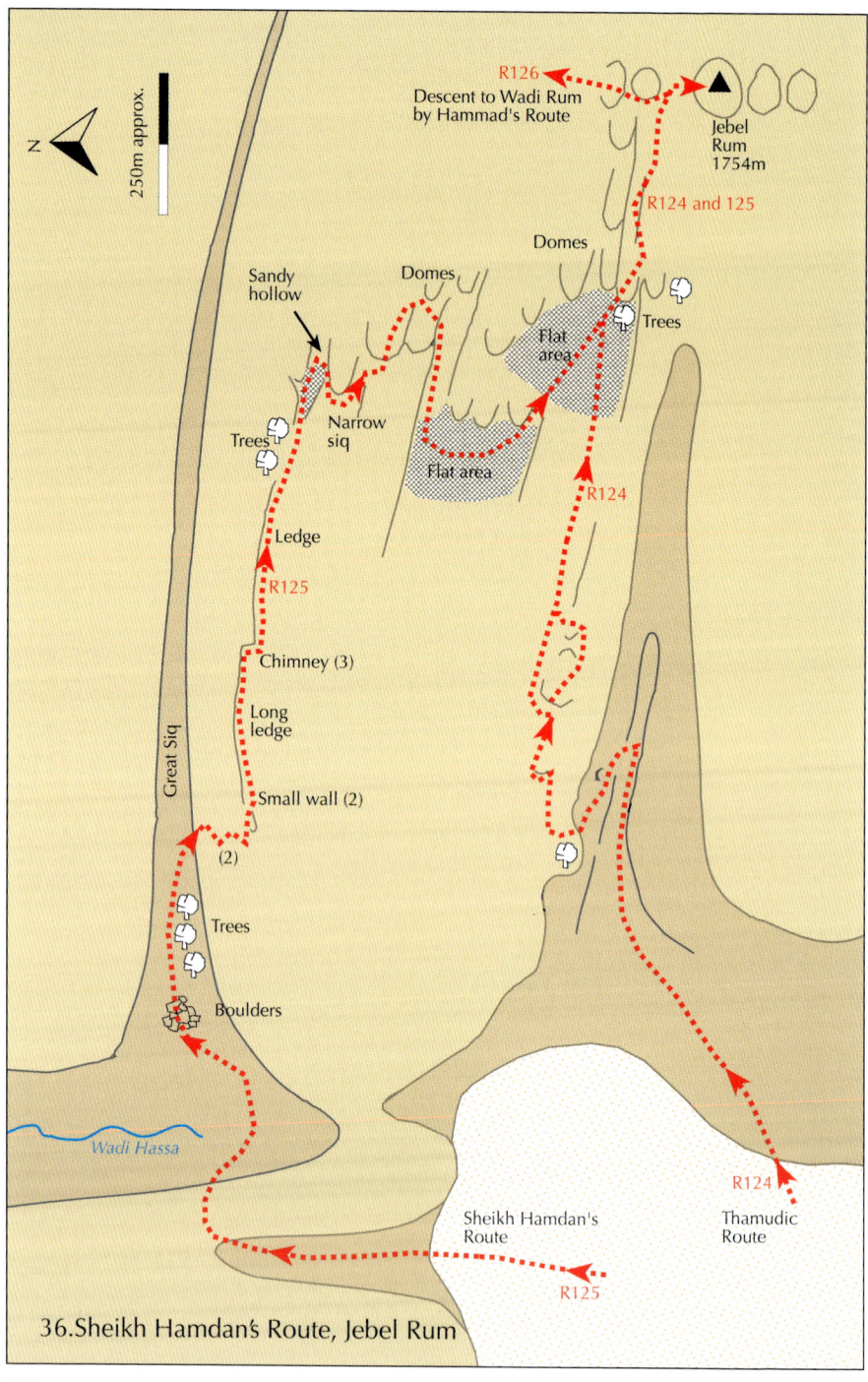

Jordan

36. Sheikh Hamdan's Route, Jebel Rum

Circuitous route finding on the domes of Sheikh Hamdan's Route

Once on the domes great care is required with route finding. The easiest way is not obvious and there are a few misleading cairns. There are a couple of awkward little descents of 2 or 3m (grade 3) if the best route is not found, otherwise there is nothing more than grade 2.

From the sandy hollow at the arrival point in the domes continue E another 50m or so, then backtrack right (W) onto the next level of domes, returning E again almost immediately through a rock crevasse to reach the next domes. Go up these on slabs, eventually crossing right (S) onto the parallel domes and down them (W) to a sandy desert area. Cross this S, then easily up SE to the next level, to meet the final ridge of domes of the Thamudic Route (Route 124) directly below the N col. There are numerous places to sleep here, with good sunset views, beyond which the short climb up the final slabby domes of Route 124 leads to the col and thence the top. Please do not add your name to the ugly collection of graffiti that has appeared there in recent years.

Descent Many people take the same way back. If you have a local guide you could also return via Route 124; either way you will need to pre-arrange a 4WD to get back to Wadi Rum. For experienced climbers the best descent is by Hammad's Route (see Route 126) to Wadi Rum, making the classic traverse of the mountain.

Route 126
The Traverse of Jebel Rum

Grade	Serious scramble; don't underestimate
Detail	About 6km
Time	Allow 8–12hrs for ascent and descent (possibly more), climbing 750m and descending 850m. Getting lost will almost inevitably entail a bivouac; be prepared.

259

Rum rock rules! A magnificent excursion. The route crosses Jebel Rum from W to E ascending either of the above Bedouin hunting routes then descending Hammad's Route, which requires abseils (where Bedouin traditionally climbed both up and down without ropes and in bare feet). Both possible ascent routes are excellent. The route then passes through more stunning rock architecture, first on high domes, then with unbeatable views down into the chasm of the Great Siq. Why not enjoy a bivouac on the mountain either on the W side, on the last sandy plateau (see above), or on the E side, on the little desert halfway down? See maps 34, 36 and 37.

Special requirements Climbing and abseil gear, trainers or lightweight footwear, plus route-finding ability, confidence to move with ease on grade 3–4 rock and abseil experience.

Guide Recommended for inexperienced parties.

Approach Ascend either Routes 124 or 125 to the summit.

The route

From the summit return to the N col, then follow the N ridge making frequent detours to the right or left to circumvent the many *siqs* that cut through the ridge. The first main barrier wall is descended near its right (E) end, downclimbing 5m (grade 3) past a curious hole. The next obstacle is a *siq* that has to be climbed into (grade 3) and out of near a tree. The final impasse is another *siq* approached down the convex bulge of a dome. It is best passed by a bold leap for the opposite dome or it can be climbed into trickily (grade 4), escaping out again up a tree.

Beyond, the domes of the N ridge flatten out and a sunken corridor (not really seen until you step over it) leads E just before the final flat-topped dome, down onto an ocean of undulating slabs. Run down grooves in the slabs to reach a sandy wadi at the bottom. After 50m or so along the wadi walk up rocky slabs to the right to reach small domes below a N-facing barrier wall. Head E along these passing a large bushy tree and descending to a sandy passage directly under the barrier, continuing E past more trees to emerge in a small 'desert'.

The upper domes of Hammad's Route

Still following the barrier cliff, the desert closes again to another sandy corridor. Leave this after 50m or so, at the second tree, and go up onto domes on the left. Follow the ridge of domes E, with *siqs* on either side, eventually descending slightly right (grade 2–3) to a sandy hollow.

Go left here along a ledge 5m up on the W side of a dome for about 50m, then through a small *siq* to emerge on the domes above Wadi Rum. Follow these first SE, rising and falling and zigzagging down with superb views (cairns, some steps of grade 2–3). Eventually a 5m barrier wall is reached; this can be downclimbed (grade 4), but there is an abseil ring above it that makes life easier. After the abseil go out E and up the next domes, then N and down them to another vertical drop. Pass it by a 10m abseil on the right, near a tree, or continue a little further and descend into a bottomless concealed chimney on the left (5m, grade 3). Step out of the chimney onto the ledge below the dome and contour E to the foot of the above abseil variant, then scramble down to a juniper with the first set of abseil chains nearby. Abseil 20m to a hollow from where the next abseil goes 10m down to a big ledge, past 'Hammad's tree'. (This dead juniper was wedged in place by Hammad to climb the overhang.)

You are now entering the confines of the Great Siq. Walk W down a chimney for 10m to another tree. The next chains are above it for a 40m abseil down into the depths of the chasm. Follow the bed of the *siq* down to the E, often with water in it, which can be fun: some precarious grade 2–3 including a 6m descent over a pool! After the last pool – and before the *siq* plunges to greater depths – walk out right up a corridor and go up left at the end onto a ridge. Scramble E along this (some grade 2) to emerge on a shoulder directly above the village.

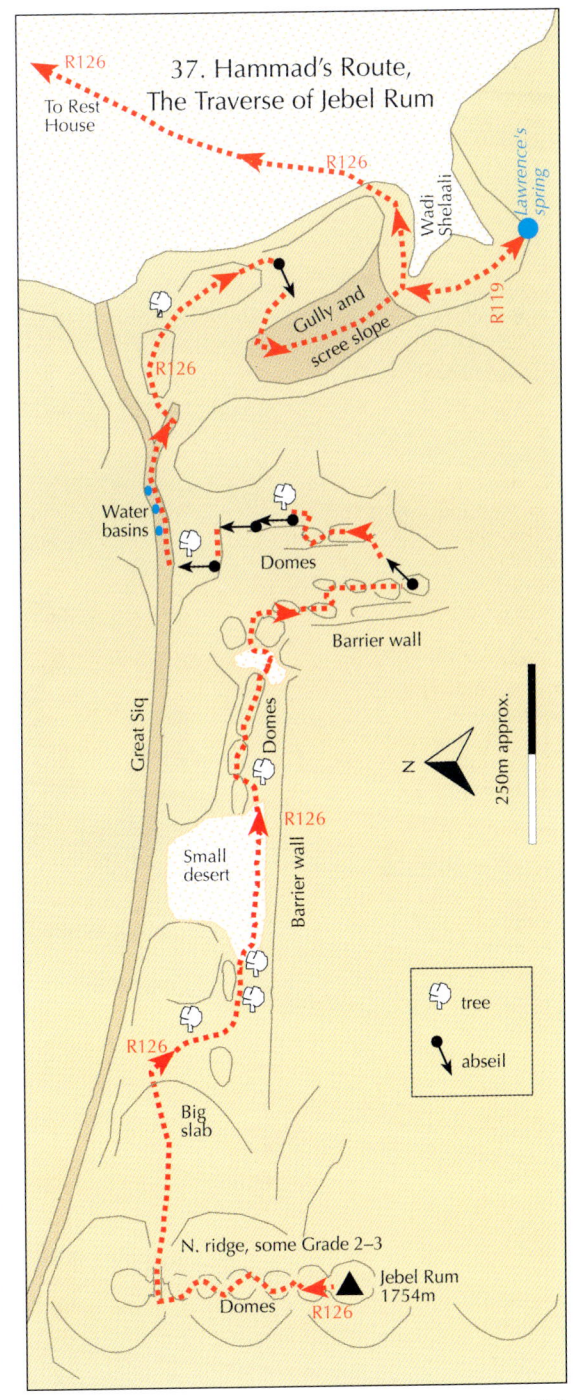

37. Hammad's Route, The Traverse of Jebel Rum

261

View down Hammad's Route to Wadi Rum and the Nassrani Towers

Follow the shoulder S descending in an increasingly exposed position (some grade 2) to reach a platform on its W side where chains mark the last 40m abseil down a knobbly slab to a rock pedestal. (Take care when pulling the ropes.) From the pedestal descend NW through large boulders squeezing under or climbing over the last one (exposed grade 3) to reach a recess. A short exposed traverse (grade 2) then gives access to a big ledge. Follow this along over a small tower and down a steep ramp (grade 3) to reach a big scree-filled gully. Go down the gully to emerge amongst the mint-filled springs in Wadi Shelaali, 200m N of Lawrence's Spring. Follow Route 119 down to Wadi Rum for a shower and cold beer!

Jebel um Ishrin, the next destination, is found E across the Rum Valley.

JEBEL UM ISHRIN, 1753m

The skyline east of the Rest House is formed by the west face of the massif of Jebel um Ishrin. Without resorting to climbing, there are two ways through it. The first is at the north end, not far from the Visitor Centre, where a *siq* divides the main summit of Jebel um Ishrin from its northern outlier, Jebel Makhras. Not so long ago it was claimed – presumably for purposes of tourism – that T. E. Lawrence named his book *Seven Pillars of Wisdom* after this mountain, which supposedly has seven pillars; but as any reader of Lawrence will know the title was originally intended for an earlier book on archaeology, and has nothing whatsoever to do with Wadi Rum.

Route 127
Wadi Siq Makhras (Valley of the Stony Canyon)

Grade	Easy walk
Details	8km; take care with route finding through the mountain
Time	Allow 3hrs for the round trip

This pleasant little valley and subsequent return journey make a nice round trip with ever-changing vistas of Wadi Rum, Wadi um Ishrin and the mountains near Barrah Canyon, which are usually hidden from view. A good introduction to Rum. See map 38.

The route
From the Visitor Centre – which is about 8km N of Rum village – head SE across the desert for just over 1km towards the low point in the skyline. From the mouth of the valley (GPS alt. 870m N29° 37.670' E35° 26.893') it is an enjoyable walk of no more than 45mins to the pass, initially following the wadi bed generally SE, taking care to scramble up left into the left branch of the wadi after a few hundred metres (GPS alt. 875m N29° 34.463' E35° 27.010') where the main valley goes S. Continue along as it narrows to a small ravine. Not long after it bends right and then left, rising though a narrowing *siq* to emerge suddenly just above the red sands of Wadi Um Ishrin, with views E to the Barrah Massif (GPS alt. 980m N29° 36.820' E35° 27.479').

About 200m or so further on and slightly right a light-coloured flat-topped mushroom of rock can be easily gained. On its top are inscriptions of feet, two separate from the rest and pointing in different directions, and another set which appears to be a family group. From here go N up an unmistakable big dune (easiest on its right) to arrive at a pass between Jebel Makhras and Jebel Reha, then descend the valley and return W round Jebel Makhras to the Visitor Centre.

Alternatively, to make a full day, connect this route with a return through Rakabat Canyon (Route 128).

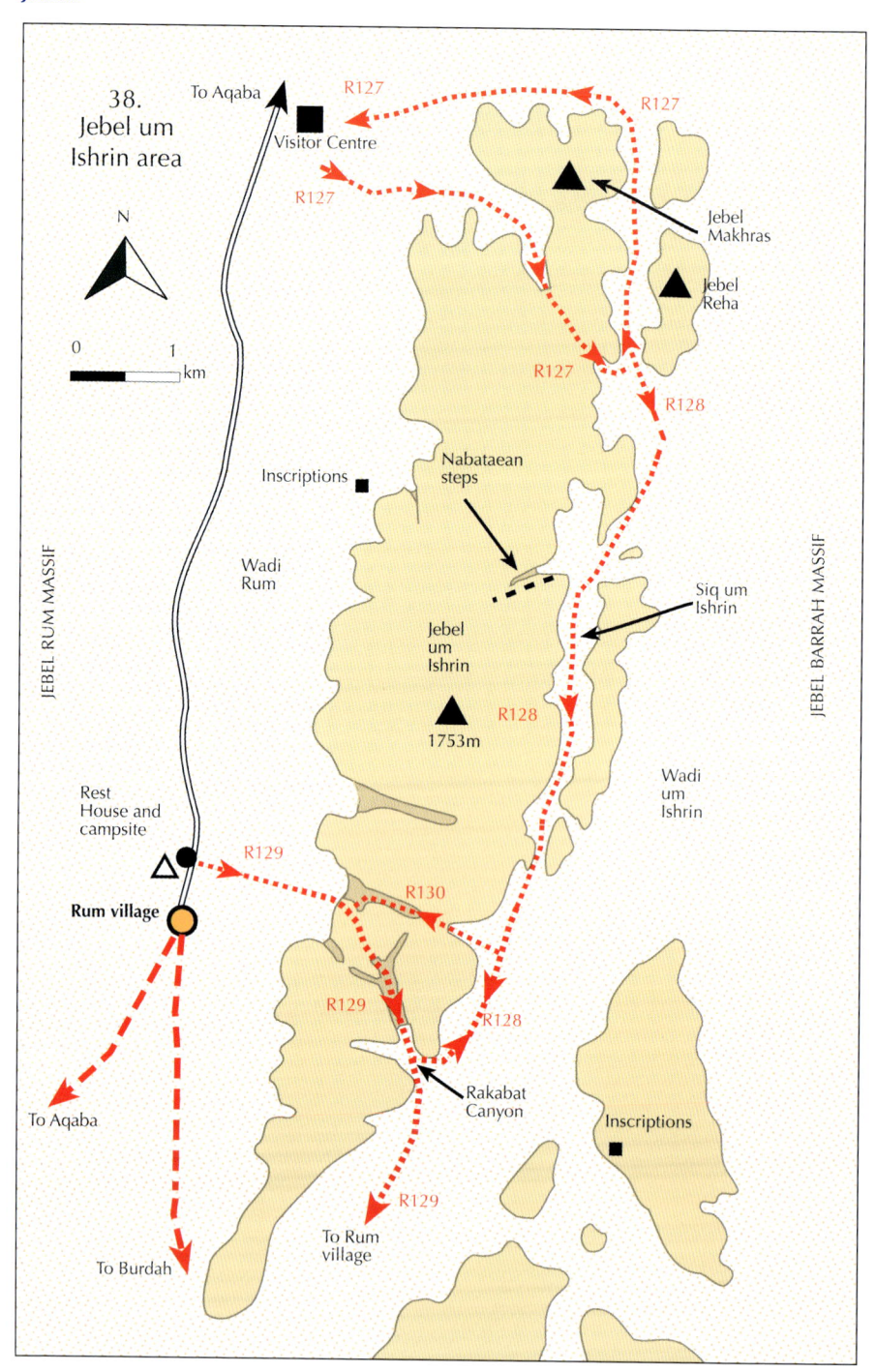

Jordan

38. Jebel um Ishrin area

Route 128
Round Jebel um Ishrin

Grade	Moderate trek and scramble; take care with route finding through Rakabat Canyon
Details	Approx 14km
Time	Allow 5–6hrs

A good round trip in wild mountain scenery, but quite a long day with considerable desert walking. See maps 38 and 39.

Special requirements If you return by Rakabat Canyon you should have a rope for emergencies, ability to climb grade 2 and a head for heights.
Guide Recommended for inexperienced groups.

The route
Follow the previous route to its exit into Wadi um Ishrin (1hr max) then head S, keeping close to the E flank of Jebel um Ishrin to reach a little side valley right of the N end of the desert canyon of Siq um Ishrin. The Nabataean steps are cut into the rock on the left side of the valley and rise diagonally across the cliffs into the upper canyon, giving access to pools of water which linger for much of the year.
 Once in Siq um Ishrin its undulating sandy floor continues S for about 2.5km before rejoining Wadi um Ishrin 1km further on near the impressive ravine of Zernouk el Daber. This cleaves its way dramatically W towards Wadi Rum but is not passable without ropes (Route 130). Just over 1km further S again the bushy entrance to Rakabat Canyon will be found just before the big red dune.
 Rakabat Canyon makes a fascinating way back through the mountain to the Rest House, reversing Route 129. Otherwise, continue S to pass round the end of the massif before returning N to Rum village (longer but easier and no route-finding problems).

Looking NE from the Rest House two massive canyons appear to split Jebel um Ishrin, but they are deceptive: you can scramble into them amongst awe-inspiring rock scenery, but you cannot cross to the other side without climbing equipment. The way through this end of Um Ishrin – Route 129 – is via a remarkable maze of concealed canyons almost directly opposite the Rest House.

Route 129
Rakabat Canyon

Grade	Moderate scramble
Details	3km from Wadi Rum to Wadi um Ishrin
Time	1½–2hrs and the same to return S round the mountain

JORDAN

A magical mystery tour! The canyons of Rakabat um Ejil now provide an increasingly popular route from Wadi Rum to the beautiful orange dunes of Wadi um Ishrin. Though the way is getting worn, route finding is not always straightforward and there are some exposed steps of grade 2. A wonderful half-day in amazing mountain and desert scenery. See maps 38 and 39.

Special requirements A rope for emergencies, ability to climb grade 2 and a head for heights.
Guide Recommended for inexperienced groups.

The route
From the Rest House cross the desert towards the right side of the giant ravine of Kharazeh Canyon, reaching the screes at GPS alt. 940m N29° 34.566' E35° 25.872'. Above to the left (about 200m right of the main canyon) a small gully will be seen (not too obvious at first) cutting through a band of cliffs and with a large overhang on its right. This is 'Goat's Gully' and provides access to a plateau (½hr from the Rest House; GPS alt. 980m N29° 34.570' E35° 25.960').

Walk almost S along the plateau (bearing 160°) towards the smaller (left hand) of two gullies. Scramble up this, still in the direction of a thumb-shaped tower on the distant skyline, to arrive in a bay.

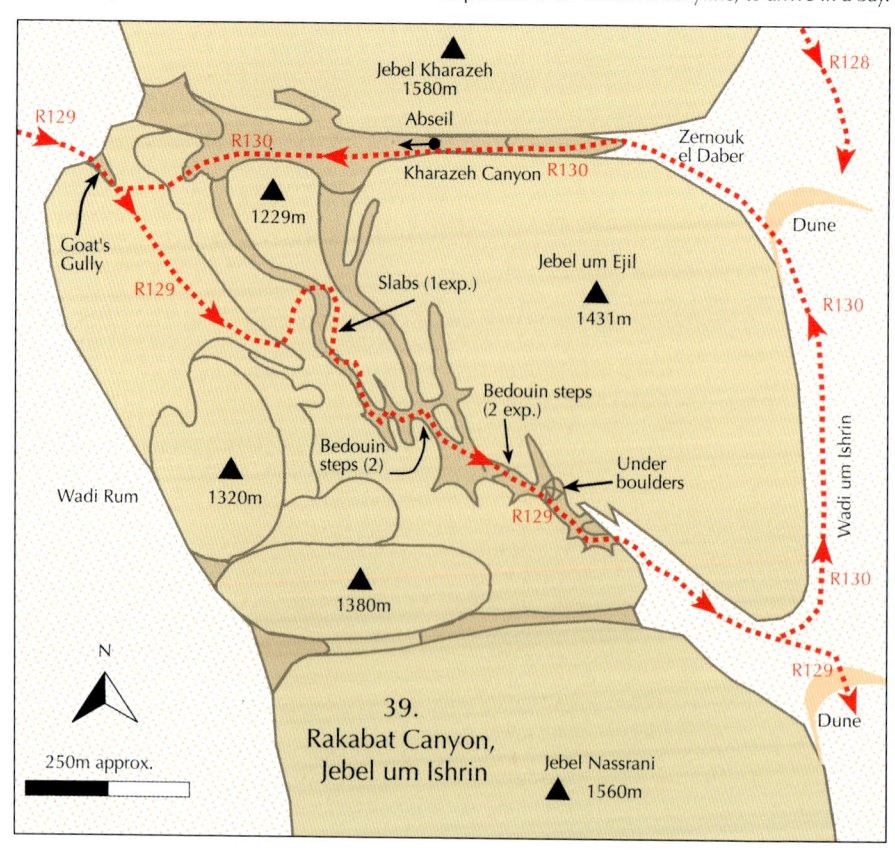

39. Rakabat Canyon, Jebel um Ishrin

Looking down from the rock climb 'Houdini' to trekkers in Rakabat Canyon (top right)

On the left is a saddle above a ravine that marks the entrance to the canyons but they cannot be entered directly. Instead go left and down to cross the little streambed at an S-bend and climb up some smooth pink slabs (grade 1) on the opposite side. Walk right along their top (exposed) and descend into the ravine above the first barrier.

About 50m further on is another small steep barrier. Either ascend it directly (grade 2), or pass it on the left (sandy). Continue, until 10m before the end where Bedouin steps lead up left to enter a side canyon. At the next junction turn right, then almost immediately left and up a narrow ravine (more Bedouin steps) to reach the pass. Descend an awkward 5m wall (Bedouin steps, grade 2), to emerge in the upper Rakabat Canyon at a 'crossroads' (GPS alt. 1160m N29° 34.239' E35° 26.213').

Here there are three options. To the left (N) is the way to the climbs on the W face of Jebel um Ejil. If this is followed to its end, a 20m abseil goes down into Kharazeh Canyon. Straight on a narrow cleft goes to a concealed canyon also with some rock climbs, while to the right is the way out into Wadi um Ishrin (this point is approximately 1hr from the Rest House). Go right, keeping to the left side and descending to a slightly lower wadi (the head of which goes back up another ravine into the concealed canyon). Continue down it, again keeping to its very left edge. Rise up over a rock bulge (do not go down the canyon), then through a defile and down steep slabs (grade 2, originally with Bedouin steps) into the lower ravine.

About 50m down this pass under a big boulder and carry on down keeping to the right side through a little defile for the first magnificent view of Wadi um Ishrin's red dunes. Descend the gully from here, squeezing past a jammed boulder (grade 2) onto slabs. Keep right, still close to the mountain, finally descending to the valley floor 10m below, through the lowest little wadi, down smooth rock (grade 1; GPS alt. 1060m N29° 34.008' E35° 26.373'). (From the opposite direction this point is opposite a tongue of rock that descends into the valley from Jebel um Ejil, and about 50m before the inner end of the valley.) From there walk out into Wadi um Ishrin, at the foot of the big dunes. Climb them with difficulty for superb views.

Return Either reverse the route to Rum village, or go S over the big red dunes of Um Ishrin, round the end of the mountain and back up the valley of Rum (6km). Either way takes about the same time.

These canyons can also be used as the start of a longer trek out to the stupendous Barrah Canyon (see *Treks and Climbs in Wadi Rum*, Appendix 2) or as part of the circuit of Jebel um Ishrin (Route 128). Alternatively, you can arrange to be met in Wadi um Ishrin with camels and combine a canyon walk with a camel trek. Route 130 is a harder option.

Route 130
Round Jebel um Ejil

Grade	Moderate scramble
Details	7km for return journey from and to the Rest House
Time	5hrs

A very enjoyable day amongst varied and continually changing rock and desert scenery, passing by many rock climbs described in *Treks and Climbs in Wadi Rum* (Appendix 2). A great introduction to walking and climbing in Rum. See maps 38 and 39.

Special requirements Abseiling equipment (2 x 50m ropes), route-finding skills and the ability to climb grade 3 in safety.
Guide Essential for anyone unfamiliar with climbing and abseiling.

Abseiling into Kharazeh Canyon

The route
Follow Route 129 through Rakabat Canyon to Wadi um Ishrin. Walk N up this in inspiring desert scenery for less than ½hr, along the foot of the E face of Jebel um Ejil, to enter the canyon of Zernouk el Daber. From the secluded basin scramble right up a boulder-filled gully to a tree with many branches. From behind the large boulder on its left make a long stride out (grade 2) onto slabs. Go up these and 10m higher move onto the top of another big boulder (grade 1), then up a ramp into a chimney and bushy gully. Leave this for the easy ridge on its left, which is crossed leftwards on slabs to the next gully. After passing a boulder (grade 1) carry on up, under a boulder and out onto the col.

An abseil chain will be found 10m down on the left. Abseil 40m into a chimney (mostly free-hanging) and descend this to the floor of Kharazeh Canyon by some awkward bridging (3) in chimneys, or by a second abseil. Walk out of the canyon between impressive mushrooming walls to where it suddenly opens out. (Route 129 – the abseil descent from Rakabat Canyon, below the W face of Jebel um Ejil – comes down the gully on the left.)

Continue out until the wadi drops down a cliff. To avoid doing the same rise left up a bushy gully to a saddle. Cross it and descend in the same direction, starting from the right, down another bushy gully that leads down to a plateau. Goat's Gully (see Route 129, GPS alt. 980m N29° 34.570' E35° 25.960') will be found across the plateau and slightly right. Descend it and cross Wadi Rum back to the Rest House.

EASTERN RUM
Moving further east into the desert the amazing defile of Barrah Canyon is reached.

Route 131
Barrah Canyon

Grade	Easy walk
Details	5km
Time	1½–2hrs

Barrah Canyon is a magnificent desert canyon with big dunes that are dwarfed by the immensity of the superlative rock architecture. There are some world-class rock climbs here (see *Treks and Climbs in Wadi Rum*, Appendix 2), but the canyon is also a great place to walk through and perhaps spend the night in. You can also go through by 4wd or with camels or horses. See maps 29 and 40.

Approach Some people walk it in half a day from the Rest House, perhaps via Rakabat Canyon; others go by 4WD, camel or horse.

40. Barrah Canyon area

The route

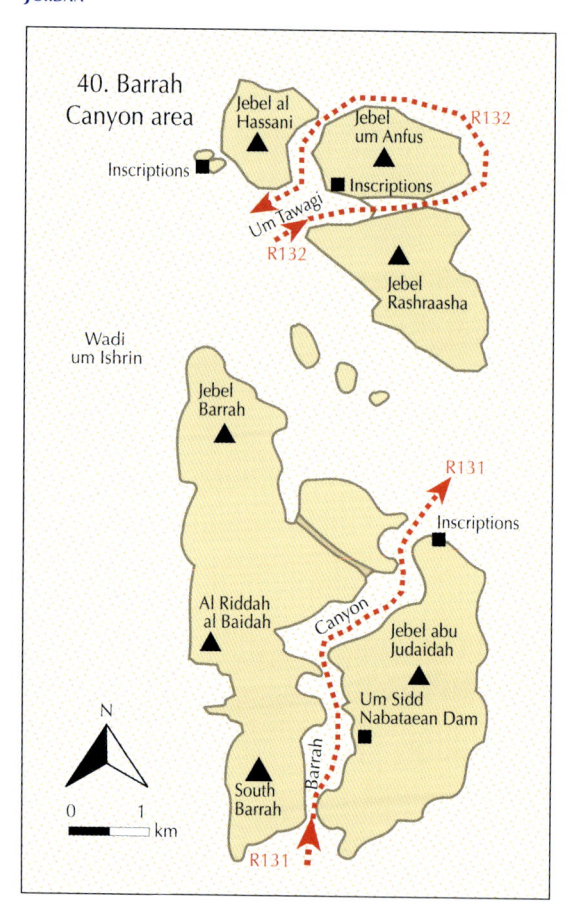

Simply head N down the canyon, making exploratory excursions en route. (There are barbed wire 'gates' near both ends; please leave these open or shut, as you find them – they either allow or prevent camels passing through.)

Near the E end of the S fence an old Nabataean dam, Um Sidd, will be found in a side canyon, whilst most of the rock climbs are in the amphitheatre inside the N fence. There are also some huge dunes there, close to the cliffs on the W side and not immediately apparent. Some of the *siqs* on the W side hold pools of water for much of the year; one, Abu Ighlakat, cuts through to another desert canyon and gives an enjoyable scramble with abseils (to go through ask a local guide or see *Treks and Climbs in Wadi Rum*, Appendix 2). Beyond the N end of Barrah Canyon and across the next desert valley another small cluster of peaks can be seen.

UM TAWAGI

This secluded desert basin is hidden away in a group of three peaks at the NE end of Wadi um Ishrin and just N of Jebel Barrah. The area may be approached by 4WD up Wadi Rum, then across an area of dunes N of the Jebel um Ishrin massif (about 15km), or it can be accessed on foot or by 4WD from Barrah Canyon, 4km to the SW. There are some pleasant walks here, including Route 132.

Route 132
Round Jebel um Anfus

Grade	Easy walk
Details	7km
Time	2hrs for the round trip

An enjoyable canyon walk with a surprising variety of scenery, and some excellent inscriptions. See maps 29 and 40.

The route
From the S entrance of Siq um Tawagi walk E along the obvious valley, coming to a surprising drop above its lower continuation and an excellent view out across the mud flats to the green oasis of Diseh. Descend into the lower valley and walk N then W round Jebel um Anfus to enter the N end of Siq um Tawagi. Walk up through dramatic rock scenery and back to the starting point.

Just W of the *siq* entrance on a black slab above a boulder slope will be seen a variety of rock drawings depicting hunting scenes. About 0.5km WSW on an isolated rock tower more inscriptions will be found on a black slab, on its SW side.

BURDAH, KHAZALI AND THE SOUTH
South of Barrah Canyon is a unique rock feature that has become one of Jordan's most famous natural landmarks, unknown to the outside world before 1984 (see below).

Route 133
The Rock Bridge of Burdah

October 21. Whilst gathering wood for a feast at Sabbah Atieq's tent, Sabbah and Defallah took us out to the southeast of Rum. On rounding the end of a mountain they pointed up to the skyline and said with mischievous grins 'Maybe this is of interest?' There, arching across the horizon, three hundred metres above the desert was a magnificent natural rock bridge, perhaps the most significant discovery of our trip to Rum.

'A Report on Wadi Rum for the Tourism Ministry' Tony Howard (1984)

Grade	Moderate scramble
Details	1.5km, climbing about 160m to the bridge
Time	Allow 3hrs, including the return journey and time to enjoy it

A truly delightful scramble on good rock, well marked with cairns but sometimes a little exposed and with some moves of grade 2. The bridge is a must for any fit visitor. The views around the Rum area are superb and even better from the actual summit, though to reach it 20m of grade 3 rock has to be climbed just after the bridge (see Route 134). Most people stop at the bridge. See maps 29 and 41.

JORDAN

Special requirements Safety rope (50m is more than enough) and associated equipment, also route-finding ability, good footwear and confidence on exposed and sandy grade 2 rock. Abseiling ability could be useful.

Guide Recommended for inexperienced groups.

Approach Take a 4WD for the 15km drive down Rum and the long valley of Khor el Ajram to the start of the route in a little valley 200m right of the N end of Burdah's W face (GPS alt. 1200m N29° 28.747' E35° 29.803'). This journey is well worthwhile in itself. The driver will meet you on your return and can visit the canyon of Khazali (Route 138) with its rock inscriptions – as well as other sites of antiquity – on the way back, if requested.

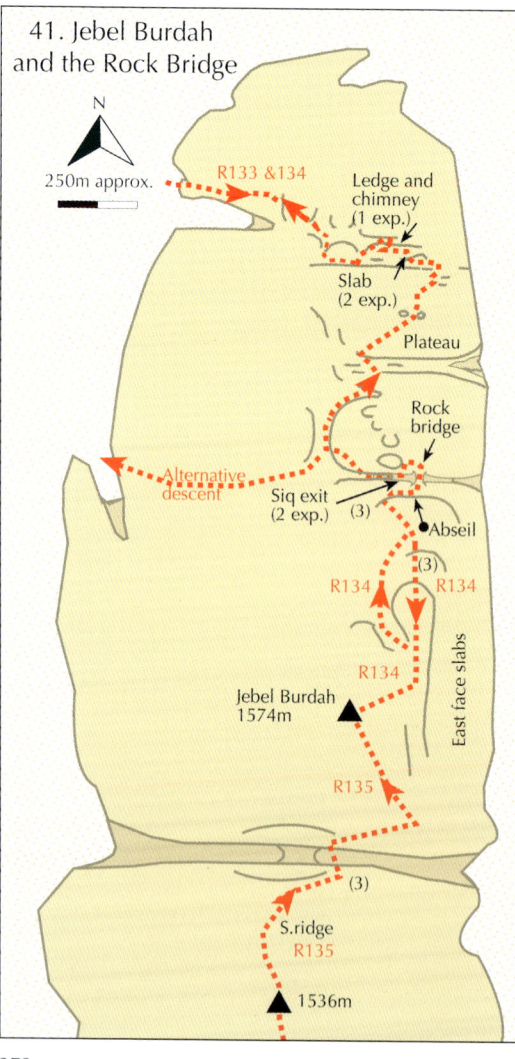

41. Jebel Burdah and the Rock Bridge

The route

Go E along a pale ridge of rock, on the left side of a little valley, with a broken white rock 'mushroom' marking the start, to the saddle above the end of the valley. Here trend left (SE) up slabs and over a dome. Carry on in the same direction and descend E for 10m to enter a gully. Go S up this, then down left at a rock barrier to a hollow.

Go up again, in the same direction, then left and right (grade 1) on a slab to pass a steep chimney, after which walk easily E again, still below the rock barrier, to two big chimneys. Avoid them by going left and across a slab to enter the next parallel ravine. Follow this up a short way to 10m before its end. Don't go up the square walled chimney ahead but step right and walk back W on a ledge (exposed, maybe some slings in place for handholds) passing under a yellow/white overhang and up a black chimney (grade 1) to ledges.

A long-suffering tree then makes it possible to climb up (grade 2) into the next gully. (Alternatively, avoid the tree by moving up left and stepping onto the left side of the slab above [exposed] and climb right across it [grade 2] to enter the gully.) Follow the gully through bushes and continue E, then go right and zigzag SW up slabs and domes above the barrier wall (some grade 2) to slabs which lead easily up past a rock tower onto a plateau (½hr from start). Go diagonally right to the far right corner, then left and up before winding clockwise

View west from the summit of Jebel Burdah (Routes 134, 135)

round the next barrier of cliffs through a small hidden valley on their left, to emerge above the next plateau.

Descend to a flat sandy area, walk S along it then left onto easy slabs and up rightwards towards the left side of a notch in the skyline, trending right below a barrier wall to enter a canyon, when the bridge will suddenly be seen ahead. Follow the canyon up, then climb its left wall steeply (exposed and sandy, grade 2, take care) to the big ledge just below the bridge (ring *in situ* at the ledge for a safety rope; GPS alt. 1360m N29° 28.393' E35° 29.960').

In 1984 there were no graffiti on or near the bridge but now the rocks are covered in carved names. Please do not add to this eyesore. It is a beautiful place – let's keep it that way.

Return By the same route; the descent into the canyon is best done with a safety rope.

If you want to go to the summit try Route 134.

Route 134
Jebel Burdah (1574m) via the Rock Bridge

Grade	Difficult scramble
Details	2.5km, climbing about 370m to the summit
Time	4–5hrs for return journey

Well worthwhile and great views. The crux is the grade 3 wall just past the bridge. Maps 29 and 41.

Special requirements Climbing and abseil equipment (50m rope adequate), suitable footwear and the ability to climb grade 3 rock.
Guide Recommended for inexperienced groups.

The route
Ascend via Route 133, then cross the bridge to the barrier wall ahead, which is climbed by traversing right (grade 3) then up and left to easier ground (chains here for the belay and abseil descent). From here the ridge may be followed directly (grade 3), or (slightly easier) go up the little valley on its W side and regain the ridge above the steep section. The final ridge goes up to a superb viewpoint on the summit (GPS alt. 1574m N29° 28.086' E35° 29.862').

Descent Follow the easiest way down, left of the ridge at the steep section, taking particular care with route finding. Abseil from chains to reach the bridge and continue as Route 133 descent.

Burdah also offers a ridge traverse (information supplied by Andrew Moore).

Route 135
The Traverse of Jebel Burdah

Grade	Moderate scramble (a few grade 3 moves)
Details	3km, climbing from 1200m to 1536m before descending about 100m and climbing up to the main summit at 1574m; approx 450m of ascent and descent in total for the full S–N traverse
Time	About 5hrs

Unlike most of Rum's routes the ascents of the two summits are up boulder-strewn slopes rather than clean undulating slabs, but as always on Burdah the views are unbeatable. See map 41.

Special requirements As Route 134.

The route
Start below the W side of the low col of Rakabat Burdah (GPS alt. 1200m N29° 27.615' E35° 29.205'), which separates the main massif from its extreme S summit. Once at the col go N up Burdah's S ridge to the first top at 1536m then along until a long descent is necessary to the right, with a few grade 3 moves to reach the gully just right of the col. From there traverse out and up right to the SE ridge and up to the main top.

Descent Via Route 134.

W of Burdah there is a delightful area of small domes.

The abseil to the Burdah bridge on the descent from the summit

THE DOMES OF ABU KHSHEIBAH

A beautiful region of small peaks and domes, 12–15km SE of Wadi Rum, interwoven by a maze of narrow and sometimes hidden valleys. The small and easily accessible Bridge of Um Fruth is here. It is a splendid area for walking or travelling through with camels or horses, and there is also a pleasant little canyon trip (Route 136).

Route 136
The Canyon of Jebel abu Khashaba

Grade	Easy scramble
Details	Just over 1km through the mountain (from where you could return) or 5km round trip
Time	1½hrs for the round trip

The narrow passage, which splits the mountain in two, provides an entertaining little trip in some of Rum's best desert scenery. See maps 29 and 43.

Approach Ask to be driven to the S end of the mountain (GPS alt. 1100m N29° 29.159' E35° 28.159') about ½hr from Rum village.

The route
Walk into what seems a dead-end valley, with a huge dune on its left side. Continue into the narrowing canyon; just before it becomes too restrictive scramble up right to ledges that continue N a short way before descending to re-enter the widening continuation of the canyon. Continue N between impressive cliffs to emerge in the open desert (GPS alt. 1120m N29° 29.740' E35° 28.228').

Return Either return the same way, or continue out, trending left across orange dunes (covered in flowers in springtime), with small rocky hills to the left. Two passes through them look tempting (one is marked by a cairn) but these have not been checked out by the authors. Instead continue along, down, round and gently back up, circumnavigating the hills in an anti-clockwise direction to arrive back at the start.

Hidden in the domes S of here, W of the large dome of Jebel abu Khsheibah, is Route 137.

Route 137
The Rock Bridge of Um Fruth

The location is easily accessible by 4WD, the photogenic bridge being just above the desert floor on Jebel um Fruth. A ride out there by horse or camel is excellent, whilst the grade 2 scramble to its top is popular. See map 43.

Next is the huge tabletop massif visible at the S end of Wadi Rum. Its N end is Jebel Khazali, whilst its S summit is Jebel Khush Khashah.

JEBEL KHAZALI AND JEBEL KHUSH KHASHAH, 1420m AND 1514m

My mind used to turn me from the direct road, to clear my senses by a night in Rumm and by the ride down its dawn-lit valley towards the shining plains, or up its valley in the sunset towards that glowing square which my timid anticipation never let me reach. I would say, 'Shall I ride on this time, beyond the Khazali, and know it all?' But in truth I liked Rumm too much.

Seven Pillars of Wisdom T. E. Lawrence (1926)

Route 138
Khazali Canyon

The canyon splits Khazali's N face and is about 8km S of Rum village and on the 4WD tourist trail (maps 29 and 43). It can also be visited on foot, or with camels or horses, and is entered by steps to a ledge on its right after which the first hieroglyphics will soon be seen above the left wall. Others will be found on both sides of the ravine at various levels. As one goes up the canyon it gets progressively narrower, often with pools, and the rock walls are worn smooth by water. It is possible to continue for 200m or so, with some climbing (grade 2) to reach the final box canyon, where there is a bull carved on the rock.
    The canyon has been descended from the summit by abseil by Bedouin guide Atieq Auda (see Appendix 1) and the big N-facing cliff to its left has a traditional Bedouin route up it that is supposed to be very good, but we have no information; ask one of the Bedouin mountain guides. There is also another Bedouin route to the S summit, described below as Route 139.

Route 139
Jebel Khush Khashah by Sabbah's Route

Grade	Difficult scramble
Details	About 1km
Time	1½–2½hrs to the summit; slightly less in descent

A pleasant rock scramble up slabs and grooves on the right of a canyon, always interesting and in great desert scenery. Popular as a guided route; we did it with Sabbah Atieq, who told the tale of an old lady who was coming down nearby with her goatskin full of water in a time of drought when a rock broke and she fell into the canyon below. There are some wooden branches sticking from the rock, placed there as handholds. See maps 29 and 42.

Special requirements Route-finding skills and the ability to climb grade 2–3 in safety.
Guide Recommended.
Approach With 4WD down Wadi Rum and up Wadi Khush Khashah to the canyon near the S end, marked by a huge smooth black wall on its left.

The route
Follow a meandering line up gullies, slabs and walls on an easy angled ridge on the right side of the canyon (a few cairns). Eventually a shoulder is reached, and above a corridor leads up through sometimes steeper rocks (sections of grade 2) to the upper slabs. Cross these, trending right (some exposed moves) to the summit plateau. The final dome is larger and trickier than it looks!

Return By the same route.

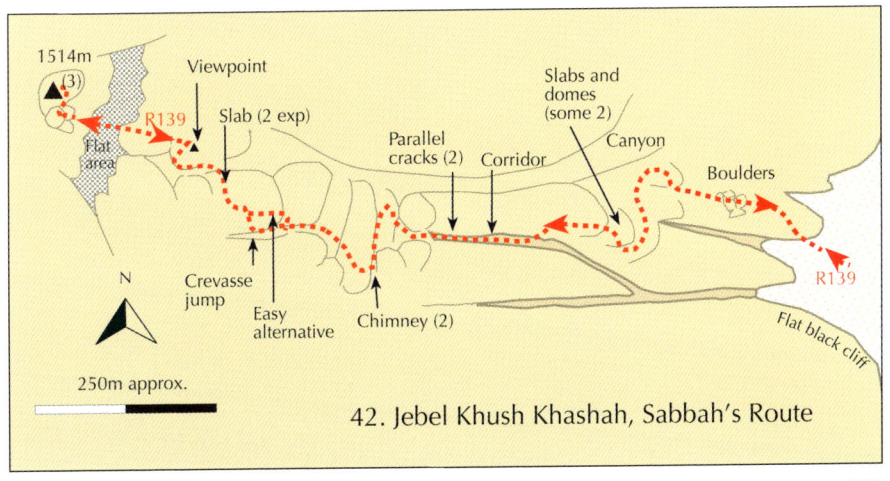

42. Jebel Khush Khashah, Sabbah's Route

Beyond Khazali there are some Bedouin tourist camps ideally located for the sunset views (see Appendix 1). Moving S again the desert, its rock domes and mountains are less frequented by tourists but as pretty as any in Rum, especially in spring. There may be camps of semi-nomadic Bedouin from Rum and Saudi Arabia, which is now close. Jordan's highest summit is here.

Route 140 goes to Jordan's highest summit, situated in an extremely remote part of the desert, 40km from Rum and only 2km from Saudi Arabia. Defallah Atieq (see Appendix 1) – who took us there many years ago – identified Adaami as Jordan's highest mountain.

Sabbah Atieq, Bedouin mountain guide, with friends on his eponymous climb of Jebel Khush Khashah

Route 140
Jebel um Adaami, 1830m

Grade	Easy scramble
Details	2km
Time	2hrs for ascent and descent, plus driving time 1½–2hrs each way

An excellent desert drive and a great day out. The ascent to the top is a pleasant scramble and the views magnificent in all directions, especially S into Saudi Arabia and N across the whole area of Rum. See maps 29 and 43.

Guide/driver Required.

Approach The enjoyable 40km 4WD journey passes through ever-changing rock and desert terrain and past isolated Bedouin camps. The last 3 or 4km are particularly difficult, up an increasingly narrow and tortuous sandy wadi, and require considerable driving skill. You will need even more time if you want to visit the petroglyphs on the N and S sides of Wadi Saabit (shown to us by Sheikh Mohammad who often had his camp nearby).

The route
From the drivable end of the narrow sandy wadi (GPS alt. 1420m N29° 18.717' E35° 26.778') scramble approx SE up a worn path on the boulder-covered hillside and into a rocky basin. Either go left to meet the summit ridge directly or, more easily and with nice views, continue ahead to meet it lower down, about 0.25km NNW of the top. Follow the ridge left round the basin to the main summit ridge, then go up it – with increasingly fine views – to the summit (GPS alt. 1840m N29° 18.551' E35° 26.040').

Return By the same route.

Siq um el Barrid, a narrow and steep-walled canyon with carved hand- and footprints, is 5–6km N of Jebel um Adaami. There are more inscriptions on the NW tip of Jebel Albzouri about 9km W of Jebel um Adaami, and others near some olive trees belonging to Sheikh Mohammad. You may find his campsite and be invited for tea and coffee.

Whilst in this delightful and far-flung corner of Rum you might consider extending your trip by 4WD or with camels or horses to include a great journey to the SE through **Wadi Salaada** (see below). This is a very pleasant walking area, a quiet and peaceful spot just N of the Saudi border. There are some very nice trekking summits on the way here from Rum via Burdah or the domes of Abu Khsheibah and the desert canyon of Nogra. You will need a competent local guide (see Appendix 1) for any of these routes. Some groups spend days here on foot or on horses or camels.

Route 141 is located further to the E.

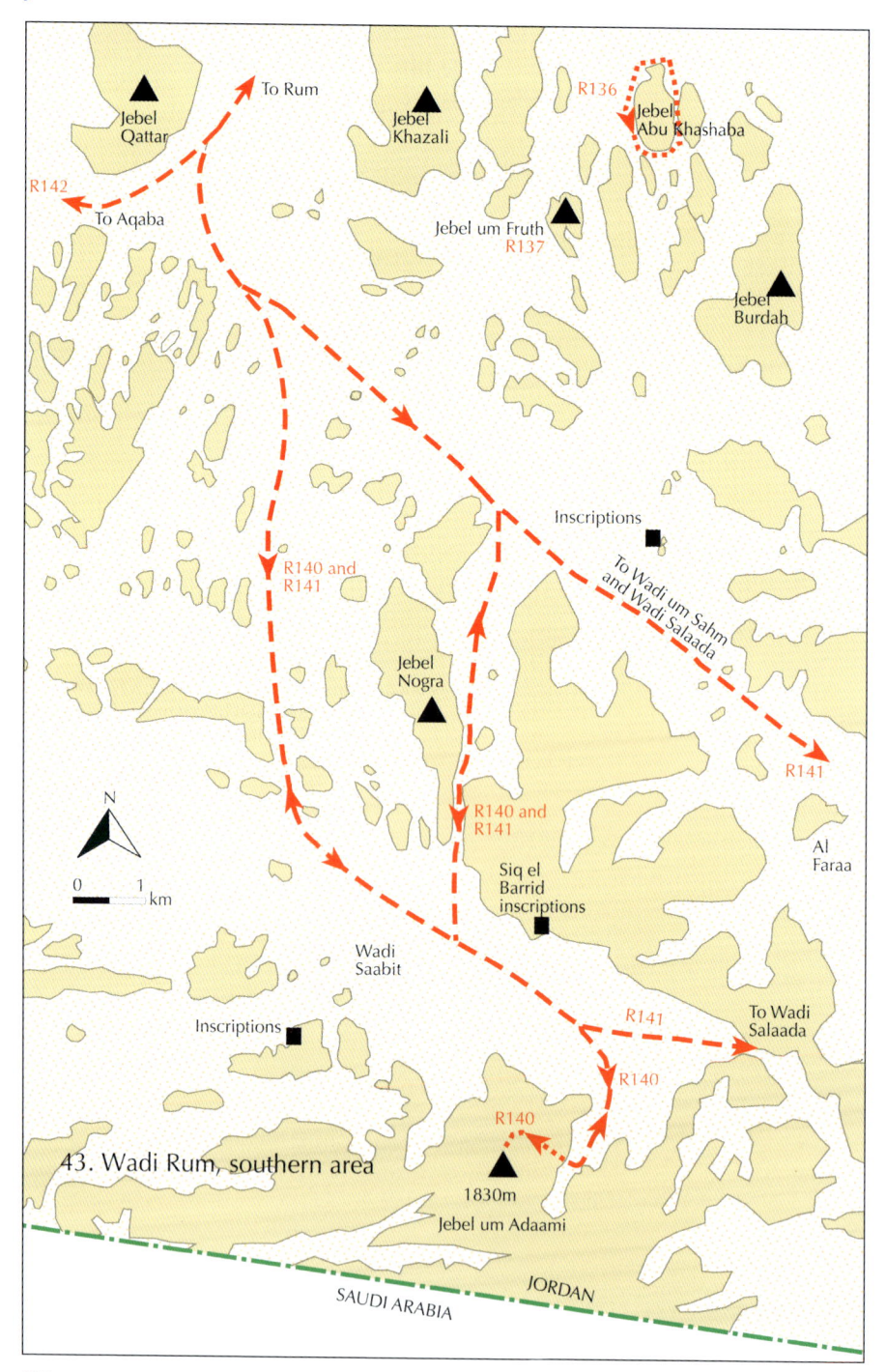

Jordan

43. Wadi Rum, southern area

Route 141
The Sand Canyons of Wadi Salaada

These remote desert valleys can be reached and travelled through by a wonderful desert drive of 100km or more, eventually winding through a tortuous 'sand canyon' – lots of fun! There are some excellent fossils of worm tubes and other shallow prehistoric marine life in this area. Do not remove these – leave them for others to photograph and enjoy. This is also a good area for horse and camel safaris and desert treks, and the following route makes a great day out. This area is part of the traditional grazing lands of the Zalabia tribe of Rum, known to all the Rum desert guides (see Appendix 1). See map 43.

Guide/driver Required.

The route
Follow the above route for 40km to Wadi Saabit, then go E up the rocky pass of Shraif Saabit to M'saiq al Khail and on down the superb 30km sand canyon of Wadi Salaada. The trick is knowing when to leave it to go back W to the low mountains of Jebel um Sahm and so to Burdah. If you miss the way or you really want a long desert journey and continue SE you will arrive after about another 50km of remote desert driving at the border post and old Turkish fort of Mudawarah. Alternatively, 20km to the NNE you will finally emerge on the Mudawarah–Diseh track in the area of Abu Suwaneh.

The other classic 4WD trip in the S of Rum was once assumed by some to be the way Lawrence and the Arab forces took en route to their capture of Aqaba, but the quotation below makes it clear that he did not follow this route until later. (His original route was down from the Ma'an plateau via Abu el Lissan and Naqb es Shar to the Quweirah plain, thence down Wadi Itm.)

Route 142
Lawrence's Way to Aqaba

In the beginning it was clean sandstone country, of pleasant rock shapes: but as we went spines of granite, the material of the shore, rose up in front of us, and after thirty miles of good trotting gradient we passed, by the southern Itm, into the main valley, just above the well of the surrender of Aqaba. The journey took us only six hours.

Seven Pillars of Wisdom T. E. Lawrence (1926)

This is a fun way to get from Rum to Aqaba with 4WD, involving about 50–70km of desert travel, dependent on route. It may also be done with camels or horses or on foot, the time taken ranging from 2–5 days. Start of route on maps 29 and 30.

Guide/driver Required; take a local guide or arrange a trip with an adventure travel company (see Appendix 1).

281

The route
The desert track to Aqaba. The start of the route is obvious, out of Rum village, heading S down the valley, past the springs of Abu Aina, then on to the SSW with the steep W face of Khazali 2km to the E, and directly below the SE face of Jebel Qattar with its beautiful 'dripping spring' in a cave once used by Nabataeans. The route continues W and finally NW through Wadi Umran to reach the main highway in Wadi Itm about 15km NE of Aqaba, after about 50km. Alternatively the highway can be avoided by branching SW and then W to reach the Red Sea in the South Beach area. This adds about 20km.

NORTH OF RUM

There are some areas to the north that are of interest and passed by Route 118.

The rock arch of Jebel Kharaz
This is 15km directly E of Quweirah and a 27km drive N of Rum village, in a remote and beautiful setting with vast desert panoramas. A visit from Rum to this huge natural rock arch, combined with a small detour to the petroglyphs at Abu el Hawil, makes a wonderful journey through a variety of desert scenery. The high desert N of Diseh is also a good place to view the sunset. There is also a climb here (see the chapter Climbing in Jordan).

The petroglyph of Abu el Hawil
There are a number of petroglyphs on the walls of this mountain, part of the Jebel um Rathah Massif 7km N of the Diseh–Rum road junction near the Visitor Centre. They include some long-horned cattle but the most bizarre are two anthropomorphic figures, over a metre high and reputedly 5000 years old, which are well worth seeing.

From Wadi Rum leave the road 12km N of the village (1km past the Diseh Junction) at Shakriyeh. Go N and NW past Jebel abu Rashrasha for 10km to find the petroglyphs on the SW side of a small mountain, with recent excavations below. The return journey to the road is about 12km, first E, then S down mudflats to pass under a railway bridge onto the Rum–Diseh road.

'The world's first map'
The rock map of Jebel Amud is just E of Diseh village at the foot of the mountains. Hidden in a cave formed by fallen blocks is a huge table-top stone marked by indentations believed by resident archaeologist Professor Borzatti to be a map of the area dating from around 3000BC, making it the 'world's first map'. Using it he was able to locate several previously unknown archaeological sites.

The whole of this quiet northern area can be visited by 4WD, on foot, on horse or camel. There are some nicely situated camping areas for a two-day journey. Also, a one-week safari by camel or horse from Wadi Rum through this area and all the way to Petra (Route 118) can be done by prior arrangement. Contact any of the Rum guides or Jordanian adventure travel companies (Appendix 1).

Our journey continues S down the Desert Highway to the Aqaba Mountains.

THE AQABA MOUNTAINS

Approaching Aqaba down the Desert Highway through the confines of Wadi Itm you feel dwarfed by the harsh-looking granite and basalt mountains that dominate the skyline north and east of Aqaba. Travelling south, the first route out of Wadi Itm is west of the road, up Jebel el Yitm. This was probably recorded by the late Dr Charles Tilstone Beke as Jebel Naur, also referred to by him as 'Mount Barghir' east of Araba and west of 'Wadi Ithm', 'overhanging the latter'. He rated it as 5000ft high and wrote of visiting it with Sheikh Muhammad bin Ijad of the Alauwin Bedouins. Another identification was a link with a notable Muslim saint Sidi Ali bin Alim from Jaffa. Beke's companion and Sheikh Muhammad found sheep skulls and bones on the summit, said to be from sacrifices, after which the sheep were eaten.

Route 143
Jebel el Yitm, 1593m

We all remarked its towering stature and trifid head-piece... the Bedawin visit it, to make sacrifice, according to universal custom, at the tomb of a certain Shayk Bakir.

The Land of Midian Richard F. Burton (1879)

Grade	Moderate scramble
Details	2km from the head of Wadi Mizfir to the summit

The peak, also known as Jebel Ahmad el Bakir, the highest of the S Shara Mountains, crowns the jagged granite skyline NE of Aqaba and no doubt has excellent views of the surrounding region. (Not checked by the authors but should be worth a visit.)

Approach 12km up the road from Aqaba in Wadi Itm, a valley ascends 4km N to a col on the W side of the peak. This col can also be reached from 25km up the road, where the wide stony valley of Wadi Mizfir goes 5km W, after which a branch goes 2km S to the same col.

The route
No details available concerning the route, grade or rock quality.
Route 144 is on the E side of Wadi Itm and is perhaps a foretaste of things to come.

JEBEL MAHAT AL HATHRA, 660m

This summit is on the left side of the road, going S to Aqaba. The name of the mountain was supplied by Defallah Atieq, a guide in Wadi Rum (see Appendix 1). Brian Hodgkinson climbed to the summit alone in November 2006 and provided the following information (not checked by authors).

Route 144
Hodge's Black Snake Route

Grade	Moderate scramble with some grade 3, or possibly 4 or 5 (though that can be avoided)
Details	About 320m of ascent and descent
Time	3hrs from the road to the summit, 2hrs down

The route provides a surprisingly enjoyable scramble in impressive surroundings. There are great summit views out E to Wadi Rum and W to Aqaba. Some of the higher pitches of the 'black snake' could be grade 5 or more if taken direct. The totally different nature of the two types of rock is amazing: the black basalt of 'the snake' generally has flat ledges often inclined downwards, whereas the surrounding pink and grey mottled granite tends to have sharp incut holds.

Special requirements The ability and confidence to climb at least grade 3 without ropes makes for a fast ascent, but climbing gear could be useful especially if trying the harder possibilities, plus abseil gear; 50m of rope should suffice for any descent abseil(s).

Approach Coming from Aqaba follow the main road towards Wadi Rum for approximately 8km. Just before a sweeping right-hand bend in the gorge of Wadi Itm a three-arched bridge can be seen, supporting the railway across the valley. A convenient gap in the crash barrier used to give car access down into the usually dry riverbed, providing a convenient parking spot (GPS alt. 340m N29° 33.669' E35° 06.287'). Unfortunately there are currently excavators in the vicinity, so it may be necessary to drive further out of Aqaba towards the Wadi Itm interchange, park on one of the other tracks which can be seen on the right of the road, then walk back down the riverbed or the railway line. Alternatively get a lift to the original starting point and scramble over the workings.

Coming S from the Wadi Rum junction, drive to the gorge of Wadi Itm and down it to opposite the three-arched railway bridge and a view of the route with its basalt dykes (30km) then another 4km to the U-turn enabling you to drive back up the other side of the road towards Rum, then follow the above directions. You could also take a taxi from Aqaba.

On the opposite side of the riverbed a track leads up to and through a distinctive railway bridge with three small arches, probably a culvert for occasional floodwater coming down the gully beyond. Follow the boulder-strewn gully, passing a few stunted trees and a particularly large smooth-sided rock, to reach the foot of the prominent black lines snaking their way up to the summit. Allow 30mins from the riverbed to the start of climbing.

The route
At the foot of the 'black snake' there is a little branch gully on the left, which gave better climbing up the granite, as the black basalt was a bit loose at its foot. Above, bear right to re-join the black snake, crossing a couple of gullies on the way, and then generally just follow the black lines to the top, the rock getting steeper and quite exposed towards the summit. Although the climbing is generally grade 3-4 some of the more tricky parts can be bypassed by climbing out on to the adjacent granite walls. The black lines eventually lead to a subsidiary peak with the main summit a further 100m to the W.

Bedouin hospitality, Wadi Rum

Descent Follow the main ridgeline W for about 1hr until a steep gully is seen on the right leading back towards the gully at the foot of the climb. On the descent two quite large drops were encountered which meant first traversing out to the left and then back to the right. Assuming a decent belay point can be found near the edge, a 50m rope should allow two abseils down these two steep pitches thereby saving a lot of time. Once down the car can be reached within ½hr.

Return to Aqaba Drive up the wadi towards Wadi Rum for about 4km until a U-turn is possible near the intersection of the Aqaba city road and Aqaba port road; the whole trip including the climb is around 6hrs.

Having arrived in Aqaba there are opportunities to enjoy some superb snorkelling and diving in the Red Sea: for hire of gear contact any local diving company or hotel such as The Alcazar, whose reef-side Club Murjan is free to guests, or try the Royal Jordanian Diving Centre (see Appendix 1). If you need more mountain adventures see the following chapters on caving and climbing.

Inside Zubia Cave (Route 145)

CAVING IN JORDAN

Caving in Jordan is in its infancy. A few caves have been found and there are rumours of more, but no major discoveries to date; sadly the best cave so far discovered – Zubia Cave – has been partially destroyed since the publication of the first edition of this book (in which it was Route 13!). It seems that well-meaning locals decided to make things easier for people visiting the cave. In doing so they removed the fun of the entrance descent and subsequent squeeze into the main chamber, enabling people to enter who have no understanding of caves, and as a consequence some of the best features have been damaged. However it's still worth a visit, and with perseverance more passages may be discovered.

Guides
There are no specialist caving guides in Jordan, but those listed in Appendix 1 may be able to help groups looking for subterranean adventures.

Route 145
Zubia Cave

Grade	Easy cave
Details	500m round trip
Time	Allow 2hrs or more if you want to explore all the 'squeezes'

The cave is in a beautiful location in karst limestone and Mediterranean-type hill country, dominated by open woodlands of oak and pistachio at an altitude of 800m. The cave has taken hundreds of thousands of years to form and was once well decorated. It is also a refuge for bats and, at times, people: we found some ancient pottery inside.

Rumour has it the cave goes 3km to water; there is also supposed to be another cave nearby where 'a shepherd lost all his goats'. These stories may well be true, but we never found more than 200m or so of passages in the Zubia Cave, nor another cave in the area, though we were told recently that 'there is a cave nearby with nice features, but very small'. Anything's possible in the caving world!

A very long time ago there was substantial roof-fall in the cave (indicated by stalagmites forming on the collapsed roof), perhaps during the earthquakes that shook the Jordan Valley 1500 to 2500 years ago. Some of the original stalagmites (which are more than 2m thick) are actually cracked through. The roof-fall, tumbled blocks and numerous columns make for sometimes difficult going and quite complex terrain – make sure you can find your way out again.

Please respect the cave environment and the bats and other creatures which live in Zubia Cave, and do not damage the formations or add to the painted arrows. If you discover any new passages please take care – and let us know. See maps 6 and 7 and cave topo 44.

Special requirements Good torches are essential; headtorches are best. Carry spare batteries and make sure you have power for at least 3hrs; otherwise old clothes and trainers are all you need. If you suffer from claustrophobia or don't like bats flapping past Zubia Cave is not the place for you!

JORDAN

Guide Recommended for non-cavers.

Approach The cave is approx 43km by road from Jerash and 2km W of Zubia village on the opposite bank of Wadi Wara. From Jerash take the road NW to Suf, 9km, then Ibbri, another 7km. About 2km after Ibbri go for 7km (passing Khirbet Afara) to a signed turn to Zubia on the left. After 3km the Zubia road goes straight on. Take the left fork here and after about 1km another small road goes right to Zubia. Pass this and go another 3km to where a small road forks right along a wooded hillside above a wadi. Follow this, ignoring another small road that goes right, for about another 3km until opposite a house set back on the left of the road (GPS alt. 830m N32° 26.171' E35° 44.506'; just beyond, the road starts to descend on the left side of the hill). You are now a couple of hundred metres from the cave, which is across walled fields to the NE and down the slope to the foot of a 3m cliff, where recently scarred rocks can be seen that have been forcibly removed to open up the entrance (GPS alt. 800m N32° 26.209' E35° 44.634').

The route

It was originally necessary to enter down a 3m drop, then a 1m drop, but these have been removed and entry is now down an easy slope. The Entry Passage has also been drastically changed; it originally

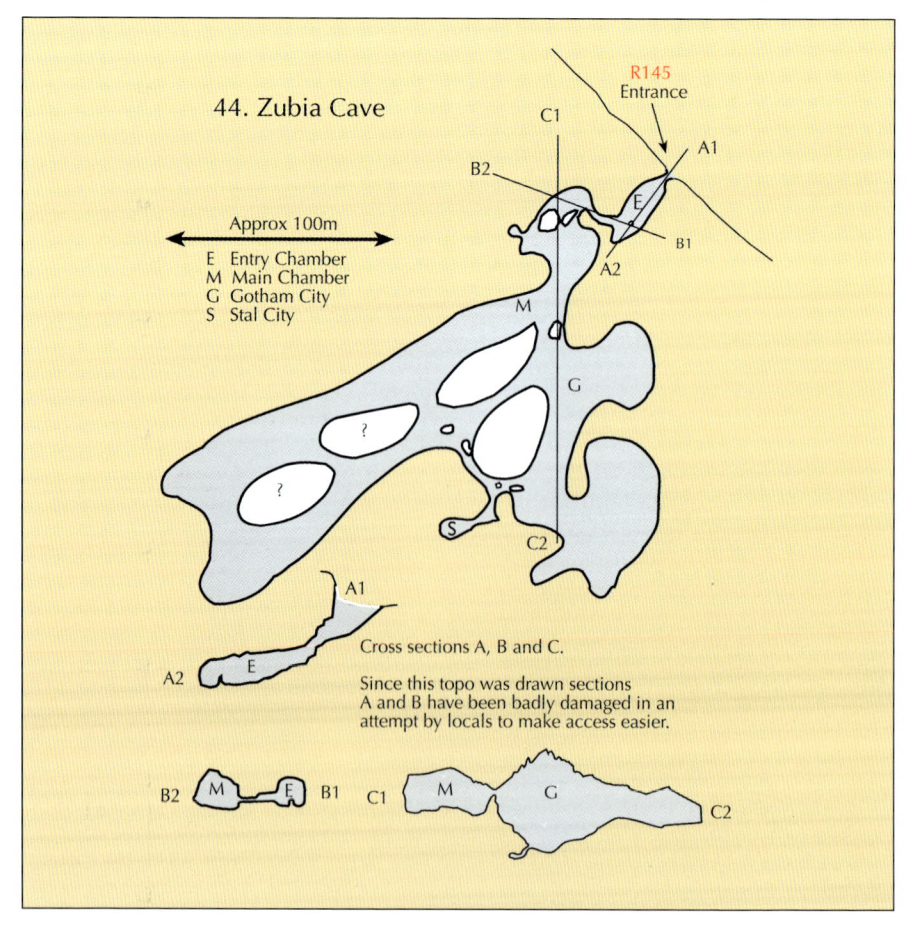

44. Zubia Cave

Approx 100m

E Entry Chamber
M Main Chamber
G Gotham City
S Stal City

R145 Entrance

Cross sections A, B and C.

Since this topo was drawn sections A and B have been badly damaged in an attempt by locals to make access easier.

Inside Zubia Cave

finished with a squeeze through to the right for 5m to enter the Main Chamber, but now you simply walk in. Once there life gets more confusing; topo 44 (done before the cave entrance was 'remodelled') is what cavers call a 'Grade 1 Survey' – a rough layout of the cave, not an accurate map.

The Main Chamber opens out almost immediately. Much of the floor is covered with ancient fallen blocks, whilst the roof rises to about 10m with bats roosting in the highest chamber, Gotham City. This is reached by going 50m or so diagonally left past stalagmites of various sizes (some 3m or so high).

Beyond Gotham City there are a number of passages, some with quite large formations. A narrow passage split by stalagmites along its centre goes back right to the Main Chamber. A tight squeeze goes left from this passage and down a tube for 5m before opening out briefly into the prettily decorated Stal City. There are also some squeezes under some of the blocks forming the cave floor, but they all seem to close after a few metres. Further into the Main Chamber there are more large stalagmites and arches dividing the chamber into different passages, but we found no way on. Surely there must have been an on-going system at one time?

There are a couple of reports of caves N of Zubia.

Wadi Yabis
Apart from the 'Roman caves' (see Route 5, map 7) Roberto Massis, a Jordanian guide (see Appendix 1), reports other caves in Yabis (no details).

Wadi Shellaleh
Wadi Shellaleh (Route 13, map 8) descends to the Yarmuk Gorge and there are said to be caves here; check locally. The nearby Caves of Al Habis Jaldak (Route 11, map 8) are hand-hewn from Crusader times.

Moving back S the Ajloun area has some caves that have been at least partially explored, the first not far from Ajloun Castle, which is 2km NE at almost 1000m. The olive groves and orchards of Wadi Kufrinja are less than 0.5km below to the S, at 550m. (Point of interest for cavers: the Jordan Valley is 14km W, at 300m below sea level – a drop of 1000m – and Zubia Cave – Route 145 – is 14km N at 800m.) The

JORDAN

huge cave entrance of Iraq al Wahaj is at the left end of Cave Cliff (see Climbing in Jordan), sometimes with a shepherd's camp at its mouth.

Route 146
The Cave of Iraq al Wahaj

Grade	Moderate cave
Details	200m round trip
Time	Allow 1hr or more if you want to explore all the squeezes thoroughly

The cave is in karst limestone and at first sight looks very promising – even the name implies it is deep. On closer inspection, however, it proved disappointing, and our only 'reward' was to be infested with thousands of fleas from a herd of goats that were being kept in the cave entrance at night. Being choked by dust and bat droppings lower down the cave didn't help much either! Whether or not perseverance through the bottom boulder chokes would bring dividends in the way of an undiscovered cave system remains to be seen. See cave topo 45 and map 46.

Special requirements Headtorches, old clothes and trainers, abseil equipment and the knowledge to use it (45m is more than enough rope to reach the lower chamber). Route finding is very straightforward. See topo 45 for cave layout – this is a Grade 1 Survey (a first impression of the cave, not an accurate map).
Approach As for Cave Cliff to GPS alt. 740m N32° 18.701' E35° 42.775'.

The route
Just inside the cave entrance we found a nicely made clay oven for baking bread, used by the shepherds who were camped outside. The initial chamber, otherwise known as the Flea Pit, is about 10m wide and maybe 5m high, the floor descending for 50m at about 30° to big boulders of old roof-fall debris. Beyond is a hole of about 3m in diameter and 10m deep. There is an expanse of flowstone down the left wall and numerous bats were flying in and out of the shaft.

A 10m abseil leads to more large boulders in the bottom of the shaft where the chamber opens out again, to about 10m high and wide and maybe 15m long – the Bat Hole. There is a dead tree at the foot of the shaft (probably thrown down by shepherds trying to rescue goats, or simply being curious about what is down there). The voracious fleas were the main problem here, a situation exacerbated in the lower chamber as the air was also full of dust and bat droppings.

We found no promising continuation passages – a search around and various struggles down between boulders for a further 5m or so always led to tighter squeezes. Nevertheless the usual cave stories exist: 'It's supposed to go all the way to the castle', or 'A long time ago some people went down with torches but after a long way, the air was bad.' (There were some initials on the rock at the start of one of the squeezes.) The cave is also reputed to have four lower chambers, one with some old carvings.

NEARBY CAVE POTENTIAL

There are said to be other, smaller cave entrances in the area as well as a 'window' through the cliff into the big cave. This seems impossible as the cave descends steeply from the entrance, rapidly

45. Iraq Al Wahaj

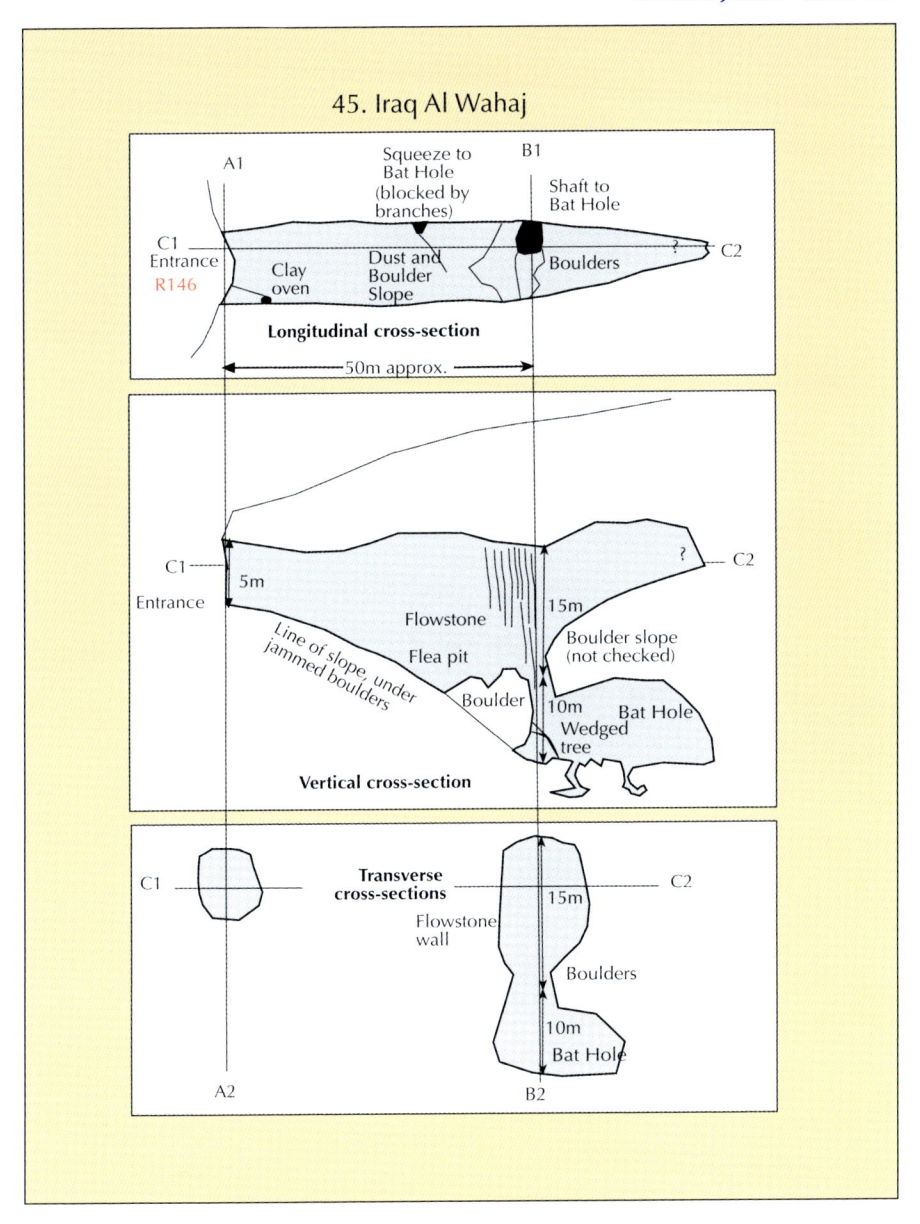

Longitudinal cross-section — 50m approx.

- A1: Squeeze to Bat Hole (blocked by branches)
- B1: Shaft to Bat Hole
- C1: Entrance R146
- Clay oven
- Dust and Boulder Slope
- Boulders
- C2

Vertical cross-section

- C1 Entrance
- 5m
- Line of slope, jammed boulders under
- Flowstone
- Flea pit
- Boulder
- 15m
- Boulder slope (not checked)
- 10m Bat Hole
- Wedged tree
- C2

Transverse cross-sections

- C1
- A2
- Flowstone wall
- 15m
- Boulders
- 10m Bat Hole
- B2
- C2

dropping below ground level, but curiously, at the far E end of the cliff, there is a 3m deep man-made hole (or tomb?) carved into the cliff about 10m up, with overhanging rock above and below (see Cave Cliff, below) but no ongoing passages.

Route 147 is found over on the S side of Wadi Kufrinja and high on a headland towards its W end.

JORDAN

Route 147
The Cave of Ras Ed Duweira

This big NW-facing crag (see Climbing in Jordan) has a cave entrance 15m up in the cliff face. The cave mouth is about 3m in diameter. Unfortunately we had no climbing gear so made no attempt to access it up the steep, loose rock. A long diagonal abseil could probably be rigged from trees in a gully just below the top. See map 46, GPS alt. 550m. N32° 16.445' E35° 40.770'.

Approach As for the cliff of Ras Ed Duweira. The way to the crag passes Ain el Birka, a fast-flowing spring appearing between rocks. Don't bother to crawl in up the stream – it sumps after 3m.

The next cave is on the plateau high above and accessible from Kufrinja or Wadi Rajib (see chapter on Climbing in Jordan).

Route 148
Kufrinja Pot

Grade   Easy cave

This is nothing more than a big hole in the ground apparently caused by the collapse of a cave roof. If so there should be ongoing passages. See map 46.

Approach From the Mahmud Cliff (see Climbing in Jordan) go 2km further down the road and turn right, signed Anjara, then follow signs to the village of Ballas, at the entrance to which a lane is taken steeply down right into a wadi and up the other side. About 2km after Ballas a large tree-filled hole will be seen on the left, just below the road (GPS alt. 840m N32° 16.743' E35° 42.809'). From here the road then passes over Ras Munif and continues to reach Kufrinja, about 3km N of the cave.

The route
The opening is approx 8m by 6m with a depth of approx 7m to the top of the boulders that form the floor (the remains of a collapsed roof?). Any ongoing passages are choked by the boulders, though a small hole on the north side may hint at one. Trees growing in the hole may indicate a stream in a cave passage below (or may thrive simply because the sheep and goats can't get at them). The hole is close to the top of wadis that descend W into Wadi Kufrinja, so any water could emerge in Wadi Haramiya or at the spring of Ain el Birka below Ras ed Duweira, which is about 500m below and 3km away.

    Climb down one of the many fig trees that have taken root in the hole, a couple of which can just be reached from the rim. Remember that you will have to climb out again!

Next, far away in the black basalt Eastern Desert near Azraq Oasis is a geological idiosyncrasy formed during a period of lava flow.

Route 149
The Lava Tube

Grade	Easy cave
Details	We only had time to look at about 70m of passageway; it may continue after the roof lowers to within 0.5m of the floor
Time	Allow 1hr max to get in and out (unless you find ongoing passages)

Geologists believe that this was created around five million years ago when a channel or river of molten lava flowed out of a volcano or fissure, cooling around the outer rim and forming a lithified crust whilst the molten lava in the middle continued to flow. When the flow shut off, the lava poured out of the end and the tube was left empty.

Not worth a special journey until the nearby rough track is surfaced (said to be happening soon – 2006), it is nevertheless an interesting curiosity not yet fully explored.

Special requirements Information on the tube varies: it was said to be either '200m long' or '2km long with a resident hyena'. Neither informant said it had to be entered through a hole about 10m wide, 6m deep, and overhanging on all sides, making a rope necessary; we had no climbing gear handy, so entered it by sliding down a vehicle towrope and were hauled out manually afterwards. (Happily, there was no hyena!) Having the right equipment would be better; headtorches essential.

The Lava Tube near Azraq oasis

JORDAN

Guide A local guide would be useful. Hussain el Hamood and Sami Tarabeek (RSCN Azraq Wetland Reserve tourism office) helped us find the lava tube at GPS alt. 770m N32° 07.957' E36° 49.414'.

Approach Follow a rough pipeline track N for 35km from Azraq, starting not far W of the traffic lights. Once the track is surfaced the tube should be accessible from Azraq in ½hr, otherwise it's a very bumpy 1hr drive. It could be a curiosity of interest en route between the antiquity sites of Um el Jimal, the castle of Qasr Huwaynit near Bishriyyeh and Azraq oasis, making possible a circuit linked to the desert castles SE of Azraq.

The route

A vehicle makes a useful belay for a rope enabling access to and egress from the entrance hole. The tube, the ceiling of which is initially 3m or more high, seems blocked to the E after 50m (possible pool after rain); the other way the roof drops close to the floor after 20m (heads of basalt columns on the desert floor above). The passage seemed to be continuing, but we had no time available. It might repay further exploration.

We also checked out a rumoured cave above the Upper Hidan Gorge, adjacent to the RSCN Mujib Reserve.

Route 150
The Cave of Maghrar el Wadid

Grade	Easy cave, moderate scramble
Time	Allow 1hr from and back to the vehicle

More of a hole than a cave. See map 14.

Approach As for Route 39 to Wadi Hidan. A dirt track comes close to the cave, just to its NE; less than 2km to the cave and back from the Hidan track.

The route

A short walk leads to the foot of the cave. Scramble up from its left side across the cliff (grade 2) into the cave. Despite its huge gaping mouth – about 10m high and wide – it is little more than 10m deep, so hardly worth the effort (though plenty of pigeons and falcons can be seen).

There are similar caves in the same escarpment just to the W sometimes occupied by Bedouin. Whether or not they go further underground is anybody's guess, but it's unlikely.

Other than that there are rumours of a cave in the Dibeen Reserve (the Rangers should know about it if there is), and we spotted a possible cave near Tel Hisban (see Route 5) and an old copper mine entrance in Wadi Jamal (Route 62). There's plenty of limestone in Jordan and at least one big cave across the Jordan River in the West Bank (see *Walks in Palestine*, Appendix 2) as well as massive Show Caves in Lebanon, so with any luck more will be discovered in the future.

Mike Searle attacked by fleas above the abseil in the cave of Iraq al Wahaj, with Sami Sabat below (Route 146)

Musa's Slab, Wadi Rum; young Bedouin mountain guide, Mohammad Hammad enjoys the warm granite

CLIMBING IN JORDAN

Jordan will be a climbing paradise, with all sorts of climbs – sport climbs, mainly short, on perfect limestone, and sandstone for the adventure climbs, also granite, conglomerate, and basalt... vive la calcaire!

Wilfried Colonna (April 2007)

This chapter provides information on some of the climbing areas outside Wadi Rum that are currently being explored. Anyone making any first ascents or having comments on existing climbs should e-mail Wilf Colonna at desert.guides@wanadoo.fr and tony@nomadstravel.co.uk

History
Other than a couple of early ascents of Jebel Rum by British missions (see the Wadi Rum chapter), climbing in Jordan started as a sport when we arrived to explore the mountains of Wadi Rum together with Al Baker and Mick Shaw in 1984, and soon became friends with local Bedouin hunter-climbers. Amongst them was Hammad Hamdan, son of Sheikh Hamdan, who took the Longstaff ladies up Jebel Rum in 1952. His son, Mohammad Hammad (see photo page 240), is following in his ancestor's footsteps and is currently the youngest of a new generation of Bedouin mountain guides, joining the ranks of Atieq Auda, Sabbah Eid, Talal Awad, Sabbah Atieq and his son M'salim Sabbah and others (see Appendix 1). All are held in high regard by visiting climbers and demonstrate a perfect example of a community benefiting from tourism by developing its traditional skills.

As we got to know the Bedouin in 1984 it was exciting to discover that not only had they reached almost all the summits whilst hunting the elusive and much-prized ibex, but also that they were climbing unroped and usually in bare feet on routes with moves up to French grade 5 (and occasionally even higher). Even today, with modern equipment, some climbers find these routes daunting.

A similar situation exists in the Petra area where Bedouin who once lived in the Nabataean tombs have become tour operators and guides with a unique knowledge of the mountains in which they and their ancestors have lived, shepherded and hunted.

Elsewhere in Jordan there was no climbing until we started looking around the limestone cliffs of Ajloun in the 1990s with Sami Sabat from Amman (who discovered the superb cliff originally named after him but now known by its correct name, Thôr Motlagh). Other cliffs were soon found in the same area and climbers came to enjoy them, raising the debate on how best to protect the routes which we had been top-roping since there were few cracks for the placement of safety gear (nuts, cams and so on). French guides Wilf Colonna and Bernard Domenech have been developing and carefully equipping these cliffs since 2000, accompanied by Ingrid Colonna and Mohammad Hammad from Wadi Rum. Exploration by this dedicated team continues.

Ethics and safety

If we allow the sport-climbing approach free rein in the mountains, we may wake up some day to realise that we've sold out our unique sport for... a synthetic substitute, offering virtual adventure where once we had the real thing.

Pat Littlejohn OBE, Director, International School of Mountaineering, Leysin

Following hard in our footsteps a few ex-pats from Amman started placing bolts, essential for leading on the blank walls, to create sports climbs. Unfortunately (in our opinion) they also bolted some of the natural lines that we had climbed, using nuts for protection. If Jordanians want to learn how to climb before experiencing the more serious adventure routes in Wadi Rum they need to learn how to place 'traditional' protection, and what better spot than the cliffs near Amman? This is therefore a plea to climbers to respect the rock, place fixed gear where it is needed (as it often is on limestone), but

Saqeb Cliff: Tony Howard climbing his 'Shivering Crack'

do it professionally; where a route can be climbed traditionally let it remain 'clean' for the benefit of others.

Conversely, we would like to thank Wilfried Colonna, a French guide we first met by chance in the Taghia Canyons of Morocco in 1979 and who came to Wadi Rum with us on our second visit in 1985. Wilf has spent much of each year in Jordan since then, working as a guide (see Appendix 1). In recent years, together with friends from France and Wadi Rum, he has not only climbed on many of the cliffs around Ajloun but also discovered others elsewhere in Jordan of granite, basalt, sandstone and conglomerate, some with multi-pitch routes. Supported by Petzl equipment they have started to professionally equip these cliffs, for which future climbers should be indebted. (Other climbers from elsewhere in the Middle East have placed fixed gear in Rum and on other Jordanian cliffs with no regard for local ethics and with insufficient experience to place it well – please leave it to the professionals.)

Although we have never met with any problems regarding access, all the cliffs are on state-owned or private land, so please act accordingly. Equally important, please park any vehicle with consideration for the local people and do not block access to fields or orchards. As Wilf says, 'Always ask permission if local people are present and in all cases be discreet, but friendly. The locals are very nice people. Do not hesitate to have a chat, or a tea together.' Finally, before getting into the route descriptions, it is important to say that we have been unable to discover the local names for most of these cliffs so, where necessary, have named them ourselves.

The cliffs and climbs

The climbs in Wadi Rum are documented in *Treks and Climbs in Wadi Rum* (see Appendix 2). French climbing grades were used and the same system has been kept in this guidebook (see Introduction). One, two or three stars are used to denote the quality of the better routes. Outside Rum the most popular and best-developed area to date is around Saqeb and Ajloun, just over 1hr drive N of Amman. See map 46.

The canyon of Wadi Weida'a, which cuts through Wadi Weida'a slabs, a recently discovered climbing area

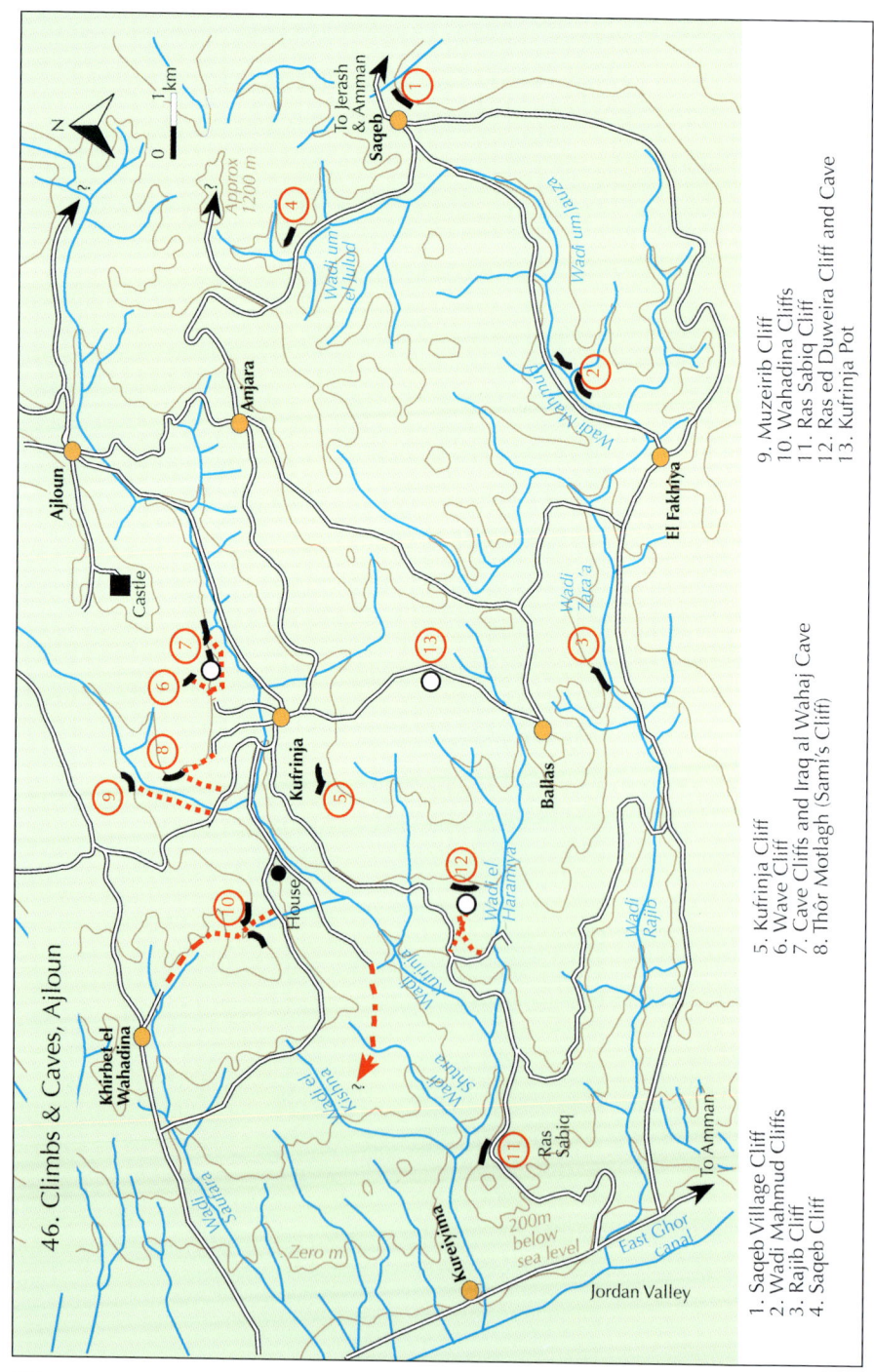

JORDAN

46. Climbs & Caves, Ajloun

1. Saqeb Village Cliff
2. Wadi Mahmud Cliffs
3. Rajib Cliff
4. Saqeb Cliff
5. Kufrinja Cliff
6. Wave Cliff
7. Cave Cliffs and Iraq al Wahaj Cave
8. Thôr Motlagh (Sami's Cliff)
9. Muzeirib Cliff
10. Wahadina Cliffs
11. Ras Sabiq Cliff
12. Ras ed Duweira Cliff and Cave
13. Kufrinja Pot

THE SAQEB AREA

The first cliff seen when heading towards Ajloun from Jerash is just below the hilltop village of Saqeb.

SAQEB VILLAGE CLIFF

This SE-facing cliff is just below the houses on the left of the road near the top of Saqeb, 9km beyond Jerash on the Ajloun road. It is first seen over to the left as you enter Saqeb coming from Jerash (GPS alt. 860m N32° 17.090' E35° 48.967'). The various buttresses look about 10–15m high and there are rumours of bolted routes here put up by ex-pats based in Amman. (Not visited by the authors.)

Approach Park on the road at the upper end of Saqeb, just after the final bend, where the footbridge over the road comes into view. From there, walk back down below the bend and descend a loose dirt slope to reach a path that goes to the foot of the cliff.

The next cliffs are down a pretty side valley SW of Saqeb.

WADI MAHMUD CLIFFS

One of Sami Sabat's discoveries, partially concealed in trees in a beautiful location; a small wadi divides the W-facing North Cliff from the N-facing Main Cliff. The cliffs receive plenty of welcome shade and are around 10m high (rather higher on the Main Cliff) and generally of good limestone with many potential lines, a few protectable by wires. There are tree belays above, but try to use rock belays to avoid damaging the trees.

The cliffs – and a smaller one on the opposite side of the road, in a little side valley – contain some small but neatly carved caves 1–2m deep. Local legend says (inevitably) they are of Roman origin; the Council of British Research in the Levant, which is involved in research on chalcolithic burial sites, confirms this opinion. There are also iron-smelting remains nearby.

Wildlife The area is full of flowers in spring, in particular cyclamen and anemones; we also saw hawks, jays, a large brown owl and squirrels (which horde acorns and nuts in the numerous 'caves').

Approach From the S Jerash roundabout turn left onto the Ajloun road. Saqeb is reached after 9km; at 10km, just over the pass at the top of the village, turn left (signed Kushayba; GPS alt. 990m N32° 16.725' E35° 48.300'). Drive down the pretty, forested valley, past orchards and olive groves and past a very small crag on the right with bouldering potential (2km from the junction), after which there is a small village. The cliff will be soon be seen on the left, 5km from the turn-off, just 50m across a field and on the other side of Wadi Mahmud (usually, though not always, dry). Park here (approx 1hr from Amman; GPS alt.770m N32° 15.394' E35° 45.646').

Mahmud Cliff: Di Taylor has high hopes on 'Pipe Dreams'

MAIN CLIFF

To date (November 2007) four routes have been done (T. Howard, D. Taylor and M. Khano). The climbs are described from right to left. Natural protection is possible on the two easiest climbs. A top rope is necessary on the two other routes as there is no protection; the grades need confirmation. Descents are at either end of the crag (try to avoid entering the olive grove behind the left end of the cliff).

To reach the first climb walk left along the foot of the crag to a large rockfall with a yellow wall above. On its left is a superb grey wall, with a vertical wall on its left undercut by a large roof. Two cracks form a V on the left edge of the grey wall, beneath which two trees grow from the crag. A route has been explored on top rope up this wall starting from a small boulder beneath the lower tree.

Rhapsody in Grey*** 18m, 6b

A delectable and varied climb on excellent rock. Climb the gently overhanging wall to the left side of the lower tree (4m, 5+). From above the tree traverse right for 4m on pockets to a footledge. Above is a vague groove; follow it slightly left up the centre of the wall on diminishing pockets until they disappear and a sequence of precarious moves leads to better holds and the top of the right-hand V crack to finish.

Descent Walk off to the right end of the crag and scramble down.

Left of this there is a 50m-long roof at head level, with another good grey wall above. Left again is a tree-choked gully and immediately left of that an arête, yellow at the bottom where it overhangs and where the next route starts.

Pipe Dreams 12m, 6b

Ascend the yellow edge on large but doubtful holds, moving left immediately onto better grey rock with good holds. Ascend diagonally left to a fluted groove (optional step left to rest on a tree) and climb the 'pipe' directly – a long reach required (or try small holds on its right).

Descent Walk to either end (or possibly scramble down the tree-filled gully?) or by abseil.

Mahmud Cliff: 'Pipe Dreams' climbs the wall on the left, and 'Rhapsody in Grey' ascends the big grey wall on the right

The extreme left of the Main Wall turns left into a secluded side valley, and presents a pleasant square buttress with a cave and two tombs.

Tomb Raider* 10m, 3+

Pleasant and unusual with traditional protection. Traverse left below the cave and tombs before moving up to the mouth of the left tomb. Stride out left to ascend the mossy slab on good holds.

Descent Easily down the right side of the buttress past another tomb near the top of the crag (to the left looking down).

Raid Direct 8m, 5

From the foot of the wall 1m left of the left tomb ascend steeply on small holds to join the mossy slab of the previous route.

The next cliff is further down the valley.

RAJIB CLIFF

Wadi Rajib is the lower continuation of Wadi Mahmud as it descends to the Jordan Valley. About 6km down the road beyond the cliffs of Mahmud is an army checkpoint. Opposite, across the deep valley of Rajib, are some steep 20m S-facing cliffs with overhangs that are said to be used by the army for climbing and therefore likely to be out of bounds. Viewpoint from just before the checkpoint (GPS alt.580m N32° 14.859′ E35° 42.953′).

Continuing W the road descends towards the Jordan Valley then crosses the wadi and curves N to meet the road from Ajloun at the lower end of Wadi Kufrinja. Or, returning E from the checkpoint, another small road soon forks down left to cross the wadi and wind over the hills past the village of

JORDAN

Ballas to the town of Kufrinja, just S of Ajloun. Kufrinja Pot is by the roadside about halfway along (see Caving in Jordan).

Moving on again from Saqeb the next cliff along the Ajloun road is Saqeb Cliff.

SAQEB CLIFF (UM EL JULUD)

A small but easily accessible and good-quality SW-facing limestone cliff reached in less than 1hr from Amman. Only a few climbs have been recorded, but there is room for more at all standards. It would be a nice place to learn the rudiments of climbing, abseiling and so on. We first visited here with Hannah Jahshan at the end of March 1999 when an icy wind was blowing – hence Shivering Crack – and again with Mark Khano and Brian Hodgkinson in April 2007. Others had visited in the interim, leaving their mark on the rock.

Approach Take the Ajloun road from the roundabout on the S side of Jerash, passing through Saqeb at 9km. After a total of 13km from Jerash a lay-by is reached on the right and the crag will be seen quite close, above orchards and below the pine-covered hillside (GPS alt. 1030m N 32° 17.842' E 035° 47.203').

From the lay-by take the track which goes back right for a short distance, then turns sharply left. About 100m further on is another small lay-by. Park here, or on the lay-by at the junction with the main road. (The little valley hidden from view a short way further up the track is sometimes used by the army and

Saqeb Cliff: 'Shivering Crack' climbs the central crack

may be closed to access.) Walk up the wooded hillside, keeping left of an orchard before contouring right above it to reach the cliff in around 5mins.

THE CLIFF

Though not high (7–10m) it is steep with good rock and in a picturesque setting with some large entertaining boulders below. The most obvious feature is a huge overhang towards the right side.

Bolted Crack 9m, 6a

Right of the huge roof, a big boulder leans against the crag. Go through the passage beneath it and scramble up the boulder to below the crack in the steep wall above the roof. Climb this past a bolt (superfluous as wire placements are possible) to the top. First ascent unknown.

Moving back left there is a corner rising from a tree left of the big overhang. Just left of this a tempting finger-crack goes all the way to the top.

Shivering Crack* 9m,

A steep fingery start leads to nice well-protected climbing up the crack above. Tree belay. Someone has placed unnecessary bolts alongside the crack.

About 40m to the left of here, just past a corner left of a long yellow overhang, is an easier angled buttress above a semi-detached block.

Beginner's Buttress 7m, 4-

Up the block from its right side and up the blunt nose of the buttress (small wires for protection).
Immediately left is another boulder with a crevasse behind.

Fleeting Visit 8m, 4

Climb the boulder and step across into a corner. Go up a short way before making a rising diagonal traverse to the arête on surprising incuts (wires for protection).

Descent 10m left of here (to the right looking down).

Heading towards Ajloun again, the next town is Anjara, then (not much further on) Kufrinja is reached with its deep valley immediately below to the N and Ajloun Castle crowning the hillside beyond.

305

THE AJLOUN AREA

Numerous cliffs have been discovered in and above the 20km-long dramatic Kufrinja Valley, which descends SW from the castle to the Jordan Valley. We discovered some when trekking, have seen others in the distance or have visited some briefly to have a closer look. They are generally 10–30m high, vertical to overhanging; some have excellent pocketed limestone but few cracks, others are more featured. They all have climbing potential, but most routes will need fixed gear if they are to become popular. Thôr Motlagh (Sami's Cliff) – the first to be discovered – is being professionally equipped by Wilf Colonna and friends.

Approach Coming from Amman drive N to Jerash, taking the Ajloun road at the roundabout on the S side of town. About 20km further on, past Saqeb, the road reaches Anjara where the Ajloun road forks right. For the cliffs of the Kufrinja Valley go straight on for about 6km to the small town of Kufrinja, which has a strange little four-columned monument capped by a miniature castle in the town centre. The first cliff is almost directly above Kufrinja.

KUFRINJA CLIFF

This N-facing 20m-high cliff rims the hilltop above Kufrinja at 750m. There are great views into the valley, across to Ajloun, down to the Jordan Valley and over to the West Bank. Though much of the rock seems poor quality, some traditional nut-protected lines look possible near the right edge (GPS 750m N32° 17.421' E35° 41.346').

Approach Follow narrow roads that wind very steeply up through the town and park at the top, W of a new mosque, taking care not to block the narrow road. The main clifftop is just a short walk to the W along the top of the escarpment. An easy descent down the W side leads to the base of the cliff.

Facing Kufrinja on the opposite hillside are a number of S- and SW-facing cliffs, all in beautiful scenery and culminating in Thôr Motlagh, concealed in a side valley WSW of the castle.

WAVE CLIFF AND CAVE CLIFFS

Worth a visit although no climbing has been done yet; any routes would be medium to high standard. The Cave of Iraq al Wahaj is here (see the section on Caving in Jordan).

Approach As you descend either of the roads from Anjara or Ajloun to Kufrinja, the cliffs are visible on the hillside to the N at around 700m. Most obvious is the S-facing Cave Cliff, high on the valley side, whilst above it is the smaller Wave Cliff, facing W; right of Cave Cliff there are two small S-facing cliffs, one above the other in a little valley with orchards below.

From the roundabout with the ornamental castle in the centre of Kufrinja go down the hill to the bend at the lower end of town (less than 200m). Turn right here down a narrow lane, then left after 100m and steeply down through ancient olive groves to cross the stream of Wadi Kufrinja. The road then ascends steeply to stop near a white house (1.5km from the roundabout).

Both cliffs are visible to the NE: Wave Cliff (approx 0.75km away) and Cave Cliff (less than 0.5km). The former will be seen as the white crest of a wave curling over the oak forests on top of the hill. The latter is just visible in profile below and to the right, facing S over Wadi Kufrinja.

WAVE CLIFF

Though well over 100m long, the cliff is small in height (5–9m) but overhangs cornice-like in a graceful curve for most of its length. The rock quality is excellent, but very compact with very few lines though there could be some extremely difficult problems. The situation is idyllic and the views marvellous.

Approach Walk along the left (N) side of the white house and its fields on a wide track which ends at an olive grove. Scramble up the hillside above, between two small valleys, to reach the crag on the crest of the hill in a beautiful location facing W towards the Jordan Valley (GPS alt. 780m N32° 18.838′ E35° 42.719′).

CAVE CLIFF

Hidden in the forest down to the E of Wave Cliff, this fairly extensive cliff varies from 6–15m in height and is steep but of variable quality. Despite scattered vegetation there are some obvious lines on both cracks and walls, none of which we had time to attempt as the cave proved (regrettably) irresistible (see the chapter on Caving in Jordan).

Cave Cliff, near Ajloun Castle

Approach There are two options.

Option 1 From the R end of Wave Cliff scramble down approx E through the trees to a shallow valley. Cross this in the same general direction, with some unusual glimpses of the castle of Ajloun about 2km away up the hill to the NE. After about 5mins emerge from the woods onto a flat grassy area just right of the tree-covered top of Cave Cliff and close to its left (W) end where the descent is.

Option 2 From the car park by the white house walk along the left (N) side of the house and its fields to the end of the wall, then follow vague paths up and slightly right through the oak woods to reach the open flat area, the left side of which is above the W end of the cliff (GPS alt. 740m N32° 18.693' E35° 42.819').

In spring 1999 a shepherd was camped there with his family, their goats penned in the massive cave at the left end of the cliff of Iraq al Wahaj. If the family is still there barking dogs will greet you, but you will be made welcome, and will probably be offered the inevitable cup of tea.

Towards the right end of the crag, high in a gently overhanging wall, there is what appears to be another cave mouth. Below is a row of holes cut in the rock face (once used to support roof beams?). Abseiling down the hanging wall to the 'cave' reveals it to be hand-hewn, about 3m wide and deep, and 1.5m high. Interestingly it's full of rubbish – one wonders how it got there! To its left is a nice-looking wall and an impressive corner crack. There are also other features of interest.

There are two more small crags about 0.5km to the E, S facing and about 20m high. A track traverses the hillside between them and probably descends SW from near Ajloun to meet the approach road to Cave Cliff near Wadi Kufrinja. No routes to date, but one or two possibilities (GPS alt. 730m N32° 18.620' E35° 41.827').

About 1.5km W of Cave Cliff there are two more S-facing cliffs on the same hillside, both visible from Kufrinja. They are passed en route to the best cliff in this area – Thôr Motlagh – which is hidden 1km further on in the side valley.

THÔR MOTLAGH (previously known as Sami's Cliff)

The SW-facing 10–30m high cliff is on the end of the ridge 4km WSW of the castle of Ajloun in beautiful wooded country. It was found by Sami Sabat and offers excellent sport on superb Mediterranean-style limestone: solid rock, sharp holds, steep or overhanging, technical, fingery climbing on 'new' rock, which can be quite harsh on the fingers. There are also some easier cracked buttresses. Belays on top can be excellent, otherwise there are some fixed double-ring belays/lower-offs just below the top (max pitch length 25m), but it is necessary to be belayed to reach them from above (this not only keeps the top 'clean' but prevents misuse by local children and non-climbers). The central area is in shade until midday. A good place to learn abseiling and climbing on easy routes, or to hone and test your skills on the hard ones (GPS alt. 670m N32° 19.092' E35° 41.488').

The cliff is being equipped by Wilf Colonna, who says 'Everything will be glued – no bolts, no slings, no pegs. The starts of the routes are often difficult so it needs perfect protection to avoid a ground fall. This has to be calculated and tried – not estimated. Ajloun should be a perfect example for Jordanian and other Middle East climbers.'

Wildlife We have twice seen eagles above this valley as well as numerous other birds, tortoises and a viper sneaking into a hole at the bottom of the cliff.

Approach There are two possible approaches, the best being Option 1.

Thôr Motlagh (previously Sami's Cliff) near Ajloun Castle

Option 1 From the roundabout with the ornamental castle in Kufrinja go past the turning for Cave Cliff (see above) and go steeply down the next little lane on the right to cross over the stream and rise up to the prominent green-domed mosque. Just beyond the road bends up left. (**Musheriefa Cliff** is concealed below and left of this hill, just above an olive grove. It has a little climbing potential though trees are encroaching; limited parking above at GPS alt. 580m N32° 18.620' E35° 41.827'. The W continuation of this cliff reappears after 200m or so, but is even smaller.)
From above Musheriefa Cliff continue up, keeping left at a road junction before going downhill. Ignore the next left turn and keep on alongside a fenced field. At the end go right on an extremely steep uphill section between stone walls until the asphalt ends on the last level track. Park just before two water cisterns (GPS alt. 630m N32° 18.926' E35° 41.579').
The cliff is out of sight, but walk up the track for about 150–200m, passing two turns, to where the first stone wall on the left, covered by branches, indicates the start of a small path. This eventually descends to the karst plateau at the top of the crag (a few cairns), 10–15mins. Descend left to reach the bottom of the cliff.

Option 2 About 1km from the ornamental castle in Kufrinja take the third turn down right (N) towards a narrow wadi and old olive groves. Just over 1km along this lane, cross a bridge (GPS alt. 420m N32° 18.287' E35° 41.190') and take the right fork. About 0.7km further on the small road passes the spring of Ain ez Zughdiya emerging from rocks on the right. This is fed along a channel, across the road and over a small wadi via an aqueduct. Just beyond Wadi Muzeirib (usually dry) is reached on the right (N) in a wooded valley (GPS alt. 480m N32° 18.648' E35° 41.271'). Limited parking. The S end of the cliff is just visible on the skyline to the right and a white house can be seen halfway up the hillside. Walk up left of the house, and left of a field on small paths until level with the cliff, then contour left to reach the bottom (about ½hr from the road).

Special requirements 10 quickdraws max for the equipped routes; 60m rope necessary for the routes on the left-hand side. If equipping new routes use glue-in rings only.

The routes
As at April 2007 there are seven equipped routes and one top-roped route. After two easy scrambles, grades from right to left are 4a and 5b (10m top rope), 6a, 6b, 4b, 6a/6a+, 6b, 6b+/6c, 6a. A total of 20 routes are planned for the end of 2007, max grade 7b/c.

How the above routes correlate with the original routes described below and first climbed by us with Mick Shaw in spring and autumn 1998 is uncertain. The hardest routes were top-roped as there was little or no protection. The first two easy routes are at the right end of the crag and have big sharp holds, perfect for beginners.

Route 1 10m, 2

Start behind and left of a tree and climb the left edge of the buttress.
Route 2 is just 3m to its left.

Route 2 10m, 2

Climb the tower, starting at cracked blocks.
About 3m left again is a corner with a steep left wall and an undercut prow.

The Infidel* 10m, 5b

Climb diagonally left from the corner onto the nose, move left and up the steep cracked wall above.
About 7m further left past a steep wall, with a very tempting crack line in its centre, is a superb arête up the left edge of the wall.

Saladin's Nose*** 15m, 6a

Start behind a tree, left of the nose, and move diagonally across the wall to gain the impending arête above the undercut lower wall. Follow it steeply on small, sharp holds. Superb.
Above the starting point of the previous route is a narrow buttress with deep cracks on either side, which should offer a pleasant climb up its centre. The next route starts at the foot of the left crack.

Baldric 15m, 5

Move up a broken crack and then left below an overhang to reach the next clean crack. Ascend this steeply to a ledge then the corner above to the top (or from the ledge pull out left onto the exposed upper wall to finish).
Left of here the crag eventually becomes blood red, offering two steep provocative crack lines. The right-hand one starts high up the crag. The left one finishes in a hole just under the top and provides the next route.

Tony Howard vanquishing 'The Red Lion', Thôr Motlagh

The Red Lion* 20m, 6b

Ascend the lower crack, then move delicately and steeply right to reach its continuation. Up this on good holds to the cave, which is left with difficulty up the overhanging groove.

Immediately left again is an impeccable grey wall undercut by a huge overhanging prow, after which the crag continues for about 30m with a selection of steep grey walls, cracks and corners: plenty to go at!

We also visited a neighbouring cliff, which is visible across the valley and about 1km to the NW, in 1998.

MUZEIRIB CLIFF

Although quite extensive there is not much quality rock. The cliff faces SE; its right side is quite high but broken and yellow, and contains some caves where we found some old pottery. A small cliff of good steep grey rock extends to the left and gives numerous short climbing problems, enjoyed but not recorded.

Approach Park discreetly as for Sami's Cliff in Wadi Muzeirib, but instead of going up the steep forested hillside follow the path up alongside the wadi for 15mins or so until the crag is visible above to the left.

Continuing SW down Wadi Kufrinja, the next cliff, high on the N side, is Wahadina.

WAHADINA CLIFF

The SE-facing cliff is quite extensive, with a ravine splitting it towards its left and clearly visible from 2km down the road from Kufrinja. Route 1 from Ajloun to Kureiyima passes up this ravine before reaching the 740m summit high above the left end of the crag. The E cliff is around 20–30m high and more than 100m long with some possibilities for climbing on a grey wall. The W cliff is smaller but sometimes overhanging, and with a few crack lines. As far as we know no one has climbed here yet (GPS alt. 630m N32° 18.229' E35° 40.065').

Approach Via the Kureiyima trek (Route 1) from the house just up the road from the point where Wadi Muzeirib meets it (GPS alt. 480m N32° 18.648' E35° 41.271'), or via the alternative start to Route 1 from Khirbet el Wahadina (easiest if you have a car). From the end of the drivable track (GPS alt. 710m N32° 18.634' E35° 40.246') go over the shoulder and descend the increasingly wooded hillside rightwards (S) into a little valley. This closes down into the rocky ravine that emerges between the cliffs.

Alternatively approach the cliffs directly up the hillside from the little road that passes less than 0.5km below the cliffs halfway up the N flank of Wadi Kufrinja. This road leaves Kufrinja as for Sami's Cliff as far as the bridge over the wadi (GPS alt. 420m N32° 18.287' E35° 41.190'). Turn left there and follow the track SW alongside the wadi for about 2km to a right fork. Park about 0.5km up here. (Not checked by the authors but seen from Route 1 and whilst visiting other cliffs along the ridge to the SW, some of which have been climbed on.)

The cliffs on the S side of Wadi Kufrinja are fewer and more scattered than those on the N rim. Kufrinja Cliff, on the highest point of the skyline and quite prominent when seen from the road just W of Kufrinja, has already been mentioned. Next, still high up, but much further W, is a big yellow cliff with a cave in its centre.

RAS ED DUWEIRA

This impressive W-facing crag, which is about 60m high at an altitude of 550m, is 200m above the road and high above the lower end of Wadi Kufrinja, on its S side. Unfortunately its yellow limestone is mostly loose so climbing opportunities are few and no routes have been done to date. The intriguing thing is the big cave mouth about 3m in diameter, 15m up the cliff, which has not yet been entered (see the section on Caving in Jordan).

Approach From approx 6km down the road from Kufrinja (GPS alt. 350m. N32° 16.558' E35° 40.404') a huge crag will be seen high above, with a gaping cave mouth low down in the centre. If coming up from the Jordan Valley this point is 5km up the road from the Ras Sabiq Cliffs (see below). Depending on transport availability there are now two options: if you have a 4WD take the left turn just a short way down the road and drive up it for about 1km until the point where a hairpin bend comes into view. Turn steeply up left and follow a worsening track for 1km to the gushing spring of Ain el Birka. Alternatively, from the viewpoint on the road, walk up a steep rough track past a house and old olive groves to reach the spring in about 0.5km. From the spring, a path rises up diagonally towards the left side of the cliff then zigzags back just below it, to reach the bottom (GPS alt. 550m. N32° 16.445' E35° 40.770').

This path and another lower one appear to continue up towards the hilltop and may continue to the top of Kufrinja village. If so, starting from Kufrinja should provide a fine walk with great views, which could probably be continued down to Kureiyima.

About 5km further down the road are some cliffs hidden directly below.

RAS SABIQ

A couple of pleasantly shaded N-facing cliffs 2km SSE of Kureiyima, which we first saw from the Kureiyima trek (Route 1). They are next to and directly below the road and the best two cliffs are at the right end looking down, one above the other, each about 20m high; no routes done yet other than a pleasant grade 3 solo scramble on excellent quality rock at the right end. Worth checking out, with very easy access.

Approach Either drive about 11km down from Kufrinja or follow the winding road up from the Jordan Valley for about 4km onto the hill of Ras Sabiq with its view N down Wadi Haramiya into Wadi Kufrinja. The clifftops are exactly on the side of the road (GPS alt. 90m – 300m above Jordan Valley – N32° 15.939' E35° 37.862').

Further N only one other potential climbing area has been reported.

YABIS UPPER CLIFFS

Visible to the N across the valley from the road between Ishtafeina and Kur Abil (viewpoint GPS alt. 490m N32° 23.365' E35° 42.431'). There is also a NW-facing cliff directly opposite, visible from lower down the road. Neither has been visited by climbers.

YABIS LOWER CLIFFS

John and Petra Smith visited the 'cliffs with Roman caves' (see Route 5) but reported no real climbing potential. However, there are other cliffs on both sides of the valley further down Wadi Yabis, which may provide some entertainment.

THE KARAK AND SHAUBAK AREAS

The following information on south Jordan was largely supplied by Wilfried Colonna from *Climbing and Mountaineering in Jordan* (see Appendix 2).

WADI WEIDA'A SLABS

The extensive cliffs face NW, with morning shade, its brown slabs of tilted strata rising 50–150m just above and E of the road from Ghor Mazra'a to Karak (map 16). The excellent compact limestone is similar to that of Todra in Morocco. Its sculptured slabs have huge erosion holes, cracks, small overhangs and unsurpassable friction: very featured, very solid and very abrasive! Two routes have been climbed to date (August 2007), one of seven pitches (200m) starting right of the canyon mouth and trending right, below the skyline, the other up the centre of the highest slabs left of the canyon. There is natural but sometimes spaced protection in cracks and solution pockets though it's sometimes possible to place pegs. Double ropes recommended.

Approach As for Route 56 to GPS alt. minus 20m N31° 14.560' E35° 34.602' (remember your passport for the checkpoint) or, from the Dead Sea, about 6km up from the Ghor Mazra'a junction.

Descent Walk off, steep and a bit loose. It's possible to abseil down certain routes such as 'Les Pirates'.

Sectors
Left of Wadi Weida'a Three big slabs above the road. The steeper slab on the right has a crack route up the centre 'Les Pirates'.
Right of Wadi Weida'a, the S pinnacle 'Dieu Ludik' starts from the bed of the wadi. **Below the S pinnacle** A jumble of blocks, slabs and arêtes, one-pitch routes, not equipped.

The routes
The first is on the left sector, 10mins above the road:

Les Pirates** 100m, 2½ big pitches, 4b/c max

Follow the obvious central crack, moving right or left as necessary to avoid the difficulties or to find protection.

Special requirements Quickdraws, slings and tape/cord for threads, 4 or 5 medium nuts, 4 or 5 assorted cams, 2 x 50m ropes.

Descent Abseil from threads and a spike.

Next is the S pinnacle sector, approached by a 5min walk following the water pipeline to the foot of the pillar/arête forming the left (N) edge of the face.

Dieu Ludik*** 150m high, but at least 200m of climbing, 4c max

Pitch 1 (25m) is the steepest and 4c, the next, is similar. The route then ascends rightwards with some belays on the arête. Six pitches of 40–45m, then 150m of scrambling with some steps of easy climbing to reach ruins on the summit.

Special requirements 15 quickdraws, slings and tape/cord for threads, 4 or 5 medium nuts, 4 or 5 assorted cams, 2 x 50m ropes; 1 peg in place at the first belay, and some threads.

Descent From the summit go down the back (E side) to a broad saddle. Follow traces of an ancient track to the SE, then a track S back to the foot of the face.

Other cliffs are being developed in the Karak area but, moving south, the next information available is for Wadi Hasa.

WADI HASA

Wilf Colonna has added some new climbs 45mins walk up the wadi from Safi, through water all the way. He writes 'Just marvellous, not high – 30 to 60m max, but just like an Eldorado canyon, full of obvious beautiful sandstone lines. We climbed two so far, Pirhanas (6b/c) and Eux Claires (?). Mostly clean climbing with some glued rings (they have to be discreet... the rock is so red!). No bolts with metal hangers, please. Swimming is always possible, as well as shade... it's a pure winter spot, altitude minus 225m!'

S again, the next cliff is between Dana and Shaubak.

BAD'DA

This extensive cliff is a conglomerate of limestone with pebbles, 15–50m high, almost 1km long and fairly solid after cleaning. The less steep parts tend to be less solid. The climbing is delicate and technical on steep walls, ribs and arêtes, and the routes to date were equipped in 2006 with 10mm expansion bolts by Wilfried Colonna, Bernard Domenech and Mohammed Hammad. Single 80m rope, or double 45m recommended, together with 15 quickdraws. There is plenty of room at the base of the crag. Access from above not recommended. The cliff faces W, with morning shade.

Approach See map 21. From the bus shelter in the upper part of Qadissiya, at the fork in the road leading down to Dana village, go down S through the village towards Shaubak, reaching a military camp on the right after 8.3km. Just before, up against the fence of the camp, take a dirt track towards the edge of the plateau, and go round the camp (do not park near the military camp). After 0.8km go down a steep track on the right and park 300m beyond. It is possible to continue down right in a 4WD for 200m on a stony track to a level wooded area. The crag is visible to the N. Traces of paths lead down and across, 20mins to the crag, 30mins to return.

The routes
In April 2007 three bolted routes were ready:
• 'Put your money on me', 6b+, 6a (2 pitches)
• 'Spicy', 6c+ (1 pitch)
• 'Women in Black', 6a+ (2 pitches)
Ten routes planned for the end of 2007.

THE PETRA AREA

In December 2007 we received details of three new climbs in the north Petra area, namely at Sh'karet M'Said, Baaga Siq and on the cliffs south of Wadi Ghurab, all of which are inside the boundaries of the Petra Archaeological Park. We were also coincidentally contacted by the PNT (Petra National Trust) to collaborate on their 'Trails' project, following on from which the subject of climbing was discussed.

The PNT is a Jordanian NGO dedicated to the preservation and protection of the archaeological, cultural and natural heritage of Petra and its region. They seek a balance between the requirements of tourism and the conservation of Petra, and are working closely with the Petra Archaeological Park authorities to improve the management of this fragile site. For more information about their work and the threats facing Petra see website: www.petranationaltrust.org or e-mail pnt@petranationaltrust.org

The PNT does not set policy on what is and isn't allowed on the site, but works very closely with director of the park Suleiman Farajat. He has confirmed that climbing is not permitted inside the boundaries of the Petra Archaeological Park. Whilst both organisations recognise the environmental and cultural awareness of climbers and the additional income that they bring to Jordan, there still remain issues of safety and management that need to be addressed before climbing can be allowed or encouraged.

PNT is developing a zoning management plan for the park, which will address these crucial issues. Discussions are ongoing and any developments will be found, together with route information, on www.nomadstravel.co.uk/Jordan.update.html

THE WADI RUM AREA

The Bedouin and Jordanians we encountered were the most gracious and generous hosts imaginable. 'Welcome to Jordan' is how all visitors seem to be greeted. Americans, still fearful of travelling to a Muslim country, are missing out. A gentle, friendly, and safe land, with unforgettable climbs, where Moses once walked, awaits.

James Garrett, Utah, USA

James Garrett also noted that 'Just 10km from Rum village it is still similar to the unclimbed American South West that greeted such activists as Harvey T. Carter and George Hurley in the 1960s.'

JEBEL KHARAZ

In November 2006 James Garrett from the USA and Res von Känel from Switzerland climbed a route on Jebel Kharaz to the left of, and minutes from, the Kharaz Rock Bridge (see Route 118 and the section North of Rum). Generous and friendly Bedouin waited at the base, offering tea!

Amidst Difficulty lies Opportunity*** 6a

This 4-pitch sandstone route climbs the obvious corner on off-widths reducing to hands then fingers followed by some face-climbing pitches; well protected with bolts at the very beginning protecting the off-width, up to a pleasant right-facing corner 5a, and the slab at the top.

Descent Abseil points equipped.

In Rum itself there are some 15–25m granite cliffs sandwiched between the big sandstone cliffs and the desert floor. We found Musa's Slab (see *Treks and Climbs in Wadi Rum*, Appendix 2). Other more recent discoveries have been made. (Sport climbers please note: please do not place fixed gear in the traditionally 'clean' sandstone climbs in Rum.)

THE AQABA MOUNTAINS

The only routes known to us are described in the chapter on Wadi Rum and the Aqaba Mountains, though to an optimistic eye there are some intriguing features. Please contact us if you find anything.

There is lots waiting to be discovered all over Jordan – have fun, and send us any new routes. Information will be added to the website at www.nomadstravel.co.uk/Jordan.update.html

And that's it. We hope you have learnt as much, and have had as much pleasure as we have, whilst wandering the hills and deserts and meeting the people of Jordan.

The late Sheikh Atieq who, together with his family, welcomed us to Wadi Rum in 1984

APPENDIX 1
Guides and Adventure Tourism Operators in Jordan

Not all Jordanian guides and trekking companies are aware of adventure routes throughout the country, or are competent to guide them. Some of those listed below specialise in their own area (Petra or Rum, for example), whilst some have a good knowledge of the whole country. There will, inevitably, be others, to whom the authors apologise for their lack of inclusion.

Adventure activities in RSCN Reserves
The RSCN provide or approve guides for routes in their Reserves. Contact:

The Royal Society for the Conservation of Nature
PO Box 1215
Jubeiha-Abu-Nusseir Circle
Amman 11941
Jordan
E-mail: rscn@rscn.org.jo, website: www.rscn.org.jo

RSCN guides can also be booked via their partner company:

Wild Jordan
Tel: 00 9626 4616483
Fax: 00 9626 4616523
E-mail: mervat.khawaja@rscn.org.jo or tourism@rscn.org.jo, website: www.rscn.org.jo/AdventuresVisit.asp

Caving guides
There are no specialist caving guides in Jordan, but Arabian Escape, Roberto Massis, Terhaal and Yamaan Safady (see below) may be able to help groups looking for subterranean adventures. All are based in or near Amman.

Climbing companies and guides
Not many Jordanian guides have the necessary skills and equipment to guide on rock climbs; even fewer know the location of the climbing areas, especially those outside Wadi Rum. All Jordanian climbing guides are currently based in Wadi Rum; only Mohammad Hammad has some knowledge of climbing in other areas. For contacts see guides marked with an asterisk in the Wadi Rum information below.

Wilfried Colonna of Desert Guides knows most about all aspects of climbing in Jordan, whist Mark Khano and David Gauchez of Arabian Escape know some route locations in Rum and elsewhere and have done some climbing. See contacts below.

Mountain biking companies
Nyazi Tours, La Bedouina and Petra Moon have worked with mountain biking groups, as have Bedouin Roads, Rum Guides and Desert Guides (the latter based in Aqaba at the Alcazar Hotel, and in France). There are also two companies in Amman and Madaba, Cycling Jordan (a branch of Arabian Escape) and Terhaal. See contacts below.

Trekking and canyoning guides and companies
Arabian Escape (Mark Khano and David Gauchez) website: www.arabianescape.com and www.cycling-jordan.com
Desert Guides (Wilfried Colonna) e-mail: desert.guides@wanadoo.fr, website: www.desertguides.com
Discovery tel: 00 9626 5697998, website: www.discovery1.com
Roberto Massis (guide) e-mail: salsa_roberto@yahoo.com
Terhaal e-mail: team@terhaal.com, website: www.terhaal.com
Yamaan Safady (guide) e-mail: yamaan@adventurejordan.com, website: www.adventurejordan.com
Pierre Voignier www.lizard-life.com with Saleem Ali e-mail: saleemali@jordantracks.co

Petra and Dana trekking and safari companies, guides and tourist camp operators
In addition to the RSCN (Wild Jordan) in Dana, the following guides and companies know these areas well.

APPENDIX 1 – GUIDES AND ADVENTURE TOURISM OPERATORS IN JORDAN

Many also organise safaris from Dana or Petra to Rum as well as operating elsewhere in Jordan. All except one are based in Wadi Musa:
Ammarin Bedouin Camp and Guides mob: 07 9566 7771, website: www.bedouincamp.net
Harun Daqlalah mob: 07 9559 8966, tel: 03 215 7491, e-mail: haron200@wanadoo.jo
Helali Bedouin Camp mob: 07 7790 3265, website: www.helalibedouincamp.com
Jordan Beauty Tours mob: 07 9558 1644, website: www.jordanbeauty.com
Jordan Inspiration Tours (Sami Hasanat) mob: 07 9555 4677, website: www.jitours.com
La Bedouina Tour tel: 03 2157 09, website: www.labedouinatours.com
Mahdi Hasanat tel: 03 2157 893, website: www.mahtours.tripod.com
Mohammed Hasanat tel/fax: 03 2156 567, e-mail: explorerone69@yahoo.com
Nawaf Awad al Fageir mob: 07 9553 7109, e-mail: nawafpetra@yahoo.com
Nyazi Tours, Aqaba tel: 03 2022 801, website: www.nyazi.com.jo/Default.htm
Petra Moon Tourism Services tel: 03 2156 665, website: www.petramoon.com
Petra Caravan Tours tel: 03 2156 925, e-mail petravan@go.com.jo
Via Jordan Tours tel: 03 2012 299, website: www.viajordan.com
Zaman Tours tel: 03 2157 723, website: www.zamantours.com

Wadi Rum trekking and safari companies, guides and tourist camp operators (* also climbing and mountain guides)
Ali Hamd mob: 07 7694 3692
Anne and Mattar Auda, Teva Services mob: 07 7204 215, e-mail: mauveanne@yahoo.fr
*Atieq Ali, Bedouin Roads mob: 07 9589 9723, website: www.bedouinroads.com
*Atieq Auda, Bedouin Guides mob: 07 9583 4736, website: www.rumguides.com
Auda Abdullah mob: 07 9561 7902, website: www.aodeh.de/index.htm
Bait Ali mob: 07 9554 8133, website: www.desertexplorers.net
Eid Atieq mob: 07 7730 9249
Eid Mohamed Swelhen mob: 07 9562 4671, website: www.bedouinlifestyle.com
Defallah Atieq and Mohammad Defallah mob: 07 7730 9239, website: www.thebedouinguide.com
Mazied Atieq mob: 07 7730 4501, website: www.mzied.com
*Mohammed Hammad mob: 07 7735 9856, website: www.bedouinguides.com
Mohammed Sabah mob: 07 9989 2446, website: www.mohammedwadirum.8m.com
*M'Salim Sabbah, *Sabbah Atieq and Suleiman Sabbah mob: 07 9566 0362, website:
    www.bedouinofwadirum.com
*Sabbah Eid mob: 07 7789 1243, e-mail: sabbah_alzlapeh@yahoo.com
Saleem Ali, Jordan Tracks mob: 07 9529 8046, website: www.jordantracks.com
Salem Eid mob: 07 7425 423
Saoud Auda mob: 07 7492 523
* Suliman and Salem Motlaq mob: 07 7742 4837, website: www.wadirum.org
*Talal Awad mob: 07 9578 9689
Wadi Rum Rest House tel: 03 2018 867, fax: 03 2014 240
Yasser Mohammed mob: 07 7766 7052
Zedan Zalabia mob: 07 9550 6417, website: drschef.de/zedane

Riding stables in Wadi Rum
In common with some of the above companies, Wilf Colonna of Desert Guides also organises treks and horse or camel safaris from Petra to Rum and vice versa as well as in Rum: Wadi Rum Horses & Camels (Wilfried Colonna and Atallah Sweilhin) fax/phone 03 2033 508, e-mail: rumhorses@yahoo.co.uk
Also check out the Alcazar Hotel, Aqaba tel: 03 2014 131, e-mail: alcsea@alcazar.com.jo or refer to website: www.desertguides.com. The stables are at Salhiyeh, which is signed on the approach from the Desert Highway about 10km before Rum village. Another company, Jordan Tracks, run by Saleem Ali in Rum village (see above), also has horses and can organise treks in the Rum area.

Other local guiding contacts
Pella
Abu Bassem, Rest House and Countryside Hotel, mob: 07 9574 145, e-mail: dheebjawahreh575@hotmail.com

JORDAN

Selah
Fahad Shabatat, Ministry of Tourism representative, Ain Al Beidah, tel: 03 3663 33
Shaubak
Abu Seif Camping mob: 07 7799 6834

Red Sea diving contacts
Alcazar Hotel website: www.aboveandbelow.biz and www.seastar-watersports.com
Aquatours website: www.aquatours.com/Jordan/index.htm
Dive Aqaba website: www.diveaqaba.com
Royal Diving Club and Coral Bay Hotel and Resort website: www.rdc.jo

For further information
Gilles Rappeneau's Rum website: http://wadiram.userhome.ch
Jordan Tourist Board website: www.visitjordan.com
Ruth's Jordan website: www.jordanjubilee.com
The authors' website: www.nomadstravel.co.uk
Walter Neser's Rum website: www.wadirum.net

APPENDIX 2
Relevant Reading

The following are listed by date of first publication. Note that some of the older books may be difficult to obtain unless they have been republished.

Background information
The Land and the Book W. M. Thompson (T. Nelson & Sons 1859)
With the Bedouins Gray Hill (T. Fisher Unwin 1890)
In the Steps of Moses the Conqueror Louis Golding (Rich & Cowan 1938)
The Land of Midian Richard F. Burton (Kegan Paul & Co 1879; Oleander Press 1984)
Archaeology of Jordan Dr Fawzi Zayadine (Department of Antiquities, Amman 1985)
Travels in Arabia Deserta Charles M. Doughty (1888; Dover Publications Inc 1979)
Palestine Past and Present L. Valentine (Frederick Warne & Co c1919)
Seven Pillars of Wisdom T. E. Lawrence (Jonathan Cape 1922, 1935; Penguin 1962; also Wordsworth Classics and Castlehill Press)
A Soldier with The Arabs Glubb Pasha (Hodder & Stoughton c1930)
In the Steps of The Master H. V. Morton (Rich & Cowan 1934)
In the Steps of Moses the Conqueror L. Golding (Rich & Cowan 1938)
Through Lands of the Bible H. V. Morton (Methuen & Co 1938)
A History of Jordan and its Tribes F. G. Peake (Coral Gables, University of Miami Press 1958)
Portrait of a Desert G. Mountfort (Harper Collins 1965)
In the Footsteps of Lawrence of Arabia Charles Blackmore (Harrap Ltd 1986)
Dancing at the Dead Sea Alanna Mitchell (University of Chicago Press 2005)

Guidebooks
Petra Ian Browning (Chatto & Windus Ltd 1982)
Petra – a guide to the capital of the Nabataeans Rami G. Khouri (Longman 1986)
The Antiquities of the Jordan Rift Valley Rami G. Khouri (Al Kutba 1988)
The Birds of the Hashemite Kingdom of Jordan Ian J. Andrews (I. J. Andrews 1995)
Jordan Revealed Anthony King (Boxer Publishers 1997)
Landscapes of The Holy Land Susan Arenz (Sunflower Books 1997)
Jordan, Syria and Lebanon Travel Atlas (Lonely Planet 1997)
Walks and Scrambles in Wadi Rum Di Taylor and Tony Howard (JDA, revised edition 1998)

APPENDIX 2 – RELEVANT READING

Wild Flowers of Jordan Dawud M.H. Al-Eisawi (National Library, Jordan 1998)
Petra Jane Taylor (Aurum Press, revised edition 1999)
Petra: Rose Red City Christian Auge and Jean-Marie Dentzer (New Horizons 2000)
Mammals of Jordan Zuhair S Amr (Zuhair S. Amr 2000)
Petra – A Traveller's Guide Rosalyn Maqsood (Garnet Publishing Ltd 1994, 3rd edition 2002)
Jordan, Syria and Lebanon Handbook Ivan Mannheim (Footprint 2000)
Jordan Blue Guide Rollin & Streetly (A. & C. Black 1996, revised edition 2001)
Petra and the Lost Kingdom of the Nabataeans Jane Taylor (I. B. Tauris, 2005)
Jordan Bradley Mayhew (Lonely Planet, revised edition 2006)
Jordan Mathew Teller (Rough Guide, revised edition 2006)
Insight Guide to Jordan (APA 1997, revised edition 2007)
A Field Guidebook to the Plants and Animals of Petra (Petra National Trust 2007)
Treks and Climbs in Wadi Rum Tony Howard (Cicerone 1987, 4th edition 2007)
Trekking and Canyoning in the Jordanian Dead Sea Rift Itai Haviv (Desert Breeze Press 2000, update due 2009)
Climbing and Mountaineering in Jordan Sabbah Atieq, Wilfried Colonna and Bernard Domenech (not yet published)

Trekking, climbing and caving guidebooks to other Middle East and North African countries
Rock Climbing in Oman Alec McDonald (Apex Publishing 1993)
The Ala Dag, Climbs & Treks in Turkey's Crimson Mountains O. B Tüzel (Cicerone 1993)
The Mountains of Turkey Karl Smith (Cicerone 1994)
An Introduction to the Caves of Oman Samir Hanna and Mohammed el-Balushi (Motivate Publishing 1996)
Adventure Trekking in Oman Jerry Hadwin and Anne Dale (Gerry Hadwin, UK Cordee 2001)
The Nativity Trail & Walks in Palestine Tony Howard and Di Taylor (Cicerone 2001)
Climbing in the Moroccan Anti-Atlas Claude Davies (Cicerone 2004)
St Paul's Trail, Turkey Kate Clow with Terry Richardson (Upcountry [Turkey] Ltd 2004)
The Lycian Way, Turkey Kate Clow with Terry Richardson (Upcountry [Turkey] Ltd 2005)
Trekking in the Atlas Mountains, Morocco Karl Smith (Cicerone 2005)
Greece and the Middle East Rock Climbing Atlas Wynand Groenwegen and Marloes van den Berg (Rocks Unlimited Publications 2006)
South Western Europe and Morocco Rock Climbing Atlas Wynand Groenwegen and Marloes van den Berg (Rocks Unlimited Publications 2007)

Advice on safety and technique
Complete Caving Manual A. Sparrow (Crowood Press 2001)
The Hillwalker's Guide to Mountaineering Terry Adby and Stuart Johnston (Cicerone 2003, 2007)
Rock Climbing Essential Skills and Techniques Libby Peter (Mountain Leader Training UK 2004)
Canyoning in Southern Europe J. Bull (Cicerone 2008)

The black iris, national flower of Jordan

APPENDIX 3
Some Useful Arabic/English Words

Topographical words

ain	spring (of water)	tilal	hills
araqib	ridges	wadi	seasonal river, desert valley
bilad	village, town		
bir	well (of water)	**A few other useful words**	
birkat	pool	water	maya (maa)
bustan	garden (usually of vegetables)	here	huna
dhahrat	flat-topped hill	there	hunak
ghor	low-lying desert	where?	wayn?
hammamat	hot spring	left	yssar
hudeib	hill	right	yemeen
jebel	mountain	straight on	dughri
khirbat	ruins	north	shamal
maghrar (magharah)	cave	south	jannub
masial	seasonal river	east	sharq
mazar	shrine	west	gharb
mazraa	fields (agricultural area)	road	tareeq
qaa	mudflat	path	tareeq turabi
qasr	castle	where is the	
qattar	dripping spring	path to...?	min wayn el tareeq ila...?
raqaba	ridge	thanks	shokran
rijm	cairn, tower	hello	marhaba
seil	wadi, stream	how are you?	kayf halak? (to a man) kayf halik? (to a woman)
siq	rock crevasse, narrow canyon		
tell	hill, mound (from antiquity)	very well thanks	quais el hamdulillah (m)
		very well thanks	quaisa el hamdulillah (f)

APPENDIX 4
Climber's Glossary

abseil	method of descending ropes
Bedouin steps	heaped stones or branches to ease ascent or descent
bivouac	sleep out without a tent
bolt	fixed protection on a cliff (expansion bolt; French *goujon*)
cairn	pile of stones to mark the way
cams	camming devices for climbing protection
chimney	vertical fissure in the rock wide enough to get body into
cirque	valley closed on three sides by mountains
col	low area of land between two hills
couloir	*see* gully
crack	vertical fissure in the rock narrower than body width
crag	cliff
defile	*see* siq
gully	narrow, possibly steep, ravine down a hillside

karst	limestone affected by water dissolution
nuts	metal wedges used for climbing protection
pass	see col
pegs/pitons	metal spikes hammered into cracks
pro	protection placed by climbers
prusik	method of ascending a rope
quickdraws	small tape loops
rappel	see abseil
ring	drilled and glued fixed protection on a cliff (eyebolt)
saddle	see col
scree	slope of loose stones
siq	narrow canyon or rock crevasse
slab	less-than-vertical rock
stals	stalactites
wadi	river (possibly seasonal) or desert valley
wires	nuts on wire, for climbing protection

APPENDIX 5
Index of Routes

The Jordan Valley Hills
Route 1 Ajloun Castle to Kureiyima in the
  Jordan Valley.............................. 50
Route 2 Ajloun Castle (Qal'at er Rabad)
  to Pella (Tabaqat Fahl).................... 55
Route 3 The Prophet's Trail, Ajloun Reserve..... 59
Route 4 The Orchards Trail, Ajloun Reserve..... 61
Route 5 Wadi Yabis........................... 62
Route 6 Lower Wadi Yabis from the
  Jordan Valley.............................. 66
Route 7 The Natural Bridge and Hot Springs
  of Pella................................... 67
Route 8 Jebel Sartaba from Pella............. 68
Route 9 Wadi Salih to Pella.................. 70
Route 10 Walks near Um Qais.................. 73
Route 11 The Crusader Caves of
  Al Habis Jaldak............................ 74
Route 12 Wadi Quweiliba, Abila and
  Wadi es Sijn............................... 76
Route 13 Wadi Shellaleh to the
  Yarmuk Gorge............................... 78

The North Eastern Desert
Route 14 Azraq Marsh Trail, Azraq Reserve..... 80
Route 15 Burqu Lakeside Walk,
  Burqu Reserve.............................. 81
Route 16 Thlaithukhwat....................... 82
Route 17 The Meteorite Crater................ 83

The Capital Area
Route 18 Dibeen Forest Walks,
  Dibeen Reserve............................. 85
Route 19 Rumeimin Waterfall.................. 87
Route 20 Walks in The Sumiya Hills........... 87
Route 21 The King Talal Dam
  Lakeside Walk.............................. 87
Route 22 Walks in Wadi es Sir................ 88
Route 23 Walks near Old Fuheis............... 89
Route 24 Walks in Wadi Shu'eib............... 89
Route 25 Walks near Tell Hisban.............. 90
Route 26 Wadi Mukheiris...................... 92
Route 27 Wadi Manshala....................... 92
Route 28 Wadi Himara......................... 93

The Madaba Area
Route 29 Walks near Mount Nebo............... 98
Route 30 Libb to Hammamat Zerqa Ma'in....... 100
Route 31 The Canyon of Zerqa Ma'in.......... 103
Route 32 The Roman Road from the
  Jordan Valley to Wadi Mujib............... 104
Route 33 Wadi Wala to Wadi Libb and
  Zerqa Ma'in............................... 105
Route 34 Wadi Wala to Mukawir............... 106
Route 35 A Short Walk to Mukawir............ 106
Route 36 Lahoun............................. 107

The RSCN Mujib Reserve
Route 37 The Roman Road from Mukawir

JORDAN

to Zerqa Ma'in and Zara 109
Route 38 Mukawir to the Dead Sea 111
Route 39 The Upper Hidan Gorge 112
Route 40 The Lower Hidan Gorge 114
Route 41 The Hidan Siq 116
Route 42 The Hidan Siq Bypass 118
Route 43 Wadi Nimr to the Dead Sea 119
Route 44 The Malagi Pools 119
Route 45 Qaser Riyash Trail 120
Route 46 Mujib Circuit Trail 120
Route 47 Mujib Gorge Trek 120
Route 48 The Upper Mujib Gorge 122
Route 49 The Lower Mujib Gorge –
  the Mujib Trail 124
Route 50 The Mujib Siq 126
Route 51 Wadi Shuqeiq 128

The Karak Area
Route 52 Wadi el Jarra 129
Route 53 Wadi ibn Hammad 129
Route 54 The Canyon of Wadi ibn
  Hammad 131
Route 55 Wadi Karak 132
Route 56 Wadi Weida'a 133
Route 57 Wadi Numeira (Wadi Hudeira) 135
Route 58 Wadi Hasa 138
Route 59 Jebel Tannur 138
Route 60 The Hot Springs of Hammamat
  Borbita and Hammamat Afra 139

The Northern Dana Area
Route 61 Selah 144
Route 62 The Canyon of Wadi Jamal
  and Wadi Khnaisser (Wadi Khanzira) 146
Route 63 Wadi Labun – Wadi Jamal –
  Wadi Khnaisser 148
Route 64 Wadi Dhalal to Wadi Araba 149
Route 65 Selah to Buseira and Dana 149

The RSCN Dana Nature Reserve
Route 66 Rummana Mountain Trail 155
Route 67 The Steppe Trail 156
Route 68 Feynan Copper Mine Tour 156
Route 69 Dana Cave Trail 156
Route 70 Khirbet Sarab Trail 157
Route 71 The Feynan Trail, Dana to
  Feynan 157
Route 72 Dana to Feynan via Wadi
  Hamra (the Red Valley) 160

The Shaubak Area
Route 73 Feynan to Shaubak via
  Wadi Hammam Adethni 163
Route 74 Wadi Ghuweir to Feynan 164

Route 75 Feynan to Mansourah
  (and Shaubak) via Um el Amad 166
Route 76 Shaubak to Beidah 168
Route 77 Wadi Feid 169
Route 78 Feynan to Beidah via Wadi
  abu Sakakin and Wadi abu Mahmud 169
Route 79 Dana to Petra via Ras Feid 172
Route 80 Dana to Petra via Um el Amad 173

The Petra Area
Route 81 The Petra Siq 181
Route 82 The High Place or Attuf Ridge 182
Route 83 Ed Deir (the Monastery) 183
Route 84 Beidah to Ed Deir
  by the High Route 184
Route 85 Um el Biyyara 185
Route 86 Jebel umm al 'Amr 187
Route 87 Jebel Khubtha via Jebel
  umm al 'Amr 187
Route 88 Petra via Wadi al Mudhlim 188
Route 89 Petra via Wadi Shib Qays 190
Route 90 Wadi al Mataha and
  Al Wu'ayra Fort from Petra 191
Route 91 Jebel Baaga 194
Route 92 Beidah to Shaubak or Feynan 194
Route 93 Siq el Barrid (Little Petra) 194
Route 94 Beidah to 'the Three Valleys' 195
Route 95 The Monastery Round Trip 196
Route 96 Ed Deir to Beidah via
  Wadi Maruan 197
Route 97 Beidah to Petra via Wadi
  Muaysra al Gharbiyya 198
Route 98 Beidah to Petra via Wadi
  Muaysra as Sharkiyya 199
Route 99 Petra to Beidah via Wadi
  Abu Ullayqa 199
Route 100 Wadi es Siyyagh to Petra 201
Route 101 Ed Deir to Wadi
  Siyyagh and Petra 204
Route 102 Wadi Maqtal to Petra 205

The Southern Petra Area
Route 103 Petra to Jebel Harun 206
Route 104 Ancient Trails to and from
  Wadi Sabra 210
Route 105 Petra to Jebel Harun and
  Wadi Sabra 210
Route 106 Petra to Wadi Sabra and
  its Roman Theatre 211
Route 107 Wadi Sabra to Wadi Musa 213
Route 108 Wadi Sabra to Wadi Tibn
  via M'zayla Siq 214
Route 109 The Sabra – Tibn Connection 216

APPENDIX 5 – INDEX OF ROUTES

Route 110 The Ascent of the Siq of Tibn
　to Taybeh or Wadi Musa 217
Route 111 The Waters of Tibn to
　Wadi Musa via Wadi Raqi. 218
Route 112 Taybeh to Wadi Musa via
　Tibn, Sabra, Jebel Harun and Petra 219
Route 113 Rajif to The Waters of Bahra 221
Route 114 The Rajif – Tibn Connection 223
Route 115 Lower Wadi Sabra 225
Route 116 Wadi Heimar 227
Route 117 Wadi Heimar from
　Wadi Araba. 227
Route 118 Trails from Petra to
　Wadi Rum and Aqaba. 229

Wadi Rum
Route 119 Wadi Shelaali –
　The Real Lawrence's Spring. 244
Route 120 Wadi S'bach to Wadi es Sid 246
Route 121 Jebel el Mayeen 246
Route 122 Jebel Ahmar al Shelaali. 249
Route 123 Round Jebel Rum Trek 251
Route 124 Jebel Rum,
　The Thamudic Route 253
Route 125 Jebel Rum,
　Sheikh Hamdan's Route 256
Route 126 The Traverse of Jebel Rum. 259
Route 127 Wadi Siq Makhras (Valley of
　the Stony Canyon). 263
Route 128 Round Jebel um Ishrin 265
Route 129 Rakabat Canyon. 265
Route 130 Round Jebel um Ejil 268
Route 131 Barrah Canyon 269
Route 132 Round Jebel um Anfus 270
Route 133 The Rock Bridge of Burdah 271
Route 134 Jebel Burdah
　via the Rock Bridge. 273
Route 135 The Traverse of Jebel Burdah 274
Route 136 The Canyon of
　Jebel abu Khashaba 275
Route 137 The Rock Bridge of Um Fruth 276

Route 138 Khazali Canyon 276
Route 139 Jebel Khush Khashah
　by Sabbah's Route. 277
Route 140 Jebel um Adaami 279
Route 141 The Sand Canyons
　of Wadi Salaada 281
Route 142 Lawrence's Way to Aqaba. 281

The Aqaba Mountains
Route 143 Jebel el Yitm 283
Route 144 Hodge's Black Snake Route 284

Caving in Jordan
Route 145 Zubia Cave. 287
Route 146 The Cave of Iraq al Wahaj. 290
Route 147 The Cave of Ras Ed Duweira. 292
Route 148 Kufrinja Pot 292
Route 149 The Lava Tube. 293
Route 150 The Cave of Maghrar el Wadid 294

Climbing in Jordan
Saqeb Village Cliff 301
Wadi Mahmud Cliffs 301
Rajib Cliff 303
Saqeb Cliff. 304
Kufrinja Cliff 306
Wave Cliff 307
Cave Cliff 307
Thôr Motlagh (Sami's Cliff) 308
Muzeirib Cliff 311
Wahadina Cliff 311
Ras Ed Duweira. 312
Ras Sabiq 312
Yabis Upper and Lower Cliffs 313
Wadi Weida'a Slabs 313
Wadi Hasa 314
Bad'da. 315
The Petra Area 315
The Wadi Rum Area 316
Jebel Kharaz 316
The Aqaba Mountains 317

2000-year-old inscriptions on the Thamudic Route, Wadi Rum, one of the world's oldest known rock climbs (Route 124)

APPENDIX 6
Place name Index

Abila 76
Abraham Path 58
Abu Aina 231, 244–245, **250-252**, 282
Abu el Hawil (inscriptions) 229, **282**
Abu Khsheibah Domes........... 232, **275**, 279
Agraba 48, 75, 77
Ain el Beidah 141–149
Ajloun................. 28, **47–61**, 289, **297–311**
Al Kharja (Byzantine ruins) 70
Amman............... 18, **33–41**, **47–58**, **84–104**
Aqaba **31–42**, 231, **281–285**, 317
Azraq Oasis 47, **79–81**, 293
'Ayy 134, 135

Barrah Canyon 40, 243, **269**
Ba'un 56, 63–65
B'dul 178, **191–200**
Beidah 163, **168–185**, **192–202**, 226
Bir Hamad 178, 213, 223–229
Bir Madhkhur 178, 181, 193, **201–205**, 209
Buseira 146, **148–154**, 192

Caves
  Iraq al Wahaj **290–291**, 300, 306
  Kufrinja Pot **292**, 300, 304
  Lava Tube 81, **293–294**
  Maghrar el Wadid 113, **294**
  Ras Ed Duweira **292**, 300, **312**
  Zubia 63–65, **286–289**
Climbing areas (outside Rum)
  Bad'da 158, **315**
  Cave Cliff 290–300, **306–308**
  Jebel Kharaz (north of Rum) 316
  Kufrinja Cliff 300, **306**, 312
  Musheriefa Cliff 309
  Muzeirib cliff 300, **311**
  Rajib Cliff 300, **303**
  Ras Ed Duweira **292**, 300, **312**
  Ras Sabiq...................... 300, **312**
  Sami's Cliff (Thôr Motlagh) .. 52, 55, 300, **308–311**
  Saqeb Cliff (Um el Julud) 300, **307**
  Saqeb Village Cliff 300, **301**
  Thôr Motlagh 52, 55, 300, **308–311**
  Wadi Mahmud Cliffs 300, **301**
  Wadi Weida'a Slabs.............. 130, 133, **313**
  Wahadina Cliff................. 53, 54, 300, **311**
  Wave Cliff 300, **306–307**
  Yabis Upper and Lower Cliffs.............. 313
Crusader Caves of Al Habis Jaldak **74**, 77

Dana................... 26, 28–34, 38, **141–175**
Dead Sea 23–27, **28**, 49, **90–140**
Dead Sea Panoramic Complex 104
Deir 'Alla 50, 53–54, 64, 66, 84, 87
Delagha 209, 229
Dhiban 104–107, 122
Dibeen..................... 18, 26, 47, 84, **85**
Diseh 231–233, 237, 242, 271, 281–**282**

El Iraq 133–135
El Qasr 129–130, 132
Es Sil 144, 146–148, 150–151

Faqua 109, 121–124, 128–130
Feynan 141–142, 153–172, 192–194, 226
Fuheis 84, 88, **89**

Gargur waterfall 148, 150–151
Gharandal 142, 209–210, 213, 225, 228
Ghor Mazra'a 41, 132
Ghor Safi 24
Gregra 154, 163, 166, 171

Halawa 56, 62–65
Hammam Adethni 158, 160–165, 173
Hammamat Afra 139
Hammamat Borbita 139
Hammamat ibn Hammad 129
Hammamat Zerqa Ma'in 98, **100**, 102
Harta 74–78
Hisma......................... 175, 227, 229
Humeimah 175, 210, 213, 223, **227–229**

Iraq el Amir 84, 88
Irbid 47, 48, 66, 72–77
Irjan (Orjan) 56, 61, 63–65
Ishtafeina 54, 56, 59, 62–65, 313

Jebel
  abu Khashaba 275, 280
  abu Mahmud (Black Mountain) 171
  abu Rashrasha 282
  Ahmar al Shelaali 249, 250
  Amud 282
  Baaga 170, 194
  Barra 158, 160–161
  Barrah 232, 270
  Barrat Salama 216
  Barwas 170–171

326

Appendix 6 – Place Name Index

Burdah 232, 271–275, 279–281
el Khandaq 89
esh Shubeil. 87
Harun. 201–202, **205, 221**, 226
Khazali 243, 271, **276–278**
Khubtha 180–181, **187–188**
Khush Khashah 232, **276–278**
Mahat Al Hathra 283
Makhras 263–264
Mayeen 242, **246–248**
Rum 232–235, 242–250, **251–262**
Rumman 242, 251–257
Rummana 150
Sarab 152–153
Sartaba 68–72
Shara 175, 192, 227
Sufaha 170, 173
Tannur 138–139
um Adaami 279–280
um Anfus 232, **270–271**
um Ejil 232, **266–269**
um Fruth. **275–276**, 280
um Ishrin 230–232, **263–269**
umm al 'Amr 180, **187–188**
Yitm 237, **283**
Jerash 47–49, 84–87

Kahf el Messih (the Jesus Cave) 68
Karak 95–97, **129–142**, 209, **313–314**
Kathraba 133
Khanzira Hellenistic temple 70
Kharazeh Canyon 266–269
Khazali Canyon. 276
Khirbet Tannur 138–139
King Talal Dam 84–85, **86–87**
Kufr Abil 55–57, 62–65, 68–70
Kufr Rakib 63, 68–71
Kureiyima 50–54

Lahoun 107–108, **120–121**
Libb 98–99, **100–101**, 105–106
Lot's Cave 137

Ma'an 142, 227–228, 237, 281
Madaba 84, **95–105**, 109
Mahas 84, **88–89**
Ma'in 98, 100–102
Malagi Pools 115–118, **119**, 124
Mansourah 158, 163–169
Mar Elias. 56, 59–60
Mazra'a 41, 130–133, 137
Meteorite Crater 39, 83
Mount Nebo 98
Mouta 133–135

Mudawarah 142, 229, 281
Mujib Dam 108, 121
Mukawir 99–101, **105–111**
M'zayla Siq. 214

Nabataean Trail. 186, 194, 210, 225
Naqb er Rubai 178, 207–210

Pella (Tabaqat Fahl) 47–48, **55–58**, **62–72**
Petra 172–173, **175–227**, 229
Pilgrimage Trail 98

Qadissiya 141, 153–154, 315

Rajif 177–178, 215, **219–226**
Rakabat Canyon 263–269
Ras Feid 172
Rock Arch (Kharaz) 229, **282**
Rock Bridge (Burdah) 271–275
Rock Bridge (Um Fruth) 275, **276**, **280**
RSCN 23–26
    Ajloun Woodland Reserve 56, **59–61**
    Azraq Wetland Nature Reserve 79–80
    Dana Reserve. 149, **152–163**, 226
    Dibeen Forest Reserve 84–85
    Jebel Mas'uda Reserve 177–178
    Mujib Reserve. 97, 107–108, **109–128**
    Qasr Burqu Reserve 79, **81**
    Rum Protected Area 231–233, **242–243**
    Shaumari Reserve. 26, **80**
    Yarmuk River Basin Reserve 24
Rumeimin waterfall 86, **87**

Safi 137
Salt 26, 48–49, 84, 89
Saqeb 85, 298–300, **301–305**
Selah 144–154
Shakriyeh 237, 240, 243, 282
Shaubak **173–174**, 192, 194, **313–315**
Siq el Barrid (Little Petra). . . . 179, **192–196**, 200–201
Siq el Ma'jan (Petra aqueduct) 181
Sumiya Hills 87
Suweileh 48–50, 84, 86, 89

Tabaqat Fahl (Pella) 47–48, **55–58**, **62–72**
Tafileh 141–144, 147, 153
Taybeh 177–178, **217–219**, 224
Tell Deir 'Alla 50, 84, 87
Tell Hammeh 87
Tell Hisban 90
Tell Hism 68, 72
Thlaithukhwat 82

Um el Amad (Dana) 158, **166–167**, 170, **173**

JORDAN

Um el Amad (Yarmuk) 78
Um Qais 48, 66, 68, **72–74**
Um Tawagi 270–271
Umm el Biyyara 181, **185–186**, **193**, 206

Wadi
   abu Ghurabah 158, 166
   abu Khusheibeh 209
   abu Mahmud 169–171
   abu Sakakin 169–172
   abu Salih 68
   abu Ullayqa 180, 193, 196, 199–200
   Araba 24–31, 141, 153, 201–229
   Bahra 215–6, **221–225**
   Batahi 211–215, 221
   Ba'un 63–65
   Buseira 146, **148–154**, 192
   Dana 150, **153–159**, 165–167
   Dhalal 149–150
   Feid 169–172
   Ghurab (Karak) 134–135
   Ghurab (Petra) 184, **192–196**, 202, 205
   Ghuweir (Shaubak) 158, **162–165**, 167, 173
   Hammam Adethni 158, **160–165**, 173
   Hamra 158, **160–162**
   Hasa (Karak) 95, 97, 133, **137–139**
   Hassa (Rum) 257–258
   Heimar 227–229
   Hersh 146, 150
   Hidan 44, 96, **105–108**, **111–126**
   Himara 91, **93**, 104
   Hudeira (Numeira) 133–137
   ibn Hammad 96–97, **129–132**
   Itm 237, **281–284**
   Jamal 146–150
   Jamal Khudeira 105
   Jirm 67, 68–72
   Karak 96, 130, **132**
   Khnaisser (Khanzira) 144, **146–148**
   Khusheiba 69
   Kufrinja 51–54, 289–292, 307–313
   La'ban 139
   Labun 146, 148–149, 150–151
   Libb **99–101**, 105, 113
   Manshala 91–92
   Maqtal 201–202, **205–208**
   Maruan 184–185, 193, **197–198**, 205
   Mataha 180, 188, **190–191**, 193
   Muaysra al Gharbiyya 180, 193, **196–198**
   Muaysra as Sharkiyya 180, 193, **196–199**
   Mudhlim 180, **188–191**
   Mujib 24–28, 94–97, **104–128**
   Mukheiris 91–92
   Musa 171–178, **191–213**, **218–221**

Muzeirib 52–55, 309
Namala 170–171, 201, 209
Naum 55–57, 65
Nimr 113, 116, **119**
Numeira 133–137
Quweiliba 74, **76–78**
Raqi 215–217, **218–219**
Rum **227–285**, 296–299, **316–317**
Rumman 242, 251–253, 256–257
Saada 215–6, 219, 223–4
Sabra 175–182, 206–229
Salaada **279–281**
Salih 63, **70–72**
S'bach 245–248
Shelaali (Rum) 239, **244–246**, 261–262
Shellaleh (Yarmuk) 76–78, 289
Shib Qays 180, **190**
Shtura 51, 53
Shu'eib 84, **89**
Shuqeiq 96, 109, 121, **128**
Sid 245–247
Sijn 76–78
Siq Makhras 263
Sir (Amman) 84, **88**
Sir (Pella) 63, 72
Siyyagh 178–186, **201–205**, 209
Suweid 215, 221–222
Thugra 169, 194
Tibn 174, 177–8, **214–225**
um el Elda 170–173, 194, 201
um Ishrin 230, 263–270
Wala 96, 99, **105–108**, 111–113
Weida'a 130, **133**, **313–314**
Yabis 55–57, **62–70**, 289, 313
Zerqa (Jerash) 50, 84, 86–87
Zerqa Ma'in 96–99, **100–105**, 109–110
Wahadina 51–56, 300, 311

Yarmuk Gorge 72–78, 289

Zara Hot Springs 99, 106, **109–111**
Zernouk el Daber 265, 269
Zerqa Ma'in (hot spring) 91, 97, **100–102**
Zerqa Ma'in Canyon 99–100, 102, **103–104**

Main page references shown in bold type

APPENDIX 7
Index of Maps in the Guide

Jordan location map 7
1 Areas covered in this guidebook 9
2 The Hashemite Kingdom of Jordan 18
3 RSCN Nature Reserves and Protected Areas 23
4 Jordan Valley and the Northern Highlands 48
5 Ajloun to Kureiyima 51
6 Ajloun to Pella and the Ajloun Woodland Reserve 56
7 Yabis and Pella area 63
8 The Yarmuk Gorge area 77
9 The Capital area 84
10 Northern Dead Sea area 91
11 The Dead Sea Hills 96
12 Wadi Zerqa Main and Wadi Wala 99
13 RSCN Mujib Nature Reserve 110
14 The Hidan Gorge and Wadi Wala 113
15 The Mujib Gorge 121
16 Wadi ibn Hammad 130
17 Wadi Numeira 134
18 Dana and South Jordan 142
19 Selah, Buseirah and Dana area 150
20 The RSCN Dana Nature Reserve 154
21 Dana, Feynan, Shaubak area 158
22 Wadi abu Sakakin, Wadi abu Mahmud and Wadi Feid 170
23 The Petra area 178
24 The Petra Basin 180
25 Petra, northern approaches 193
26 Petra to Jebel Harun 207
27 Petra, southern approaches 215
28 Petra to Wadi Rum 228
29 Wadi Rum central area 232
30 Wadi Rum Protected Area 243
31 Wadi Shelaali and Rest House Area 245
32 Jebel Mayeen 247
33 Jebel Ahmar al Shelaali 249
34 Jebel Rum 252
35 The Thamudic Route, Jebel Rum 254
36 Sheikh Hamdan's Route, Jebel Rum 258
37 Hammad's Route, The Traverse of Jebel Rum 261
38 Jebel um Ishrin area 264
39 Rakabat Canyon, Jebel um Ishrin 266
40 Barrah Canyon area 270
41 Jebel Burdah and the Rock Bridge 272
42 Jebel Khush Khashah, Sabbah's Route 277
43 Wadi Rum, southern area 280
44 Zubia Cave 288
45 Iraq Al Wahaj 291
46 Climbs and Caves, Ajloun 300

APPENDIX 8
Animals and flowers of Jordan

APPENDIX 8 – ANIMALS AND FLOWERS OF JORDAN

SAVE £££'s with

tgo
THE GREAT OUTDOORS

Britain's leading monthly magazine for the dedicated walker. To find out how much you can save by subscribing call

0141 302 7744

HILLWALKING • BACKPACKING • TREKKING • SCRAMBLING

Get ready for take off

Adventure Travel helps you to go outdoors over there

More ideas, information, advice and entertaining features on overseas trekking, walking and backpacking than any other magazine - guaranteed.

Available from good newsagents or by subscription - 6 issues £15

Adventure Travel Magazine T:01789-488166

LISTING OF CICERONE GUIDES

BACKPACKING
Backpacker's Britain Vol 1 – Northern England
Backpacker's Britain Vol 2 – Wales
Backpacker's Britain Vol 3 – Northern Scotland
Book of the Bivvy
End to End Trail
Three Peaks, Ten Tors
BRITISH CYCLE GUIDES
Border Country Cycle Routes
Cumbria Cycle Way
Lancashire Cycle Way
Lands End to John O'Groats – Cycle Guide
Rural Rides No.1 – West Surrey
Rural Rides No.2 – East Surrey
South Lakeland Cycle Rides
CANOE GUIDES
Canoeist's Guide to the North-East
DERBYSHIRE, PEAK DISTRICT, EAST MIDLANDS
High Peak Walks
Historic Walks in Derbyshire
Star Family Walks Peak District and South Yorkshire
White Peak Walks Northern Dales
White Peak Walks Southern Dales
FOR COLLECTORS OF SUMMITS
Mts England & Wales Vol 1 – Wales
Mts England & Wales Vol 2 – England
Relative Hills of Britain
IRELAND
Irish Coast to Coast
Irish Coastal Walks
Mountains of Ireland
ISLE OF MAN
Isle of Man Coastal Path
Walking on the Isle of Man
LAKE DISTRICT AND MORECAMBE BAY
Atlas of the English Lakes
Coniston Copper Mines
Cumbria Coastal Way
Cumbria Way and Allerdale Ramble
Great Mountain Days in the Lake District
Lake District Angler's Guide
Lake District Winter Climbs
Roads and Tracks of the Lake District
Rocky Rambler's Wild Walks
Scrambles in the Lake District (North)
Scrambles in the Lake District (South)
Short Walks in Lakeland 1 – South
Short Walks in Lakeland 2 – North
Short Walks in Lakeland 3 – West
Tarns of Lakeland Vol 1 – West
Tarns of Lakeland Vol 2 – East
Tour of the Lake District
Walks in Silverdale and Arnside AONB

MIDLANDS
Cotswold Way
NORTHERN ENGLAND LONG-DISTANCE TRAILS
Dales Way
Hadrian's Wall Path
Northern Coast to Coast Walk
Pennine Way
Teesdale Way
NORTH-WEST ENGLAND
Family Walks in the Forest of Bowland
Historic Walks in Cheshire
Ribble Way
Walker's Guide to the Lancaster Canal
Walking in the Forest of Bowland and Pendle
Walking in Lancashire
Walks in Lancashire Witch Country
Walks in Ribble Country
PENNINES AND NORTH-EAST ENGLAND
Cleveland Way and Yorkshire Wolds Way
Historic Walks in North Yorkshire
North York Moors
South Pennine Walks
Yorkshire Dales – South and West
Walking in County Durham
Walking in the North Pennines
Walking in Northumberland
Walking in the South Pennines
Walking in the Wolds
Walks in Dales Country
Walks in the Yorkshire Dales
Walks on the North York Moors, books 1 and 2
Waterfall Walks – Teesdale and High Pennines
Yorkshire Dales Angler's Guide
SCOTLAND
Ben Nevis and Glen Coe
Border Country – A Walker's Guide
Border Pubs and Inns – A Walkers' Guide
Central Highlands: 6 Long Distance Walks
Great Glen Way
Isle of Skye, A Walker's Guide
North to the Cape
Pentland Hills: A Walker's Guide
Scotland's Far North
Scotland's Far West
Scotland's Mountain Ridges
Scottish Glens 1 – Cairngorm Glens
Scottish Glens 2 – Atholl Glens
Scottish Glens 3 – Glens of Rannoch
Scottish Glens 4 – Glens of Trossach
Scottish Glens 5 – Glens of Argyll
Scottish Glens 6 – The Great Glen

Scrambles in Lochaber
Southern Upland Way
Torridon – A Walker's Guide
Walking in the Cairngorms
Walking in the Hebrides
Walking in the Isle of Arran
Walking in the Lowther Hills
Walking in the Ochils, Campsie Fells and Lomond Hills
Walking the Galloway Hills
Walking the Munros Vol 1 – Southern, Central
Walking the Munros Vol 2 – Northern and Cairngorms
West Highland Way
Winter Climbs – Ben Nevis and Glencoe
Winter Climbs – Cairngorms
SOUTHERN ENGLAND
Channel Island Walks
Definitive Guide to Walking in London
Exmoor and the Quantocks
Greater Ridgeway
Isles of Scilly
Lea Valley Walk
North Downs Way
South Downs Way
South West Coast Path
Thames Path
Walker's Guide to the Isle of Wight
Walking in Bedfordshire
Walking in Berkshire
Walking in Buckinghamshire
Walking in Dorset
Walking in Kent
Walking in Somerset
Walking in Sussex
Walking on Dartmoor
UK GENERAL
National Trails
WALES AND WELSH BORDERS
Ascent of Snowdon
Glyndwr's Way
Hillwalking in Wales – Vol 1
Hillwalking in Wales – Vol 2
Hillwalking in Snowdonia
Lleyn Peninsula Coastal Path
Pembrokeshire Coastal Path
Ridges of Snowdonia
Scrambles in Snowdonia
Shropshire Hills – A Walker's Guide
Spirit Paths of Wales
Walking Offa's Dyke Path
Walking in Pembrokeshire
Welsh Winter Climbs

AFRICA
Climbing in the Moroccan Anti-Atlas
Kilimanjaro
Trekking in the Atlas Mountains
THE ALPS (Walking and Trekking)
100 Hut Walks in the Alps
Across the Eastern Alps: E5
Alpine Points of View
Alpine Ski Mountaineering
   Vol 1 Western Alps
Alpine Ski Mountaineering
   Vol 2 Eastern Alps
Chamonix to Zermatt
Snowshoeing: Techniques and Routes
   in the Western Alps
Tour of the Matterhorn
Tour of Mont Blanc
Tour of Monte Rosa
Walking in the Alps (all Alpine areas)
CROATIA AND SLOVENIA
Julian Alps of Slovenia
Walking in Croatia
EASTERN EUROPE
High Tatras
Mountains of Montenegro
Mountains of Romania
Walking in Hungary
FRANCE, BELGIUM AND LUXEMBOURG
Cathar Way
Ecrins National Park
GR5 Trail
GR20 Corsica – The High Level Route
Mont Blanc Walks
RLS (Robert Louis Stevenson) Trail
Rock Climbs Belgium and
   Luxembourg
Tour of the Oisans: GR54
Tour of the Vanoise
Trekking in the Vosges and Jura
Vanoise Ski Touring
Walking in the Cathar region
   of south west France
Walking in the Cevennes
Walking in the Dordogne
Walking in the Haute Savoie, Vol 1
Walking in the Haute Savoie, Vol 2
Walking in the Languedoc
Walking in Provence
Walking in the Tarentaise and
   Beaufortain Alps
Walking on Corsica
Walking the French Gorges
Walks in Volcano Country
GERMANY AND AUSTRIA
Germany's Romantic Road
King Ludwig Way
Klettersteig Scrambles in
   Northern Limestone Alps
Mountain Walking in Austria
Trekking in the Stubai Alps
Trekking in the Zillertal Alps
Walking in the Bavarian Alps
Walking in the Harz Mountains

Walking in the Salzkammergut
Walking the River Rhine Trail
HIMALAYAS – NEPAL, INDIA, TIBET
Annapurna – A Trekker's Guide
Bhutan – A Trekker's Guide
Everest – A Trekkers' Guide
Garhwal & Kumaon –
   A Trekkers' Guide
Kangchenjunga – A Trekkers' Guide
Langtang, Gosainkund and
   Helambu: A Trekkers' Guide
Manaslu – A Trekkers' Guide
Mount Kailash Trek
ITALY
Central Apennines of Italy
Gran Paradiso
Italian Rock
Shorter Walks in the Dolomites
Through the Italian Alps: the GTA
Trekking in the Apennines
Treks in the Dolomites
Via Ferratas of the Italian
   Dolomites Vol 1
Via Ferratas of the Italian
   Dolomites Vol 2
Walking in the Central Italian Alps
Walking in the Dolomites
Walking in Sicily
Walking in Tuscany
NORTH AMERICA
Grand Canyon and American South
   West
John Muir Trail
Walking in British Columbia
OTHER MEDITERRANEAN COUNTRIES
Climbs and Treks in the Ala Dag
   (Turkey)
High Mountains of Crete
Jordan – Walks, Treks, Caves etc.
Mountains of Greece
Treks and Climbs Wadi Rum, Jordan
Walking in Malta
Walking in Western Crete
PYRENEES AND FRANCE / SPAIN
Canyoning in Southern Europe
GR10 Trail: Through the
   French Pyrenees
Mountains of Andorra
Rock Climbs in the Pyrenees
Pyrenean Haute Route
Pyrenees – World's Mountain Range
   Guide
Through the Spanish Pyrenees GR11
Walks and Climbs in the Pyrenees
Way of St James – Le Puy to
   the Pyrenees
Way of St James – Pyrenees-Santiago-
   Finisterre
SCANDINAVIA
Pilgrim Road to Nidaros
   (St Olav's Way)
Walking in Norway

SOUTH AMERICA
Aconcagua
SPAIN AND PORTUGAL
Costa Blanca Walks Vol 1
Costa Blanca Walks Vol 2
Mountains of Central Spain
Picos de Europa – Walks and Climbs
Via de la Plata (Seville To Santiago)
Walking in the Algarve
Walking in the Canary Islands 1 West
Walking in the Canary Islands 2 East
Walking in the Cordillera Cantabrica
Walking the GR7 in Andalucia
Walking in Madeira
Walking in Mallorca
Walking in the Sierra Nevada
SWITZERLAND
Alpine Pass Route
Bernese Alps
Central Switzerland –
   A Walker's Guide
Tour of the Jungfrau Region
Walking in Ticino, Switzerland
Walking in the Valais
Walks in the Engadine, Switzerland
INTERNATIONAL CYCLE GUIDES
Cycle Touring in France
Cycle Touring in Spain
Cycle Touring in Switzerland
Cycling in the French Alps
Cycling the River Loire – The Way
   of St Martin
Danube Cycle Way
Way of St James – Le Puy to Santiago
   cyclist's guide
MINI GUIDES
Avalanche!
GPS
Navigation
Pocket First Aid and Wilderness
   Medicine
Snow
TECHNIQUES AND EDUCATION
Adventure Alternative
Beyond Adventure
Hillwalker's Guide to Mountaineering
Hillwalker's Manual
Map and Compass
Mountain Weather
Outdoor Photography
Rock Climbing
Snow and Ice Techniques
Sport Climbing

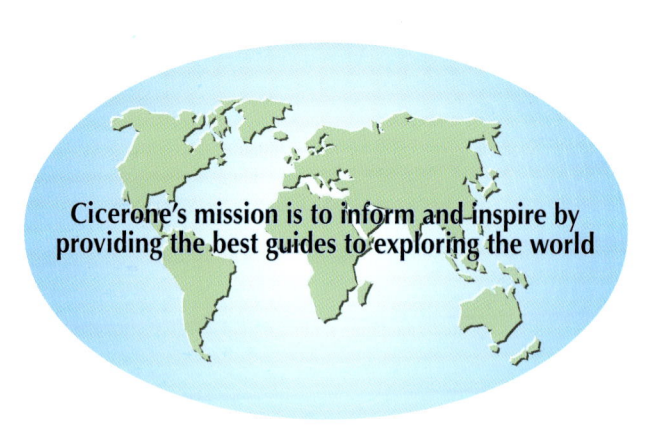

Cicerone's mission is to inform and inspire by providing the best guides to exploring the world

Since its foundation over 30 years ago, Cicerone has specialised in publishing guidebooks and has built a reputation for quality and reliability. It now publishes nearly 300 guides to the major destinations for outdoor enthusiasts, including Europe, UK and the rest of the world.

Written by leading and committed specialists, Cicerone guides are recognised as the most authoritative. They are full of information, maps and illustrations so that the user can plan and complete a successful and safe trip or expedition – be it a long face climb, a walk over Lakeland fells, an alpine traverse, a Himalayan trek or a ramble in the countryside.

With a thorough introduction to assist planning, clear diagrams, maps and colour photographs to illustrate the terrain and route, and accurate and detailed text, Cicerone guides are designed for ease of use and access to the information.

If the facts on the ground change, or there is any aspect of a guide that you think we can improve, we are always delighted to hear from you.

Cicerone Press
2 Police Square Milnthorpe Cumbria LA7 7PY
Tel:01539 562 069   Fax:01539 563 417
e-mail:info@cicerone.co.uk   web:www.cicerone.co.uk

CICERONE